SOCIAL ENTROPY THEORY

SOCIAL ENTROPY THEORY

KENNETH D. BAILEY

STATE UNIVERSITY OF NEW YORK PRESS

Thanks to the following publishers for permission to quote from their works:

Excerpts from *Systems Research*, Volume 1, Number 1, Kenneth D. Bailey, "Equilibrium, Entropy, and Homeostasis: A Multidisciplinary Legacy." Copyright © 1984 by Pergamon Press PLC. Reprinted with permission from the publisher.

Excerpts from *The British Journal* of Sociology, Volume XXXV, Number 1, Kenneth D. Bailey, "Beyond Functionalism." Copyright © 1984 by Routledge. Reprinted with permission from the publisher.

Excerpts from *Systems Practice*, Kenneth D. Bailey, "Social Entropy Theory: An Overview." Copyright © 1989 by Plenum Publishing Corporation. Reprinted with permission from the publisher.

From *Behavioral Science*, Volume 26, Kenneth D. Bailey, "Abstracted Versus Concrete Sociological Theory," Copyright © 1981 by Behavioral Science. Reprinted with permission from the publisher.

Kenneth D. Bailey, "Post-Functional Social Systems Analysis," taken from *The Sociological Quarterly*, Volume 23. Copyright © 1982 by Jai Press Inc. Reprinted with permission from the publisher.

Excerpts from *Quality and Quantity*, Volume 18, Kenneth D. Bailey, "Sociological Entropy Theory: Toward a Statistical and Verbal Congruence." Copyright © 1983 by Elsevier Science Publishers. Reprinted with permission from the publisher.

Excerpts from *Quality and Quantity*, Volume 18, Kenneth D. Bailey, "A Three-Level Measurement Model." Copyright © 1984 by Elsevier Science Publishers. Reprinted with permission from the publisher.

Kenneth D. Bailey, "Micro-Macro Analysis of Status Inconsistency: Toward a Holistic Model," taken from *Status Inconsistency in Modern Societies* edited by Hermann Strasser and Robert W. Hodge, Sozialwissenschaftliche Schriften 33. Reprinted with permission from the publisher.

Published by
State University of New York Press, Albany

©1990 State University of New York

Library of Congress Cataloging-in-Publication Data
Bailey, Kenneth D.
    Social entropy theory/Kenneth D. Bailey.
       p. cm.
    Bibliography: p.
    Includes index. ISBN 0-7914-0056-5. ISBN 0-7914-0057-3 (pbk.)
    1. Sociology—Methodology. 2. System theory. 3. Social systems.
  4. Social structure. I. Title
    HM24.B296 1990
301'.01'8—dc19

88-30109
CIP

10 9 8 7 6 5 4 3 2 1

TO   JNB   AND   SJB

Contents

List of Tables

List of Figures

Preface

Social entropy theory is based upon the premise that understanding of society as a whole is the central task of sociology. We must return to classical concerns. Chapter 1 discusses this task in more detail. Chapter 2 critiques functionalism, and introduces system theory. Chapter 3 critiques the equilibrium concept, and presents the concept of social entropy. Chapter 4 presents the basic dimensions that society utilizes in its day-to-day operations. Chapter 5 analyzes the role of the individual within complex society. Chapter 6 discusses the organizational level with the framework used in earlier chapters. Chapter 7 studies order in some detail, while Chapter 8 deals with quantitive aspects of entropy, and Chapter 9 concludes the volume with reflections and hypotheses.

This volume uses a systems perspective to present the "big picture." I feel that, although specificity abounds in modern sociology, general analysis is sorely neglected but is crucial to our discipline. The level of generality in this volume is such that the model is meant to be applied to any society at any stage of development.

Social entropy theory cannot specifically include every middle range approach but makes an effort not to preclude any. For example, many sociologists felt that classical functionalism hindered analysis of social change and conflict. I have made an effort to ensure that such exclusions are avoided in this model. Rather, I simple seek a general model that presents concepts suitable to the comparative analysis of disparate societies.

I am indebted to the editors of *Behavioral Science, British Journal of Sociology, Quality and Quantity, Sociological Quarterly, Systems Practice, Status Inconsistency in Modern Societies,* and *Systems Research* for permission to include in this book some material that was originally published in their journals. I am also indebted to colleagues too numerous to mention at both the University of California, Los Angeles, and Tulane University for helpful comments, criticisms, and encouragement. I particularly wish to thank

Dr. James Grier Miller for his invaluable assistance with the systems approach. Finally, special thanks go to Rosalie M. Robertson and Diane Ganeles of SUNY Press for their excellent editorial direction.

Chapter 1

Constructing a Theory of Complex Society

Our goal in this volume is to construct an adequate model of complex society. It will be taken as axiomatic that a complex model is necessary in adequately understanding complex society. More specifically, the model must be isomorphic with the society and so must be as complex as the society it models. This will be discussed in detail in this chapter and the next.

To be adequate such a model must enable us to understand how a complex modern society functions on a day-to-day basis. That is, it must specify the macrosocietal variables important to society's functioning and specify the important interrelationships among such variables. In addition to specifying the salient characteristics of the total society, the model must specify the salient individual characteristics (micro variables) that will help us understand how the individual functions within the societal context. Finally, the model must show us how the micro variables (individual characteristics) and macro variables (societal characteristics) are interrelated to form a functioning whole. In short, the model must successfully deal with the micro-macro problem, which at least since the time of Durkheim has been recognized as a major but yet unresolved issue in sociology.

In addition to successfully linking the micro-macro aspects of a complex society, the model must also be adequate for the analysis of change over time. It must be able to specify the salient variables at a given point in time and identify the relationships among them in a cross-sectional analysis; it must also be suitable for studying individual action over time, for showing changes in macro (societal) variables over time, and for showing how the two spheres interrelate.

The successful model of complex society must recognize and encompass the strains and pressures within society as well as the factors that lead to social coherence and help ensure societal survival and continued day-to-day functioning. Thus, the model must allow for conflict as well as for consensus. Finally, the successful model *must not* emphasize material existence and the observation of empirical reality at the expense of the subjective factors of human

existence. No matter how scientific it may become in the pursuit of explanation and prediction, the model must remain humanistic enough to deal with a
human society. A model of human society that lacks a place for values may
be scientific but it is not realistic.

Social entropy theory (SET) is first and foremost a macrosociological approach. We follow Durkheim's (1950, 1951) dictum that society exists sui
generis. Thus, much of our analysis will utilize the holistic society as the basic
unit of anlaysis, and the variables of interest are those that can be considered
properties of the society as a whole. However, since we also include the study
of components of the society, we will at times be utilizing organizations,
groups, and individuals as the respective units of analysis. Thus, we parallel
Miller's (1978) multilevel approach in *Living Systems* but with at least two
exceptions. One exception is that unlike Miller we begin at the level of the
society and "work down" to the individual. Further, we put somewhat greater
reliance upon relationships between levels and less upon structural similarities
across levels.

In our attempt to understand the society sui generis, we are clearly returning to concerns of the founders of our discipline. Thus, the problem is not
new. Questions then arise as to whether the sort of theoretical problems that
interested the founders have been solved through the course of time, and if
not, whether they are still worthy of solution. It is clear to me that they have
not been solved, and that they are still important (indeed fundamental, and in
fact vital). It is clearly trite (but nevertheless important) to reiterate that modern sociology directs surprisingly little of its intellectual effort toward the
holistic understanding of society. Few would deny that the study of the society
as a whole is central (if not definitional) to sociology as a discipline and (at
least partially) is the basis for distinguishing sociology from other social sciences. It is a mixed blessing that so much contemporary work in sociological
theory deals directly with the reexamination of the works of nineteenth century theorists such as Marx, Weber, Durkheim, and others. We are fortunate
that the works of these scholars provide such a sound basis for our discipline
and that they have stood the test of time. On the other hand, we sorely miss
newer theories that extend these classical works or reach beyond their boundaries with original formulations.

Social entropy theory rests upon the assumption that the study of the society as a whole is important. Indeed, it is not the central concern of any other
discipline: if sociologists do not study it, who will? Thus, the question becomes not *whether* to study macrosociology but *how* to study it. The model
presented in this volume attempts to bring contemporary tools—both theoretical and methodological—to the study of macrosociology. Many new tools
have been developed since the masters wrote, and we will combine them in a

fresh approach to old problems. Prominent among these developments are systems theory, entropy theory, Guttman's (1959) facet theory, and a number of other formulations. In addition, various methodological developments will be useful. Also, we will build upon many contemporary theoretical formulations.

The Direct Strategy

Construction of a holistic model could be approached in a number of ways. This model will be a macrosociological model of the sort described by Merton (1968) as "total" theory. Conceivably, we could use a *divisive strategy* to break a still-larger theory into a theory of the desired size. This begs the question, as such a "total-total" theory has not been conceived. More realistically, we could adopt an *aggregative strategy* in which smaller theories (middle-range or less) are combined into one theory of the needed complexity. Although this seems to be the strategy recommended by Merton (1968), attempts to aggregate have proven difficult (see Opp, 1970). If these strategies seem impractical, some might simply abandon the quest for a macrosociological complex theory; however, this is unwise. Today more than ever there is a clear need for an integrative large-scale theory rather than the middle-range theories advocated by Merton (1968). This leaves as our chief hope the *direct strategy* which entails examining the salient features of complex society and deigning a macrotheory that attains point-by-point isomorphism with all of its salient features.

Sociologists of the 1940s and 1950s probably did not feel the lack of global theory but in fact had a substantial amount of unverified theory available. They probably relied on this stockpile for theoretical support more than they realized. Sociologists of today are without this reservoir of large-scale theory. Although earlier sociologists would agree with Merton that the discipline can afford to be patient in its search for unified theory, sociologists of today see a greater urgency for the construction of such theory. Aiken (1981; 449) states the case well:

> One of the factors that, in my estimation has contributed most significantly to the erection of boundaries and the absence of bridges for the discipline is the absence of an overarching theoretical paradigm which gives the discipline direction and focus. . . . I recall my training during the 1950s when Parsonian functionalism was dominant and set the tone for discussion and debate. While one could argue in retrospect that the hegemony of this particular theoretical perspective was stifling, it nevertheless channeled scholarship and debate toward a more social science orientation, and it provided

sociologists with a sensitivity to the contributions and insights that could be
drawn from other social science disciplines.

Thus, while Merton placed no emphasis on the costs incurred in waiting
for the construction of the unified theory through aggregation, there are
clearly some costs today. Sociology needs a unified theory. The longer it is
delayed, the more likely we are to see an increase in the number of substantive
paradigms and the use of quantitative techniques. Many of these are developed outside of sociology, and so it is unclear whether we can rely upon their
application to point out the salient problems of the discipline. Inasmuch as the
increasing pluralism creates anomie and a sense of powerlessness for some
people, because of a lack of central focus, a further delay in constructing unified theory can be psychologically costly.

The basic reason that SET must be directly formulated stems from a central premise of this volume: *the model must be isomorphic with the social
phenomenon being studied.* Thus, the character and degree of generality of
SET is designed to be isomorphic with the degree of complexity in the social
phenomenon (the unitary, holistic society) being studied. In other words, the
generality of SET does not emanate from a desire to write a theory that is general, unified, total, grand, or global. Rather, the degree of generality is specified the perception of society as a unitary functioning whole, and the attempt
of the model to be isomorphic with this phenomenon.

This process of perceiving the phenomenon holistically and constructing
an isomorphic model of equal complexity is clearly a direct strategy, very
similar to that Merton advocates for middle-range theory (see, for example,
his discussion of the formulation of reference group theory in Merton 1968,
40). Chapter 2 will demonstrate that there are really three "levels" to this approach: the conceptual (the perception of the society), the empirical (the actual society), and the operational (the model designed to explain certain features of the society). Further, the complex model portrays societal members
in the process of interaction. In other words, within a given society, the basic
system unit is the *individual person.* This is a classical approach but is a rather
radical departure from Parsonian systems theory, in which the basic unit of
the social system was the *social role* rather than the *individual actor.* Miller
(1978, 17) refers to systems with organisms as the basic unit of analysis as
concrete systems. Systems such as Parsons' social system, with the social role
as the unit of analysis, are called *abstracted systems* by Miller (1978, 19).

SET is a concrete systems model, as the primary isomorphism is between
it and the society as a set of interacting social actors. However, this does not
mean that we eschew conceptual analysis, such as the analysis of social roles.
Rather, once our basic concrete systems model is formulated, we use it to gen-

erate various abstracted (conceptual) systems, just as various symbol systems are generated by social interaction among societal members as the empirical level.

In contrast, most middle-range theories are "abstracted" in Miller's terms, meaning that their basic units are concepts rather than concrete individuals. Parsons (1979, 705; Parsons and Shils 1951, 190) adamantly supported this approach as the optimal analytical strategy. It does have some advantages, as we have determined elsewhere (Bailey 1981). However, *the fact that most middle-range theories are abstracted theories is another reason why we cannot aggregate them to construct the general theory isomorphic with the phenomenon being studied.* In other words, aggregating two or more abstracted theories will result in a more-general abstracted theory but can never yield a concrete theory. The aggregative strategy would only yield a general concrete theory if the middle-range theories to be aggregated were themselves concrete. Due to the paucity of middle-range concrete theories, this strategy is not feasible at the present time. For further discussion of cumulation see Turner (1989).

The basic SET model is concrete but abstracted systems are generated as needed. The concrete model describes interaction or relationships among human actors. The abstracted subsystems describe relationships, too; but these are relationships among variables rather than actors. Thus, a primary task of SET is to also explore and explain the congruence between social relationships (among societal members) and variable relationships (among the characteristics of these members).

The analysis of relationships among objects or organisms is generally called *Q-analysis* (Sneath and Sokal 1973; Bailey 1972). The analysis of relationships among variables is generally called *R-analysis* (Sneath and Sokal 1973; Bailey 1972). Thus, it can be shown (Bailey 1980) that concrete systems are generally Q-systems and abstracted systems are R-systems, although other names have been used for these distinctions. Kuhn (1974) refers to concrete systems, such as systems where the basic units are human social actors, as acting systems. Conceptual (abstracted) systems in which the basic units are concepts, symbols, or signs are referred to as *pattern systems* by Kuhn (1974). Facet theory (Guttman 1959; Lingoes 1968) provides still another set of terms: the population of N objects is called the *P-facet*, while the set of M items, or variables analyzed for each object, is called the *I-facet*. Actual societies encompass both facets, of course, and they are closely interwoven. Thus, an adequate isomorphic model also encompass both facets. It is analytically simpler to study one or the other, as it generally done, but this represents an inappropriate simplification of reality and lacks sufficient complexity to generate an isomorphic model. That is, if both facets exist in society they must both exist in an adequate model, and that model must be isomorphic with the society being modeled.

Unfortunately, most analyses in sociology are either Q (P-facet, concrete system, acting system) or R (I-facet, abstracted system, pattern system) but not both. Thus, they are not isomorphic with the actual societal situation in which human actors (P-facet) utilize symbols or signs (often in the form of characteristics of themselves or others such as gender, age, race, and so forth) to help guide their interaction. Classically, verbal theory has focussed on the action of human actors and has also utilized symbols, so it has come the closest to isomorphism. However, Parsonian functionalism departed from this with its emphasis on abstracted systems. Actors (P-facet) were still used by Parsons, but the stress was put upon the analysis of the social system as an abstracted system, or pattern system, utilizing primarily the I-facet (Parsons 1979, p. 705; Parsons and Shils 1951, p. 190).

On the other hand, virtually all statistical studies in sociology are R-studies. A few exceptions that use the individual rather than the variable as the unit of analysis include a very few Q-analyses (for example, Butler and Adams 1966); some sociometric models such as blockmodelling (for example, White, Boorman, and Breiger 1976); and some social mobility and migration models such as the mover-stayer model (Spilerman 1972). The prevailing R-models have never been isomorphic with actual society but represent only a limited analytical abstraction. Their explanatory power is thus limited to analyzing relationships among a relatively few variables abstracted from those deemed salient in the society at large. By utilizing both the P- and I- facets, SET escapes the limitations of these narrower models and thus has greater explanatory power.

Aiken (1981, 449) makes basically the same point in different words: "I would argue that the underlying logic of sociology is a conceptual one, that is, research and scholarship are organized fundamentally into conceptual categories and relationships." He notes that although some other social sciences are also conceptually organized (for example, economics), many *do not* share the purely conceptual basis. For example, history has a temporal and spatial organization, whereas political science has a conceptual and spatial organization.

Sociology's purely conceptual organization has limitations, according to Aiken. Principally, a spatial organization would be less isolating. "One of the consequences of having a spatial logic as the basis of organizing a discipline is the openness to incorporating insights and information from other disciplines into research and scholarship" (Aiken 1981, p. 449). Aiken's "conceptual organization" is just another way of saying that sociological anaylsis is generally limited to R-analysis (abstracted system, pattern system, or I-facet).

The SET model, elaborated in Chapter 2, studies human actors as they interact in physical space within (and across) societal boundaries. This does not hinder conceptual analysis (as some might argue) but in fact facilitates it, as well as provides the advantages of the spatial variable discussed by Aiken.

Relation to Other Formulations

Beginning with an isomorphic concrete system, SET generates six macro-sociological variables. This is done in the basically inductive manner (although deduction is used in SET as well) described by Merton (1968, p. 40) for the derivation of the middle-range theories of reference groups and relative deprivation. Thus, although clearly macrosociological, SET deals with a limited set of variables and would seem to meet Merton's criteria for a middle-range theory. But even if SET is not middle-range, it seems impossible to formulate such an isomorphic model, which integrates both the P-and I-facets, by adding together a number of formulations that are chiefly limited to one facet but not both. Thus, the direct strategy seems to be the only feasible approach.

However, Merton also implies that the direct approach to general theory, if premature, is doomed to failure and pretentious as well. This requires clarification. For one thing, macrosociological formulations, like microsociological formulations, will probably succeed in some respects and fail in others. There will not likely be consensus on their degree of success, as criteria for evaluating theories vary widely in sociology. Further, it is not clear that an attempt to formulate macrosociological theory is more pretentious than an attempt to formulate microsociological theory. The "larger" task is not necessarily always the best or the most difficult. It is surely easier to perform an appendectomy than to perform certain types of microsurgery, even though the former is more macro in nature.

The Relation of SET to Middle-Range and Micro Theory

We have noted that, as Opp (1970) pointed out, Merton gives us no logical rules by which middle-range theories can be converted into a more general theory. In other words, Merton never really said that middle-range theories were literally to be aggregated into a general theory. However, he hints at aggregation by saying that total theory results from "sustained, disciplined, and *cumulative* research" (Merton 1968, p. 47, italics added) and quotes Henderson to the effect that in natural science total theory does not stem fully formed from the mind of a single researcher but is formulated and revised by many researchers (Merton 1968, p. 47).

An alternative view posited by Miller (1978, p. 5)—and one that seems quite reasonable to me—is that a general theory is not a mere aggregation of existing theories but a new formulation that organizes existing theories and bridges gaps in knowledge. SET would seem to help bridge the gaps between some less general theories. When conceiving SET I was careful *not* to read existing theories, in order to maximize the isomorphism between SET and my perceptions of the existing society, rather than depend upon (and thus be limited by) a narrower formulation that was insufficiently complex to be isomorphic with the holistic society. Thus, SET is clearly not a simple aggregation of existing theories. However, it cuts across many, although it is doubtful that it exhausts any, and it probably does not utilize the same terminology. SET does rely heavily, as will be seen, on many familiar concepts in sociology; for example, the division of labor, technology, role, norm, and so forth. Among the middle-range theories that clearly overlap with SET are role theory, norm theory, status theory, and symbolic interactionism. An attempt will be made in the respective chapters to provide references to relevant middle-range theories, even though these will often not be directly represented in SET. Rather they may sometimes be seen as parallel formulations that utilize a different conceptual armory but with similar goals, or indeed in some cases they may be seen as contradictory to SET.

The Relation of SET to General or Macro Formulations

It has been stressed here that it is unclear where the dividing line lies between Merton's middle-range theory and total theory. In addition to *total*, Merton interchangeably uses the terms *unified theory* and *general theory*, although it is not clear that these are actually synonyms. SET would probably be classified as middle range by Merton because it relies primarily upon six macro variables. Thus, it certainly is not a total system of theory, and it is also not completely general or completely unified (and again the demarcation line for these terms in unclear and seems to be arbitrary). However, it is more unified and more general than many extant theories. It particularly goes beyond most formulations in integrating the P- and I-facets and in the general integration of theory and methodology.

There are clear parallels between SET and a number of extant macro-sociological formulations. As a systems theory, SET attempts to build upon the best-known macro systems theory in sociology: structural functionalism. It was formulated as a model that utilizes the advantages of systems formulation without the flaws of functionalism. SET can also be compared with another systems theory, James Grier Miller's (1978) *Living Systems*. A number of principles central to SET, such as the emphasis on isomorphism between the system and the society and the advocacy of concrete systems, are also found in *Living Systems* (LS). However, LS is clearly more of an exercise in general systems theory than is SET. While LS emphasizes the common features of systems at every level (e.g., organism, group, organization, society), SET applies systems theory to derive a sociological explanation of the aspects of each level, be they common to other levels or unique. There are also some parallels between SET and the various extant world systems models, most of which are based either on the Forrester-Meadows (Meadows 1972; Forrester 1973) Club of Rome model or on Wallerstein's (1974) theory. The overlap is relatively slight, as neither of these formulations utilizes general systems theory to the extent that SET does nor utilizes the society as the basic unit of analysis. Probably the clearest point of overlap is between the Forrester-Meadows model and SET's formulation of the six basic macro variables, discussed in Chapter 4.

SET also parallels, overlaps, or draws upon a number of systems theories. It draws quite heavily upon *General System Theory* (Bertalanffy 1968). It also draws somewhat upon the work of Buckley (1967), but is much more macrosociological than his formulation. Similarly, there are parallels with the systems theory of Kuhn (1963; 1974), and this work was quite helpful in the development of SET.

Another formulation having some overlap with SET is the work of Bates and Harvey (1975); a number of points of overlap here, including the critiques of Parsonian theory. SET also parallels at least two other recent volumes. Blalock and Wilken's (1979) formulation can be seen as parallel to SET in a number of respects, including the goals of various chapters, although the conceptualization and terminology are quite different. Also, the Blalock and Wilken formulation shares SET's concern with the integration of micro and macro factors, but with quite a difference in emphasis. While Blalock and Wilken concentrate on micro issues and only really discuss macro issues toward the end of the volume, SET generates the macro variables before the micro. The other recent volume is Blau's *Inequality and Heterogeneity* (1977), which can be seen to parallel certain chapters of SET and have a certain degree of methodological overlap.

Plan of the Chapters

Chapter 1 has been devoted to establishing the nature of the task and the general mode of procedure. As already noted, we plan to utilize the systems approach because it seems optimal for macrosociological analysis. Chapter 2 presents the specific systems model I think is optimal for macrosociological analysis. It must escape the pitfalls that were the bane of functionalism (such as the equilibrium trap) and in general must meet all the myriad challenges to a macrosociological systems theory. Two basic epistemological features of the model are its use of the three-level model of conceptual, empirical, and operational isomorphism, in conjunction with a dual usage of the P-facet (persons and their social interaction) and the I-facet (variables or characteristics of persons and their intercorrelations). I contend that the three-level model (Bailey 1984c, 1986, 1988b) is minimal for satisfactory analysis, replacing the usual dichotomy that is variously described as *theory/data, conceptual/empirical, abstract/concrete,* or *theory/research.* Three levels are necessary, as dichotomies either neglect one level or merge two levels together. Yet, the two-level model is so commonplace and familiar (for example, see Blalock 1968; Costner 1969) that it is never challenged.

The two level model presents a good illustration of why the extension and aggregation of middle-range theory is so difficult. Once one accepts the notion there are only two levels, there is neither mechanism nor motive for broadening the model. Yet, if one eschews the two-level model, thus escaping the limitations posed by its assumptions and concepts, cursory examination of the actual measurement process clearly reveals three-levels of analysis rather than two. Chapter 2 also presents the details of the systems model, including such crucial features as boundaries, the proper unit of analysis (including reasons for using the individual actor instead of the social role), and the notion of isomorphism.

Chapter 3 deals with the crucial issue of the measure of system state. Even a conceptually sound systems model is of little use for empirical research (and theoretically limited) without an adequate measure of system state. Verbal macrotheorists in sociology have generally referred to the state of the system by such terms as *system integration* or *system order.* These terms can be vague, arbitrary, and rather difficult to use rigorously. Thus, at first glance, the functionalists' use of such terms as *functional prerequisite, system survival,* and particularly *equilibrium* would seem to be a more rigorous way of dealing with the problem. Unfortunately, the concept of equilibrium proved unsound both theoretically and methodologically and became one of the primary weaknesses of functionalism. It is clear that SET requires a measure of system state other than the concept of equilibrium. This is available in the concept of entropy. Entropy is a measure of system structure that has both theoretical and statistical interpretations, as well as widespread applications in other disciplines (including general systems theory). It is a sibling concept of equilibrium and generally subsumes it, so that the concept of equilibrium can still be used when appropriate but need not be when it is inadequate (unlike the case for functionalism, which had no alternative).

The six basic macrosociological variables, and other ways of measuring them (for example, distributional measures), are presented in Chapter 4. These variables are also presented in the form of simultaneous equations representing an *abstracted system* in Miller's terms or a *pattern system* in Kuhn's terms. However, instead of being isolated, as is generally the case when an abstracted system is presented *in lieu of* a concrete system, this (and other abstracted systems generated within the course of the analysis) is firmly situated within the context of the concrete system.

Chapter 5 studies the role of the individual in complex society. That is, individual action is analyzed within the context of the set of macrosociological variables generated in Chapter 4. Different societies may have different configurations of these macrosociological variables, thus providing different contexts for individual action, leading to different goals, motivations, and expectations for societal members. For example, an individual might well have different goals and expectations in a society with a particular population size, technology, and occupational division of labor than in one with different values of these and the other strategic macrosociological variables. Obviously, however, individual actions are not set only within the context of the macro variables but within the context of his or her own characteristics (including those both ascribed and achieved). In fact, individual action occurs within the context of a host of intermediate variables representing the characteristics of groups intermediate to the individual and the societal levels of which the individual might be a member (discussed in Chapter 6). Chapter 5 discusses individual action within the context of such notions as role theory, goal theory, and expectation theory. These subtheories can be readily identified as "middle-range theories," even though they were not formulated in a direct manner and as precursors to the more general theory but in fact were formulated after the macro theory and are set within its context. This facilitates the study of micro-macro relationships. Beyond that, it shows that general theory does not only develop cumulatively from less general theory, as Merton implies, but in fact the prior formulation of the general theory can aid in the formulation of middle-range theory and may be necessary for the development of such theory. Thus, it is possible to get the middle-range cart before the unified horse.

Social interaction between two or more actors, as well as individual action within the context of groups and organizations, are discussed in Chapter 6. As in Chapter 5, Chapter 6 deals with the action of concrete individual actors (concrete system, acting system, P-facet, Q-analysis) within the context of symbol systems (abstracted system, pattern system, I-facet, R-analysis). This achieves a degree of theoretical and methodological unification not found generally but necessary for the model to be isomorphic with empirical reality, and thus to explain the phenomenon holistically. Any less complex formulation may explain a portion of the phenomena (though probably in artificial fashion) but surely will not yield an adequate explanation.

Chapter 7 culminates the integration of the P- and I-facets by discussing their interrelationship for all levels of the society as a whole: entire society as a unit, individual level, and intermediate levels such as group and organization. This chapter seeks a generalized theory of social order and includes a discussion of power. The concept of entropy is used and yields theoretical explication as well as facilitating operationalization. The resulting explication of social order is more holistic than is usually found and not limited to a single middle-range perspective like consensus or equilibrium theory (functionalism), on the one hand, or conflict theory, on the other. However, the reader is forewarned that no definitive theory of social order is forthcoming. This is the "cutting edge" of the SET model; and along with operationalization and empirical testing, it is the primary arena for future research.

Chapter 8 is the quantitative counterpart of Chapter 7. In Chapter 8, the cutting edge of the operationalization of entropy is examined in more detail, and the statistical literature on entropy is analyzed. Various entropy measures are discussed, as well as the application of the concept to various substantive areas. Also, the relationship of entropy to various extant statistical measures in sociology is analyzed. Together Chapters 7 and 8 seek to contribute more fully to the understanding of the relationship between the substantive and statistical interpretations of entropy and to the relationship between sociological theory and method in general.

SET is summarized in Chapter 9. Problems of operationalization and verification are discussed, and selected hypotheses suitable for testing are presented. The central focus of this book is a consistent, unified presentation of the basic SET model at the societal, individual, and intermediate levels. However, this does not ignore the problem of verification. Utilization of the entropy concept greatly facilitates the operationalization process, as the concept has both substantive theoretical significance and amenability to multivariate statistical operationalization. Thus, hypotheses are presented in Chapter 9, and more will be derived later, to form the basis for future efforts of extended use and testing. Although the problems of verification of a macrosociological model such as SET can be immense—primarily because of the effort and expense involved in data collection—use of the entropy concept minimizes problems of operationalization substantially. Further, although a given model should be potentially testable, it is not necessary that all testing be accomplished immediately. We have strived mightily to ensure that SET is in a form amenable to operationalization and testing.

Chapter 2

The Isomorphic Concrete Systems Model

In its most general sense (to be defined later in much greater detail) a system is a set of interrelated parts. A complex society certainly displays many interrelated parts, so minimally it meets the definition of an empirical system. This being the case, it seems logical that a systems model be adopted for the analysis of the social system. Unfortunately, however, systems analysis in sociology has been more promise than product. Although the concept of system is a rather old one in sociology, systems theorizing has encountered a number of problems that must be solved, resolved, or simply avoided if a systems model is to be successful.

Beyond Functionalism

The two most prominent systems approaches in sociology have been functionalism and general systems theory (GST). Functionalism is a relatively old approach; GST is a more modern interdisciplinary approach. Our approach is basically a postfunctional one that draws quite heavily from GST. We also draw on functionalism. Unfortunately, functionalism has been plagued by a number of problems, which have limited its success considerably. In order to escape some of these problems in the model, we will review the history of systems theory (most prominently, functionalism) in sociology and attempt to move beyond functionalism.

Functionalism

Functionalism in sociology is approximately as old as the discipline itself. According to Turner (1978), Comte's (1875) organicism helped lay the foundation for early functionalism. Spencer ([1885] 1966, p. 473) distinguished between structure and function, and Durkheim ([1893] 1933) in the *Division of Labor* developed functionalism quite explicitly.

With the development of American sociology in the early twentieth century, systems theory was barely visible, seen chiefly in the early writings of the students of Pareto (1935), Cannon (1929; 1932), and Henderson (1928; 1935). Most prominent among these students were Homans and Curtis (1934) and Parsons (1937). Durkheim's influence on early American sociologists was minimal since his work was not available in English until the 1930s, with the publication of the *Division of Labor* in 1933 and Parsons' *Structure of Social Action* in 1937. But functionalism was alive and well in anthropology, most notably in the work of Radcliffe-Brown (1935; 1948; 1952) and Malinowski (1944; 1948). Functionalism reemerged in sociology in 1945 with the publication of the Davis-Moore hypothesis (Davis and Moore 1945). The immediate critical reaction to this theory (for example, see Tumin 1953) was to serve as a harbinger for functionalism. Doom was not immediate. The search for functional requisites (Aberle et al. 1950) met with some acceptance. Merton's (1949) "Manifest and Latent Functions" seemed to alleviate, if not cure, some of functionalism's ills. Parsons' systems theory (1951; Parsons and Shils 1951) received considerable acclaim. The president of the American Sociological Association (Davis 1959) attacked, claiming that functionalism was ubiquitous. Goldschmidt's *Comparative Functionalism* (1966) seemed to offer a viable comparative framework for anthropology. Moreover, Stinchcombe's (1968) characterization of functionalist explanation as a causal loop showed a promising way out of the ever-present illegitimate teleology trap that had proved so treacherous to functionalist adherents since Durkheim.

Unfortunately for functionalism, these promising developments were countered by a torrent of criticism of virtually all facets of functionalism. Because of emphasis on such concepts as system order, integration, and equilibrium, functionalism has been attacked on ideological grounds as a conservative rationale for maintenance of the status quo (Gouldner 1959, 1970; Horowitz 1962; Lockwood 1956; Lopreato 1971). The logic of the approach has also been widely questioned. Homans (1964) flatly asserts that functionalism is inadequate as explanation both because it generally is not reductionist and because it is not deductive, as deduction to Homans is the only adequate explanatory form. The vulnerability of functional models to charges of illegitimate teleology have long been recognized. Sociologists ask how a structure can be explained by something that occurs after it does (Dore 1961)?

Functionalists have sought to defend against these charges. One approach has been to provide a causal explanation of the structure in addition to an analysis of its function. A more modern model that seems to be relatively free of teleology is Stinchcombe's (1968) graph model, in which a functional explanation is portrayed as a causal feedback loop. Another strategy is to expunge the language of all words that smack of teleology, such as *purpose* (Turner 1978; Gouldner 1959; Merton 1949). A third strategy (perhaps a variation of the first) is to explain the origin of the structure in a nonteleological, if noncausal, fashion. The most popular way is to evoke evolution and say that the structure serving the particular requisite function was "socially selected" and other less adequate structures may have existed, but if so failed to maintain their respective societies, leading to their demise. Turner and Maryanski (1979) feel that since it is virtually impossible to test for societal survival, the social selection approach can easily become a gloss for illegitimate teleology. A final way to legitimate teleology is to avoid seeking an explanation for the existence of a function in a particular society, because this generally leads into the teleology trap. Goldschmidt (1966) successfully avoids teleology by eschewing explanation altogether and limiting his functional approach to a comparative framework, but most sociologists have explanation as their goal and are unwilling to relinquish it. In addition to teleology, functionalism has been charged with tautological reasoning. As with teleology, a common defense is to invoke the notion of selective social survival.

The functionalist's valiant efforts to avoid logical traps have seemingly failed to stop the flow of criticism. Criticism of functionalism's logic has been substantial (for example, see Dore 1961; Erasmus 1967; Gouldner 1959; Hempel 1959; Isajiw 1968; Bergman 1962; Canfield 1964; Deutsch 1951; Sztompka 1969, 1974).

In spite of all the valiant efforts to repair their model, functionalists seem now to be bloodied, if not bowed. Few if any explicitly functional explanations seem now to be published, and Turner and Maryanski (1979, p. 141) feel that functionalism as explanatory theory is "dead" and should be abandoned. It seems safe to say that all of the critical smoke would indicate the existence of at least some fire of functional deficiency. The critics' unanimity and consensus is sometimes artificial because, although both persons A and B are critical, they are criticizing different things. What critic A likes, critic B abhors, and vice versa. This is similar to a child and her father both disliking their pony; the child because it is too large to ride, and the father because it is too small to ride. Nevertheless, so many criticisms from so many directions are difficult to ignore, and we must conclude that none of the several variants of traditional functionalism in either sociology or anthropology seems viable enough to justify a great deal of effort at the present time.

General Systems Theory

Does the death of functionalism spell the doom of all systems analysis in sociology, or is there a viable nonfunctional systems approach? The only nonfunctional systems approach since Pareto to command any substantial attention from social scientists has been general systems theory (Bertalanffy 1956, 1968; Buckley 1967, 1968; Churchman 1968; Maruyama 1963; Wiener 1948).

General systems theory as developed by Bertalanffy (1968) and others is a basically content-free multidisciplinary approach. It is largely derived from models and principles in biology and physics. As such its application in sociology is certainly not without precedent, as organic and mechanical models have been applied since the writings of Comte and Spencer. However, the unsophisticated use of such models in sociology is sure to elicit criticism.

Further, much of GST will appear to the careful observer to be neither a physical nor organic analogy but rather a very general, essentially content-free set of basic definitions and programmatic statements. Critics may not see the value of this approach unless they realize, as Klir (1969) has pointed out, that, as a relatively content-free paradigm, GST is incomplete unless complemented by content from some content-specific substantive discipline. The gist of GST is that such a content-specific discipline will reveal empirical entities that can be seen as systems and that the principles of GST can elucidate. This is the premise upon which our application of the systems model to the complex social system is based.

So far, this somewhat cursory review of the sociological systems literature shows that neither functionalism not GST has achieved the goal of explaining how a complex society operates on a day-to-day basis. However, nothing in the literature concludes that a viable approach to systems analysis in sociology cannot be constructed. GST has never been specifically applied to this task, the foci of the books by Buckley (1967), Kuhn (1974), and Miller (1978) being quite different. Functionalism, on the other hand, is probably more suitable for the analysis of simple social systems (e.g., mechanical societies in Durkheim's terms). Functional models were viable in some anthropological applications but were never adequate for the analysis of complex social systems, even if the ideological and logical pitfalls discussed earlier could have been avoided. The time seems right to attempt a move beyond functionalism through a synthesis based on the several valuable concepts to be found in the rubble of this earlier systems approach. This is the goal of the present volume:

1. Detail the problems inherent in any systems approach designed to analyze complex social systems;
2. Detail the strengths of a systems approach, to demonstrate that such an approach is worthwhile (and perhaps even necessary) in spite of all the difficulties it encounters;
3. Present an optimal approach designed to maximize the strengths listed and minimize the weaknesses listed;
4. Evaluate the approach and indicate the direction of future research.

The approach to be presented is a synthesis based largely on functionalism and GST. Exploitation of the universal general principles in GST will help avoid some of the problems in functionalism, stemming from its many different variants. Similarly, functionalism, with its comparatively rich content, will help repair the overly general and sometimes apparently vacuous nature of GST. The synthesis will be further enriched by borrowing from existing substantive systems models, most notably the POET model of the ecological complex (Ogburn 1951; Duncan and Schnore 1959) and Parsons' systems model (1951).

The Challenges

Theorists attempting to successfully model complex social systems face many challenges. Some of these pitfalls have been recognized in functionalism and GST and some have not. Those that have been recognized have been solved with varying degrees of success, as the review indicates. We will be concerned with thirteen basic problems:

1. An adequate definition of the system.
2. An adequate specification of the boundaries for the system as a whole, for system components, and for subsystems (if any) and their components.
3. An adequate measure of system state and adequate operationalization of such a measure.
4. The attainment of isomorphism between the theoretical systems model and the actual operating, empirical, complex system.
5. The selection of a suitable set of explanatory variables out of the almost infinite number that could be identified in a complex social system.
6. An adequate understanding of the relationship among the components of the system and between each component, and the whole, to overcome the problem of unwitting displacement of scope.
7. An adequate analysis of both micro and macro levels and their interrelationships to solve or avoid problems such as reductionism and emergence.
8. A recognition of the needs of the individuals and subgroups within the system and of the system as a whole.
9. An adequate defense against the almost certain criticism that the systems analysis is an inappropriate organic or mechanical analogy.
10. The recognition of individual, subgroup, and system goals and an understanding of how they are attained.
11. An understanding of the role of matter-energy and information in ongoing system functioning.

12. An adequate diachronic analysis of the system, to understand change over time.
13. The adequate explanation and prediction (including verification) of salient aspects of the complex system via the social systems model.

Meeting The Challenges

The discussion in this chapter has centered upon a host of problems that have confronted sociological systems theorists. These myriad problems range from illegitimate teleology, to system boundary problems, to displacement of scope. When confronted with such an array of difficulties, one might be inclined to agree with Merton that general theory is doomed to failure. Conversely, though, the difficulties to be overcome by a theory merely underscore the low probability of arriving at precisely the fortuitous combination necessary to solve these theoretical ills by aggregating extant middle-range theories.

It might also be argued that some of these problems (for example, boundary delimitation) are a function of a systems formulation and would disappear if systems theory were eschewed. This argument is countered relatively easily. A perusal of the thirteen challenges shows that the bulk of them are clearly problems to be met by any complex theory, systems theory or otherwise. The general systems formulation being utilized is so skeletal that it fosters few problems in isolation, and the majority of the problems are encountered in the particular application; that is, they are problems of content, or are problems stemming from the size and complexity of the model rather than problems of general systems theory.

For example, the concept of functional prerequisite was clearly responsible for many of the logical problems, specifically problems of illegitimate teleology and tautology, experienced by functionalism. This concept is foreign to general systems theory and unique to a particular application of systems theory—functionalism. Similarly, Chapter 3 will show that the concept of equilibrium is not foreign to systems theory, but it is used in quite a different fashion than it is in sociology. Thus, although the particular usages of equilibrium in sociology caused tremendous problems, the use of the concept in nonsociological systems formulations (for example, in economics) has not encountered such problems. Further, Parsons' use of abstracted systems caused a number of problems (Miller 1978; Bailey 1981). This is once again a case where problems arose not from a general systems model but from a particular application. Whereas abstracted systems are not unknown outside of sociology, the concrete model is much more widely used and has many advantages (Miller 1978).

It is true that we could to a certain extent avoid certain problems (such as boundary delimitation) by the use of a nonsystems model or even by the use of an abstracted, as opposed to a concrete, systems model. However, boundary delimitation is not merely a systems problem, it is also a content problem. That is, societies, as well as systems models, have boundaries, and indeed this is one of the points of isomorphism between the model and the data. Thus, using a model that does not include boundary analysis simply means neglecting an important macrosociological problem. In extreme cases, it also means losing model-data isomorphism, thus risking an inability to verify the model. Of course, a further strategy toward these challenges is to simply refuse to deal with them (at least with so many of them) and to direct all energy toward smaller tasks that offer a greater potential for success. Unfortunately, smaller tasks yield smaller rewards. Further, the challenges outlined in this chapter are so central to the discipline of sociology that they cannot be ignored, particularly when a complex, isomorphic, concrete systems model might prove efficacious in dealing with them.

We now turn our efforts to sketching such a model. Obviously a model sufficient to deal with all thirteen issues will be broad and quite complex. Also, obviously, the model cannot deal with every issue of interest to sociologists. The crucial criteria is that the model be sufficiently broad not to preclude the study of a broad array of topics. In other words, it is not necessary that the model include an exhaustive array of middle-range concerns at this time but only that it be broad enough, in a skeletal form, to have the potential for the analyzing such topics. Only by beginning with a sufficiently large model can we safeguard the potential for studying both rational and random action, both process and product, both positivism and idealism.

The Isomorphic Concrete Systems Model

This section deals with the formulation of a systems model adequate for the analysis of complex society. As stated earlier, we have decided to construct a concrete model isomorphic with the society being studied. Specifically, to be successful, it must be as complex as the phenomenon being modeled. The first task is to discuss the epistemology of the endeavor, specifically the relationship between the systems model and the actual society.

Epistemology

The task at this point is to define isomorphism and specify clearly the systems that are said to be isomorphic. In both regards the discussion by Miller (1978) is used and extended.

Isomorphism

We will follow Miller's (1978) usage of the terms *function, formal identity,* and *isomorphism. Formal identity* can be defined in terms of function, and *isomorphism* can be defined in terms of formal identity. Miller (1978, pp. 16–17) says that: "A *function* is a correspondence between two variables, x and y, such that for each value of x there is a definite value of y, and no two y's have the same x, and this correspondence is determined by some rule (e.g., $x^2 = y, xn = y, x + 3 = y$). . . . This sense of "function" is the usual mathematical usage." We must stress that the term *function* is being used here in the mathematical sense, as opposed to its substantive usage in *structural functionalism.*"

Now that *function* has been defined, we can follow Miller (1978, p. 17) in defining *formal identity*.

> One system may have one or more variables, each of which varies compara-
> bly to a variable in another system. If these comparable variations are so
> similar that they can be expressed by the same function, a *formal identity*
> exists between the two systems. If different functions are required to express
> the variations, there is a formal *dis*identity.

Isomorphism between two systems A and B exists, in principle, when (1) the components of system A are represented by corresponding components in system B; and (2) when the relationships between the components of system A are represented by corresponding relationships (identical mathematical functions) between the corresponding components of system B.

Thus, if the empirically occurring society (for example, the United States) is seen as a system with a set of components and with relationships between them, a systems model can be made isomorphic with the social system if it has a component to correspond to each of the society's components, and if the relationships between the components of the systems model are the same as the relationships between the corresponding components in the society. Basically, the idea of isomorphism is simple enough and only refers to a one-to-one correspondence between the components and their interrelationships for each of two or more systems. Isomorphism between two systems would not exist if the systems differ in the types of components or if the relationships between components were different for the two systems.

The value of a true isomorphism should be evident. If we can construct a model—whether verbal, mathematical, or a combination of both—that truly represents all societal components and their interrelationships, then in effect by understanding the model we should be able to understand the society that it represents. Miller (1978, p. 17) says that

> Science advances as the formal identity or isomorphism increases between a theoretical conceptual system and objective findings about concrete or abstracted systems.
>
> The chief purpose of this book is to state in prose a conceptual system concerning variables—units and relationships—which have important formal identities or isomorphisms to concrete, living systems.

We, too, wish to construct a model—SET—that is isomorphic with the complex society. This is the principal reson why the model must be as complex as the phenomenon being modeled.

The Two-Level Model

To this point the establishment of isomorphism has been shown to be central to the endeavor and, in fact, to all social research. Sociologists use the principle of isomorphism frequently, even though they may not use the term. Next we discuss how model-data isomorphism may be achieved. It is customary in social science to distinguish between the conceptual and empirical levels of analysis (Blalock 1968; Costner 1969). This dichotomous formulation (or variants of it) has been presented repeatedly in the sociological literature, with various substantive applications and a wide variety of names for the two levels.

Blalock (1968, p. 12) speaks of these two levels as "underlying or unmeasured concepts, on the one hand, and indicators or composite indices, on the other." Later (p. 24) he speaks of "theoretically defined concepts" versus "the operational level". Costner (1969) also utilizes the two-level approach, expressing this dichotomy alternatively as "abstract concepts and concrete implications," "abstract conceptions and concrete events," and "abstract and empirical levels" (p. 245). Variants of the two-level distinction have been widely applied in typology construction. Winch (1947) distinguishes between heuristic and empirical typologies; Capecchi (1966) contrasts abstract and non-abstract types; whereas Hempel (1952) speaks of ideal versus classificatory types; and McKinney (1966) refers to ideal versus extracted types. In theory construction, Coleman (1964, p. 9) distinguishes between synthetic and explanatory types. Sociologists also utilize the two-level dichotomy widely in discussions of validity. Bohrnstedt and Knoke (1982, p. 12) speak of "establishing links between concepts and their empirical referents." They say further that "*Validity* refers to the degree to which an operation results in a measure that accurately reflects the concept it is intended to measure."

Many other researchers have applied the two-level dichotomy in various ways. The distinction used earlier between an uninterpreted calculus and an interpreted calculus (Brown 1963, p. 174) is itself an application of this dichotomy. Among other variants of this dichotomy are Northrop's (1947) distinction between concepts by intuition and concepts by postulation; Bierstedt's (1959) nominal versus real definitions; and Coomb's (1953) distinction between phenotypic and genotypic levels of analysis. Blalock (1968, p. 12) feels that most of these terminological differences are primarily sematic in nature. Still other expressions of this same basic dichotomy are found in such familiar distinctions as theory-data, theory-method, and so forth. Among the terms that have been used to signify the conceptual level are *conceptual, abstract, ideal, heuristic, theoretical, definitional,* and *construct.* Among the terms applied to the other level are *empirical, concrete, operational, data,* and "*real world.*"

Given the pervasiveness of this seemingly ubiquitous dichotomy, it seems likely that it would have made its way into general systems theory (GST) as well. Such is indeed the case. Miller (1978) makes a basic distinction between a conceptual system and a concrete system. According to Miller, "*Units of a conceptual system* are terms, such as words (commonly nouns, pronouns and their modifiers), numbers, or other symbols, including those in computer simulations and programs" (1978, p. 16). In contrast, "*A concrete, real, or veridical system* is a nonrandom accumulation of matter-energy, in a region in physical space-time, which is organized into interacting interrelated subsystems of components" (1978, p. 17).

Whereas concrete systems are by definition empirically occuring systems, conceptual systems are never empirically occurring;

> A conceptual system may be purely logical or mathematical, or its terms and relationships may be intended to have some sort of formal identity or isomorphism with units and relationships empirically determinable by some operation carried out by an ovserver, which are selected observable variables in a concrete system or an abstracted system. (p. 17)

Miller's (1978, pp. 19–20) abstracted system is an intermediate type in that its components may or may not be empirically observable "The units of *abstracted systems* are relationships abstracted or selected by an observer in the light of his interests, theoretical viewpoint, or philosophical bias. Some relationships may be empirically determinable by some operation carried out by the observer, but other are not, being only his concepts" (p. 19).

A chief task of scientific research, then, becomes the attainment of isomorphism between conceptual systems, on the one hand, and concrete or abstracted systems, on the other. Miller (1978, p. 17) says that:

> The observer selects the variables of his conceptual system. As to the many variables in the concrete or abstracted system that are not isomorphic with the selected variables in his conceptual system, the observer may either (a) observe that they remain constant, or (b) operate on the concrete or abstracted system in order to ensure that they remain constant, or (c) "randomize them" *i.e.*, assume without proof that they remain constant, or (d) simply neglect them.

At this point the establishment of isomorphism would seem to be relatively straightforward. Society can be seen as an empirically occurring concrete system and the model as a conceptual system. To attain ismorphism between the two simple means that all components of the empirical system and the relationships among them must be identified and represented in a direct one-to-one fashion at the conceptual level. Unfortunately, the situation is not that simple. For one thing, as discussed in Chapter 1, both relationships among human actors (Q-relationships) and relationships among variables such as race or gender (R-relationships) must be represented in the isomorphism. The Q- and R-analyses either can be formulated as two separate systems or combined holistically in one model, depending upon the analytical strategy. We utilize the latter strategy in this book. The former strategy, if chosen, allows at least four types of potential analysis: Q-analysis at both the conceptual and empirical levels; and R-analysis at both the conceptual and empirical levels. This complicates the establishment of isomorphism somewhat. However, the situation is seen to be even more complex when one realizes that there are not merely *two* necessary levels on which social research takes place but *three* minimally distinct levels. Thus, instead of four types of analysis, we are now faced with six.

Anomalies in the Two-Level Model

We have seen that the two level model has been widely applied and accepted, despite some indications of problems in certain applications of the model, such as Blalock's (1968, pp. 12–13) suggestion that there is some confusion concerning the concept of validity and at least two separate types of validity exist.

> From the logical or theoretical standpoint, a measure is said to be valid to the degree that it measures what it is supposed to measure. . . . Validity is

used in a very different sense, however, when one is attempting to interrelate two operational procedures or two concepts by intuition. . . . It might serve to lessen the confusion over these two types of validity if they were given completely different names. (Blalock 1968, p. 13)

Although it may not be completely clear at this point, the confusion that Blalock noted is an anomaly, or symptom, of an inadequate model of measurement and research. Other hints of anomalies are evident upon closer examination of the two-level model. For example, Blalock (1968, p. 127) presents the two-level model as a contrast between "underlying or unmeasured concepts, on the one hand, and indicators or composite indices, on the other". A later discussion of ostensibly the same two-level model (p. 19)—remember that Blalock contends that there is one basic two-level model and terminological differences among various authors are largely semantic differences—does not speak of concepts and their indicators as the earlier discussion did, but rather refers to "the true value" and "the measured value." Perhaps these representations are merely two different ways to say the same thing or semantic differences that a writer might utilize to improve readability. Closer examination shows that this is not the case, and the different presentations have distinctly different connotations that essentially mirror, although he did not note this fact and apparently did not realize it, the distinction between the two types of validity that Blalock said should have different names. In the earlier discussion, Blalock is certainly speaking of a relationship between a concept and its indicator. This representation of the two-level model clearly parallels Northrop's (1947) distinction between concepts by postulation and concepts by intuition. The former can never be found empirically but the latter can. Concepts by intuition are linked to corresponding concepts by postulation through *epistemic correlations* (Northrop 1947, p. 119; Blalock 1968, pp. 10–12). This is essentially the same situation as the first type of validity that Blalock (1968, p. 13) discussed.

Blalock's (1968) later discussion, however, is quite different and similar to his second type of validity. This is the contrast between the true value and the measured value. The "true value" of something seems clearly an empirical entity rather than a concept, as was the case earlier. Further, although it is not really accurate to speak of measurement error between a concept and its empirical indicator (the correct term here would be *epistemic correlation* or *isomorphism*), it is completely appropriate to speak of measurement error between a true value and a measured value, as they both refer to empirically occurring entities. Thus, apparently Blalock inadvertently switched from a concept to an empirical entity without realizing it. This is extremely easy to do within the confines of the two-level model. The fact is that there are really three levels on which research is conducted. An attempt to analyze this situation with only two levels, for example in the study of measurement and validity, will result in either the unwitting merger of two of the three levels or the neglect of one level.

The Three-Level Model

In spite of the anomalies present in the two-level model, to my knowledge, it has never been challenged. There are probably a number of reasons for this. One is that the two-level model suffices (at least to a certain extent) in certain limited applications. If the concern is with only one or two of the three levels, the full model may not be needed. Another reason is that all three levels are sometimes utilized (but not simultaneously or correctly) without the analyst even realizing it. That is, the analyst maintains one level as Blalock did (the measured level) and shifts from the second level to the third level (from the conceptual to the empirical) without even realizing it. This is generally possible only within the relatively nonrigorous confines of a verbal discussion.

Still a third reason is that acceptance of the notion that only two levels exist precludes the search for a third. Recall the discussion in Chapter 1 of the aggregative and direct approaches to theory construction. A clear limitation of the middle-range strategy is that acceptance of the borders of the limited model often precludes any reason to reach beyond them. If one sketches a very broad skeletal model, as we are doing—with very wide borders—"holes" or neglected areas of research within those borders are readily apparent. However, if one utilizes a limited "middle-range" model, then attention is not focussed upon problems outside of its borders, as researchers are more concerned with resolving issues within the borders of the paradigm. This apparently was the case with the two-level model. Researchers focussed upon its application, for example, in measurement (Blalock 1968; Costner 1969), and apparently saw no reason to look beyond the model for three or more levels. I wish to make it clear here that these criticisms of the two-level model are directed at the logic of the model not at any particular application of it by a particular author. The model has been used widely by many methodologists, including, of course, me (see Bailey 1978, pp. 44–49).

However, once removed from the restrictive confines of the two-level model, the researcher can immediately see three levels quite clearly. Consider the familiar but oft abused example of the concept of intelligence. A researcher who wishes to measure and study intelligence has a mental perception, or cognitive image, of what is meant by intelligence. At this point the concept is merely a perception in the mind of the researcher. We symbolize this conceptual level by X. It is further assumed that the phenomenon of intelligence is actually possessed by human individuals and thus exists empirically. We symbolize this empirical occurrence with X'. We also hope to measure this phenomenon of intelligence with a scale or intelligence test. We symbolize such a scale with X''.

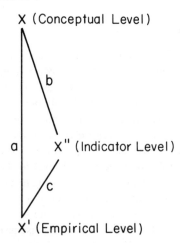

Figure 2.1 The Three-Level Measurement Model.

These three levels together form the three-level model, shown in Figure 2.1.

We can use standard terminology to refer to three levels, illustrating that all three levels are known to sociologists. However, unfortunately they are not all distinguished and utilized simultaneously as they must be to avoid confusion such as that noted by Blalock. The level signified by X, we label the *conceptual level*. This level refers *solely* to a mental image in the mind of the investigator and not to a word or definition of a concept transferred to paper or other medium. The level symbolized by X' is called the *empirical level*. This represents an actual occurrence of the phenomenon that can be studied with the senses. The third level is called the *indicator level* or *operational level*, symbolized by X''.

Perhaps an editorial note on the term *level* is in order. The conceptual, empirical, and indicator-operational levels are separate dimensions, which perhaps can be thought of as orthogonal. One dimension can be mathematically mapped into another, but the dimensions will always remain distinct and will maintain their original positions relative to one another. Thus, we can speak of the degree of isomorphism among phenomena represented in the three levels, but it is inappropriate and misleading to speak, as is sometimes done, as if the "distance" among these levels can be decreased or increased. For example, Blalock (1968, p. 24) says that sometimes the conceptual level will be "close" to the operational level. This is misleading, as the levels cannot "move" or become "closer," although there *can* be a high degree of isomorphism, or a strong "epistemic correlation" in Northrop's (1947) terms.

Further, the use of the term *level* in this context should not be confused with other applications of the term by writers such as Miller (1978). Miller's levels—such as the individual, group, and society—are levels of a hierarchy, and formed through aggregation, with a higher level subsuming a lower in the sense that the lower is a subsystem of the higher. For example, an individual can be a component of a group, a group can be a component of an organization, and an organization can be a component of a society.

The conceptual, empirical, and operational-indicator levels are not hierarchical in this sense. It would probably be preferable in some cases to eschew this particular application of the term *level* in favor of some other term, such as *dimension*. However, the term *level* has been used so widely that it is difficult to think in other terms. Such internalization of terms is perhaps still another example of why Merton's strategy of building larger theory through aggregating smaller theories is difficult—people become dependent upon certain terms and find it difficult to relinquish them. It may be easier to begin with a brand new outlook and brand new terms than to alter established terms and viewpoints.

It is clear in Figure 2.1 that the relationship between the conceptual (X) and the empirical (X') levels (path a) is what is known as an *epistemic correlation* in Northrop's (1947) terms. Path b in Figure 2.1 refers to the relationship between the conceptual level (X) and the indicator level (X''). Path c shows the relationship between the empirical occurrence of a phenomenon (X') and its measured value (X'').

Path b represents the classic definition of *validity* (Blalock 1968; Bohrnstedt and Knoke 1982), the degree to which the indicator (X'') measures the concept (X) it is designed to measure. This is the link between theory and research that Blalock (1968) was discussing when he spoke of a concept and its indicator (p. 12). However, he also confused it with path a when he spoke in terms of an epistemic correlation (Blalock 1968, p. 13). Path c indicates the amount of measurement error. This was the situation that Blalock was discussing later (p. 19), but the switch from discussion of path b was subtle and there was no indication of a switch to the reader, so it was apparently inadvertent. In effect, Blalock merged and confused all three paths—a, b, and c. This is extremely easy to do with the two-level model, and in fact, it may be inevitable because the model simply is not adequate for its task.

Mathematically, we can see the operational or indicator level (X'') as the mapping of both the conceptual (X) and empirical (X') levels into this third level. This dual nature of X'' is the source of its importance in analysis but is also a major reason why it is so easy to confuse it with either of its parent levels, X or X'. For example, when Blalock (1968, p. 12) contrasts "underlying or unmeasured concepts" with their corresponding "indicators or composite indices," the three-level model makes it clear upon reflection that he is not merely speaking of an indicator (X'') but of an indicator that has been used to measure empirical content (X'). That is, an indicator in which X' has been mapped into X'' (path c). This can be clearly illustrated by examining Figure 2.1. Let us assume that the "underlying or unmeasured concept" to which Blalock refers is represented by X, the unmeasured concept of intelligence. We can map X into the indicator level X'' simply by writing a definition or description of X on some physical carrier, such as paper. If the description of intelligence in X'' is a faithful representation of the concept of intelligence X, then X and X'' are isomorphic.

Now we have an underlying concept (X) and its indicator (X''). Does this illustrate the relationship that Blalock (1968, p. 12) was describing? If we take him literally, it clearly does. However, notice that the situation as described so far, while isomorphic along path b, does not entail any empirical representation and indeed does not enable verification. Thus, while Blalock merely said, "indicator," he clearly was assuming an indicator (X''), which was not only a mapping of X into X'' (clearly a necessity) but *was also* a mapping of X' into X'' (also clearly a necessity). This is done by constructing an indicator that, while maintaining its isomorphism with the concept X along path b, is also suitable for measuring the actual empirical value of intelligence exhibited by some human being in X', thus establishing isomorphism along path c of Figure 2.1 as well. Thus, although the two-level model does not clearly illuminate both aspects of an indicator X'', the three level model does.

How can X and X' be mapped into X''? This is generally accomplished through some sort of physical carrier, called a *marker* (Miller 1978, p. 12), that can receive and store information on both X and X'. Both information and matter-energy are central concepts in general systems theory (Bertalanffy 1968; Miller 1978). A marker is some form of matter-energy (Miller 1978, pp. 66–67):

> These might be the stones of Hammurabi's day which bore cuneiform writing, parchments, writing paper, Indians' smoke signals, a door key with notches, punched cards, paper or magnetic tape, a computer's magnetized ferrite core memory, an arrangement of nucleotides in a NDA molecule, the molecular structure of a hormone, pulses on a telegraph wire, or waves emanating from a radio station. (Miller 1978, p. 12)

Probably the most common visual marker, and that we will employ most frequently in our development of SET, is common writing paper. The most common audio markers are the sound waves that carry voices during conversation. However, the medium for conveying information increasingly is a piece of film or a computer tape or disc. Further, as we shall see, human beings are often utilized as markers themselves.

At least two sociologists have used some form of the concept of marker, although neither used the term *marker*, this term being coined in information theory. Durkheim's (1954) concept of the totem is clearly a form of marker. The Australian totems he studied were generally living objects such as birds or trees. These objects had great symbolic significance, as they represented religion as well as the clan. A modern example of such a marker is a national flag that elicits feelings such as patriotism. Sorokin also discussed markers without using the term.

> *Any empirical sociocultural phenomenon consists of three components: (1) immaterial, spaceless, and timeless meaning; (2) material (physiochemical and biological) vehicles that "materialize, externalize, or objectify" the meanings; and (3) human agents that bear, use, and operate the meanings with the help of the material vehicles.* (1943, p. 4, italics in the original)

Sorokin's material vehicle is clearly a marker.

It is clear from a perusal of Figure 2.1 that now we are not dealing with a single isomorphism between a conceptual model and empirical reality, as in the two level model. Rather, the three-level model contains three pairs of levels and thus three types of isomorphism. For want of better terms, these three types of isomorphism will be distinguished simply as *type A* (between the conceptual X and the empirical X' levels), *type B* (between the conceptual X and indicator X'' levels), and *type C* (between the empirical X' and the indicator X'' levels). Ideally, all three types should be fully isomorphic.

It might be possible in certain very simple research situations (for example, with "middle-range" research) to achieve full type A isomorphism (between X and X') without any need for an indicator X'', and thus without any need for types B and C isomorphism. This, however, would essentially entail the researcher having a point-by-point mental image of every facet of the empirical situation (X') and a full understanding of all interrelationships among these facets. If the researcher had a complete mental picture of the empirical reality, then perhaps an indicator would not enhance understanding. Thus, in some respects, the chief goal of social research can be said to be establishment of type A isomorphism, because if this could truly be done, then in effect the researcher would have an accurate perception of society.

However, even if type A isomorphism could be established without an indicator (X''), and thus without types B or C isomorphism, an indicator is still useful. For example, even with complete isomorphism between X and X', the indicator level (X'') is convenient for storing information, and facilitates communication between two or more individuals about the nature of society.

Further, only rarely (if ever), can such direct type A isomorphism be achieved. Certainly, in dealing with a complex society, as in the present case, it seems impossible for any individual to perceive the whole of society at one time. It is not sufficient to merely have an opinion as to the nature of society. To have direct type A isomorphism, one must comprehend simultaneously all components of society and all of the interrelationships among these components. This alone would provide full type A isomorphism (or a perfect epistemic correlation in Northrop's terms). In the present instance I will not even attempt to directly establish full isomorphism between X and X' (type A). This would entail correctly perceiving and memorizing simultaneously all of society's components and their relationships. I cannot do it. Does this mean, then, that Merton was right? Is the task is too complex and thus our efforts doomed to failure? No, not at all. Although I cannot directly map all of the complex society X' into X (for example, because I cannot simultaneously observe and perceive all of society), I can hope to establish the link between X and X' indirectly. That is, I perceive limited aspects of the society X' that are stored in my mind as X. These selected aspects can be mapped into the indicator level as X''. Assume for the present that my marker for the X'' level is ordinary ink on writing paper. My first task is to map X into X''. If I can do this successfully I can establish type B isomorphism. All that is required to establish type B isomorphism is to faithfully represent my mental images, or X (whatever they are), on paper (X''). For example, assume that my sole mental image is the symbol X, without any "empirical referent." Merely by writing the symbol X on paper I have established type B isomorphism. An important point that may be difficult to understand is that I can attain type B isomorphism merely by faithfully representing (mapping) X on X'', *whether or not type A isomorphism has been established.*

Another way to say this is that even though X'' may accurately represent X, it may not accurately represent X', because X may not represent X'. How can I ensure that X'' is indeed isomorphic with X'? This is done by mapping X' directly into X'', or establishing type C validity. An example of this is when I collect data to verify an hypothesis. Now the situation is quite different. If I have both type B and type C validity, then I will have type A validity, even if I cannot establish it directly. This is the usual research procedure. I have some perception (X) of X'. I cannot establish type A validity directly. However, I can map my perceptions X into X'' by writing some specific model on paper. This model can be either qualitative or quantitative. It can be a verbal theory, a mathematical model, a deductive sequence, or an indicator such as an alienation scale or authoritarianism scale. The next step is to "verify" the theory or hypothesis or to "measure" the phenomena with the indicator, by mapping "actual data" (X'') into X. Another way to say it is that I arrive at X'' from two directions—from X' and from X. If the two X''s are identical, the hypothesis is said to be verified; it the two X''s are divergent, the hypothesis is said to be contradicted.

The two mappings, b and c, undoubtedly account largely for the tendency to reduce the three-level model to a two-level model. For example, "substantive theory" (Leik and Meeker, 1975, p. 10) is often contrasted with "data." Assuming that *data* refers to the empirical situation X', or perhaps a mapping of X' into X'', what is *substantive theory*? It is really not clear, but in most cases it is probably a verbal formulation resulting from mapping X into X''. Thus, when Miller (1978) talks of the "conceptual system" he is not speaking merely of X alone, or X'' alone but is assuming a mapping of X into X''. Similarly, when Blalock (1968) uses the terms *empirical level* and *operational level* interchangeable, he is essentially not referring to X' alone, on the one hand, or to X'' alone, on the other hand, but to the mapping of X' into X''. Thus, the situation is much more complicated than most previous discussions have indicated. These discussions have not only neglected some levels but have compared mappings without so indicating. Instead of only two levels to deal with, there are actually three distinct levels plus three distinct mappings. Although the full import of this extended model may not be clear at the present time, any researcher who chooses to neglect any of these six aspects of social research is inviting confusion and the failure that an inadequate model invites.

The two-level model is an oversimplification and so by definition cannot provide holistic understanding of society. Although while it is sometimes difficult to work with all six aspects of the three-level model, this is necessary. The conceptual (X) and empirical (X') levels are distinct and relatively easy to understand. The indicator level (X'') is more difficult to understand, as in a sense it has no identity of its own but merely stores and conveys information from either the conceptual or empirical levels. Thus, we generally are not interested primarily in the physical characteristics of the marker (X''). That is, we are not interested in a piece of writing paper per se. However, we are interested in the mapping of X into X'' (type B) and the mapping of X' into X''. Thus, we are interested in the information about the conceptual and empirical levels stored on the piece of writing paper.

The role of the indicator level X'' is much broader than many readers may realize. Sociologists have been most familiar with this level through work on measurement and scaling and through discussions of operationalism

(Bridgman 1927; Lundberg 1939; Blalock 1968). Thus, some persons may assume that the indicator level or operational level refers solely or primarily to quantitative information, such as the quantified scores on an intelligence test or some other sort of scale. Although quantified scale scores may be the most familiar examples of information that can be stored and processed on the indicator level X'', they are only one example of many. *The indicator level is not limited to quantified information.* A verbal theory, such as Parsons' (1951) *The Social System* is a mapping of perceptions (X) onto a physical marker (the paper pages of the book or X'') and thus constitutes a perfectly legitimate type B mapping. To reiterate, isomorphism can be established between X and X'' any time the type B mapping is entirely accurate so that X'' faithfully represents X. This is true whether or not X is isomorphic with X' and whether or not the concepts from X that are mapped into X'' have "empirical referents." Further, I can easily perceive of a set of numbers. As purely cognitive perceptions these are components of X. I can map them into X'' by writing them on the page—again, this is true whether or not they refer to any empirical phenomena (X'). Thus, when conceiving both words and numbers in the mind (X), and mapping them into X'' by writing them on a page, there is relatively little difference between "verbal theory" that is "qualitative," and "quantitative analysis" in the form of numerals or specified relationships among "variables".

Further, the conceptual level X can encompass not only perceptions of words, numbers, or other symbols but also perceptions of the relationships among them. For example, I can perceive of a set of symbols and a deductive sequence among them. I can also conceive of a set of variables and relationships among them, as in a path diagram. All of this is contained in my mind and is thus all conceptual (X) level for the present. However, there is a limit to the complexity of the formulation (for example, the number of symbols, relationships among them, and assumptions about them) that I can store in my mind. Thus, at some state of complexity I want to map X into X''. After the formulation is secure on paper, I can more easily add to it and revise it. If the symbols that were mapped from X into X'' have empirical referents (as, for example, when the symbols in X were conceived inductively from observation of X' so that type A isomorphism exists), then I can map X' into X''. This is the verification of verbal theory, or administration of scales to individuals, or testing mathematical and statistical models.

We do not wish to specify any sequence of mappings in the three-level model, as many different sequences are used. Much usage will proceed from X' to X (for example through induction), then from X to X'' (specification of verbal theory or a mathematical model), and then from X'' back to X' (verification). However, many other sequences are used in addition to this basic path a, path b, and path c sequence. For example, prior theorizing may result in the establishment of a new concept through deduction (Northrop's [1947] "concept by postulation") rather than from direct observation of X' (Northrop's "concept by intuition"). Further, after we have formulated our complex systems model X'', there may be occasion to revise it. One such occasion, for example, is when the actual society (X') remains unchanged but we gain an improved perception (X) of it, so that the degree of type A isomorphism is improved. This revised X will necessitate subsequent changes in X''. Another occasion for change is when we perceive that changes have occurred empirically in the actual complex society (X'). This will, of course, necessitate subsequent change in both X and X''.

Extensions of the Three-Level Model

The importance of this model extends beyond mere measurement problems. It is probable that all the ramifications of this model will not be adequately clarified in this volume. It is clear, however, that the three levels are in general usage in society. For example, an architect who wishes to build a new structure begins with a perception (X). This perception is merely a cognitive phenomenon or mental image at this point. It may or may not be based upon observation of some already existing building (X'). The perception (X) is then mapped into a marker, generally in the form of blueprints (X'') and perhaps in the form of a scale model (X'').

There is a premise from early ethnomethodology to the effect that sociologists use essentially the same methods (though perhaps in a somewhat different form or described in different ways) that the lay public uses (see Zimmerman and Pollner 1970). The three-level model is perhaps an example of this. This model is primary in sociological research and measurement but is also used daily by individuals as they function in society. The way in which these three levels are used by members of society is quite complex, and can be difficult to understand. This matter will be discussed in more detail throughout this book and particularly in Chapter 7. The basic elements for understanding this situation involve a population of concrete individuals interacting in a given spatial location within societal boundaries. This is basically Miller's (1978) concrete system. As individuals interact with each other in this spatial location, over time, they exchange a great deal of information and matter and expend a great deal of energy. This basically involves all three levels, X, X', and X''.

For example, suppose that you wish to apply for a job. The employer has a perception (X) of the successful applicant. You send him or her your resume

(X'') in advance. The resume is, of course, an information-bearing marker. Generally, this is not sufficient to obtain the position; you also must attend an interview, in which the prospective employer observes you (the actual empirical person or X'). *You* are now serving as a marker, and the employer utilizes information gained from observing you in this role. Such information (physical appearance, grooming, "attitude") is used to supplement the information on your resume (X'') and to check its veracity.

One basic sequence is as follows: individual members of concrete society (X'), through their actions over time, form perceptions of other individuals and of the society (X), store these on markers (X''), and use the information from these markers in a later time period as the basis for new ("rational"?) actions. The information stored on the markers (X'') is generally in the form of a system of symbols, either alphabetical or numeric. These are used to form symbol systems, what we have been calling *abstracted systems* (Miller 1978), which are otherwise known as *pattern systems* (Kuhn 1974), *R-systems* (Bailey 1972; Sneath and Sokal 1973), or *I-facet systems* (Guttman 1959). The human actors and their interrelationships, over time, form a concrete system (Miller 1978), which is otherwise known as an *acting system* (Kuhn 1974), *Q-system* (Bailey 1972; Sneath and Sokal 1973), or *P-facet system* (Guttman 1959). Over time, then, there is a cyclical reciprocal relationship (a "dialectic" if you will) between the human acting (concrete) systems and the symbolic pattern (abstracted) systems that they generate, with many (but not all) of these symbol systems being stored on markers (X'') of various sorts.

Thus, there is a sequential process-product relationship. The human actors use pattern systems or symbolic information that was produced by past human action as "data" to guide their actions. Then the current *process* of human action results in a new *product*, or symbol system on a marker, which can then be used in the next sequence to guide the actions (process). As will be shown in Chapter 7, this reciprocal relationship of process-product-process, and so on, between acting systems and pattern systems is found in the larger society but is also the link between verbal theory and statistical analysis in sociology (thus illustrating the ethnomethodological notion that the methods used mirror actual actions in society).

If it is indeed true that sociological methods and theory mirror the methods and theory of the lay public, and use of the three-level model mirrors its use in the society at large, then it follows that the "person on the street" will also have some perception (X) of the actual society (X'). This undoubtedly is true and, to the extent that these perceptions are isomorphic with each other (shared by all persons in the society), then a "collective conscience" (or consciousness, as the term can be translated into English both ways from French) can be said to exist sui generis in the Durkheimian sense. The salient question at this point is how these respective perceptions (X) of society are derived and what they consist of. Undoubtedly the lay public derives many of its perceptions about the nature of society from information carried on various markers, principally television and the print media. To the degree that this information provided by the various sources is identical and is perceived identically by the public, an identical shared perception of society (X) will exist. In other words, this is the case of type B isomorphism, or isomorphism between the shared perception (X) and the media (X''). But notice in this case the information proceeds from X'' to X. If such type B isomorphism exists, then a collective conscience exists *regardless of whether type A isomorphism (between X and X'') exists*. Essentially what this latter statement says is that a collective conscience (X) could exist if an identical shared conscience was derived from markers, even if this perception of society (X) *was not* congruent with the concrete society (X'), or perhaps even if the latter did not exist empirically. This, of course, is one case of the "social construction of reality" (see, for example, Berger and Luckman 1967) in which the social reality exists in the relationships between the conscience (X) and the salient markers (X''). The analysis of this type B relationship thus greatly facilitates understanding certain ontological aspects of society.

However, we would suspect that society is not *totally* constructed in the sense that it exists only on the conceptual (X) and the indicator (X'') levels and in the type B isomorphism among them. In this case direct type A isomorphism would not exist. Actually we expect some degree of direct type A isomorphism between the conceptual (X) level (for example, the collective conscience) and the concrete or empirical level (X'). One form of type A relationship occurs when persons first have a perception of society (X) and then shape the empirical reality (X') to conform with this perception, thus establishing direct type A isomorphism. This is another example of the "social construction of reality" and is an X to X' link. The link in the other direction $(X'$ to $X)$ is also important. In this case we would expect that the lay public and sociologists as well would derive some of their knowledge of society (X) through direct observation of the empirical level (X') or the actual concrete society. If society exists empirically (X') and we can observe it accurately, then our perception (X) of society can be derived inductively and should have a high degree of type A isomorphism.

However, the salient question at this point is, How much of society is actually empirically observable? According to Collins, a large portion of society is not observable:

> Much of traditional sociology conceives of its subject matter as consisting of "society," "organization," "classes," "communities," "roles," and "sys-

tems." None of these, in fact, is observable. All we can ever see are real
people in real places, or the writings and artifacts they have made. (1975,
p. 7)

The implication would seem to be that if we can observe society (X') we can
perceive it accurately and understand it (X), thus achieving type A isomorphism. If we cannot see it (and according to Collins, this is largely true), then
our hopes for direct understanding and achievement of type A isomorphism
are dim.

This point requires clarification. We observed in Chapter 1 in the discussion of middle-range theory that, whereas the view is widely accepted that
small-scale studies are easier to conduct than large-scale studies, this is not
always true. It is true, as Collins says, that we cannot observe "society" but
we can observe "real people." However, it is well known that many aspects
of these "real" people (for example, personality factors) cannot be directly observed but must be inferred or studied from their supposed effects. Further,
these "real people" are not as amenable to observation as one might think.
Even cursory reflection will show you that you cannot even observe *all* of
yourself (or all of any other person) simultaneously. In fact, there are parts of
your own body that you have *never* observed directly and never will (for example, the back of your head), though you may detect them with senses other
than sight (for example, touch). The only way that you can see all of yourself
is by mapping yourself (X') into a marker (X''), such as a mirror or film.

Observation of a large aggregate of persons is even more difficult.
Whereas we cannot see a "society," we also cannot simultaneously observe a
population. Thus, even a demographer wishing to count the population of a
country cannot simply observe all people simultaneously but must map the
information onto markers (X''), such as census forms, and aggregate it to
reach the total tally. Until recently, the only way we could observe a large
aggregate of persons at all (such as a crowd) was from the top of a building
or some other vantage point. Recently, however, the development of markers
like film (X'') enables us to map crowds onto the marker and then observe
them indirectly by viewing the marker.

The point of all this is that even Collins's "real people" are not so easily
observed, particularly at the aggregate level. Thus, although we have emphasized that our basic systems model is a concrete system based on these
"real people," we often have to rely upon establishing type A isomorphism
indirectly, through the establishment of both type B and type C isomorphism,
rather than directly, through observation of the concrete population. Further,
we said that the pattern system, or symbolic content of the society, will not
be neglected but will be derived within the context of the concrete system. It
also should be pointed out that this symbolic content is not as "unobservable"

as Collins' statement might imply. It is true that we cannot see a "class." However, we can observe many factors that are correlated with class. Moreover, these factors are often recorded on markers (X''). Thus, while we cannot observe them directly, we can observe them indirectly through observing the marker. Notice that in this case they are no different than the population of "real people" that also can only be observed indirectly through a marker.

One example of such an indicator of class of course is amount of money possessed. We can observe directly that an individual possesses money (X') or more likely observe it indirectly after the amount of money is mapped numerically into a marker, such as a bank balance or an income tax form (X''). Thus, Collins's observables are not as observable as often assumed, and his unobservables are not as unobservable as is often assumed. However, it is still relatively easy to study both if they are mapped into X'' and if we concentrate on establishing types B and C isomorphism, as well as striving for the direct establishment of type A isomorphism when possible.

From the standpoint of SET, the key to understanding society as both a constructed (symbolic) and concrete phenomenon is to understand the three-level model in combination with the distinction between relationships among persons (concrete systems) and relationships among variables (pattern systems). *The congruence between the concrete and pattern systems can be seen in the cyclical relationship between the two systems over time, as societal members sequentially utilize all three levels of the three-level model.*

This sequence can be characterized in terms of *action* involving one actor and one or more markers, and *interaction* involving two or more actors who are interrelating (exchanging information or matter-energy). One salient example of action is when an actor (X') observes himself or herself in a mirror (marker, or X''), thus gaining a perception (X) of his or her appearance—a basic X' to X'' to X sequence. In this sequence we first strive for type C isomorphism, which is achieved if the mirror (X'') provides an accurate reflection of the person's body (X'). We next strive for type B isomorphism, which is achieved if X is an accurate perception of the image in X''. In this case the perception (X) of the body is derived indirectly or deductively. Thus, X is not a direct image of X' but only is achieved indirectly through X''. Additionally, one can directly observe portions of his or her body (type A isomorphism), thus checking the accuracy of the mirror's reflection. Notice that in each case the perception (X) is affected by past perceptions. For example, perhaps "cultural conditioning" or "internalization of norms" (a la Parsons 1951) led the person to focus on socially salient characteristics of his or her appearance, such as age or gender. Another basic action sequence involving path b is when a person's perceptions (X) are formed and altered by information gathered from a marker, as when one reads a book (X''). This action process involves no interaction with another person, except perhaps indirectly as when one forms a perception (X) of another person (X') by reading about him or her as a character in the book (X'').

In interaction, two or more persons use their perceptions (X) of the situation and markers (X'') in dealing with each other within a given environment (X'). In place of the mirror just described, the marker (X'') may be the other person, as in Cooley's 1922, p. 184 "looking glass self," in addition to other markers that may be useful in the interaction, such as books, maps, money, blueprints, scripts, or company reports. The actors (at least partially) use the synchronic structure afforded by existing symbol systems, which were in turn produced by past diachronic actions, to order their interactions. Thus, a present interaction is partly a function of such things as socialized expectations, internalized norms, and so on (a la Parsons 1951) and partly a reaction to the present situated context (a la symbolic interactionism, as in the work of Blumer 1969, and ethnomethodology as in the work of Garfinkel 1967). The result is (relatively) ordered or *replicated interaction*, an important term in SET. To the degree that such interaction is not random, it is an *orderly process*, and the result of such diachronic interaction by the acting system will be a synchronic symbolic structure that, as will be shown in Chapter 3, displays a degree of entropy well below the maximum. This lower degree of social entropy will be characterized in terms of structure or organization. This is discussed in detail in Chapter 3, and action and interaction are discussed in Chapter 5 and 6.

The three-level model has many other ramifications (as in the analysis of validity) that are tangential to our present analysis but are being pursued in work in progress. Now that the role of our systems model (X'') within the three-level model is understood, we can turn toward specification of this model. The first task is to discuss the decision to focus initially upon the concrete system (remembering that we will subsequently study pattern systems as well and in fact will study the relationship between concrete and pattern systems). Parsons has argued forcefully against the use of the concrete system situated in physical space-time, but the analysis so far should have proved the necessity for studying both concrete systems and pattern systems and their congruence, and a case will be made for this strategy in the next section. After all of these preliminaries are concluded, the chapter ends with a brief sketch of the skeletal systems model.

Abstracted versus Concrete Sociological Theory

Early sociological systems theorists and equilibrium theorists generally used the individual or some aggregate of individuals as the basic unit of analysis (Spencer 1892; Pareto 1935; Henderson 1935). Parsons (1951; Parsons and Shils 1951) departed rather dramatically from this practice, choosing the social role rather than the concrete individual organism as the basic unit of analysis of the social system. Parsons and Shils (1951, p. 190) say: "The 'individual actor' as a concrete system of action is not usually the most important unit of a social system. For most purposes *the conceptual unit of the social system is the role*" (italics in the original). Parsons has no intention of denying or neglecting the importance of the concrete individual actor. Empirically, there is little doubt that the individual actor is of central concern in Parsons' framework. Indeed, *"The frame of reference of the theory of action* involves actors, a situation of action, and the orientation of the actor to that situation" (Parsons and Shils 1951, p. 56, italics in the original). Further, Parsons seems to consider the concrete individual the "ultimate" empirical unit of the society, as when he says that: "In the limiting conception a society is composed of human individuals, organisms; but a social system is not, and for a very important reason, namely, that the unit of a partial social system is a role and not an individual" (Parsons 1967, p. 328).

The point is basically whether the concrete individual or the social role is best suited as the unit for a theoretical analysis of the social system. In Parsons' mind the latter is clearly preferable as long as it is understood that the unit is purely analytical. Thus, Parsons and Shils (1951, p. 190) say that: "The social system is made up of the actions of individuals. The actions which constitute the social system are also the same actions which make up the personality systems of the individual actors. The two systems are, however, analytically discrete entities despite this identity of their basic components." Parsons' analysis entails abstracting not only the notion of a social system, with the social role as the basic unit, but also the interrelated notions of a cultural system and personality system (Parsons 1951; Parsons and Shils 1951) and later an organismic system as well (Parsons 1961a).

The basic rationale of Parsons' analytical strategy is clear: the empirical world need not be analyzed holistically. The action theorist should concentrate on the basic components, such as social system, personality, and culture, and leave the analysis of the organism to biologists. The inclusion of the organismic system guards against criticism that Parsons overreacted. One could hardly quarrel with a sociologist emphasizing analysis of the social role. Beyond this general rationale, there are several more specific reasons for utilizing the role rather than the concrete individual as the basic unit of social systems analysis.

Although there has been some confusion in empiricist thought of the concrete and analytic frames of reference, and although Parsons' utilization of the latter has sometimes been misunderstood (Alexander 1978, p. 180), there was no sustained challenge of his strategy until publication of *Living Systems* (Miller 1978). Miller (1978, pp. 16–21) distinguishes between abstracted systems and concrete systems. In this formulation, Parsons' social system, with the role as the unit of analysis is an abstracted system, whereas Miller's living system with the concrete individual as the basic unit of analysis is a concrete system. According to Miller (1978, p. 17): "A *concrete, real,* or *veridical* system is a nonrandom accumulation of matter-energy, in a region in physical space-time, which is organized into interacting interrelated subsystems or components" (italics in the original).

In contrast,

> The units of *abstracted systems* are relationships abstracted or selected by an observer in the light of his interests, theoretical viewpoint, or philosophical bias [italics in the original].
>
> . . .
>
> The verbal usages of theoretical statements concerning abstracted systems are often the reverse of those concerning concrete systems.
>
> . . .
>
> A theoretical statement oriented to concrete systems typically would say 'Lincoln was President,' but one oriented to abstracted systems, concentrating on relationships or roles, would very likely be phrased, 'The Presidency was occupied by Lincoln.' (Miller 1978, p. 19)

Miller (1978, pp. 20–23) argues forcefully that theorists should concentrate upon concrete rather than abstracted systems and gives a number of reasons for this argument. The debate is continued in the review of *Living Systems* in *Contemporary Sociology* and in *Behavioral Science*, with all four reviewers (Kuhn 1979; Boulding 1979; Parsons 1979; and Rapoport, 1980) commenting upon the abstracted-concrete distinction and with Miller (1979; 1980) answering. In one of the last works written before his death, Parsons (1979, p. 705) concludes with an eloquent plea for the use of abstracted systems:

> Above all, my questions go back to the choice he [Miller] made at the very beginning to emphasize concrete rather than abstracted systems. I am quite content to rest my case on a refusal to accept this path of analysis. The path that leads through a series of abstracted systems seems to me much more fruitful. I only hope that there will be another Miller who will explore this alternative path as thoroughly as Miller has explored his.

Both abstracted and concrete systems have advantages in sociological analysis, and this has been thoroughly discussed elsewhere (see Miller 1978;

Bailey 1981). The overall conclusion is that both roles and their incumbents are proper—and indeed necessary—objects for sociological analysis. They must be studied simultaneously. To eschew the study of either would greatly hamper the task of sociological explanation. But once having decided to analyze both roles and concrete individuals, the question of the position each is to occupy in systems analysis still remains.

The Complex Isomorphic Systems Model (X'')

There is general agreement on the basic definition of a system. Bertalanffy (1956, p. 3) defines a *system* as "a set of elements standing in interaction." Miller (1978, p. 16) says:

> A *system* is a set of interacting units with interrelationships among them. The word 'set' implies that the units have some common properties. These common properties are essential if the units are going to interact or have relationships. The state of each unit is constrained by, conditioned by, or dependent on the state of other units.

Parsons and Shils (1951, p. 107) say:

> The most general and fundamental property of a system is the interdependence of parts or variables. Interdependence consists in the existence of determinate relationships among the parts or variables as contrasted with randomness of variability. In other words, interdependence is *order* in the relationship among the components which enter into a system.

Hall and Fagen (1956, p. 18) say that: "*A system is a set of objects together with relationships between the objects and between their attributes.*" And finally, Berrien (1968, pp. 14–15) says that: "A system is defined as a set of *components* interacting with each other and a *boundary* which possesses the property of filtering both the kind and rate of flow of *inputs* and *outputs* to and from the system." All of these definitions are similar in referring to a system as a set of similar components related in some nonrandom fashion. The differences are largely terminological, with the components of the system variously referred to as *elements, components, units, parts, objects, or variables* and the relationships referred to as *interaction, interdependence* or *relationships*.

Whereas only Berrien specifically emphasizes the existence of a boundary, the others implicitly assume it. The boundary is a very important element of the system, especially for entropy analysis, as it is central to the crucial distinction between open and closed systems. Basically, an open system has relatively permeable boundaries that allow flows of various sorts into and out of the system, while closed systems are impermeable and do not allow such flows.

In classical thermodynamics a further distinction is made between closed and isolated systems. For example, according to Foster, Rapoport, and Trucco (1957, p. 9), the distinctions among these types of systems are as follows:

Isolated— where neither matter nor energy may be exchanged between system and environment
Closed— where energy but not matter may be exchanged
Open— where both energy and matter may be exchanged

Hall and Fagen (1956, p. 20) define the environment as follows: "For a given system, the environment is the set of all objects a change in whose attributes affect the system and also those objects whose attributes are changed by the behavior of the system."

In contemporary GST the open-closed distinction is a little more flexible. The term *isolated system* is rarely used. Furthermore, Miller (1978, p. 11) generally does not distinguish between matter and energy, because of their known relationship, but combines them essentially into a single entity ("matter-energy") that is contrasted with information. Thus, according to Miller (1978, p. 17): "Most concrete systems have boundaries which are at least partially permeable, permitting sizable magnitudes of at least certain sorts of matter-energy or information transmissions to cross them. Such a system is an *open system*. In open systems entropy may increase, remain in steady state, or decrease." In contrast, "A concrete system with impermeable boundaries through which no matter-energy or information transmissions of any sort can occur is a *closed system*" (1978, pp. 17–18). Miller also notes that no actual concrete system is completely closed.

As stressed throughout this chapter, symbol or pattern systems are generated, transmitted, and revised by human actors in the course of their interaction within the context of a concrete or acting system. In this chapter we sketch the concrete system. The development of pattern systems and their relationship to concrete systems will be discussed in detail in subsequent chapters, beginning in Chapter 3.

We clearly cannot include *all* aspects of the actual concrete society (X') in our model (X'') but must select perceptions (X). It seems most efficacious to ensure that the model does not preclude the future analysis of all potentially relevant factors. Thus, we prefer to sektch a skeletal model of the entire society in its most general form, even if "holes" must be left within the borders of our model to be filled later.

The task, then, is to distill the common elements of every actually empirically occurring concrete society (X'). The components of the system will be concrete individuals, or human actors. We will analyze the relationships among them (social interactions) in the course of their everyday activity. These human actors operate within societal borders.

Consider the society of the United States. It has empirical boundaries that contain a population. The citizens of the United States perform numerous roles. It seems intuitively clear that in order to understand how such a society operates holistically on a day-to-day basis we need a model that is isomorphic with the society. A systems model fills this need. The empirical society has a boundary, and a system has a boundary. The society has components (members) and the system definition has components (units). The society exhibits interrelationships of various kinds among its members, and by definition, a system contains interrelationships among its units. One sort of relationship evident in the society is the social role. Thus, the most direct way to achieve isomorphism between the concept of system and the empirical society is to conceive of the concrete individual residing within the borders of society as the basic unit of the social system and to conceive of the social role as one type of relationship between the system units (individuals).

The social system so defined is a concrete system, but it also facilitates the analysis of social roles. Such a system; (1) conforms to the definition of a system; (2) serves the goal of simultaneously studying both role incumbents (individuals in a particular spatial-temporal location) and roles; and (3) establishes a basic three-point isomorphism between, respectively, system boundaries and societal boundaries, system units and societal units, and system relationships and societal relationships. Modern complex society is so complex that it is very difficult for the sociologist to understand holistically. The systems model is more manageable, and the basic isomorphism between the model and the complex reality holds the promise that construction of a complex social systems model will enable adequate understanding of a complex society.

There are at least two other distinct advantages of such a concrete model of complex society. One advantage is that the isomorphism between boundaries, units, and relationships that holds at the societal level holds for other levels of analysis as well. That is, the isomorphism is not dependent upon the level of analysis. This means that we can use the system model to study lower levels of living systems, such as organizations and groups, which can be seen as subsystems of the society (Miller 1978, p. 747). The model can also be extended to the world system, or as Miller (1978) calls it, the supranational system.

A second major advantage, it seems to me, it that although the model advocated here is essentially a concrete, living system model very similar to Miller's and an acting system in Kuhn's terminology, I can see no way that its use precludes abstracted systems analysis (pattern systems analysis in Kuhn's terms) as advocated by Parsons. It seems that a holistic, concrete, complex social systems model that is isomorphic with the boundaries of an empirical society facilitates the analysis of all aspects of the society. This includes not only the characteristics of the societal members but the relationships between the members. It certainly would not preclude role analysis or the analysis of conceptual systems (pattern systems).

Holistic Model Adequacy

Let us briefly review the arguments for abstracted systems presented earlier in light of the holistic model just advocated. The notion of roles as relationships among units of the social system is certainly consistent with an emphasis on role permanence. Although a given example of an empirical society has a location in space-time, and thus a given role has a particular incumbent at a particular place and time, the role as relationship in the systems model is permanent and exists even when incumbents change. The holistic model also facilitates the study of multiple roles for on individual and multiple incumbents for one role. There is no restriction on the number of roles an individual may occupy or the number of incumbents a role may have. This is a matter to be determined empirically. This same basic reasoning holds for the third argument for abstracted systems, the notion that the individual is a composite of social forces rather than a singular entity. As Alexander (1978, p. 180) puts it, "when we look at an individual person, he appears to be discrete when in fact he is interpenetrated with other individuals by virtue of shared symbolic norms." In my view, the concrete model of the complex social system is entirely consistent with the notion that individuals are the composite product of a variety of social factors and that individuals share norms. The concrete individual is a marker in the sense that he or she is the concrete carrier for shared social information, such as norms. Without some concrete information carrier, such as the concrete individual, norm transmission would be impossible, and the continued existence over time of social norms and roles would be threatened. For example, the shared information processed by a group of concrete individuals generates such concepts as loyalty and patriotism, which Durkheim contended to be the epitome of the social fact or society *sui generis*, as such group concepts or cultural symbols could not, according to him, be conceived in the mind of a single individual acting in isolation.

Thus, to my mind, the use of concrete individuals as units in a holistic complex social system model does not preclude the notion of shared symbols and internalized norms but in fact facilitates such a notion. By treating the concrete individual holistically as a marker or information processer and carrier, the way is left open for the analysis of any properties of the individual, a group of individuals of any size N, or any properties of relationships among such individuals or groups. In contrast, choosing a single property of an individual or group such as personality or the role as the basic unit, makes it much more difficult, if not impossible, to consider other properties or variables that may later be deemed to have either theoretical or empirical salience.

For example, choosing the concrete individual as the basic unit in a model of complex society allows free study of any aspects of the society or its subsystems; such as culture, norms, roles, personality factors, and biological factors. Choosing Parsons' approach and use, for example, personality as the basic unit of the personality system and role as the basic unit of the social system, adds not only the problems of studying each system but those of studying the relationships between systems. We then have the added problem that abstracted systems of this latter sort have no clear isomorphism between the analytical system model and the empirical phenomena. This lack of model-data isomorphism makes operationalization and hypothesis testing difficult and leads to definite dangers of reification.

The counter to this is, of course, that the social system consists largely if not wholly of shared symbolic elements that are not empirically observable, and thus isomorphism between the system definition and the society cannot be achieved. This is similar to the fourth argument for abstracted systems, that the individual should be studied in terms of symbolic space rather than in a matter-energy–space-time framework. I certainly do not think that sociologists should limit themselves solely to the study of organisms acting in a space-time framework. In a certain sense I agree that Parsons' (1979) action level (the social system) can be seen as an emergent phenomenon over time that is on a different level than is the organism. However, I do not see how understanding this emergent phenomena is facilitated by denying the matter–space-time reality. The task for sociology is to begin with concrete grounding as a basis for the emergent analysis and then to seek other dimensions for analysis in addition to space-time.

The fifth argument for abstracted systems is that sociologists should be concerned solely with social facts and that utilization of a concrete living systems framework could lead to biological reductionism, or at least to a deemphasis of social factors. This is always possible. However, the other side of the coin is that abstraction into a number of artificial abstracted systems can lead to a set of disparate and unconnected literatures replete with reifications. The utilization of a model with individuals as units can not only reduce the number of fruitless abstractions and dangerous reifications but facilitate the establishment of interdisciplinary links, and can aid in the avoidance of needless duplications of effort in different disciplines.

In conclusion, it seems to me to be somewhat ironic that an action theorist such as Parsons would advocate the utilization of pattern (abstracted) systems rather than acting (concrete) systems. I believe that Parsons is correct in emphasizing the study of the symbolic elements of society. Sociologists must study meanings, categories, and symbols as well as other aspects of culture. However, we must not be too quick to label all models that are empirically grounded and subject to operationalization as overly empiricist and incapable of properly serving the aims of interpretive and subjective sociology.

To me, the basic question is whether the study of cultural symbols can ever be completely satisfactory if it is pursued solely in abstracted systems divorced from acting systems. Cultural symbols are not generated in a vacuum but are the result of human action in a social context. A basic issue that I think sociologists should be concerned with now is the link between acting and pattern systems or concrete, abstracted, and conceptual systems. In other words, how are conceptual systems generated, maintained, transmitted, and changed in the ongoing interaction of complex concrete societies? More specifically, how are particular conceptual categories generated by social action in concrete societies, and what role do they play in such action?

For example, consider the dual meaning of the term *relationship* in sociology, which is not coincidentally a key term in the definition of system. We speak both of social relationships, such as social interaction, and relationships between variables, such as the correlation between race and educational level. The former usage refers to human action and thus to a concrete or acting system, whereas the latter term refers to relationships between concepts and thus to abstracted, conceptual, or pattern systems. There seems to be a definite but as yet not fully explored and thus not fully explained link between the two types of relationships. We have already discussed this issue to some extent and will discuss it in more detail in subsequent chapters, particularly Chapters 3 and 7.

To summarize, I cannot directly perceive *all* of society. Thus, I will attempt to "selectively perceive" the elements that are common to *all* empirically occurring social systems. At the empirical level (X'), these are (1) components (human actors); (2) the interrelationships among them (e.g., interaction within roles and other sorts of social interaction); and (3) national boundaries, within (and across) which such interaction takes place. These three selected elements are sufficiently concise that I have perceived all of them simultaneously (X) and have mapped them (through writing) into the pages of this book (X''). At this stage we should have a relatively high degree of all three types of isomorphism (type A, type B, and type C). We can now turn to the analysis of entropy. In chapter 3, we will also have occasion to discuss further the general role of boundaries in the system, including the issue of boundary permeability.

Chapter 3

Social Entropy

The isomorphic complex systems model (X'') as sketched in Chapter 2 comprises human individuals as the components, interaction among these components, and the national (political) border of the country, with the latter serving as a boundary for the social interaction. As such, this definition is consistent with most systems definitions, which generally emphasize components, interrelationships among them, and a boundary (although the latter may be assumed rather than defined explicitly). The SET model (X'') is also consistent with Miller's definition of a concrete system. Although this definition was examined previously, it bears repeating in the interest of clarity. According to Miller (1978, p. 17); "A *concrete, real,* or *veridical* system is a nonrandom accumulation of matter-energy, in a region in physical space-time, which is organized into interacting interrelated subsystems or components."

Notice that physical space is specifically included as part of the system. Thus, in the model, all the physical, spatial area within national boundaries, including water and airspace, is part of the concrete system. This includes, of course, the contents of the spatial area such as minerals and "natural resources." I emphasize this point because such spatial characteristics are often known as the "environment," but inasmuch as they are within the boundaries of the concrete system, they are part of the system and not part of the systems's environment. The system's environment is limited to those factors beyond the national boundaries (including the "physical environment") that in some way affect the system, generally through exchange of energy or information.

If you will recall, in Chapter 1 I quoted Aiken's (1981, pp. 449–50) comment that sociology generally has a conceptual rather than a spatial orientation and his note of some advantages of the latter. Then, in Chapter 2, Parsons (1979, p. 704) was quoted as cautioning that Miller's treatment of concrete individuals as actors in physical space can lead to "the apparent belief that physical space is ontologically absolute and not subject to any kind of relativizing interpretation."

The specific inclusion of space in our model agrees with the view of Aiken and Miller (1978). Further, Giddens (1979; 1981) has emphasized the time-space constitution of social systems. Human actors *do* interact within a space-time framework. Exclusion of this from the model would do irreparable damage to our attempt to construct a holistic model. Parsons's issue of how space is interpreted is quite another matter. As will be seen, space definitely *is not* assumed to be "ontologically absolute." The specific inclusion of human consciousness (X) in the model allows for many interpretations of physical space (X'). Human societies have a large variety of conceptions of space, as Sorokin (1943, pp. 97–157) noted long ago in his discussion of "sociocultural space." Our model (X'') attempts to mirror the actual empirical society (X') by first emphasizing that humans act in a context of physical space-time and subsequently by explicating the manner in which symbol systems ($[X]$ including conceptions of space) are generated within this space-time context. Note further that this use of space is not ideographic in the sense of being unique to a particular country within a particular time period, as the use of space often is in other disciplines, such as history. Rather, the model is a general one, intended to apply to any society at any point in time.

One interesting element generated within the space-time context is the system boundary. This chapter will show that not only concrete systems but symbol systems as well have boundaries. The boundaries of concrete systems have a symmetrical or reciprocal relationship to the acting systems within these boundaries. By this we mean that human action can create boundaries (often but not always along some physical boundary such as a river), and in turn boundaries can constrain the human action within them. After the boundary is formed, even if its placement is quite arbitrary, it will constrain energy and information processing within it and thus to some extent may also shape the symbolic content resulting from social interaction. Human interaction can, of course, extend beyond societal boundaries, as in the "world system." Further, the replicated social interaction and the symbolic content that it produces may not be uniform or homogeneous within a given boundary. For example, a common language can extend across the boundary in one case, whereas different languages can be in use within the same society in another case. In general, though, we would expect more uniformity of symbolic structure within system boundaries than across system boundaries.

As Klapp (1975) emphasized, system boundaries do not remain permanently open nor permanently closed but can be regulated by societal members in order to stimulate or impede flows of information or energy. Further, regulation of flows via boundary control can be asymmetric, in the sense that a boundary may be open in one direction but closed in the other, or may be symmetric, open or closed in both directions. As a rudimentary example of the former, consider an energy source such as grain. A grain shortage within system A may motivate societal leaders to close the boundary to exports, thus conserving available internal supplies of grain, while opening it to imports. A surplus of grain within the system, of course, can lead to asymmetry of the opposite sort, opening the boundaries to exports but closing them to imports. In the case of symmetric boundary control, leaders may alternatively open (in both directions) the boundary or close (in both directions) it, to control information and matter-energy flows and thus to control the entropy level.

It is safe to assume that most societal leaders do not utilize the concept of entropy, do not set their goals in terms of entropy, and do not express the needs of their society in terms of entropy. Rather, they set societal goals in terms of some more familiar information or matter-energy source (e.g., food or oil). Societal leaders acting over time, set goals for these crucial commodities and manipulate the actions of societal members of the acting system to meet these goals. Such a system, in which one or more systems variables are controlled (often within a given range), is called a *controlled system* by Kuhn (1974, pp. 25–26).

Although leaders may not conceptualize societal needs and goals in terms of entropy, their actions and the variables they control, of course, subsequently affect the entropy level of the concrete system. The concept of entropy is efficaciously used as a continuous measure of system state. As will be shown, it is much superior to the concept of equilibrium in this regard and actually subsumes equilibrium, so that this concept may be used when appropriate. Further, entropy has a relatively precise statistical formulation, so that it can be successfully operationalized to a degree never attained (nor attempted) by the functionalists in their concept of equilibrium.

The History of Social Equilibrium

Social interaction by concrete individuals acting within social boundaries in the confines of a space-time framework results in a degree of symbolic structure that is amenable to statistical analysis. The statistical measure of entropy is proposed as an appropriate measure of system state for SET. However, although the concept of entropy has seen increased usage of late in sociology, it has long been overshadowed by its sibling concept of equilibrium. We consider equilibrium to be inadequate to our task of seeking a continuous measure of system state. The concept of equilibrium has been heavily criticized on theoretical, methodological, and ideological grounds in sociology; and this criticism will not be belabored here. However, some review of the concept of equilibrium in physics, biology, and sociology is necessary to set the stage for a discussion of entropy. Since equilibrium and entropy are sibling concepts and in some ways emphasis on the latter predates emphasis on the former (in physics if not in sociology), it is impossible to discuss equilibrium without occasionally lapsing into the analysis of entropy. Some of the present discussion is from Bailey (1984b).

Thermodynamic Equilibrium and Entropy

The development of the concept of entropy was central to the second law of thermodynamics and thus central to modern thermodynamics, which began early in the nineteenth century. As Guggenheim (1933, p. 6) says: "The Second Law of Thermodynamics was foreshadowed by the work of Carnot (1824) but was first clearly enunciated by Clausius (1850) to whom is also due the conception of entropy." Clausius (as cited in Wheeler 1951, p. 69) offered the following statements of the First and Second Laws of Thermodynamics:

First Law: "Die Energie der Welt ist constant."

Second Law: "Die Entropie der Welt strebt einem Maximum zu."

The first law is the principle of the conservation of energy. The second law says that the entropy of the world tends toward a maximum, which holds for an isolated or closed system that does not exchange matter, energy, or information with its environment.

The thermodynamic concept of entropy was defined as inversely related to energy (in the form of heat). We symbolize entropy by S and change in entropy by dS. The degree of change in entropy, dS, is inversely related to q/T, where T is the temperature of the system and q is the amount of heat being added to the system.

Notice that, although the first and second laws of thermodynamics refer to energy and to entropy, both important concepts in SET, they make no direct statements about equilibrium. In fact, Clausius mentions entropy frequently but virtually never uses the term *equilibrium*. However, equilibrium can be identified as the state of maximum entropy. In an isolated thermodynamic (heat) system, the system variables can be classified into three extensive systems variables (entropy, energy, and volume) and two intensive variables (temperature and pressure). Together, the five systems variables can be used to define the equilibrium conditions. The basic equilibrium condition is that of maximum entropy. Equilibrium can be defined for nonmaximum conditions of entropy if the values of the other variables are changed so that the system properties are mathematically equivalent to the condition of maximum entropy; for example, for a given entropy value and volume, equilibrium exists if energy is a minimum. In all, six equations use the extensive and intensive properties, all of which are mathematically equivalent and consistent with the second law (Guggenheim 1933).

If equilibrium is defined principally in terms of the second law, if a major thermodynamic theorist such as Clausius hardly even uses the term, and if it is synonymous with minimal energy (hardly an optimal state of affairs) and maximum entropy (which can be seen as system disintegration), what is so attractive about the concept? Why would Parsons (and many others) even wish to use it? Obviously, at some point equilibrium must have been cast in a more favorable light in order for it to make the long journey from early thermodynamics to twentieth century sociology.

The positive image of equilibrium was fostered by a number of early theorists, principally Pareto and J. Willard Gibbs. Although Clausius did not stress the concept of equilibrium, it was given prominence in the work of his predecessor J. Willard Gibbs. Gibbs had great influence on Henderson (1935), who taught systems theory and the equilibrium concept to a generation of Harvard social science students, most notably Homans (Homans and Curtis 1934), Parsons (1951), and James Grier Miller (1978). Gibbs emphasized the concept of equilibrium in the title of his most famous paper, "On the Equilibrium of Heterogeneous Substances," published in 1875 (see Gibbs 1874–1877). Although Clausius had analyzed homogeneous substances, no one had extended thermodynamics to heterogeneous chemical substances, and Gibbs' work had great theoretical and practical ramifications for years to come.

However, the focus of Gibbs' work is so foreign to most sociologists that it is doubtful that they would ever have adopted his interest in the equilibrium concept had it not been through Henderson's teaching. Further, it is unclear whether Henderson's great interest in equilibrium would have been sufficient to ingrain the concept so firmly within sociological systems theory had interest not been bolstered from other directions. Four other direct influences on sociological equilibrium theorists are the work of Spencer 1892 [1864], Pareto (1935), and Cannon (1929; 1932) and the several rather intuitive and appealing examples of the equilibrium concept within areas of physics outside of thermodynamics. A rather cursory review of physical equilibrium is in order before turning to a discussion of Spencer, Pareto, and Cannon.

Nonthermodynamic Physical Equilibrium and Entropy

Physics recongnizes several other types of equilibrium, all of which can be subsumed under the general theory of thermodynamic equilibrium. A particle that moves with constant or zero velocity (zero acceleration) is said to be in *mechanical equilibrium*. If the particle is at rest, the equilibrium is termed *static*. Particle statics is a special case of particle dynamics. When a rigid body has constant linear velocity and angular velocity, then both the linear and angular acceleration are zero and the rigid body is said to be in *mechanical equilibrium*. If the rigid body is at rest, the equilibrium is said to be static. Rigid body statics is a special case of rigid body dynamics. A rigid body is said to be in *translational equilibrium* if the vector sum of all force acting on the body is zero. A rigid body is said to be in *rotational equilibrium* if the vector sum of all the external torques acting on the body is zero. A rigid body in a gravitational field is said to be in *stable equilibrium* when the application of a force, *F*, will result in raising its center of gravity. The body is in unstable equilibrium if application of a force, *F*, results in a lowering of its center of gravity. The body is in neutral equilibrium if the application of a force, *F*, neither raises nor lowers its center of gravity. Two bodies are in thermal equilibrium if both are measured by an instrument to be at the same temperature or if the bodies are in states such that if they were connected the combined systems would be in thermal equilibrium.

All of these other types of equilibrium obey the second law of thermodynamics and can be subsumed under the concept of thermodynamic equilibrium. For example, a rigid-body object in stable equilibrium is at rest with its center of gravity at its lowest point. Thus, entropy is maximized and potential energy is minimized (is zero), and the body is in its most probable state. The only way that a force, *F*, can change the center of gravity is to raise it, thus decreasing entropy and increasing potential energy. This is an "unnatural process" and contrary to the second law. Such an action results in "unstable equilibrium," such as an object balanced on its edge. The tendency here is for the object to fall back to the ground, thus expending potential energy and increasing (maximizing) entropy in accordance with the second law. In general, for a system to be in thermodynamic equilibrium it must be in mechanical equilibrium, thermal equilibrium, and chemical equilibrium (Resnick and Halliday 1960, p. 533).

In addition to Gibbs, another chemical equilibrium theorist, Le Chatelier, has had considerable influence on equilibrium theorists in psychology, biology, and sociology. Le Chatelier's (1888) principle, which has been widely quoted in biology and social science, says:

> Every system in chemical equilibrium, under the influence of a change of every single one of the factors of equilibrium, undergoes a transformation in such direction that, if this transformation took place alone, it would produce a change in the opposite direction of the factor in question. *The factors of equilibrium are temperature, pressure, and electromotive force*, correspond-

ing to three forms of energy—heat, electricity, and mechanical energy. (translated by Lotka 1956, p. 281)

This quote has been widely used as justification for saying that a system in equilibrium which is disturbed by an outside force will "automatically" return to equilibrium.

After thermodynamics, the next influential theoretical development in physics involving entropy was that of statistical mechanics. Developed in part by Maxwell, Boltzmann, and Gibbs, statistical mechanics lent probability theory to the study of mechanical systems and developed a model of a mechanical system directly analogous to that of the thermodynamic systems developed earlier. Statistical mechanics linked the thermodynamic concept of entropy and the statistical concept of disorder through the equation

$$S = k \ln w$$

where S = entropy; k = Boltzmann's constant; and w = the probability that the system will exist in the state it is in relative to all the possible states it could be in (Resnick and Halliday 1960, p. 551).

Much, but not all of the equilibrium literature in sociology can trace its genesis to physical principles. However, sociologists vary substantially in their introduction to physical principles and the particular physical principles that influenced them. Elsewhere I have discussed the development of entropy, equilibrium, and homeostasis in detail for a number of disciplines (Bailey 1984b). Here I will confine myself to a more cursory history of the equilibrium concept. The task of understanding the influence of earlier work on modern sociological equilibrium theory is facilitated by eschewing a disciplinary approach in favor of a discussion of influences in (more or less) chronological order. Therefore, I begin with a look at Spencer and the dilemma he faced because of his use of the equilibrium concept.

The Spencerian Dilemma

The concept of equilibrium or "equilibration" was given prominence by Spencer in *First Principles* (1892 [1864]). Spencer wore several hats, writing on psychology (1896) and biology (1864-1867) as well as sociology. Thus, he contributed to the literature on equilibrium in both biology and sociology. Spencer was writing about the time that the first and second laws of thermodynamics were being fully developed by Clausius and others. He utilized physics but relied primarily upon the first law of thermodynamics, the conservation of energy.

Spencer distinguished among four different types or "orders" of equilibration (1892, p. 487). The first type is exemplified by a projectile that is in motion a relatively short time, does not have rhythms, and is at rest (equilibrated) as soon as its energy is dissipated or transferred to a body that it strikes. The second type is exemplified by vibrations or oscillations that are equilibrated by like vibrations or oscillations that oppose them. Both of these equilibrations are "plain" equilibrations, or simply processes of motions being brought to a state of rest through resistance. The third and fourth orders of equilibration are both moving equilibrations. The third order, called a *dependent moving equilibration*, is exemplified by the steam engine. The force that is dissipated in driving the machinery is replaced by the fuel fed into the furnace that heats the boiler. The expenditure of energy is balanced by the supply of fuel. Spencer gives this type of moving equilibrium prominence in evolutionary adaptation. It is clearly the precursor of the later concept of homeostasis. The fourth type of equilibration, called *independent* or *perfect moving equilibrium*, is used far less by Spencer than dependent moving equilibrium. Independent moving equilibrium is exemplified by the rhythms of the solar system, which have little resistance and thus experience little dimunition even in long periods of time (1892, pp. 487–88).

Both Spencer's "plain" equilibrium and moving equilibrium seem to be analogous to types of equilibrium discussed in the review of physics. The plain equilibrium state is analogous to static equilibrium in physics, whereas the concept of moving equilibrium was apparently inspired by a physical example of rotational equilibrium—the spinning top. Even the very term *moving equilibrium* was borrowed from some unnamed "French mathematicians" who had used the term *equilibrium mobile* (Spencer 1892, p. 486). The spinning top will move across the table until it finally becomes fixed in one spot, thus reaching "external" equilibrium, but still spinning and so not yet in "internal" equilibrium. Spencer's third form of moving dependent equilibrium is very similar. The society reaches equilibrium or a "fixed center of gravity" relative to the external world but still can change internally. The crux of Spencer's theory of equilibrium is summed up as follows:

> Any system of bodies exhibiting, like those of the Solar System, a combination of balanced rhythms, has this peculiarity;—that though the constituents of the system have relative movements, the system as a whole has no movement. The centre of gravity of the entire group remains fixed. Whatever quantity of motion any member of it has in any direction, is from moment to moment counter-balanced by an equivalent motion in some other part of the group in an opposite direction and so the aggregate matter of the group is in a state of rest. Whence it follows that the arrival at a state of moving equilibrium is the disappearance of some movement which the aggregate had in re-

lation to external things, and a continuance of those movements only which the different parts of the aggregate have in relation to each other. Thus, generalizing the process it becomes clear that all forms of equilibration are intrinsically the same; since in every aggregate, it is the centre of gravity only that loses its motion: the constituents always retaining some motion with respect to each other—the motion of molecules if none else. (Spencer 1892, p. 488)

This description of the general process of equilibration, written some 100 years before contemporary functional equilibrium theory in sociology, has all of its key elements and is in some ways considerably more sophisticated. The key phrase, "Whatever quantity of motion any member of it has in any direction, is from moment to moment counter-balanced by an equivalent motion on some other part of the group in an opposite direction," is very similar to Le Chatelier's principle stated earlier, which was developed for chemical systems some twenty-five years later.

The crux of the argument is that evolution is a series of progressive adaptations. Each adaptation can be seen as the establishment of a dependent moving equilibrium (form 3 of equilibrium). In the case of a society adapting to its environment, such changes (e.g., in population size) as are necessary will be made until motion relative to the environment ceases (until "the system as a whole has no movement"). After the system becomes motionless relative to its external environment, then the system becomes internally balanced. While all of this internal motion is taking place, there still is no motion relative to the external world (what is now called the *environment of the system*). This balance with the external world, or adaptation to the environment, occurs through changes in the internal structure of the society so that the particular function required for adaptation is met (Spencer 1892, p. 501). Once this adaptation is complete, there may be external changes that disrupt the equilibrium between the external world (environment) and internal world (society), thus necessitating new adaptation resulting in a new form 3 moving equilibrium (dependent moving equilibrium) accomplished only by internal structural changes. In general, these changes result in ever increasing heterogeneity. For example, degree of the differentiation or division of labor sufficient to establish a moving equilibrium at an earlier date (e.g., with a smaller population size) may be insufficient for establishment of a moving equilibrium, or balance with the environment, for a larger population.

A student of Cannon (1929; 1932) will note that this form 3 equilibrium is very similar to Cannon's concept of homeostasis developed some sixty years later. Spencer, like Cannon, discusses internal changes. He also talks in terms of supply and demand (1892, p. 508) and speaks of the *vis medicatrix naturae*, or natural healing of the body, which Cannon also notes and which Spencer presents as a prominent example of his third form of equilibration as displayed by organic bodies (1892, p. 500).

Spencer had originally felt that moving equilibrium was only a penulti-mate type of equilibrium. Each successive adaptation, representing an equilib-rium between society and the environment, would move society closer to the ultimate state of bliss. The increase of heterogeneity could cease only when equilibration stopped, but this would be when further development was unnecessary and society had adapted to its highest state. He was thus "staggered" when told by Professor Tyndall that ultimate equilibrium was sys-tem death (according to the second law). He learned this in approximately 1858, some six years before the publication of *First Principles*.

In a letter to Professor Tyndall (D. Duncan 1908, vol. I, p. 136), Spencer describes his reaction to Tyndall's statement concerning the implications of the second law (maximum entropy):

> Regarding, as I had done, equilibration as the ultimate and *highest* state of society, I had assumed it to be not only the ultimate but also the highest state of the universe. And your assertion that when equilibrium was reached life must cease, staggered me. Indeed, not seeing my way out of the conclusion, I remember being out of spirits for some days afterwards. (italics in the orig-inal)

The ultimate equilibrium referred to here is, of course, maximum en-tropy. Spencer was understandably devastated when told that according to the second law the ultimate equilibrium was the worst state of the system—sys-tem death. Working without the concept of an open system that later allowed general systems theory (Bertalanffy 1968) to escape this trap, Spencer was never able to successfully theoretically avoid the finality of the second law. In his autobiographical "The Filliation of Ideas," written in 1899, and published in Duncan (1908), Spencer acts as though the matter were cleanly resolved. In referring to his conversation with Tyndall some forty years earlier, he says that "And then, in pursuance of the same line of thought, embodying itself in the question—'What happens after equilibration is completed?' there came the reply 'Dissolution.'" (Duncan 1908, vol. II, p. 335). Unfortunately, this one-word solution is no solution at all and could hardly have been more com-forting to Spencer than it is to us now. In reality the matter was not resolved so cleanly in his discussion of equilibration in *First Principles* (see Russett 1966, p. 39). Although this quote would indicate that Spencer acquiesced and relinquished his belief in a higher state of society in accepting the harsh fate of societal dissolution, in fact he left the matter unresolved and contradictory by accepting the notion of final dissolution without giving up his sacred notion of the higher ultimate societal state. Thus, he juxtaposes (Spencer 1892, p. 517) references to "that cosmical equilibration which brings Evolution under all its forms to a close" and "We finally draw from it a warrant for the belief, that Evolution can end only in the establishment of the greatest perfection and the most complete happiness."

Pareto

Pareto was also working prior to later work in physics and GST, which allowed theorists to avoid the Spencerian dilemma. He thus was not able to escape it entirely, but as a student of physics he was able to avoid the direct confrontation with it that devastated poor Spencer. Pareto's problems with the equilibrium model are most evident in the persistent confusion between the system as heuristic and the system as empirical. Ironically, Pareto (1935, p. 1461) was cognizant of the concept of entropy but eschewed it, instead relying heavily upon the concept of equilibrium. Pareto wrote before the terms *open system* and *homeostasis* were coined. He does however say that "the equilibrium of a social system is like the equilibrium of a living organism" and refers to *vis medicatrix naturae* (Pareto 1935, p. 1436).

While eschewing the concept of entropy, Pareto discussed equilibrium in great detail. In defining social equilibrium, Pareto (1935, p. 1435) says:

> *The state of equilibrium.* If we intend to reason at all strictly, our first obligation is to fix upon the state in which we are choosing to consider the social system, which is constantly changing in form. The real state, be it static or dynamic, of the system is determined by its conditions. Let us imagine that some modification in its form is induced artificially. At once a reaction will take place, tending to restore the changing form to its original state as modified by normal change. If that were not the case, the form, with its normal changes, would not be determined but would be a mere matter of chance. (italics in the original).

Like a number of other equilibrium theorists, such as Spencer before him and Henderson after him, Pareto wore several hats. By the time he applied the equilibrium concept to sociology, he had already studied equilibrium in physics, as early as 1870 (Russett 1966, p. 88), and had worked with the concept in economics. Thus, it should be clear that Pareto's equilibrium model was surely not inductively derived from studying an empirical society but was a more general model that could be applied to sociology along with applications in physics and economics. Pareto obviously was well aware of the difference between equilibrium as a heuristic and concrete equilibrium in an actual society, a distinction that sometimes escaped his readers (Russett 1966, pp. 95-96). However, Russett (1966, p. 98) charges that "Pareto was too preoccupied with constructing a neat analytical model to worry greatly about its fit with the real world." In reaction to Homans and Curtis's (1934, p. 276) statement that Pareto believed "That most societies at most times behave in a manner which indicates that they are in equilibrium," Russett (1966, p. 97) says that "This is far too important as well as too problematic a statement to permit such uncritical acceptance." It is clear that Pareto did not empirically determine that even a single society was in equilibrium. It is also clear that he would doubtlessly say, as economists generally do, that societies "tend" toward equilibrium but that obviously there are cases where the necessary conditions are not met and thus the society is not in equilibrium. However, it is clear that in addition to using equilibrium as a concept, he thought that it had empirical applications in sociology.

Notice that in Pareto's definition, he speaks of "artificial" changes in equilibrium. This can be interpreted as being almost identical to the notion of "unnatural processes" utilized in thermodynamics (see Guggenheim 1933). Since "artificial" processes are by definition not "real" and thus will not occur empirically, the concept seems to be purely heuristic. However, Pareto (1935, p. 1436) says:

> Somewhat similar to the artificial changes mentioned are those occasional changes which result from some element that suddenly appears, has its influence for a brief period upon a system, occasioning some slight disturbance in the state of equilibrium, and then passes away. Short wars waged by rich countries, epidemics, floods, earthquakes and similar calamities would be examples. Statisticians long ago observed that such incidents interrupt the course of economic or social life but briefly; yet many scientists, who have worked without the concept of equilibrium have kept meandering about in search of imaginary causes. Mill, for one, wondered why a country afflicted for a short time by the curse of war soon returned to its normal state.

Thus, far from being merely a heuristic device, the equilibrium concept is seen to be a powerful tool in empirical analysis that can end the "meandering" of errant social scientists.

Another instance of heuristic analysis is found in Pareto's frequent use of analogies. In the course of two pages (Pareto 1935, pp. 1439–40), he says that social equilibrium is analogous to the state of a river, to the state of dynamic equilibrium in a physical system, to the state of equilibrium in a living organism, to economic equilibrium, and to "statistic" equilibrium in the kinetic theory of gases. In the case of economics, the analogy is "so close" that economic equilibrium may be considered a particular case of the general state of the sociological system (Pareto 1935, p. 1440).

Pareto apparently did not utilize the distinction between open and closed systems. His analogies referred both to physical systems and organisms. He did, however, distinguish between static and dynamic equilibrium. His definition is broad enough that neither is precluded (Lopreato 1971, p. 329).

According to Russett (1966, p. 93), Pareto considered social equilibrium to be "dynamic and incremental rather than static" but had no theoretical tools for studying dynamic equilibrium, as was done in physics, so he had to settle for the study of a series of static equilibria as a "substitute" for the study of dynamic equilibrium. Further, although Pareto emphasizes a return to equilibrium, he allows for "normal change" in the system (Pareto 1935, p. 1435). Also Pareto emphasizes the reaction of system elements in returning the system to equilibrium. This is based upon the assumption that, if the conditions initially leading to equilibrium still prevail, the changes causing disequilibrium must be essentially aberrations or "artificial." Thus, if they occur empirically they will be mild and of short duration (such as short wars in rich countries). The question of what would happen to systems in which the changes are not minor aberrations is not answered. The logical conclusion would be that major changes of long duration (such as long wars in poor countries) could cause disequilibrium and even system death.

Equilibrium between Pareto and Parsons

The majority of later American equilibrium theorists utilized generally verbal but relatively familiar equilibrium analyses. For example, Small, especially in his earlier work, offers a notion of equilibrium that would seem familiar to any student of Spencer:

> Society, in order to maintain its coherence and continue its development, must constantly readjust itself to natural and artificial conditions, for the organism sustains a relation of double reaction with its environment . . . Thus approximate equilibrium may be preserved by an endless series of social readjustments to progressive changes in external conditions. (Small and Vincent 1894, p. 336)

Likewise, Ward (1883, p. 177) presented an organic model of equilibrium, saying that: "Equilibration is the constant tendency of the organism to adapt itself, by means of morphological and physiological modifications, to the changes going on in the environment."

Ward's opinion of Spencer's equilibration theory was generally positive: "Unquestionably the most able portion of Herbert Spencer's treatise on biology is his discussion and analysis of the principles of 'Equilibration' in chapters XI and XII of Volume I" (Ward 1883, pp. 176–77). However, he was much less tolerant of poor Spencer's dilemma with regard to the second law. He says that: "We must divest our minds of the current notion that evolution necessarily implies higher and higher organization. Evolution is progress toward the condition of stable equilibrium, not necessarily progress toward higher organic perfection" (Ward 1883, p. 166). Ward contends that the "law of dissolution" will not only "perpetually antagonize" the "law of evolution" but will in fact defeat it, so that: "Dissolution forms the last act in the great cosmical drama, and completes the cycle of change. Societies are disintegrated, and the races of man scattered and extinguished" (Ward 1883, pp. 166–67).

Fortunately, a century later, the use of sociological systems analysis does not necessitate such dire predictions as either Ward's biblical-sounding apocalypse or the Spencerian dilemma. Both were later resolved in GST through an adoption of the open systems model that does not inevitably follow the second law, as the decrease of total entropy through the introduction of negative entropy from outside the system is possible. But at the time Spencer's quite sophisticated organic analogy was diluted and frustrated by his inability to adequately deal with the second law of thermodynamics. Thus, he was stymied chiefly because he mixed the organic (open systems) and physical (closed systems) models, without realizing the important fundamental difference between them with regard to production of entropy. This problem remains in writing on social equilibrium almost up to the present. Henderson (1928), for example, went so far as to even write a closed system analysis of *Blood*. Lundberg, while offering a positivistic notion of equilibrium based directly upon the second law of thermodynamics, implies that the chief difference between physical and organic equilibrium is that: "But in living systems especially, the equilibrium achieved by the adjustments of the system to its environment is a dynamic, a moving, rather than static, equilibrium" (Lundberg 1939, p. 208).

The implication seems to be that one can construct an adequate sociological systems model simply by recognizing that the society is an open system and using the notion of moving equilibrium rather than "static" equilibrium. Unfortunately, this is simply not true. Spencer used the notion of moving equilibrium so extensively that Lotka (1956, p. 262) was moved to comment that moving equilibria were emphasized "almost *ad nauseam* by Herbert Spencer" (italics in the original). Even this extensive use of moving equilibrium could not save him from the Spencerian dilemma. Further, Ward used the concept of moving equilibrium extensively, and it could not save him from predicting the Wardian apocalypse. The key to avoiding these conceptual traps lies not in the concept of moving equilibrium but in the understanding that production of entropy need not follow the second law of thermodynamics in open systems, as it must in isolated systems. The discussion now focusses on equilibrium as used by Parsons, the section, from Bailey (1984a).

Parsons

"Who now reads Spencer?" Apparently not Parsons. Although this quote from Brinton (1933, pp. 226–27) proved to be a very effective opening for *The Structure of Social Action* (Parsons 1937), its rather cruel irony cannot escape us ("Who now reads Parsons without criticizing his equilibrium concept?"). Although as a systems theorist I *do* read Parsons and admire his work greatly, I cannot help being saddened by the thought that if he had read Spencer more carefully (particularly *First Principles* 1892, and biographical works such as Duncan 1908), he might have been spared the Spencerian dilemma. Ironically, though, Parsons carried this nemesis right into his own work, so that the ghost of Spencer returns to haunt those who dismissed his work so sardonically.

Ironically, whereas Parsons (1937, p. 3) criticized Spencer as a representative of positivism, he, too, was later to use an equilibrium model that was essentially positivistic and quite similar to the isolated-system equilibrium model of classic thermodynamics. It is again ironic that, although Spencer worked without knowledge of the second law, Parsons was writing at a time when the distinction between open and closed systems and the distinction between homeostasis and equilibrium had been clearly made by Cannon (1929; 1932). Thus, he was in a position to avoid the Spencerian dilemma simply by entirely eschewing the closed system notion of equilibrium with its cataclysmic consequences and utilizing solely the more appropriate concept of homeostasis.

However, it may be that Parsons purposefully retained the closed system concept of equilibrium, even if it was inappropriate, because only the closed system concept of equilibrium ensured a return to equilibrium. Social equilibrium theorists have generally cited Le Chatelier's principle (presented earlier) as evidence that, when equilibrium is disturbed, forces within the system will work to restore it. However, even though Bertalanffy (1968, p. 80) says that this principle is valid for open systems, it is nevertheless true, as Lotka (1956, pp. 284–85) says, that this principle generally will *not* hold for living systems. Actually, we can easily show (although we will not do it here) that Le Chatelier's principle holds *only* for the state of maximum entropy and is quite consistent with the second law. Thus, its usage puts us face-to-face once more with the Spencerian dilemma. The only state of equilibrium where return is ensured if disturbed is the ultimate equilibrium of maximum entropy. This is of no use to social theorists, as it is the state of complete system disintegration or social disorganization.

The basic problem seems to be that Parsons was too uncritical in his acceptance of the equilibrium notion. He was exposed to the work of both Cannon and Henderson at Harvard (Russett 1966). Thus, although he criticized positivism, he learned equilibrium from two physiologists, as well as from the works of Pareto, who had first learned equilibrium as an engineering and physics student. He further tended to accept equilibrium virtually as a given and uncritically adopted most of its varieties rather than discriminating between appropriate and inappropriate applications.

One of his definitions of equilibrium is provided within the context of his definition of system. In an oft-quoted passage, Parsons and Shils (1951, p. 107) define the concept of system by saying that:

> The most general and fundamental property of a system is the interdependence of parts or variables. Interdependence consists of the existence of determinate relationships among the parts or variables as contrasted with randomness of variability. In other words, interdependence is *order* in the relationship among the components which enter into a system. (italics in the original)

This definition seems relatively clear and noncontroversial so far and is quite consistent with the definition of a system provided by Hall and Fagen (1956, p. 18): *"A system is a set of objects together with relationships between the objects and between their attributes"* (italics in the original).

However, Parsons and Shils (1951, p. 107) continue their definition, saying that:

> This order must have a tendency to self-maintenance, which is very generally expressed in the concept of equilibrium. It need not, however, be a static self-maintenance or a stable equilibrium. It may be an ordered process of change—a process following a determinate pattern rather than random variability relative to the starting point. This is called a moving equilibrium and is well exemplified by growth.

So defined, the concept of equilibrium is crucial to the concept of a system. Equilibrium is defined as the self-maintenance of order, regularity, and non-randomness or interdependence among variables. Without such nonrandom relationships among variables in the system, the system could scarcely be defined. However, as pointed out by Alexander (1978, p. 181), equilibrium should not be equated with order. Rather, equilibrium is stable order or, more correctly, self-maintained order within the system.

The major problem with this is that *interdependence* defined as "nonrandomness" is hopelessly arbitrary and vague. This sort of looseness of definition is common in verbal treatments of systems but is untenable when seeking to operationalize the notion of a system. That is, there are a large number of nonrandom sets of relationships among variables in a system. In a large system this number may approach infinity. Thus, a large number of conditions of stable nonrandom interdependence may be identified. Are all of these to be call equilibrium? Gouldner (1959, p. 253; 1970, p. 211) says that equilibrium implies interdependence but that interdependence does not imply equilibrium. Let us explore this matter further, elaborating statistically what Gouldner has stated verbally.

Consider the simple case of two ordinal variables X and Y, each containing a "high" category and a "low" category, and combined to form a fourfold contingency table, with the expected values shown in the cells. The expected values (in χ^2 terminology) are the values that would occur in each cell if the two variables were randomly distributed and are computed by multiplying, for each respective cell, the row marginal by the column marginal and dividing by the grand total. If this exact distribution of frequencies were to occur empirically (the "observed values" in χ^2 terminology), then χ^2 would be zero and there would be no relationship between X and Y. Thus, any measure of association used (Yule's Q, phi, and so forth) would also be zero. This is clearly what Parsons and Shils (1951, p. 107) termed the *randomness of variability* of our simple two-variable system and that they contrasted with interdependence or "the existence of determinate relationships."

Now suppose that in another case some of the observed values differ from the expected values, giving us a value of Yule's Q equal to, for example, 0.1. Suppose that this relationship exists without change for 100 years. This situation meets Parsons and Shils' definition of equilibrium, as it is nonrandom and stable over time. Thus, the definition of equilibrium is seen to have two requirements, each of which is necessary but not alone sufficient, whereas together both are sufficient for the existence of stable equilibrium. Stable equilibrium exists if (1) a nonzero (nonrandom) relationship exists among variables in the system; and (2) this relationship is constant over time.

Several things can be said about this definition. The mere existence of a relationship, usually assumed to be constant over time (but not necessarily "self-maintaining"), is commonly recognized in statistics as simply a relationship. It is likely to be tested for statistical significance but is not likely to be labeled *equilibrium*. Parsons and Shils' definition is arbitrary on both points

1 and 2. How much must a relationship depart from randomness before it satisfies criterion 1 (must it be "statistically significant"), and how long must this relationship remain constant before requirement 2 is satisfied? Is equilibrium in fact a continuum? Does not a perfect relationship (Yule's $Q = 1.0$) maintained forever represent the epitome of equilibrium? Rhetorically, which most closely satisfies conditions for equilibrium, a weak relationship that is self-maintaining and stable over a long period of time or a strong relationship that is stable for only a short period of time?

The arbitrariness of the definition of equilibrium makes it vulnerable to the same sorts of criticism that befell the functionalists' notion of system survival. Just as one could ask how much a system must change before it is said to have failed to "survive," one could ask how much, and for how long, a system could change before it is said to be out of equilibrium. No rule of thumb for such determination was ever given by the functionalists as far as I know, probably because any departure from equilibrium was considered only temporary and thus not a crucial topic of concern.

But, not only is the equilibrium concept arbitrary in its very definition, it is also arbitrary in the sense that more than one state of a system can be considered equilibrium (especially in the case of moving equilibrium). The concept of equilibrium as a measure of system state is both nonunique and arbitrary. A measure could be unique and arbitrary, indicating that any state could be equilibrium but that only one state of a given system would be labeled equilibrium. The zero point on the Fahrenheit temperature scale is unique but arbitrary. The functionalists' definition, however, is not only arbitrary in the case of moving equilibrium, it is not unique, letting any and all nonrandom states be called *equilibrium* (although only one at a given time).

Not only is the concept of equilibrium inherently arbitrary for a given system and nonunique, it is also dichotomous rather than continuous. All we can determine about a system is whether it is in equilibrium. If it is not, it should be returning to a state of equilibrium. We have no measure of the degree of equilibrium. Rather than try to make a continuous measure of equilibrium based on strength of relationship or duration of the equilibrium state, it seems more efficacious to replace the concept of equilibrium with a continuous measure of system state that will vary between determined limits. Thus, rather than measuring only whether the system is in equilibrium, which is like measuring whether the temperature is freezing, the measure will encompass all possible states of the system, just as a temperature scale measures a range of temperatures besides freezing. Interestingly enough, while gaining a measure of many system states besides equilibrium, we sacrifice nothing, as the scale being used (entropy) includes equilibrium.

Moving Equilibrium. Parsons and Shils (1951, p. 107) include the notion of moving equilibrium to account for conditions of system growth and change that clearly contradict the notion of static or stable equilibrium. Most of what was said about stable equilibrium earlier applies to moving equilibrium as well. The concept is still arbitrary and nonunique, perhaps even more so. The problems of determining how long the relationship must be constant before it can be said to be in equilibrium are perhaps even greater than with stable equilibrium. While the concept of moving equilibrium may facilitate the study of change, it will not solve the problems of measuring system state facing us here.

Equilibrium as an Analytical Device. Criticism of Parsons' equilibrium concept has been mostly from conflict theorists, who feared that the concept inhibited the study of conflict and change, rather than from any concern with measuring the state of a system. The criticism sometimes has been answered by Parsons' defenders with the statement that "Parsons' concept of equilibrated interaction is a theoretical construct and not a description of empirical reality" (Johnson 1975, p. 34) or that the equilibrium seeking tendency is partially drawn from experience but is also used for "heuristic" purposes (Devereux 1961, p. 33).

Parsons makes it very clear that the existence of a "stabilized or equilibrated interaction process" is the reference point for "all dynamic motivational analysis of social process" and is "clearly an assumption" (Parsons 1951, p. 205). He reiterates this point by saying that the proposition of a stabilized interaction process as a major point of reference is "*a theoretical assumption, not an empirical generalization*" (Parsons 1951, p. 481, italics in the original).

The use of an assumption to provide a reference point is the crux of Weber's ideal type strategy and can be a very valuable methodological tool. Especially in the absence of rigorous experimental control, one valuable way to analyze relationships is to assume that certain potentially confounding variables are constant or that the system is in a certain state and then to see what would happen if this were the case. This if-then strategy can be very valuable. It is often not well understood by sociologists, who tend to see the assumptions as "unrealistic" rather than as a tool for assuming away extraneous factors and thus simplifying the analysis.

However, use of an assumed reference point as an analytical tool does not change the criticism of the equilibrium concept as a measure of system state. Building an effective systems theory of society requires an effective measure of system state, and the equilibrium concept, as we have seen, is arbitrary, nonunique, and noncontinuous. This holds whether equilibrium is empirically verified or assumed. Further, a measure is required that can be empirically utilized not merely assumed.

But, although an assumption of stability may be a useful heuristic tool, there is no need to label it *equilibrium*, thus calling up all of the difficulties associated with this term. The "complementary interaction of two or more individual actors," described by Parsons (1951, pp. 204–205), is valuable but need not be called *equilibrium* (Buckley 1967, p. 10). The term *balanced or stabilized interaction* (the latter term is used by Parsons interchangeably with *equilibrium*, 1951, p. 205) serves quite well without the problems of the equilibrium concept. Further there is no need to assume that equilibrium is self-maintaining or that the system returns to equilibrium if disturbed. This has no role in the heuristic use.

However, even if complementary interaction is a legitimate heuristic device, it is clear that in other cases the concept of equilibrium is not assumed merely as a heuristic tool but, as has been seen, is the foundation of Parsons and Shils's (1951, p. 107) very definition of the system. If we wish to consider all usage of the concept of equilibrium (defined as a condition of self-maintained nonrandomness or interdependency among the variables of the system) as merely heuristic, then by deduction the entire concept of the social system can only be "heuristic," as the system definition depends upon the definition of equilibrium. Although it can certainly be argued that any conceptual device such as the notion of a system is essentially heuristic, I do not think that it is necessary to limit the notion of system this drastically. Systems need not be "assumed" but can be analyzed empirically, if only a measure of system state can be found that is superior to the concept of equilibrium.

Homeostasis. To Parsons, the concept of homeostasis is a special case of the concept of equilibrium (Parsons 1961b, p. 339). This can only mean that all cases of homeostasis are also cases of equilibrium but not all cases of equilibrium need be homeostasis. He provides no estimate of what percentage of cases of equilibrium are not homeostasis, but the definition by Parsons and Shils (1951, p. 107) of the system as self-maintaining sounds very much like the concept of homeostasis. Also, Parsons has, on occasion, used examples of temperature regulation in animals to illustrate his discussions of equilibrium (1961b, p. 339; 1961c), so it is not surprising that a critic should accuse him of "the indiscriminate equation of the equilibrium and homeostasis principles" (Buckley 1967, p. 14). Actually this equation of equilibrium and homeostasis in sociology is not unusual, as Buckley (1967, pp. 14–15) notes. As Cannon noted (1932, p. 24) the word *equilibrium* had even by 1932 come to have a fairly exact meaning, a meaning limited to isolated (closed) systems. Since, as shall be seen, biological organisms and social systems must be seen as open systems, a concept reserved for isolated systems will not suffice. Thus, Cannon coined the term *homeostasis* to apply to open systems only. The sole reason for coining the term *homeostasis* was so that it would not be confused with *equilibrium*, and this gain was effectively wiped out by equating the two. Probably Henderson was as much to blame for this as anybody, as he used the isolated system model in a study of blood (Henderson 1928) and apparently simply carried the isolated system notion over to social groups, where it was inappropriate. That is, the conception of the system that Henderson uses is clearly open, as he speaks of disturbances from without the system, but he retains the concept of equilibrium, which is only applicable to isolated systems (Barber 1970, p. 138).

If sociologists had followed the lead of Cannon more than Henderson or had at least not equated homeostasis and equilibrium, their analysis would doubtlessly have been better received. While I certainly cannot speak for the conflict theorists and say that they would have been pleased with a faithful rendering of Cannon's concept of homeostasis, they may find it more palatable than they had imagined. While the concept of homeostasis also utilizes the notion of self-maintenance, which the conflict theorists have found so unpalatable, at least as used by Cannon, the concept does not merely assume that the status quo will be reestablished but allows showing in great detail *how* and *why* the steady state is reestablished.

Cannon's concept is much more sophisticated than is usually presented in sociology. He distinguished between "homeostasis by regulating supplies" and "homeostasis by regulating process" (Cannon 1929, p. 403). The latter has received most of the attention in sociology, particularly his example of the regulation of body temperature. However, the concept of homeostasis by regulating supplies is fascinating and is further divided into two subtypes, depending upon how supplies are stored: "*storage by inundation*" and "*storage by segregation*" (Cannon 1929, p. 403). Cannon provides examples in which storage of material in the body is utilized as a regulatory mediation between supply and demand.

But whereas homeostasis is at the very least not as arbitrary and confusing as the concept of equilibrium and it may be used legitimately by sociologists of Parsons's persuasion (whether they can ever satisfy conflict theorists is another matter), its emphasis on self-maintenance of a steady-state keeps it from serving as the potential continuous measure of system state desired for our model. Use of the concept of social entropy, which is more suited to our needs, in no way precludes use of the concepts of equilibrium and homeostasis. In fact, it facilitates usage of these concepts by providing a reference concept, as both equilibrium and homeostasis can easily be related to the concept of entropy.

Summarizing the Breadth of Parsons' Equilibrium Concept. Parsons (1961b, p. 338) also says:

> Equilibrium in short is nothing but the concept of regularity under specific
> conditions . . . and of course its maintenance is by no means inevitable but,
> if the conditions on which it depends are changed beyond certain limits, it
> will disappear, again most probably giving way to other regularities than to
> sheer randomness.

When defined so broadly, equilibrium becomes almost synonymous with the maintenance of order or nonrandom relationships among the variables in the system. Nonequilibrium theorists, statisticians, and sociologists in general share the assumption that there will be nonrandom relationships among societal variables *without* using the concept of equilibrium. Yet Parsons (1961b, p. 338), obviously growing weary of criticism of the equilibrium concept, says that: "The denial of its legitimacy in the conceptual armory of social science is at the least, in my perhaps not very humble opinion, symptomatic of the denial that social science itself is legitimate, or realistically possible."

Parsons's equilibrium concept is very general. It is a heuristic but also represents the minimal maintenance of empirical order necessary for social science to exist. It is also part and parcel of the system concept. Further, while recognizing that the social system is an open system (Parsons 1961a, p. 30) and using the concept of homeostasis, Parsons also uses the isolated system concept of equilibrium and says that homeostasis is a "special case" of equilibrium (Parsons 1961b, p. 339). Equilibrium can also be static, stable, or moving.

Virtually every type of equilibrium reviewed here is included in Parsons's conception of equilibrium. The problem is that many of these are at least partially incompatible, especially when used simultaneously. Perhaps the most dangerous example of this is his confusion of closed (isolated) systems equilibrium and open system homeostasis. Application of the former to social systems leads the theorist squarely into the Spencerian dilemma, as equilibrium is seen as a state of societal dissolution. Application of the latter puts one on sound theoretical ground and escapes this dilemma. The overall result of Parsons's overly broad use of the concept of equilibrium is a general lack of precision that weakens the value of the equilibrium concept.

So much has been written on sociological equilibrium and the term has been applied in many ways that this cursory treatment does not do the topic justice. However, the equilibrium concept has been criticized so widely that it is doubtful how efficacious further analysis would be. Thus, we move beyond equilibrium by analyzing in some detail the concept of social entropy. For further discussion of equilibrium, as well as discussion of equilibrium in the work of other theorists (such as Cooley) neglected here, the definitive source is Russett (1966). The chapter by Lopreato (1971) is also excellent, and the discussion here is supplemented elsewhere (Bailey 1983b, 1984a, 1984b).

The History of Social Entropy

Entropy and equilibrium are sibling concepts. Clausius (1879) did much of the pioneering work on entropy in thermodynamics but scarcely felt it necessary to speak of equilibrium at all. In fact, in an admittedly casual reading of his book, I found no mention of equilibrium, although entropy is mentioned scores of times. However, as mentioned earlier, there is a direct link from the equilibrium analysis of Gibbs (1874–1877), through Henderson (1935), who was a great admirer of both Gibbs and Pareto, to Parsons (1951). Thus, the bulk of social systems analysis, particularly functionalism, is rooted in Gibbsian equilibrium analysis. As such, it was conceived without benefit of the work of Prigogine on open systems.

Prigogine

Although equilibrium analysis proved valuable in thermodynamics, it is clearly often a special case and often only heuristic. The "real world" is often *not* in equilibrium. Specifically, physicists were long troubled by the seeming paradox that some systems, including social groups, could *decrease* in entropy, rather than increase according to the second law. The precursor of this line of analysis was Maxwell's (1871) discussion of a hypothetical "demon" who could let fast molecules through a trap door and keep slow ones out. A heat engine working on this principle could violate the second law. Further work on this problem by Szilard (1929) and Brillouin (1956; 1964) led to the concept of negative entropy, or negentropy, and its relation to information.

But the major works that formed the foundation for modern systems theory were by Prigogine (1955; 1962) on the thermodynamics of irreversible processes. Prigogine went beyond the early equilibrium analysis of Gibbs to analyze entropy change, not only in isolated thermodynamic systems (where the second law holds) but also in open systems that exchange both matter-energy and information with the environment.

The Prigogine entropy equation (equation 3.11 here) shows that, although internal entropy production increases or remains constant within the system, imported entropy can be decreased by importation of energy from the environment, thus resulting in an overall decrease of system entropy or the increase of order.

The Prigogine entropy equation allows completely escape from the

Spencerian dilemma. At the risk of overstatement, I can say that the limitations of functionalist systems theory stem largely because it is based upon isolated-system equilibrium analysis, a la Gibbs, rather than the more modern Prigogine entropy analysis. Only the latter is really appropriate for open systems such as social systems. The Prigogine analysis does not change the relationship between entropy and energy nor violate the second law; it simply analyzes the open-system situation where energy can continually be imported into the system, unlike the isolated system of equilibrium analysis that is closed against energy flows. Prigogine simply shows that where energy increases, entropy decreases (and order and organization increase).

The overall conclusion is that twentieth century Prigogine entropy analysis provides a much more viable model for open systems such as social systems than the nineteenth century Gibbsian equilibrium analysis that the functionalists used. The Prigogine approach is simply more modern and based on an extension of Gibbsian analysis. Thus, there is no question that we should utilize entropy analysis in our systems formulation, as we can always utilize the special case of equilibrium if we wish to.

Use of Entropy

Why have not sociologists utilized entropy more? One reason is simply that sociology has not had a scientist that crossed boundaries and brought entropy into sociology the way that Pareto, Henderson, and others brought in equilibrium. Entropy has only recently been introduced into anthropology (see Aberle 1987; Adams 1975; Campbell, 1982). In addition, there may be several reasons why the equilibrium concept has been used more extensively in sociology than the concept of entropy. Doubtlessly, one reason is the intuitive appeal of the equilibrium concept, particularly its connotation of balance or stability. For example, as seen earlier, Pareto (1935) says that statisticians long ago noted that disruptions such as short wars waged by rich countries, earthquakes, floods, and epidemics are relatively short lived, and the country quickly returns to normalcy (equilibrium). This is surely a comforting thought for a politician or a common citizen worried about the stability of the social system.

Entropy, in contrast, has no such comforting intuitive understandability and no notion of balance. Despite some recent popularization, many scholars, including sociologists, remain unfamiliar with the concept of entropy. Those who are aware of it often associate it with thermodynamics and often consider entropy a property of heat systems. Thus, they feel that its application to social phenomena is inappropriate at worst and unfruitful at best. Most people probably have little or no intuitive understanding of entropy. Those who do may associate it with the second law of thermodynamics, which states that closed systems tend toward maximum entropy. Since maximum entropy is often portrayed graphically as "system death," the connotation of entropy is ominous and quite opposite from the secure image conjured up by the concept of equilibrium.

Thus, the concept of entropy lay slumbering in the shadows of sociology for decades while its sibling concept of equilibrium was widely applied in functionalism (see Parsons 1951; Russett 1966; Lopreato 1971), only to be severely criticized on a number of grounds, including methodological, ideological, and substantive grounds (Horowitz 1962; Gouldner 1959; Lockwood 1956). It is interesting then, that, within the last fifteen years or so, entropy has risen from its slumber like a conceptual Rip Van Winkle. It is still an exaggeration to say that the concept is widely used in sociology. Nevertheless, the list of discussions of entropy is substantial and continues to grow. Further, it is also interesting that, whereas the bulk of this literature is statistical, a number of verbal explications of the entropy concept have appeared, and some of them are quite comprehensive.

Ironically, though, whereas the entropy literature has finally begun to grow in sociology after a delay of many years, we are not seeing the accumulative effect that we like to see in science. There has been some accumulation of findings, with subsequent efforts building upon past efforts, but this accumulation seems far less than it could be. Most studies, both statistical and verbal, remain disturbingly separate, with relatively few cross-references. For example, one recent statistical article developed the PRU (proportional reduction of uncertainty) interpretation for entropy (Teachman 1980) but failed to cross-reference another article that had developed the same PRU interpretation five years earlier in the same journal (Horan 1975).

The basic cause of the lack of accumulation is the diversity and lack of integration of applications, not only between the verbal and statistical literature, but within each respective literature as well. A problem with the statistical literature is the diversity of substantive applications. Most substantive areas have seen one (or no) applications. It is rare when entropy is applied twice in the same area, as when the work of Hauser et al. (1975) in mobility builds upon the work of McFarland (1969) in the same area. Furthermore, many of the applications have come to sociology from the field of information theory, which has at least two ramifications. One is that in general the study is conceived of primarily as an application of information theory to sociology, and the researcher may apply it in an area where it has not been applied before. Further, most of the references tend to be to the information-theory literature rather than to other entropy studies in sociology. A second (and very important) ramification is that although the H measure is generally used, it often is called by different names: a measure of information or uncertainty (McFarland 1969; Horan 1975) as well as a measure of entropy (Capecchi and Möller 1968). This use of multiple names makes it difficult for researchers to locate other entropy studies, makes the literature on entropy seem smaller than it really is, and undoubtedly reduces the numbers of citations in published research. All these factors hinder the accumulation of a body of knowledge on sociological entropy. Remember, too, that all this diversity is encountered *within* the statistical literature on sociological entropy. This is somewhat ironic as a clear statistical operationalization such as *H* (discussed later) should lessen diversity.

The situation is even worse when considering the diversity within the total entropy literature, both statistical and verbal. The verbal literature, though not as large, is also quite diverse in both approach and subject matter. The continuity that does exist appears largely due to a rather consistent approach to the analysis of entropy in general systems theory (e.g., Bertalanffy 1968). But the systems literature is not always well integrated with information-theoretic approaches to entropy. Only a few studies (e.g., Buckley 1967; Galtung 1975) facilitate integration of the verbal and statistical approaches by presenting a statistical presentation of the *H* measure along with a verabal explication of entropy. Furthermore, some of the verbal studies do not even refer to entropy in the title (e.g., Klapp 1975), which further makes the literature difficult to locate and integrate.

The thesis of this book is that the sociological entropy literature, both statistical and verbal, is sufficiently large and mature to support substantial theoretical and applied advances. However, further advances are presently hindered by the diversity and diffusion evident in the literature. One function of SET is to provide a framework for integrating the verbal and statistical literature, as well as reducing the diversity within each. Thus, the first task is to review the literature, both statistical and verbal. The following section is from Bailey (1983b).

Statistical Formulations

Statistical applications of entropy began to appear in sociology in the 1960s, most of them based on the *H* measure (Shannon and Weaver 1949; Wiener 1948). For the univariate case, the formuila for entropy is (Kramer and Smit 1977)

$$S_{ave} = -K \sum_{i=1}^{K} p_i \ln p_i \tag{3.1}$$

where S_{ave} = average entropy; K = a constant; and P_i = probability of occurrence of the ith one of the K categories. Shannon and Weaver's (1949) *H* measure is strikingly similar:

$$H = -\sum_{i=1}^{K} p_i \ln p_i \tag{3.2}$$

where K = the number of categories; and P_i = probability of occurrence of each category.

The *H* measure is variously called *entropy, information,* or *uncertainty* (McFarland 1969). *H* is clearly an entropy measure, and as such does measure uncertainty, so either of these two latter terms is correct (see Kramer and Smit 1977). Thus, it is correct to apply *H* in sociology as a measure on entropy. It is also correct to refer to *H* as a measure of uncertainty. It is somewhat misleading, however, to refer to *H* as a measure of information, as it is more correctly a measure of lack of information or negative information. *H* varies between 0, when any one category has a 100 percent probability of occurrence, and a maximum value of log *K*, when each of the *K* categories has an equal probability of occurrence.

In addition to univariate entropy, one can also compute joint and conditional entropy. For the variables *X* and *Y*, joint entropy is

$$H(XY) = -\sum_{i=1}^{K} \sum_{j=1}^{L} p_{ij} \ln p_{ij} \tag{3.3}$$

where *X* and *Y* are variables, each having *K* and *L* categories, respectively. For two variables *X* and *Y*, conditional entropy is

$$H(Y|X) = -\sum_{j=1}^{L} p_{j|i} \ln p_{j|i} \tag{3.4}$$

$H(Y|X)$ gives the amount of entropy in variable *Y* if the entropy value of variable *X* is known.

A note on the type of logarithm used in the entropy formula is in order. We are using natural logarithms (base *e*) throughout. Some authors use base 2 logarithms ($\log_2$). The choice is somewhat arbitrary, as it is relatively easy to convert from one form to the other (McFarland 1969). However, more tables are available for natural logarithms than for base 2, and they can be computed readily with a hand-held calculator.

One of the earliest statistical applications of entropy in sociology was by Coleman (1964). Coleman listed the measure as "entropy" in his index but also noted that it is additionally called *information* and *uncertainty.* He derived

H and discussed its use by Shannon, but he also noted the parallel development of entropy in physical chemistry by Boltzmann. Coleman developed a hierarchical measure that indicates the degree to which entropy deviates from maximum entropy:

$$h = \frac{H_{max} - H}{H_{max} - H_{min}} \qquad (3.5)$$

Coleman applies the h measure to sociometric data and compares it with an alternative measure of hierarchization.

A number of researchers applied the entropy concept to the study of classification in the late 1960s and early 1970s. Among these were Capecchi and Möller (1968), who continued their work in the 1970s (Möller and Capecchi 1975; see also Capecchi 1964). Capecchi and Möller used entropy to classify the political participation of 108 Communist and Christian Democratic party workers. They proposed several entropy-based measures of classification. Their refined measure, presented in Moller and Capecchi (1975), is based on the ratio

$$\frac{h_{ij}}{H_{ij}} \qquad (3.6)$$

where H_{ij} is the total entropy for two tests i and j; and h_{ij} is the remaining entropy (unexplained uncertainty) after the conditional entropies $H_{i;j}$ and $H_{j;i}$ are known.

In another early discussion, Pergler (1968) was concerned with measuring the quality of prediction in sociological typology construction. He says that the concept of information is useful in this regard. For two variables, X and Y, he defines information as

$$I(X,Y) = H(X) + H(Y) - H(XUY) \qquad (3.7)$$

where H is entropy.

In still further work on classification, Sandri (1969) utilized the concept of entropy in his extensive discussion of the logic of classification, and Feldman and El Houri (1975) applied entropy widely in their discussion of homogamy measures. Among the applications presented by Feldman and El Houri are the models of independence, perfect dependence, and perfect homogamy and information dependence coefficients. In addition they discuss mutual information and information distance. All of their applications use the *H* measure, which they term *information*, while noting that it is also called *entropy* or *uncertainty* (Feldman and El Houri 1975).

In other studies, McFarland (1969) applied the *H* measure in a study of the permeability of occupational structures. He discussed both conditional and joint H measures, as well as a number of methodological issues (such as the effect of the number of categories). Vodáková and Vodàk (1969) applied the concept of "vector entropy" to the study of the validation problem. Specifically, they were concerned with the analysis of communication errors encountered in sociological research; for example, in asking and answering survey questions. Entwisle and Knepp (1970) studied the educational aspirations of high school students. They used a measure of contingent uncertainty, which is the difference between the actual joint uncertainty and the maximum joint uncertainty (i.e., degree of departure from maximum joint entropy). Entwisle and Knepp use the symbol U for uncertainty and never use the symbol H (although they do refer to Shannon, and it is clear from the text that $U = H$). Also, they never use the term *entropy*.

Theil's (1967) *Economics and Information Theory* is often cited by sociologists. Theil (1970) also contributed directly to the sociological literature. His article focussed upon logit analysis but used entropy measures (H) to supplement the logit analysis. He also compared entropy measures with multiple correlation coefficients. Theil used the H measure but referred to it as entropy throughout and did not use the terms *information* or *uncertainty*. He presented discussions of both bivariate and multivariate entropy. The bulk of the analysis utilized "average conditional entropy."

Charvat and his collaborators applied the entropy concept in an ongoing project concerning the application of systems theory to sociology. See, for example, Charvat and Kucera (1970), Charvat (1972), and Charvat, Kucera, and Soukup (1973). Charvat (1972) presents the basic H measure but uses the symbol E instead of H. He applies the concept of "semantic entropy" to social systems. This application has a substantial degree of explanatory power. For example, if semantic entropy is minimal (zero), then a single semantic value prevails and the power of the semantic decision maker is low. If semantic entropy is maximal, however, there are a large number of semantic values to choose among and the power of the semantic decision maker is great.

Charvat and Kucera (1970) and Charvat et al. (1973) also utilize a systems approach. They operationalize the concept of "entropy of behavior" of the system. For example, entropy of behavior can be used to measure the homogeneity of needs of all system activities. They also use entropy of behavior to define the notion of dependence between systems. Essentially, the dependence of the behavior of system 1 on system 2 is measured by the difference between the level of the entropy of behavior of system 1 and that of system 2, or $E(S_2) - E(S_1)$.

A number of statistical entropy applications also appeared in sociology in the latter half of the 1970s. One of these shows a direct cumulative effect,

Hauser et al.'s (1975) application of McFarland's (1969) entropy measure in the study of social mobility. However, Hauser's study presents entropy as only one of several alternative approaches to mobility analysis.

Horan (1975) applied entropy to the analysis of the structure of teaching opportunities in academic departments. This article refers to McFarland (1969) and utilizes the information-theoretic perspective. Horan never uses the term entropy, as far as I can ascertain. In fact, he never uses the symbol H but relies on the symbol U for uncertainty; however, as in the Entwisle and Knepp article, $U = H$.

In an innovative and valuable statistical derivation, Horan develops a measure of "proportional reduction of uncertainty" (PRU), based upon Costner's (1965) criteria for proportional reduction in error (PRE) measures of association:

$$\text{PRU}_{yx} = \frac{U(Y) - U(Y|X)}{U(Y)} \tag{3.8}$$

This formulation has great potential for decreasing the substantial isolation of entropy measures by clearly relating them to the larger body of PRE measures.

An article by Teachman (1980) illustrates the fragmentation, isolation, and lack of continuity that exists in portions of the sociological entropy literature. Although Teachman discusses the measurement of population diversity, a large portion of the article is concerned with various statistical derivations. He uses the H measure throughout and consistently refers to it as *entropy*, or *information*.

Teachman (1980) presents the PRU measure:

$$\text{PRU}_{x \cdot y} = \frac{H(X) - H_y(X)}{H(X)} \tag{3.9}$$

where $H_y(X)$ = the conditional entropy of X when Y is known. A cursory comparison shows that equations 3.8 and 3.9 are identical, although the symbolism differs and the positions of X and Y are reversed. Yet Teachman (1980) never refers to Horan's (1975) article even though it was published only five years before in the same journal.

I do not wish to belabor the point nor to criticize Teachman, as it is always easy to miss any given reference. However, I do want to illustrate my contention that the diversity of areas of application, terminology, symbolism, and background of the various entropy studies hinders the accumulation of knowledge. The titles of the Horan and Teachman articles give virtually no clue to the substantial overlap of their content. One sees no mention of the term *entropy* in either the title or abstract of either of these two papers. Thus, these papers easily pass like the proverbial two ships in the night.

Another recent discussion that may not be easily recognizes as a contribution to the entropy literature is by Allison (1978). Allison evaluates Theil's (1967) *T* entropy measure as a measure of inequality. He compares it with the Gini coefficient and the coefficient of variation. He finds that the entropy measure fares very well compared to the other two on criteria such as scale invariance, sensitivity to transfers (e.g., of income or wealth), and adequacy of upper and lower bounds. There is virtually no clue that an entropy measure is being discussed. The measure is symbolized by *T*, and the symbol *H* is never used. The terms *entropy* and *uncertainty* are not used either. The only clue is that Theil's measure is said to be "based on information theory."

Still another example of an entropy discussion that is difficult to locate, and thus difficult to link to the larger entropy literature, is Galtung's (1980, pp. 441–42) discussion of the operationalization of diversity. Galtung's general task here is the development of world indicators, and he wishes to measure structural and cultural variations within a society. He says that one possible measure of diversity is the "measure of information taken from information theory." Again, this is all the identification that is given, with no mention of *H*, entropy, or uncertainty. The *H* measure is given but without the symbol (i.e., only the right-hand portion of equation 3.2 is presented).

It seems clear that interest in entropy will continue in the 1980s. One study is by Magidson (1981). This article is easier to identify as a contribution to the entropy literature, as the term *entropy* is included in the title. Magidson develops and compares two qualitative analogs to R^2. One is based upon qualitative variance, and the other on entropy, based upon the work of Theil (1970). Magidson concludes that both measures are adequate.

Another recent study with interesting implications is by Katakis and Katakis (1982). They extend the traditional concept of entropy to define the concept of "telenomic entropy." The latter is said to be more useful for the analysis of complex multilevel and heirarchically ordered living systems.

Entropy in General Systems Theory

Statistical entropy theory in sociology is one-sided, as most of the continuity lies in references to the information-theoretic literature. There is another side to the entropy coin, the thermodynamic side. This side was virtually never cited in the statistical studies reviewed (one exception was Coleman's brief mention, in a footnote, of Boltzmann's work). The thermodynamic side of the entropy coin receives much more attention in general systems theory (GST) than in the statistical literature reviewed earlier. GST generally utilizes both the thermodynamic and information-theoretic aspects of entropy. Thus, attention to the systems literature may help in the effort to unify entropy theory or may at least provide insight into the neglected thermodynamic side of entropy. Unfortunately, only a relatively few of the statistical entropy studies in sociology have utilized a systems approach. Among these are the studies by Charvat and Kucera (1970), Charvat (1972), and Charvat et al. (1973).

Much discussion of entropy in GST centers around the distinction between open and closed systems. An open system allows the transfer of matter-energy and information across systems boundaries from the environment, and a closed system does not (Bertalanffy 1968; Hall and Fagen 1956; Miller 1978). The importance of this distinction in systems theory is made clear by analyzing the first two laws of thermodynamics. The first law is that of the conservation of energy. The second law says that, in a closed system, the entropy of a system tends, over time, toward its maximum value. Although an equilibrium state of sorts can be defined for all levels of entropy if certain assumptions are made, the true or "ultimate" state of equilibrium occurs when system entropy is maximized.

Thus, equilibrium and entropy are related concepts. In fact, in thermodynamics, equilibrium is generally defined in terms of entropy. But as noted earlier, sociological theorists such as Pareto (1935) and Parsons (1951) tended to emphasize equilibrium while ignoring entropy. However, they generally used equilibrium as synonymous with system integration and stability. Thus, there is a great irony here, because according the second law true equilibrium (maximum entropy) is *not* the state of system integration that sociologists envisioned but conversely is *really* the state of system disintegration (or "system death"). This is the situation that referred to earlier as the Spencerian dilemma.

General systems theorists, however, have long been acutely aware of this dilemma, although they state it in different terms. The use of the open system concept allows them to avoid this trap. For even if internal entropy does increase within a system, transfers of information, energy, or matter from without can decrease entropy, so that total system entropy may remain constant (e.g., as in homeostasis) or even decrease over time.

This is easily shown in the expanded Prigogine (1955) equation for open systems. Using the standard thermodynamic symbol S for entropy, the original Clausius equation for entropy can be stated according to the second law (see Guggenheim 1933; Bertalanffy 1968, p. 144):

$$dS \geqq 0 \qquad\qquad\qquad (3.10)$$

Equation 3.10 holds for isolated systems and shows that entropy change is irreversible (entropy can never decrease). Notice that, in terms of this equation, entropy is not a static quality but is only defined in terms of change. The equation must be integrated in order to derive the static form of entropy. The expanded Prigogine entropy equation for open systems (Prigogine 1955, p. 16; Bertalanffy 1968, p. 144) is

$$dS = d_e S + d_i S \tag{3.11}$$

where dS equals the total entropy change in the system; $d_e S$ is external entropy production that is imported into the system; and $d_i S$ is the internal production of entropy due to irreversible processes in the system. Whereas $d_i S$ will always remain constant or increase (see equation 3.10), $d_e S$ can be negative if sufficient amounts of matter-energy or information are imported into the system, and thus overall entropy can decrease.

The Prigogine equation effectively sidesteps the Spencerian dilemma. In terms of systems theory, the dilemma is this: if the second law says that entropy (disorder) will increase over time, how can social and biological systems clearly increase their degree of order or organizational complexity (decrease entropy) over time? The Prigogine equation shows how the second law is combatted for open systems. Since virtually all social and biological systems are regarded as open, the dilemma is solved for biology and social science.

Verbal Formulations of Social Entropy

The Prigogine equation and the distinction between open and closed systems avoid the Spencerian dilemma and thus open the way for analyses of both equilibrium and entropy (both statistical and verbal) that are consistent with these principles. The number of verbal entropy analyses is less than the number of statistical entropy analyses. Like the statistical literature, the verbal analyses are fragmented and in need of integration.

One of the earliest verbal explications of entropy in sociology is by Buckley (1967). This discussion is quite broad and might well serve as a model for our integrative efforts. Although basically a verbal discussion, Buckley presents Shannon's H measure. He also draws upon GST in distinguishing between closed systems as entropic and open systems as negentropic and by noting that the concept of equilibrium thus should not be applied to open systems.

Buckley follows Rothstein (1958) and George Miller (1953) in analyzing sociological organization in terms of entropy (and negentropy). His analysis includes both joint entropy and conditional entropy (although he does not use these terms) and also utilizes the Euler diagram, as do Capecchi and Möller (1968). In analyzing Rothstein's organizational model, Buckley relies upon the notion of constraints. I think that this is an effective mechanism. For example, in a closed system there are no constraints on a particular variable, Y, and thus it tends toward maximum entropy. However, in an open system a number of constraints may affect the variable and maintain it in some state of entropy that is below the maximum.

In speaking of Rothstein's definition of organization, Buckley (1967, p. 88) says that it is "simply one minus the ratio of the actual entropy of an ensemble of messages due to constraints among them, to the maximum for that ensemble without constraints." If H_a is actual entropy and H_{max} is maximum entropy, then organization is

Rothstein's organization $= 1 - H_a/H_{max}$ (3.12)

Thus Rothstein's organization is 0 when actual entropy is maximum, and 1 when actual entropy is zero. This is the information-theoretic measure of redundancy.

Bailey (1968) utilized the entropy concept quite extensively, both statistically and verbally, in a systems approach to human ecology. Bailey continued Buckley's discussion of organization in terms of entropy. He also applied the entropy concept to the study of the distribution of cities by size and related the entropy concept to various measures of city-size distribution, as well as to measures of the division of labor. Bailey generated a number of propositions written in terms of the entropy concept. These propositions concern organization, population size, technology, and the environment.

In another application of entropy to organizations, Katz and Kahn (1978) characterize organizations as open systems. They approach the study of organizations primarily from the standpoint of GST rather than from an information-theoretic standpoint. They note that living systems are characterized by negative entropy (negentropy) rather than by positive entropy and say that "The essential difference between closed and open systems can be seen in terms of the concept of entropy and the Second Law of Thermodynamics."

In a very innovative study, Klapp (1975; 1978) revises the traditional model of an open or closed system. GST has traditionally used the open and closed labels in mutually exclusive fashion—thus a given system at a given time was either open or closed and could not be both. Klapp presents a model of social systems as oscillating systems that can alternatively open or close their boundaries as the internal state of the system dictates. Specifically, systems are closed whenever the entropy level is getting too high. Notice that according to the Prigogine equation (equation 3.11), entropy imported into the system from outside can be either positive or negative. The implication is that it will often be negative and thus will offset the entropy production inside the system. The ultimate result is a living system that shows substantial levels of organizational complexity (negentropy). Klapp, however, tends to imply that entropy (rather than negentropy) is imported into the system. Thus, threats to the system often come not only from the accumulation of internally produced entropy but also from the importation of external entropy. Entropy is the opposite of information in Klapp's formulation. Thus, one source of entropy is information overload. Other examples of entropy that may be communicated into the system are "noise," "banality," "boringness of signals," "restriction," and "lack of reinforcement." Klapp feels that by successfully opening and closing its boundaries at the proper time, the social system can achieve the correct amount of information input without gaining an excessive amount of entropy. Klapp applies his model at the organismic, psychological, and social levels. The Klapp analysis is a good example of the potential of verbal entropy analysis in sociology. However, the extra rigor of definition that could be achieved by operationalizing entropy would be appreciated. Despite the relative lack of operationalization, Klapp's model has been applied quite efficaciously by Comeau and Driedger (1978) in their study of ethnic opening and closing in Canada.

Another verbal analysis is presented by Galtung (1975). Galtung presents the H measure and also talks of entropy in terms of thermodynamics; however, the bulk of the analysis is verbal and broad. All in all the analysis is innovative and provocative and again helps to demonstrate the potential of entropy analysis in sociology. Galtung uses the concept of entropy to study peace and conflict. He utilizes two basic types of entropy in his highly complex analysis: actor entropy and interaction entropy. He says that between them, these two concepts can be used to derive a large number of peace models. Galtung does not feel that the world is moving unidirectionally, either toward (in accordance with the second law) or away from maximum entropy. Rather, he feels that strong forces exist to push the system away from either extreme (maximum entropy or minimum entropy). The result can be expressed in a "pendulum theory," which sees social systems as oscillating between states of low and high entropy. Galtung, like Klapp, also analyzes entropy at both the micro and macro levels. For example, he says that macro conflicts (e.g., war between nations) will occur when the entropy level is low, while micro conflicts (e.g., cognitive dissonance) will occur when the entropy level is high.

In one of the latest verbal discussions of sociological entropy, Miller (1978) gives the rather well balanced presentation that we have come to expect from GST. Miller studies social systems at various levels (e.g., the organism, the group, the organization, the society, and the supranational system) and says that living systems:

Maintain a steady state of negentropy even though entropic changes occur in them as they do everywhere else. This they do by taking in inputs of foods or fuels, matter-energy higher in complexity or organization or negentropy, i.e., lower in entropy, than their outputs. (Miller 1978, p. 18)

An interesting feature of Miller's analysis of entropy is his inclusion of the often neglected relationship between energy and entropy. Miller discusses the important relationship between entropy and information but extends the discussion to analyze the interrelationships among entropy, information, and energy. Miller says that because the amount of energy used in a system to transmit information is only a small proportion of the system's total energy use, systems theorists tend to neglect the calculation of energy costs and thus miss an important aspect of systems theory. Miller says that it may be possible to determine the minimal amount of energy necessary to transmit one bit of information and thus to determine for the system a constant relationship among measures of energy, entropy, and information.

Evaluating the Literature on Social Entropy

It should by now be abundantly clear that I am not inventing the term entropy or merely applying a physical concept. On the contrary, there is already a substantial sociological literature, both statistical and verbal, of some twenty years standing.

However, this literature may not have been visible to the average sociologist for a number of reasons, as mentioned earlier. The primary reason is that different writers have used different terms for the same concept, principally *entropy, uncertainty,* and *information.* Some have merely presented the H measure with no identification (Galtung 1980), while other symbols such as E (for entropy), I (for information), U (for uncertainty), or S (the thermodynamic symbol for entropy) have often been used in addition to the most common symbol, H. Visibility has also been lessened because entropy has been discussed in a number of substantive areas from social mobility to population diversity with virtually no published attempts at integration. Still another reason for entropy's lack of visibility in sociology is that the verbal and statistical literatures are bifurcated, with probably relatively little dual readership. Visibility and integration are hindered further because some sociologists have come to entropy analysis through GST, which emphasizes the role of entropy within the open system, while others have come to it from information theory, which does not emphasize a systems context. The last hindrance to visibility and integration is that much of the entropy literature has been published in European methods journals (particularly *Quality and Quantity*), which may not be widely read by some non-European sociologists.

Thus, our task is not to establish a field of sociological entropy theory—that has already been done. We need only to nurture the entropy concept by providing a systematic framework for its analysis within the context of a holistic model.

Although our primary use of entropy is as a continuous measure of system state to replace the inadequate concept of equilibrium, its value goes far beyond this. SET is seen as an integrative effort for sociology, and entropy is perhaps the prime integrating concept at this time. It has potential, as will be shown in Chapters 7 and 8, for integrating the verbal and statistical literatures within sociology. It also has potential for bridging disciplinary gaps by providing a common point of reference. As Katakis and Katakis (1982, p. 118) say: "The interest in entropy is not surprising since it provides many advantages for interdisciplinary, multilevel investigations. *Its unifying potential can hardly be overemphasized*" (italics added).

As Katakis and Katakis (1982) note, the entropy concept is currently being applied more and more widely to the analysis of human behavior. Among the fields they mention in which entropy has been applied are economics (Georgescu-Roegen 1971; 1976), art (Arnheim 1971), city planning (Wilson 1970), and psychotherapy (Katakis and Katakis 1978; Katakis 1981). They could also have mentioned the work of Boulding (1978), the discussion of "entropy economics" by Samuelson (1980), and the discussion of entropy by Rifkin and Howard (1980), which deals with a number of social issues including inequality.

It is customary in GST to equate entropy with "disorder" and negentropy with "order." For example, Bertalanffy (1968, p. 143) equates "increasing entropy" with "decreasing order." He says further that living systems may be characterized by decreasing entropy, and in discussing this case he uses phrases such as "a state of high order" and "increasing differentiation and organization" (Bertalanffy 1968, pp. 143–44). However, the relationship of entropy and order is complex. Further, a plethora of definitions of *social order* exists in sociology, including such terms as *moral order, political order,* and so on. Thus, I must caution against any hasty interpretation of entropy in terms of "social order." This topic is extremely complex and must be left for chapters 7 and 8. However, at this point the statistical measurement of entropy can legitimately be interpreted in terms of "statistical order," as measured by departure from randomness (maximum entropy). It is interesting to compare this interpretation of entropy with one of Parsons' definitions of equilibrium (Parsons and Shils 1951, p. 107).

In its statistical form, entropy (H) is a content-free, continuous measure of system structure—just what we said we needed to replace equilibrium. It is *not* a measure of heat systems. At this point in time perhaps the only way to avoid confusion is to recognize that there are many types of entropy, depending upon the type of system analyzed. These types all differ in terms of the units being discussed. The only way to keep them conceptually distinct is to utilize adjectives such as *physical entropy* or *social entropy*. Many other types of entropy have been distinguished such as interaction entropy, phase space entropy, and teleonomic entropy among others (see Katakis and Katakis 1982).

However, a generic interpretation of entropy is common to all concepts of entropy regardless of the type of system in which it is applied. The maximum state of entropy in *any system* is defined as maximum disorder (randomness) or the "most probable" state of the system. Conversely, minimum entropy is *always* minimum disorder (maximum departure from randomness), regardless of the system in which it is applied. However, there can be great differences in how disorder is defined, depending upon the nature of the specific system being studied. For example, as Katakis and Katakis (1982) point out, both their concept of teleonomic entropy and thermodynamic entropy can be interpreted as measures of disorder. However, disorder means quite different things for these two types of entropy. Whereas disorder in thermodynamics refers to the positions and velocities of molecules, maximum teleonomic entropy means complete indifference to goals.

In SET, both physical and statistical entropy may be utilized. Physical entropy may be used, as is customary in GST, to refer to the entropy level of the concrete system of human actors. Statistical entropy could refer to the degree of disorder in the symbol or category systems that the physical actors construct and use in the course of their ongoing social interaction. The links between acting systems and pattern systems have already been alluded to so some links could be expected as well between physical entropy levels of the concrete acting system situated in physical space-time and the pattern entropy of the symbol system generated by this interaction. This is generally beyond the scope of this chapter and must be reserved for Chapters 7 and 8 or discussion elsewhere. However, it is clear that social interaction by the acting system can only continue though expenditures of energy and information, as increase in physical entropy entails a reduction of information and matter-energy, and thus a reduction in resources available to the acting system. A continuation of this condition can, of course, threaten the maintenance of symbolic order and may even, over the long run, lead to increases in the entropy levels of symbolic (pattern systems) as manifested in statistical entropy measures.

The statistical measure of entropy seems to suffice as the continuous measure of system state that was sought to replace the equilibrium concept. For the present, the basic H measure (equation 3.2) or various transformations of it will suffice as a statistical measure of entropy. *H* is particularly useful, since it has both multivariate (joint) and conditional forms.

Recall that earlier the concept of entropy was said not to contradict the concept of equilibrium but merely subsume it. Although the concept of equilibrium has been used in myriad ways, one can easily think of instances of social phenomena that may be termed *equilibrium*, especially in its connotation of "balance" (e.g., the shifting of persons among lines in banks so that all are of relatively the same length). Further, a situation where an entropy level remains constant over time can be referred to as equilibrium. The attendant problems that have sometimes plagued equilibrium analysis, such as heuristic-empirical confusion, should be lessened through systematic usage of a three-level model. However, the term *equilibrium* generally will be eschewed in favor of *entropy*. More important, the degree of entropy in a given society is to be determined empirically. No given degree of entropy can be assumed, except of course the assumption that entropy is somewhere below the maximum, and no stipulation is made of the return to a given entropy level if it is disturbed. The amount of change in entropy over time, like the entropy level at a given point in time, may vary greatly for different societies and thus must be determined empirically. It is noteworthy that, although the equilibrium concept has been widely criticized as hindering the study of social change, Galtung (1975) specifically chose the entropy concept for the study of conflict, and it served him very well in that regard.

Now that the basic epistemology and systems groundwork has been presented, we can begin analyzing properties of the social system with an analysis of macrosystems properties. These are properties that can only be defined for the holistic society as the unit of analysis.

Chapter 4

Macrosociology

Now that SET has been described in some detail, it can be applied to the analysis of complex society. The analysis begins with macrosociology. This chapter examines those variables that can be defined as properties only of the holistic society. One of the paramount problems of macrosociological analysis is selection of the proper set of variables for study. There seems to be virtually an infinite number of variables that could be chosen. Obviously, it is not possible to study all variables, and in fact, this is shown to be unnecessary. What is desired is some means of generating an optimal set of variables that the ongoing holistic society utilizes in its day-to-day functioning.

There are several alternatives for narrowing the number of variables to be studied without searching for functional prerequisites. One way is to begin with a large number of variables and utilize some statistical method, such as factor analysis, to reduce the total set to some smaller number of underlying dimensions. This method, although perhaps feasible in some cases, has a number of clear disadvantages. It can be overly descriptive. It does not rely upon any theoretical underpinning but simply consists of statistical data reduction. Thus, the data so derived may not lend themselves to generalization beyond the society for which the analysis was conducted. Further, it would take a great deal of time and money to even attempt to list all potentially relevant variables needed to begin the reduction procedure.

Clearly, some theoretical mechanism for selecting variables is needed. However, the analysis should not be limited prematurely. Ideally, all the variables that allow a society to operate from day to day should be included. Thus, the study should not be limited at this point to only the division of labor, for example, or to only the study of technology. There are a number of extant complexes of variables, or of classes of variables, to build upon. However, it is not clear that any of these are sufficiently exhaustive for our purposes, and it is also not clear how they could be adequately combined to form a more complex set of variables. For example, the ecological complex (Duncan and Schnore 1959) consists of the interrelated components of population, organization, environment, and technology (POET). While this complex has proven useful both as a heuristic and in applications (e.g., Duncan 1961; Schnore 1961), it is not always clear how values or norms, or the action of individuals, fit into this formulation. Similarly, Parsons's (1951; 1961a; Parsons and Shils 1951) designation of interrelated personality, cultural, social, and organismic systems has clear analytical advantages but is not sufficiently exhaustive for our purposes. Not only does Parsons's formulation exclude the environment from the primary focus of analysis, but the place of such major factors as technology is not always clear.

Thus, rather than attempting to work with existing sets of variables, we will attempt to generate our own formulation, making it as general as possible. The concept of functional prerequisite and the dichotomous notion of survival or failure to survive in a normal or healthy state must be avoided in order to escape the criticism that functionalism suffered. This can be done by recognizing that survival is just one value or level of the society's level of living. The functionalists were really interested in the level of living, and survival in the literal, subsistence sense is the lower limit of the society's level of living. Level of living can be seen as a generic concern to all societies. Furthermore, this concept should not be nearly as controversial as survival, since the concept of level of living is central to many paradigms from Marxism to conflict theory in general to ecology (Gibbs and Martin 1959) to demography to stratification. Indeed concern with social indicators (Land and Spilerman 1975) is indicative of renewed interest in the level of living.

Our general strategy will be to begin with the notion of level of living (L) and then search for all variables that are correlated with L, specifically the ways in which L can be increased or even maximized. Thus, correlates of the level of living will be substituted for the maligned notion of functional prerequisite. This strategy follows Ogburn's (1951) lead but alters the mode of analysis somewhat. Ogburn, in the analysis that led to the later formulation of the ecological complex (POET), identified technology, organization, and population as correlates of the "standard of living" and also mentioned resources.

Key Societal Variables

The functionalists' recognition that societies do have needs that must be filled if they are to function on a day-to-day basis is worth retaining. Some of these needs will be shown to be materialistic, and Marxian theory recognizes that control of these needs is a major issue in societal functioning. The challenge here is to utilize the systems framework without falling into the functionalists' trap of using equilibrium, functional prerequisites, the notion of survival, or any of the other notions that proved to be so troublesome.

Our goal is to construct a model (X'') that is isomorphic with the actual empirical society (X'). This can be achieved by utilizing our perceptions (X) of the generalized empirical society (X'); that is, to visualize the common variables that all societies utilize in their day-to-day functioning. No attempt will be made to specify levels of these variables, as such levels vary empirically from society to society, rather a model will be constructed sufficiently general to apply to societies at many different levels of development. This means being content merely to specify the salient macrosociological variables.

Perhaps, this task is not so difficult as it seems in the generic form, although it becomes more difficult when attempting to operationalize these variables. Past experience (e.g., Bailey 1982b; 1988a) has shown us that operationalization of these variables can easily become an intellectual red herring. It is sometimes difficult for readers to distinguish between the generic component and various alternative operationalizations of it. Thus, for now, the components will be specified in their most general sense.

Global Properties

In this chapter the unit of analysis is the holistic society; only variables that are properties of the society will be analyzed. Chiefly these are global and analytical properties. According to Lazarsfeld (1958) a *global property* of a society is one that can be defined without utilizing any information about properties of individuals. An *analytical property* of a society is one that is defined by aggregating properties of the individuals in the society. First, global properties will be formulated, and then the discussion will turn to analytical properties. As said earlier, our basic system is a concrete system (in Miller's 1978 terms) or an acting system (in Kuhn's 1974 terms). As such it is composed of a set of human actors who are acting, over time, in a setting of physical space. Thus, for a given point in time, two basic macrosociological properties are the *population size* of a concrete society and the *physical space* that provides the context for their action. These are macrosociological properties of our system by definition.

Spatial Area (Expansion of Boundaries)

First consider the macrosociological property of physical space. Sociology has a history of analytically separating physical, biological, and cultural factors. Chapter 2 argued strongly against such analytical separation, for it is clear that social factors are generated by humans acting in the context of physical space. It is clear that *all* social systems presently operate within a spatial area. The properties of this spatial area have been alluded to earlier and will be expounded upon in greater detail here. According to the tenets of SET, *space refers to the totality of the physical, biological, and chemical elements within the boundaries of the system.* As such it includes all energy and food resources within the boundaries, the water within the boundaries (or some "territorial limit"), and the air space above the land area. Thus, the *spatial area* of the social system refers to *everything* of a physical, chemical, or biological nature within the boundaries. This includes features that are generally referred to as the *physical environment*, or merely *environment*, of the society. However, such terminology is inappropriate here for at least two reasons. First, in the concrete system, the physical spatial area is a part of the system (is internal to its boundaries) rather than external to the system. Second, the environment in systems terms is defined residually as the set of all factors *external* to the system boundaries that can affect the system or be affected by it. Thus, factors within the spatial boundaries should not be termed *environment* if it is to be consistent with extant systems theory. Just remember that *spatial area* means not only land but everything it contains within the boundaries, including all energy sources and other natural resources. Perhaps the idea is clearer if the term used is *land area* rather than merely space.

Population Size

A second property of a concrete system, by definition, is population size. Since for a given point in time, both the spatial area and the population size of a particular system are constant, they often are assumed or taken as givens and not utilized explicitly in the analysis. In keeping with the desire to produce an integrated, holistic model, it is imperative that both the spatial area and the total population size are included explicitly within systems boundaries as basic macrosociological variables. Further, although area and population size may be constant for a synchronic analysis, they are often not constant for diachronic analysis and can be crucial or key variables that should not be taken for granted.

Level of Living

A third basic macrosociological property of any and all systems is the level of living. This property can be alternatively labeled the *quality of life, standard of living, level of well-being*, or any of many other terms that have been used. The functionalists' notion of *survival* can be recognized as the lower limit of this property (level of living). Similarly, *equilibrium* was often used to refer to some level of this property, but the level referred to was generally arbitrary. If above the "survival" level, it was often some state considered to be "normal" or "healthy" (Hempel 1959).

There are many ways to operationalize the level of living as a macrosociological global property of society. One measure is the total amount of all scarce resources possessed by the society; for example, the amount of gold in Fort Knox. Besides wealth in gold or monetary units, the level of living can be operationalized variously as the total life span of all citizens, the total amount of energy the society possesses as expressed in calories or petroleum, and so forth. Although some readers will doubtlessly protest, at this time it is necessary to resist the temptation to operationalize the level of living. There is general consensus as to what is meant by level of living, and everyone agrees that *all* societies possess some value of the level of living. One problem in operationalization is that the level of living is often multidimensional, and the particular correct operationalization is often culturally defined in the particular society. Thus, the optimal operationalization varies from society to society and is a matter to be determined in a given empirical analysis. For an example of operationalization of the level of living in terms of calories, see Bailey (1982).

Even cursory reflection will show that level of living, population size, and spatial (land) area are all intercorrelated. Let us symbolize the level of living of a society by (L). The level (L) is the total amount of resources (e.g., precious metals, energy, etc.), however, operationalized possessed by the holistic society. As such it is a global property of the society, because measurement of this property does not require information about properties of individuals. It is obvious that changes in population size affect the overall level of living, because (ceteris paribus) a given resource level (L) provides a lower standard of living for a larger population than for a smaller one. Thus, for a given level of living L, lowering the population size (P) raises the average standard of living for each person, and raising (P) lowers the average standard of living.

Only slight reflection is necessary to show that spatial area (S) is correlated with level of living (L). All of the society's energy resources are by definition contained in this land area; that is, the land area is the basic source of the society's internal wealth. Thus, decrease in land area may reduce the level of living, or may at least cause the society to be more efficient in exploiting the decreased resources. That is, a decrease in land area or space (S) does not necessarily lead to a decrease in the level of living (L) but may cause changes in other systems variables. Conversely, an increase in land area can provide increased resources and thus (ceteris paribus) can lead to an increased level of *L. Ceteris paribus* means primarily that the levels of the other key systems variables remain constant.

Notice that although level of living (L) is often thought of as a dependent variable, the relationships among the three systems variables specified so far (P, S, and L) are symmetrical. For example, a decrease in (L) can necessitate a decrease in (P) simply because the reduced level of living is not sufficient to maintain the former population size. Further, a decrease in (L) may lower energy levels to the extent that the society cannot maintain the spatial area (S) at its present size but must decrease it. Similarly, an increase in (L) can facilitate an increase in (P) and an increase in the spatial area (S) that can be maintained.

Technology

Perhaps the simplest way to derive the remaining macrosociological variables is by attempting to deduce all other factors, besides (P) and (S), that can affect (L), either positively or negatively, or can be affected by it. Remember that these must be macrosociological variables, *social facts* in Durkheim's terms or *analytical* or *global properties* on Lazarsfeld's (1958) terms.

For a given population size (P), a given land area (S), and a given level of living (L), what additional factors can affect (L)? Clearly, one such additional factor is the society's level of technology. A given population (P) that occupies a land area (S) rich in natural resources may be able to greatly expand (L) if it can obtain advancements in technology (T), whereas declines in technology may lead to decreases in the level of living L.

As with level of living, there is general consensus as to the meaning of technology but relatively little consensus on the proper means of operationalizing it. As with level of living, it seems unnecessary to specifically operationalize technology at this point, particularly since it can lead to bickering and to tangential analysis. I have discussed technology at length elsewhere (Bailey 1968) and may attempt more specific operationalization in the future in order to facilitate testing. For now *technology* will simply be defined as the tools utilized by the society. As a global property of society, the level of *technology* (T) is defined as the total number of tools possessed by the society. These can range of course from simple dibbles to lasers, microcomputers, or nuclear generators. These tools generally utilize energy and information and are used by the society in the pursuit of its goals (e.g., to raise the level of living). As such the use of these tools is primarily for what we call work but may often also be for leisure or other pursuits.

Organization

Even a wealth of natural resources in a given spatial area (S), optimal population size (P), and advanced technology (T) may be inadequate for achieving a society's potential optimal level of living (L) if its organizational structure (O) is not commensurate with these other components. Chapter 2 explained that role structure can exist somewhat independently of the incumbent; that is, a set of roles can exist *sui generis* in the Durkheim sense. This means that a given role can exist through a succession of incumbents, that a role may exist (at least temporarily) without an incumbent, and that a particular person may in some instances fill more than one role simultaneously (multiple roles).

This concept will be elaborated more fully in Chapters 5 and 6. For now an *organizational structure* (O) is simply defined as a global property of the society. Some units of this organizational structure are those generally called *jobs* or *occupations*, that is, *work roles*. However, the organization of the society can include roles other than work roles (e.g., leisure roles, retirement, unemployment). Thus, both work roles and nonwork roles are included in the organizational structure (O). Even the term role does not seem sufficiently generic. For now the unit of analysis of the organizational structure will be described as the generic "position," without defining the nature of the position but with the understanding that the bulk of these positions are occupations (e.g., a position in a bureaucracy). The number of positions in a given society will be highly correlated with the society's technology (different positions require different technological skills). Further, there will often be a high correlation between the number of positions and the population size. However, sometimes there will be more positions than persons eligible for incumbency and sometimes fewer positions than persons available for incumbency.

A *position* can be defined as a normatively regulated activity. It will generally (but not always) have specific goals and will process or extract energy and information to achieve these goals. Such information and energy expenditure and processing is generally achieved through utilization of a particular tool (technology). Different positions can have distinctly different qualifications in terms of skill level, strength requirement, and so on. *The global organizational property (O) of the society is simply the sum of all positions (of all types) in the society.* Organization (O) is clearly related to level of living (L). For a given population size (P), spatial area (S), and technological level (T), the level of living (L) can vary according to whether the society is organized (O) to utilize the talents of its population (P) and efficiently utilize the available technology (T) to optimally process the natural resources available in the spatial area (S).

We have seen thus far that, *ceteris paribus* (specifically for a constant value of all other variables), change in the level of living (L) can be affected (either positively or negatively) through change in spatial area (S), population size (P), technology (T), and organization (O) and that all of these can be defined as macrosociological properties of the holistic society as the unit of analysis.

Information

So far five macrosociological properties can be found (at one level or another) in all societies and are crucial to the day-to-day operations of the society: the society's spatial area (S), population size (P), level of living (L), technology (T), and organization (O). Although each of these seems to be necessary, the question arises as to whether they together are sufficient for proper societal functioning.

This specification basically replicates the POET model of Duncan and Schnore (1959), which includes population (P), organization (O), environment $(E$—our $S)$, and technology (T). In addition, we added a fifth variable, level of living (L). This variable was included in Ogburn's (1951) earlier formulation, which is in some respects a precursor of POET. However, it is clear that we have not yet included all relevant macrosociological variables. One glaring omission is information. Open systems have been said to allow for the importation of both matter-energy and information across system boundaries (in both directions). Further, the three-level model has been discussed in some detail, and one important social process within that model is the storing of information in markers (X''), so that it may be retained and subsequently revised or retrieved for processing.

Obviously, the information available to a society constitutes a sixth important macrosociological variable. Without information, a society could occupy a large spatial area (S) containing a wealth of resources, could have a population size (P) seemingly commensurate with this area, could have an advanced technology (T), and a complex structure (O), and yet could still have a low level of living (L), if the necessary information for utilizing these other variables were not available. In fact, the information level of a society is so strongly intercorrelated with the other variables that, for example, it seems inconceivable that a society could ever utilize advanced technology or maintain a complex organizational structure without a sophisticated information base.

What are the components of information? Obviously scientific or technological knowledge (e.g., the knowledge required to operate certain forms of technology) is included, as is nontechnical knowledge of various sorts. Further, the information component explicitly includes societal values, including (but not limited to) those that form the bases for normative proscriptions or prescriptions. Values are very important in guiding societal action and can greatly affect all of the other macrosociological variables specified, including the amount of space occupied and how it is utilized (S), the population size (P), the level of living (L), the technology (T), and the organization (O).

Notice also that although the term used is *information* this component also includes negative information: *misinformation* or *noise* in information-theoretical terms. That is, not all of the cognitive units that a society possesses represent "truth," rather some can represent "error" of various sorts. Also, not all cognitive units are useful in goal attainment; for example, some cognitive units can represent "false consciousness." Thus, the society thinks it has correct information but does not. Since it includes *all* cognitive phenomena (X), the informational component also includes ideology and religious dogma. In fact it includes what is often called *culture*. It includes beliefs, values, the proscriptions and prescriptions (norms) that attempt to guide behavior in conformity with these values, and in general includes the information component of society as embodied in the symbol system (Parsons 1951, pp. 10–11).

Generically, the information component (I) consists of the totality of all cognitive perceptions (X of the three level model) in the society. This includes some information that is directly isomorphic with the empirical world (X'), some that only relates to other concepts (X), and some that relates to markers (X''). Some of this information is stored in markers (X'') and some is not, being merely present in the conceptual (X) level. Further, the information component comprises technical information, nontechnical information, literary information, values, ideology, and so on—all cognitive components of all types.

Distributional (Analytical) Measurement

Heretofore each of these six components has been discussed as a global property of the society. As such, each is a finite amount at a given point in time (synchronic analysis). For example, a certain finite amount of scarce resources (L) is available for the total society, as is a certain finite spatial area (S), a certain population size (P), a finite number of technological instruments or tools of all sorts (T), a certain finite number of organizational positions (O), and a finite amount of information (I).

Analytical measurements can be constructed for most of these components in addition to their unitary global measurements. This can be done for the five components other than population simply by distributing the society's total population over each variable. The resulting distribution can be envisioned as a form of analytical variable in Lazarsfeld's (1958) terms. It is customary in sociology to work with these distributional measures rather than with the global indicators. For example, rather than measuring level of living as the total wealth the society possesses holistically, it is more common to measure (L) in the form of a class distribution, as when we analyze inequality. This distributional measurement is easily achieved by distributing the population over categories of wealth to form a measure of class (L). Similarly, the total population can be distributed over the other global properties. The distribution of persons over the totality of available occupational positions is the familiar division of labor. Although it is less commonly done the population can be distributed over the total range of technological instruments or tools, thus deriving a *division of technology*. Similarly, the population can be distributed over spatial areas, yielding a *division of residence*; while the total finite amount of information that a society possesses at a particular point in time can be subdivided into a rather large variety of subcategories, including religious beliefs, political ideologies, value systems of various sorts of technical knowledge, and language categories.

It is theoretically important for holistic analysis and for many national planning purposes to specify global measures of each of the six variables. It is particularly important that population size be explicitly recognized as an important macrosociological variable, as this variable is often implicitly "controlled for" in many statistical analyses in which it is used as a base for some particular computation, such as the median or the mean. Distributional measures have the obvious advantage of showing how the total population of citizens is allocated among the various categories of each of the other five variables, even though the number of categories is often drastically attenuated by analysts for ease of computation and interpretation. Distributions of each of the five variables are easily amenable to measurement in terms of entropy. One convenient measure as noted in Chapter 3 is equation 3.13, which is basically a measure of the degree to which the total population is concentrated among the various subcategories specified for each of the five variables, respectively.

Interrelationships among Variables

Global Measurement

Notice that in deriving our six variables, change in each was mentioned. That is, change in the level of living was accomplished through change in population, space, organization, technology, and information. The ability to specify change in each of the variables facilitates the extension of the model to societies of any size or stage of development. Some or all of the values of the respective variables need only to be altered to derive the model of the particular society desired. Thus postulated, all six variables are seen in continuum, which facilitates not only generalization of the model but also the mathematical operationalization of the relationships between the six continuous variables.

The level of living (L) has been discussed and five correlates of it derived. Thus, L is a function of all five.

$$L = f(P, S, T, O, I) \tag{4.1}$$

where L = level of living of the society; P = population size; S = amount of space (area) within societal boundaries; T = the type of technology; O = the particular organization of work; and I = the information level.

In addition to equation (4.1), five additional equations can be written, with each of the other five variables, respectively, as the dependent variable.

$$P = f(L, S, T, O, I) \tag{4.2}$$
$$S = f(P, L, T, O, I) \tag{4.3}$$
$$T = f(P, S, L, O, I) \tag{4.4}$$
$$O = f(P, S, T, L, I) \tag{4.5}$$
$$I = f(P, S, T, O, L) \tag{4.6}$$

Thus expressed, all six variables can be seen to be related reciprocally or in a state of interdependence or mutual causation. All six variables are related in a nonrandom or interdependent fashion such that each can vary only a certain amount without changes in one or more of the others.

Analysis of equations 4.1 through 4.6 clearly shows that (L) is not the only variable affected by the others and thus not the only variable that can be considered dependent. Equation 4.2 shows that the population size of a society is closely determined by the combined characteristics of space, technology, organization, and information. For example, if space (S) is inadequate, or if technology (T) is inadequate or if organization of work (O) is inadequate, or if the information level (I; for example, the value system) is conducive to food waste through many taboos and proscriptions, then population growth (P) will be severely limited. Similarly, in equation 4.3 the amount of space that can be utilized by a society can be seen to be a direct function of the population size, the level of living of the society, the technology available to utilize the space, the efficiency of organization for work, and the level of information. Similar statements can be made for equations 4.4 through 4.6. Note particularly that, as well as being a crucial dependent variable, L is a very important independent variable, as it is clear that all six other variables are dependent upon L. For example, a large population size, the control and utilization of a large spatial area, an advanced technology, an advanced occupational structure, and a high level of knowledge, including a complex information processing system, are all facilitated by a high level of living.

Since the six variables are all interrelated so closely, a huge increase in any one variable is unlikely, as a significant change in one variable can cause change in one or more of the others or even all six. Further, the degree that one variable can change in value without necessitating changes in the values of other variables is limited. Change occurs in sort of a "stair-step" fashion; that is, change will occur in one variable, then in all (or at least some) of the others. The amount of change in the other variables depends upon the amount of change in the first variable during the time period being analyzed. The level of a given variable imposes limits on the values of other variables due to their intercorrelations. Finally, since all six variables are related reciprocally, both positive and negative feedback are possible.

Distributions

There is also a relationship among the five distributions and among the global and distributional variables as well. For example, population size per se is not sufficient for heterogeneity (e.g., heterogeniety in the division of labor), although this was implied by Spencer (1892) and effectively disproven by Durkheim (1933). Although not alone sufficient for the existence of the respective distributions, a population of a certain size is clearly necessary for a large distribution. For example, as we said earlier, roles or positions can exist without an incumbent. It is certainly not unusual to find one or more void categories in a particular distribution, and thus it is not correct to say that the number of categories in a distribution cannot exceed the population size. However, in general, there will often be more than one person per category, and positions may not continue to exist for long periods of time with no incumbent. Thus, we would expect that the number of categories in a given distribution (e.g., the number of occupational categories) will not generally exceed, over the long run, the number of people in the population, and if it does exceed the population size, this excess will not be large. The more common case is probably that the number of categories is somewhat less than the population size, with a number of people frequently occupying the same category (e.g., having the same occupation).

We have just been discussing the relationship between the global measurement of population size (P) and the five respective distributions. There are also relationships between the other five global variables ($L, S, T, O,$ and I) and the five distributions. These interrelationships are clearest in the indirect form, where each global variable affects another global variable and it in turn affects its respective distribution. Obviously, if the global level of scarce resources (L), whether measured in food, petroleum, gold, or something else is low, then the society will not be able to afford maintenance of a large spatial area (S), a large number of tools (T), a large number of organizational positions (O), and an extensive information network (I). If each of these global variables in restricted, its respective distribution will be attenuated, and there will obviously be some correlation among the five distributions.

The relationship between global properties of the six variables, which are properties of the society *sui generis* rather than aggregated properties of individuals, and the five distributional (aggregated or analytical) properties forms the initial basis for examination of the link between macrosociology and microsociology. At a given point in time, each society has a specific value on each of the six global properties (P, I, S, T, O, L). These six global variables are related to (but do not specifically determine the value of) the five analytical distributions. Each person in the society has a position in the macrostructure by virtue of his or her position on the five distributional variables. This position is determined partially but not exclusively by the particular configuration of levels of the six global variables at a particular point in time, as this configuration of levels helps determine the size of the five respective distributions and thus affects the positions in these distributions that individuals attempt to occupy. For a given level of the six global properties and a given size of each of the respective five distributions, there are, of course, a number of more "local" factors that determine an individual's position in each of the five distributions, and these factors are examined in detail in Chapter 5. This chapter is chiefly concerned with the nature of the five distributions and the interrelationships among them.

The entropy level of each of the five distributions can be measured. Bear in mind that for a given population size, each person in the social system occupies a position in each of the five distributions. If the assignment of persons to distributions is random on all five dimensions, which is not likely, then the entropy level of each distribution would be maximum, the joint entropy for the five distributions would be maximum, and there would be no correlation among the five distributional variables. Conversely, if the position of *every* person in the population were completely orderly and determined and, further, if every person occupied the same category in each distribution (all persons were in one category), then individual and joint entropy would be minimal, and there would be perfect intercorrelations among the five variables.

Again, although the exact level of intercorrelation varies empirically among actual systems and depends upon a number of factors, such as the level of the six global variables (and, as shall be shown in the next chapter, characteristics of individuals and intermediate groups), the intercorrelations generally will be intermediate—with entropy levels being below the maximum but considerably above the minimum. As said earlier, the levels of the six global variables and their interrelationships affect the size of the five distributions, thus partially determining the position of persons within those distributions. For example, if the resource level is very low (L), the spatial area is small (S), the number of tools is small (T), the number of occupations is small (O), and the information level is low (I), then there may not be much variation in occupation and everyone will have about the same occupation. If the levels of these six variables are large, the distributions also may be large. In any case, but especially the latter, there are some "degrees of freedom" (in statistical terms) regarding a person's position in the five distributions for a given size of each of the six global variables and each of the five distributions. That is, if the six global variables and five distributions are fixed, these partially determine the position of a particular person (and of the whole population) on each of the five distributions, but there are some (empirically variable) degrees of freedom, meaning that the individual's position is partially determined by other factors. As will be shown in Chapter 5, these include both ascribed (e.g., race and sex) and achieved (e.g., education) variables.

Since each individual has a position on all five of the distributions simultaneously, if the distributions are really correlated, then the individual's position on each respective distribution will partially determine his or her position on a given one of the remaining distributions. Further, the more that positions are fixed, the less may be the degrees of freedom remaining for predicting the individual's position on each of the remaining distributions.

Although the individual's position on one distribution partially (but not entirely) determines his or her position on the other distributions, two persons with the same position on one distribution may vary rather widely on the other distributions. However, there is a tendency for intercorrelation or "consistency" between the distributions. Thus, a person with a high position on one of the five distributions can be expected to have relatively consistent positions on the other four distributions. For example, someone who scores high on I (e.g., a high educational level) can also be expected to score high on O (a high occupational level), thus have a relatively high commensurate technological skill (T), make a rather high salary (L), and reside in a relatively affluent neighborhood (S). This is, of course, an example of what has been termed *status consistency*. Someone who has, for example, a high educational level but low occupational level is said to be experiencing status inconsistency. (Lenski, 1954).

The person's positions on each of the five distributions are what are generally termed *achieved characeristics*, as distinguished from *ascribed characteristics*. However, this terminology may not be sufficiently precise, as each person is "born into" some position on each of the five distributions, at least in terms of parents' status. For example, each person has a region of birth (*S*), and a level of living (*L*), technological skill (*T*), organizational position (*O*), and information level (*I*) that his or her family possesses. Thus, there is a "beginning point" in the five distribution framework for each person. So to say that that person's present status is achieved is imprecise. His or her status is changed, compared to the configuration of five birth statuses, but how much "achievement" this constitutes is empirically variable.

The point is that the term *achieved status* has the connotation that the status is achieved entirely by the person, when in fact he or she had some beginning set of five statuses "ascribed" at birth. A better distinction for our purposes is between mutable and immutable characteristics. The five distributional statuses are *mutable characteristics*, meaning that even though a person is born into such a status, this status can be changed over time, and different statuses can be "*achieved.*" In contrast, many individual personal characteristics are essentially *immutable* and cannot be effectively changed during the course of life. Salient among these are race, gender, time of birth, and other physical characteristics. Chapter 5 will show that immutable characteristics also partially determine a person's position in the overall structure of the five mutable distributions.

Thus, a person's position in the five mutable distributions is affected by three factors, each of which only partially determines the individual's position, leaving some degree of freedom for determining position by factors of the other two levels. These three factors are

1 The set of values on the six global variables, which partially determine the shape of the five distributions. These are purely *macrosociological* factors, requiring no information on the characteristics of individuals.

2 The individual's position on each of the other four distributions partially determines his or her position on each distribution, as the five mutable distributions are intercorrelated. *These five mutable distributions are intermediate factors that mediate between purely macrosociological factors (global properties) and purely microsociological factors (immutable properties).* These analytical variables are considered macrosociological factors by Lazarsfeld (1958) but differ from the global properties in requiring information about individuals.

3 The individual's position in the set of immutable individual characteristics (e.g., gender and race) deemed socially salient by that particular social system and used as a basis for allocation into the mutable distributions.

The mutable properties already have been described intermediate properties that link both the global macrosociological properties and the immutable microsociological properties. If global properties are characteristics of societies sui generis and immutable properties are characteristics of individual human actors, would not "intermediate" properties thus have characteristics of each (i.e., both of society and of the individual)? This is exactly the case. The mutable properties are routinely recognized as legitimate microsociological properties just as the immutable properties are, because, they too, are genuine characteristics of individuals. Thus, mutable properties such as occupation and education are *micro* properties that can be aggregated into *macro* properties (distributions). Bear in mind, though, that the resulting distributions are analytical properties of societies. While being legitimate *macrosociological* properties, they are distinct from global properties and can never themselves be global properties.

As we have seen, the five mutable distributions have clear relationships to both the global and micro properties within the boundaries of the concrete social system. The explication of this link between micro and macro phenomena has been facilitated by our broad systems framework. A narrower framework would probably have lacked the breadth to show the links between the global, analytical (mutable), and immutable realms and would probably have focussed on the analysis of one of these realms.

The interrelationships between acting and symbol systems, working through the levels of the three-level model, are used to allocate persons to various positions in the five mutable distributions. This allocation is consistent with the norms of the given system and also determined partially by emergent phenomena within the immediate social context. This will be pursued in detail in Chapter 5.

Exhaustiveness

A salient question in evaluating the six global variables and their five distributional forms is whether this is an exhaustive set of such variables or whether more exist that have not been mentioned. It is also possible, of course, that too many have been included and some should be omitted.

That all six factors are clearly interrelated already has been demonstrated. The salient question now is whether any have been omitted. In other words, each of the six is apparently necessary for day-to-day societal operation but are the six together sufficient? Although there may be no definitive way to prove that these six factors constitute an exhaustive set of global properties, there is some evidence that this seems to be the case. For one thing, although these six properties are generally not combined as they are here, they all are certainly familiar, and no other global property of this nature immediately comes to mind. If we quickly examine various macrotheories, we see that most of them have dealt with some of these six factors, although often the analyses were relatively narrow, dealing with only one or a few of these factors at a given time. For example, Durkheim dealt with the occupational division of labor (O), including its relationship to population size (P) and density (P/S), and also dealt extensively with information (I; e.g. his analysis of totems in *Elementary Forms*). Similarly, Weber studied bureaucracy (O) and Protestant ideology (I), whereas Malthus was preoccupied with population size (P). Marx studied technology (T) and ideology (I), with less emphasis on the occupational division of labor (O), and he mentioned population (P) almost only in passing.

The point is that the major concerns of the classical writers seem to be included in the six global factors, although their terminology may be quite different. It is true, however, that almost always their frameworks were narrower, comprising a subset of our six factors. Further, this set of six global variables replicates and extends the most comprehensive ecological frameworks, such as POET (Duncan and Schnore 1959).

Thus, the set of six seems to be exhaustive. To test this, simply see if there is anything else that an acting concrete society can do to affect its level of living in addition to altering its land area (physical environment), altering its population size, altering its technology, altering its occupational structure, or altering its information base. I have repeated this analytical exercise a number of times and cannot generate any other components, so I conclude tentatively that each is necessary and that the set together is sufficient for day-by-day macrosociological functioning.

However, it must be emphasized that although these six are described as variables, they perhaps should be labeled *components* or *factors*, because they are inherently multivariate (with the possible exception of population size) and each can be split. We have already noted that (L) comprises many measures of different types of scarce resources, such as food, gold, money, energy sources such as petroleum, and so on. Further, there are many types of technology, many types of information (ideology, religious dogma, values, norms, technical knowledge, etc.), many types of organizational positions (including occupational and nonoccupational positions), and many variables within the spatial area. Also, many variables that might at first glance seem to be excluded from this framework do fall within the framework, although this may not be immediately clear. For example, population density is clearly recognizable as a combination of population size (P) and spatial area (S) and is really a variant of the spatial distribution, one of the five mutable distributions.

All in all, the set seems to be exhaustive. It is important that an exhaustive set of global properties be derived, not only because of the additive effects of each independent variable upon the particular dependent variable but because of interaction effects as well. For example, suppose for purposes of illustration that we are interested in (L) as a dependent variable and are utilizing the remaining five global properties as independent variables. Each of the five has an additive effect on L. In addition, there is very probably an interaction effect. For example, the particular effect of population size (P) on L may well depend upon the particular levels exhibited by other variables (e.g., the size of the spatial area $[S]$, and the level of technology $[T]$). Lack of the right set of variables makes it impossible to accurately determine the interaction effects. For this reason the set of global properties must be exhaustive.

Control

Since macrosociological systems models often fall prey to the criticism that they exhibit "determinism" of some sort or another (biological, economic, environmental, etc.), it is important to briefly discuss the role that decision making plays in setting the levels of the six global variables and the five mutable distributions. Discussion of decision making concerning the immutable characteristics, as well as further discussion of mutable characteristics, is found in Chapter 5.

The human social system is a form of "controlled system" (Kuhn 1974). Control over the six global variables is probably imperfect in most societies, and obviously the difficulty of control can vary greatly, depending upon the level of the six variables and the complexity of their five distributions, among other things. Control takes a number of forms. The first is attempted direct control over the levels of the six global values. It is probably safe to say that most societies attempt to monitor these six levels in some fashion but do not necessarily attempt direct control over all six. For example, the United States government clearly monitors aspects of all six. It attempts direct control over some, particularly various aspects of (L)—for example, control over the money supply—but does not attempt direct control over others; for example, population size. In addition to direct control over the level of the global variables for the entire society, there are various forms of partial control. These include control over the particular distribution for a particular level of the global variable. For example, whether there is direct control over the global level of technology (total number of tools the society possesses), there can be direct control over some *types* of tools out of the total number. Further, there may be control over some types of technology but no attempt to control other types (e.g., control over the number of weapons and who possesses them but no control over the number or type of computers). Another form of partial control is control by local region. Here the distribution may be controlled on the local level (e.g., by a state) but not for the whole society.

In addition to direct and partial control, macrosociological global variables and distributions are also subject to indirect control, which is accomplished via the interrelationships among global variables and distributions. One example is the familiar example of "implicit" population control where a society does not directly control the number of births in each family but affects this variable indirectly through tax exemptions that directly affect the family's income (L). Similarly, affecting the level of education (I) a person has can indirectly affect his or her occupation (O) and income (L). Because of the strong intercorrelation among the six global properties, the optimal value of a given variable is often determined by the values of the remaining variables. For example, whether a society's population size should optimally be large depends upon whether its spatial area (S), level of living (L), technology (T), organizational level (O), and information base (I) are all at levels sufficient to support such a population size (and to support each other). Thus, one of the reasons there has been so much difficulty in specifying optimal population size in demographic theory is that it is very difficult to specify one optimal population independently of the values of the other five variables.

The interrelationship among the six variables means that the range of values a particular variable can take on is determined, at a given point in time, by the values of the other variables. This is simply statistical order but is an example of what Parsons (Parsons and Shils 1951, p. 107) sometimes called *equilibrium*.

Internal versus External Relationships

Internal Relationships

Human living systems are open systems. As such they transmit energy and information across their boundaries. However, the analysis of global properties and distributions in this chapter has emphasized only internal properties of systems, with no discussion of flows across systems boundaries. Obviously, relationships across systems boundaries can affect not only the six global properties but their five distributions as well. Due to the importance of such flows across boundaries, it is necessary to first summarize the analysis of the holistic society's internal operations and subsequently discuss external relations and their effects on the six global properties and the five distributions.

To summarize the internal workings of the social system, a concrete human social system can be said to consist of a population of actors (P), who act within a given spatial area (S). This area and its natural resources in all forms constitute the forum for social action (one actor) and social interaction (two or more actors in relation to one another). This concrete society processes and utilizes energy and information, within the context of its boundaries, to achieve its various goals. Among these goals are the attainment of a certain standard of living (L). The scarce resources gleaned from the spatial area and information (I), including both technical information and values, ideology, and norms, enable the society to achieve a certain level of (L). This is done by establishing organizational positions (O) and utilizing certain tools (T). The human actors who compose the population are allocated among each of the other five global variables to compose the five mutable distributions.

The human actors utilize all levels of the three-level model $(X'$, X, and $X'')$ extensively in shaping and monitoring the values of the six global variables and the five distributions. Information in the form of symbols (words, numbers, etc.) is stored on various forms of markers (paper, videotape, computer disks, etc.). This information is accumulated, utilized, and revised extensively in the process of changing or maintaining levels of the six global variables and five distributions to achieve societal goals. For example, a government planner may set a target figure (X) for the optimal amount of grain to be produced five years hence. This figure will be mapped onto markers in the form of government planning documents (X''), a type B mapping. The actual amount of grain currently produced (X') will be measured, and this figure can be mapped onto the same documents (X''), a type C mapping. The disparity between the two (surplus or deficit) guides the actions of the farmers in the intervening period.

Much of the information used for planning and change or maintenance of the six global variables and the five distributions is numerical; for example, total barrels of petroleum production desired or number of persons working in a particular occupation. In addition to such quantitative information, societies also depend upon nonnumerical symbols in managing the six variables and the people in the five distributions. These symbols are often nominal categories used to divide people and to allocate them into positions in the various distributions (as will be shown in the next chapter). A primary need in this regard is to distinguish societal members from nonmembers. Basically all persons in the society have only one piece of information in common, their citizenship. For example, all members of the United States' society share the status of American citizen. This information is mapped into a marker (X'') in the form of a passport, voter's registration card, or other citizenship designation.

Among the nonquantitative symbols generated by the acting society within societal boundaries are various totemic representations, in Durkheim's (1954) terms. Totems are hardly limited to unindustrialized societies or to religious applications. Generically a totem is the type C mapping of a symbol for a common empirical entity (X') onto a marker (X'') representing some other empirical entity or some aggregation of one of the six global variables. For example, consider the Detroit Lions. The Detroit Lions are merely a subsample of the population (P) who have a particular occupation in common (O). They are not literally lions but simply utilize this totem to represent their collective consciousness as imbued in a certain geographical (S) location (Detroit). All societies have national totems, generally flags or symbols of some sort, including animals (the eagle and the bear). Totems are also often mapped onto technology, which thus serves as a marker (X''), as in the case of the Flying Tiger Airlines, in which the symbol representing an animal is mapped onto a piece of technology (an airplane). Such totems and other qualitative symbols serve to distinguish various categories in the five mutable distributions.

There is a reciprocal or symmetrical relationship between societal action and the social system's boundary. In a sense, the boundary is both cause and effect. That is, social action constructs the boundary originally, then maintains it or changes it. In this sense the boundary is an effect of social action. However, social action is itself constrained by the boundary, and in this sense, the boundary is a cause. The location of the boundary determines spatial area (S). It is thus not unusual that it is symmetrically related to the other five global variables, as we have indicated that all six are symmetrically related.

Open Boundaries

To say that human societies are open systems means that actually they control their boundaries and can open them or close them. However, the discussion in this chapter was confined to internal variables. The internal analysis is important, as societies function as a unit to control and maintain the six global variables and the five mutable distributions. All societies have these eleven variables. However, virtually no society depends *solely* on internal production of these eleven variables, rather the society interacts with other societies when needed. Thus, if levels of food such as grain are deemed too high (L), a surplus exists and the boundaries may be opened to exports. If levels of grain are too low (L), the boundaries are opened in the other direction (to imports). In this manner, societies attempt to rectify internal deficiencies (be they in P, S, T, etc.) or surpluses by interchange with other societies.

The societal boundary serves as an entropy break, meaning that entropy levels on one side of it are different than on the other side. For example, we said that entropy was minimal on the variable "nationality" within the system, as there is only one category (American). For this reason, citizens in some countries such as the United States may not even have a permanent identification card (X''). They may have only state identification, as entropy levels on state citizenship do not show minimal entropy but show variation within the society. It may only be when the system boundaries are opened and citizens are allowed to cross into other societies that a national identification on a marker (X'') is even needed.

Summary

We can see that our discussion to this point is quite cumulative. Human actors in concrete living social systems utilize all three levels of the three-level model, over time, to construct the coordinated sets of six global variables and the related five mutable distributions. This is done by relationships between human actors (Q-system) who manipulate sets of related or correlated variable characteristics (R-system). The synchronic symbol set created by action at one point in time is used to guide action at a later point in time. This is done by storing the symbol set in the indicator level (X'') of the three-level model. Thus, for example, a government planner can use a previous symbol set stored on a marker, such as petroleum production in a given year (X''), as a basis for forming a mental perception about what level of petroleum production is feasible for a future year (X). This goal is then mapped into the indicator level (X'') so that the information on the given goal can be transmitted to others. When the target time arrives, actual production (X') is checked against the recorded goal (X'').

Thus, to this point we have sketched a rather complex relationship between symbol and acting systems, over the three levels, and have discussed the macrostructure that results from this systemic action. This macrostructure, of course, takes the form of the six global variables and the five mutable distributions. The latter form the link between the six global macro variables and the micro (immutable) properties of individuals. The next task is to show in greater detail how systemic action, again using the interrelationship between the synchronic symbol system or R-system and the diachronic acting system (Q-system) working over the three levels, allocates individuals to particular positions in the five mutable distributions. This allocation is made on the basis of both mutable and immutable characteristics of individuals and, of course, is affected by the relationship between the six global variables and the five mutable distributions. The details of this allocation are the topic of Chapter 5.

In the transition from Chapter 4 to Chapter 5, remain ever cognizant of the micro-macro link (e.g., Alexander et al. 1987; Eisenstadt and Helle 1985; Helle and Eisenstadt 1985; Knorr-Cetina and Cicourel 1981; and Fielding 1988).

Chapter 5

The Individual in Complex Society

So far, the holistic model has been sketched in some detail, and the macrosociological properties of society, both global and analytical, have been specified. These societal properties form the context for *individual* action and interaction. Different levels of the six global properties form quite different arenas for individual action. Individual options may be quite different in a society with a high level of living, a large technological base, a large land area, and many organizational positions than in a society with a smaller population, a smaller land area, a limited technology and organizational structure, and so on. Although both the global properties and analytical properties are true macrosociological properties, in the sense that the entire society is the unit of analysis for each, the crucial difference between them is that global properties are defined without knowledge of individual characteristics, whereas analytical properties are defined by aggregating properties of individuals. The analytical or distributional properties utilize knowledge about individuals: each individual is seen to have a residence, a standard of living, a technological skill, an occupation, an educational (information) level, and so forth.

Clearly, the analytical properties function as intermediaries between the group characteristics and the purely individual characteristics. Since the five analytical distributions are aggregated from information about individuals, in a real sense they function as dual macrosociological and microsociological properties. They thus serve as links between the global properties that provide no information about individuals, and individual micro properties, specifically the immutable properties of individuals such as gender and skin color, that provide no information about the society sui generis. Of course, immutable properties (e.g., percentage of the population that is black) can be aggregated into analytical properties of sorts, however, these structural properties can never have the dual character of the five mutable distributions. This is because each of the defining characteristics of the five mutable distributions *exists separately from the individual*, yet can be linked to individuals. Thus, the mutable distributions can be linked to both the global macrosociological properties of societies sui generis and the immutable microsociological properties of individuals. For example, levels of living, spatial areas, tools, value systems, and organizational positions all exist independent of a given individual. Unlike the immutable characteristics, these properties are separate and distinct from individual actors, and when summed for the whole population they (along with population size) constitute the six global variables. Yet, each of these five properties (level of living, spatial area, technology, organization, and information) can be linked to the individual. From the individual standpoint, these characteristics of individuals, such as the individual's level of living, are *relational characteristics* in Lazarsfeld's (1958) terminology; thus, they have dual aspects, macro and micro. From the societal perspective they are analytical properties of societies; from the individual perspective they are relational properties of individuals. An example should make this clear. While each society has an occupational division of labor (O) that is an analytical property of the society, each individual has an occupation (O) that is a relational (mutable) property of the individual. This is a key link between macrosociological and microsociological aspects of the concrete, human living social system.

In chapter 4, the key macrosociological properties of the society sui generis were elucidated. To this end the six global properties and the five mutable distributions were discussed in some detail. In this chapter, the microsociological properties of individuals are discussed, and the relationship between the micro and macro properties elaborated in greater detail—(a task that continues in Chapters 6 and 7.

Sorokin's Ten-Dimensional Structure

It may be of interest in passing to compare our five-dimensional structure with Sorokin's ten-dimensional structure of sociocultural space. Sorokin says that

> the sociocultural position of any human agent is satisfactorily determined if we know: (1) the language system to which he belongs; (2) his scientific position: whether he is of elementary, high-school, college, or university level, what his specialty is (such as chemistry or history), what his scientific position is with regard to the main problems of science, his total scientific mentality, his status as a scientist if he is such, and so on; (3) his religious position: what his religious attitude, credo, or denomination is and so forth; (4) his esthetic tastes and preferences: in what kind of art he is particularly interested (music, painting, literature, and so on), what kind of style and form

he particularly favors or disfavors, who are his favorite masters, what he does himself in that field, and so forth; (5) his ethicojuridical position: his total social status, ethical codes, juridical attitude and convictions, the totality of his rights and duties, and so forth; and then the main derivative and mixed systems with which he is affiliated, namely: (6) his economic position and economic occupation; (7) his family (kinship) status; (8) his citizenship and political status; (9) his "philosophy"; (10) his membership in other associations and organizations. (1943, p. 133)

Notice that although Sorokin says that this ten-dimensional space tells us all that we need to know to properly classify each person as a sociocultural agent, close reflection shows that this space cuts across our five-dimensional space and is in fact considerably narrower than our space. Since Sorokin is primarily concerned with the transmission of sociocultural meaning, it is understandable that many of his dimensions deal with information (I). Positions 1, 2, 3, 4, 5, and 8 all deal at least partially with information components of some sort (religious beliefs, scientific knowledge, political ideology, etc.). Thus, all fall within our information (I) component. Although the reference to "economic position" in position 6 is rather vague, it probably refers to the person's level of wealth or income, and thus to his or her position in the class structure (L). The second part of position 6 (economic occupation) clearly refers to the person's position in the organizational structure of the society (O). Position 8 refers to residence (citizenship) and is thus within the spatial component (S). Positions 7 and 10 refer to the individual's membership in groups that are intermediate to the individual and the holistic society as it exists sui generis. Such groups have their own positions in the five-dimensional structure. Further, the individual has a number of intermediate positions in the five-dimensional structure depending upon the number of intermediate groups in which he or she holds membership. Such group statuses are discussed in Chapter 6.

Overall, Sorokin's ten-dimensional structure seems quite compatible with our five-dimensional structure, despite the differences in emphasis. Whereas our typology is meant to portray all of the positions of the individual in the everyday operation of the holistic society, Sorokin's emphasis is on the individual as a sociocultural agent and thus is somewhat narrower. Nevertheless, his property space, while concentrating on (I), specifically covers four of the five mutable distributions. It omits specific mention of T and does not refer to the total population size (P) of the society, which is one of our six global variables and a component of all of the five mutable distributions composed by combining P with the other five global variables.

. . .

Discussion of the six macrosociological variables was the main topic of Chapter 4, and they will not be belabored at this point, but only mentioned in passing. They are discussed again in the analysis of allocation. The chief point is that concrete acting societal systems *as a unit* possess six variables within systems boundaries: population size (P), level of living (L), spatial area (S), information (I), organization (O), and technology (T).

The global levels of these six variables can affect the five mutable distributions. One clear example is afforded by population size. If the population is very small, the five mutable distributions will be necessarily attenuated. If population is large, then more variation is possible in the particular shape of the distribution and thus in the entropy level.

The Mutable Distributions

The five mutable distributions can be seen as property-space, to use Lazarsfeld's (1937) terms. Although the mutable properties are not physical microsociological properties of the individual's body, as many immutable or ascribed properties (e.g., skin color) are, each individual is generally linked to each of the five mutable ("achieved") properties and thus can be identified in terms of them. Space (S) is a convenient example. Each individual must have a residence within the political boundaries of the concrete social system. Allocation to residence is not random but based on a number of things and correlated with the other four mutable properties. Therefore, each person in the society has a residence and occupies a position in the mutable spatial area (S) distribution at a given point in time. Similarly, consider level of living (L) as operationalized in wealth. Each person in the society has a certain value of wealth (even if it is zero) and occupies a position on the mutable level of living (L) distribution. Similarly, each individual can be linked to each of the other three mutable properties (especially, if we assume the existence of a zero point on each continuum). Each individual has some level of information or knowledge (I). This information is used in the individual's cognitive processing and includes not only technical information or the sort generally learned through formal education but also religious dogma, political ideology, values of whatever sort (patriotism, loyalty, etc.), superstitious beliefs, and the totality of all other information, whether "rational," "factual," "verified," and so on.

Each individual has some position in the overall organizational structure (O). Further, each individual utilizes some sort of technology (T). These latter two are more complicated than the other three in a complex society because of their frequent multiplicity. All the properties can be changed, over time, for both the society as a whole and for each individual—hence, the term mutable. Thus, an individual can change his or her residence, level of living, and information content. However, for a relatively short period of time (e.g., one day), a person's residence, information, and level of living are generally relatively constant, although multiplicities can exist (a person can have more than one residence and more than one source of income, for example). Evidence of multiplicity is even clearer in the case of technology and organization. Persons may have a variety of technological skills that allow them to operate a variety of technologies in the course of a day. Similarly, persons may occupy a variety of organizational positions ("roles"). Although SET must be sufficiently comprehensive to accommodate the most complex society, we need not presently consider a multiplicity of roles or technologies for each individual. We will simply recognize the existence of such multiplicity and assume that each individual has a "chief" organizational position and technology (e.g., the ones that afford "principal identity"). For example, these may be the organizational position of "hospital physician" and the correlated skill of operating X-ray equipment (radiologist), although we recognize full well that the same individual might also have the organizational position of "real estate investor" and the technological skill of "airplane pilot." The point is that the existence of multiple statuses is recognized and the SET model is designed to accommodate analysis of this complexity. However, in the interest of sketching the full model, the intricacies of multiple positions in all their complexity will be ignored at this time.

Each person in any society is born into a particular configuration of five statuses in the five-dimensional space, where each dimension is a mutable distribution: space, level of living, technology, organization, or information. The newly born child is cared for by a person or persons with a particular residence, level of living, technology, organizational position, and information level. Later, he or she will often change position on one or more of the five dimensions, often on all five. Furthermore, this change is position will be intercorrelated among the five variables. The comparison of a child's position in the five-dimensional structure with his or her family's position is recognized in the sociological literature as *intergenerational mobility*, whereas change of position within the person's own lifetime is recognized as *intragenerational mobility*. However, the analysis is often limited to changes in level of living ($[L]$, wealth or income), information ($[I]$, education), or organization ($[O]$, occupation). It is sometimes applied to residential change (S) but less often to technology (T). Of course, from the standpoint of a holistic perspective such as SET, the only adequate analysis is one that studies change on all five dimensions simultaneously.

Although each person is born into a particular group (e.g., the nuclear or extended family) that has a position on each of the five mutable dimensions, he or she can,—and often will,—change position on one or more dimensions. An important factor affecting the amount and direction of change (generally called *achieved characteristics*) is the beginning configuration of five mutable properties. That is, where one is at any given point in time in the five mutable distributions is partially determined by where one started. Some persons move on all five dimensions, some on none, some on only one, some on two, and so forth. Similarly, some move a relatively long distance from their origin on one or more variables (so-called long-distance mobility), some a short distance. Some move "up" (and are "socially mobile"), while some move "down" (and are "sliders"). Therefore, one set of factors that determines a person's position in the achieved or mutable characteristics is that person's starting point in those characteristics. In addition to achieved or mutable characteristics, immutable micro characteristics and structural (global) properties also are instrumental in determining a person's position, at a given point in time, in the five-dimensional property-space of mutable properties. Let us consider the latter first.

Not only are the mutables distinct from the individual, necessitating a link of some sort, they also are generally not amenable to direct type A observation, at least not in their entirety. That is, one cannot easily observe, at a single point in time, the totality of the spatial area of the system (S), the global value of all technology (T), all organizational positions (O), or even the entire population (P). Even on the individual level, the mutables generally are not directly observable. One generally cannot see an individual's educational level, values, and so forth (I), nor occupation, nor generally even wealth. Usually, these mutable properties are mapped into markers (X''). Thus, many individuals do not even directly see their *own* wealth but only see the aggregate in numerals mapped onto a bank statement or other financial document. Their perception (X) of their own wealth at any point in time is thus not directly generated by seeing the money or other commodities (X'), which could form the basis of type A isomorphism, but only based on perception (X) of numbers on bank statements (X''). This type B isomorphism substitutes for type A isomorphism. The individual thus takes on faith that type C isomorphism actually exists (e.g., that the actual money exists $[X']$, which is equal to the amount shown on the marker $[X'']$). Of course, this assumption sometimes is true and sometimes not (e.g., in the case of bank insolvency).

It is a tenet of SET that the mutable properties exist apart from the individual and are linked to the individual through a process of social interaction. The initial social interaction comes about when the individual is born into a family structure having a particular configuration of the five mutable variables. By changing on one or more variables, he or she is establishing new link with the configuration of the five mutable distributions. Thus, the spatial area exists independent of the individual, as do other persons in the population. Wealth (L) also exists independent of the individual, who may alter his or her share of it. The same is true of the tools within societal boundaries, organizational positions, and the information system (although it may be more difficult for some readers to accept that these latter two exist sui generis independent of the individual). However, anyone who thinks that organizational positions do not exist sui generis must argue that each position is always synonymous with one incumbent. This seems hardly tenable and has been discussed elsewhere (Bailey 1981). During Durkheim's time it was, perhaps, more difficult to argue that information systems existed independent of the individual. Durkheim's major point was that social consciousness (group consciousness) exists independent of the individual, as evidenced by concepts such as patriotism and loyalty, which Durkheim contended do not apply to a single individual and would have no meaning for an individual in isolation. The point is that information exists external to the individual and can be transmitted to him or her. This is a basic assumption of the whole education system. With contemporary storage of information on computers it is easy to show that information exists independent of the individual. The whole population coud disappear and the information stored in a computer would still exist (although there would be no one to process it.)

The Immutable Variables

In contrast to mutable properties (S, L, T, O, and I), immutable properties are not distinct from the individual. Immutable properties include gender, age (time of birth), skin color, and various other physical properties such as eye color, hair color, and facial features. Some of these are not strictly immutable and are subject to some degree of change. These include weight, hair color, grooming, and perhaps the appearance of age. These semimutable characteristics are generally not subject to major change at a given point in time and are generally not crucial in social interaction.

While the mutable characteristics are often not directly observable, and thus not subject to type A verification, the immutable characteristics are. One's skin color, height, and gender generally are readily observable. Thus, in the process of social interaction, one achieves his or her perception (X) of the immutable characteristics of the other (X') by direct observation and thus achieves type A isomorphism. There are at least three reasons why the immutable properties such as skin color and gender are effective in social control:

1. They are not subject to change, so persons in less desirable positions cannot escape their fate by changing their characteristics.

2. They are always present, and cannot be separated from the individual.

3. They are quickly discernible by direct, type A verification.

Like the mutable characteristics, the immutable characteristics can also be mapped from the empirical realm (X') onto markers (X''). That is, an individual can write a resume that lists not only mutables such as residence (S) and educational achievement (I) but also immutables such as gender and skin color. When mapped onto a marker (X''), the immutable characteristics can be omitted or distorted, just as mutable characteristics can be. Thus, for example a prospective employer who has an applicant present can utilize type A verification for the immutable characteristics but must rely upon markers (type B verification) for the mutable properties and must assume that the marker, such as the resume, accurately portrays reality (type C isomorphism.). If the applicant is not present, type C isomorphism must be assumed for both the mutable and immutable characteristics. Bear in mind that although immutable properties cannot be changed (at least not to a great degree), their social salience can be. Whether a given property is considered to be a criterion in social interaction is, of course, subject to change.

For example, it is possible that change could occur so that a racial designation that was previously a hindrance in job selection is now favored. Although the social definition of an immutable characteristic might conceivably change from negative to positive (or vice versa), it could also change to neutral, meaning that it is no longer a salient criterion, monitored and utilized in the course of social interaction. Often the utilization of a particular immutable characteristic in the allocation of persons to particular positions in the mutable distributions is purported to be functional. Thus, for example, police, fire, and military organizations may not only limit hiring to men but may utilize further immutable criteria, generally age, height, and weight as well. The rationale behind the utilization of such immutable criteria is that the persons selected will be better equipped to fulfill the function of police officer, fire fighter, or soldier. At other times the functional basis for utilization of a particular immutable characteristic in the allocation process is not so clear but may still be claimed. Often this is done in terms of various components of the mutable variables. For example, persons of a particular skin color may be purported to be cognitively inferior (I) or it may be claimed that women cannot adequately operate certain forms of technology such as machinery (T) or would not wish to do so if this necessitated violation of feminine norms (I) such as cleanliness.

The question arises at this point as to whether a distribution of immutable characteristics exists in the concrete acting social system, in addition to the five mutable distributions. There is no doubt that one could structurally classify societies in terms of immutable characteristics. For example, it is customary in demography to compute a sex ratio for a given society, to compute the percentage of the population that is female or black, or to arrange the population into age groupings.

It is clear that there is a fundamental conceptual and statistical difference between these latter immutable distributions (by sex, race, etc.) and the five mutable distributions. Although the *persons* were mapped into an external property-space in the case of the five mutable distributions, here the *immutable characteristics are mapped onto the persons*. Thus, the mutables represent a Q-mapping of persons into a variable property-space, whereas the immutables represent an R-mapping of variable characteristics onto a property-space of persons.

The mutable and immutable distributions could simply be summed. For example, assuming three basic immutable characteristics (perhaps, race, gender, and age), we would have an eight dimensional property-space, composed from five mutables and three immutables. However, this would be conceptually and statistically cumbersome—if not illegitimate. We would be adding Q oranges (the mutables) to R apples (the immutables), and this would be very difficult to interpret. Thus, we conceptualize the mutable and immutables as two distinct property spaces. Another reason for separating the mutable and immutable property-spaces is that the number of immutable properties that are socially salient in a given society is not clear at this point and in fact may vary from society to society. That is, although it was argued in Chapter 4 that the set of six global properties (which form the five mutable distibutions) is exhaustive and satisfactory for the classification of all societies in any stage of development, it would be a monumental task to offer an exhaustive set of immutable properties. It is easy to argue that all societies have at least a minimal set of immutable properties considered salient in day-to-day societal operation. Durkheim (1933) found that even "mechanical" societies seemed to utilize sex and age in assigning persons to positions in the mutable structure (primarily work roles). It is also clear that race is very salient in many societies. However, it is unclear how many societies recognize other immutable variables in addition to gender, age, and race in allocation to the mutable structure. Doubtlessly, other immutables such as height, weight, and physical attractiveness are used extensively in many societies.

In summary, all societies contain a Q property-space of five mutable variables, and a separate R property-space in which a set of immutable variables in distributed over the population of individuals. These immutable variables are distinctly micro variables. They can be defined only as properties of individuals, never as global variables of societies, and they are distinct from the mutable micro properties, which are intermediate between the global and immutable properties. However, the immutables are utilized in allocating persons to positions in the mutable property-space. Thus, they are directly correlated with the five mutable distributional variables, and indirectly correlated with the six global variables. The acting individual is of course the diachronic link between the set of synchronic immutable variables and the set of synchronic mutables. The immutables are mapped onto the actors, and the actors are mapped into the mutables. These two distinct mappings can be illustrated in tabular form, as done in Chapter 8, when the statistical aspects of entropy analysis are explored in greater detail.

It might be mentioned in passing that the mutable characteristics are all at the interval level of measurement and actually seem always to be ratio. In contrast, the immutable characteristics often tend to be dichotomous nominal variable (e.g., race and gender), but some are ratio, such as age, height, and weight. Thus, the distinction between mutable and immutable parallels (but is not synonyumous with) Blau's (1977, p. 45) distinction between "graduated parameter," such as income inequality, and "nominal parameter," such as gender. These different parameters form the basis for two different types of differentiation in Blau's terms: inequality based on graduated parameters and heterogeneity based on nominal parameters (Blau 1977, p. 77).

Allocation Theory

Thus far this chapter has focussed upon the global and mutable structures that provide a context for individual action and the immutable microsociological characteristics that, along with the globals and mutables, constrain and affect individual action. Attention now turns to the process, already alluded to, by which *individuals* are allocated to particular *positions* within the structure composed by the five mutable distributions.

Global Constraints

Chapter 4 alluded to the relationship between the levels of the six global variables in a given society and the form of the five mutable distributions. The six global variables and the five mutable distributions are interrelated, and thus the levels of the former can affect the position of an individual in the latter. Bear in mind that the five mutable distributions are essentially *ratios* of population size to the other five variables: space, level of living, technology, organization, and information. The particular levels of these six variables, at any given time, are important in affecting the allocation of the individual into the five mutable distributions. Remember that not only are the absolute levels of each of the global variables important, but also their levels relative to the levels of the other five. As said in Chapter 4, there often is no given optimal level of population size, for example, except in relation to the levels of the other five global variables. The optimal population size is one commensurate with the other five variables and that facilitates the optimal use of information, technology, organization, and space, so as to maximize the level of living of the society. While the levels of all six variables and their relationships to each other are important, the relationship of population size to the other five is particularly important in allocating individuals to positions in the five mutable distributions. In particular, if the population is too large for the available space, for the current technology, for the information capabilities, for the organizational positions, and for the resource level, not only will the society's level of living suffer, but it will be difficult to allocate individuals to positions in the five distributions. Conversely, if the population (P) is small relative to the levels of the other five global variables, then it will generally be easier for a given individual to move to a given position in the property-space formed by the five mutable distributions.

For example, if the population greatly exceeds the number of organizational positions $(P > O)$, then there will be intense competition for positions and various selection criteria will be implemented to determine how persons are allocated to positions. Such "survival of the fittest" can be somewhat avoided, or at least localized, by conversion from a mechanical to an organic form of society (increased division of labor) where competition is now for various specialized organizational positions rather than mass competition for all positions (Durkheim 1933). The excess of population over jobs $(P > O)$ was said by Marx to be the "capitalist law of population," with the capitalist form of control of technology spawning excess population so that a "reserve army" of surplus workers is readily available to be exploited.

Conversely, if the global level of population is smaller than the number of jobs $(P < O)$, then specific selection criteria may be relaxed, as when women were hired as welders and riveters in the United States during World War II. Thus, the picture that emerges is that excess population leads to stringent criteria for selection to a given position, including both mutable criteria (e.g., "qualifications" such as education $[I]$) and immutable criteria (e.g., such as gender, skin color, and age). However, more available societal positions (e.g., organizational positions) than persons in the population to fill them leads to relaxation of selection criteria. In the former case, where more stringent selection criteria is due to pressure on the relatively few structural positions, there will be a stronger statistical correlation between selection and various mutable and immutable characteristics (e.g., education, or race).

Thus, the joint and contingent entropy between these criteria and position in the five mutable distributions will be lower, as the allocation of persons to the distributions departs more strongly from randomization. However, if the number of available positions exceeds population size, then entropy levels, both joint and contingent, will increase. That is, as selection criteria are relaxed there will be less correlation between selection to a particular position in the five dimensional structure and the various immutable and mutable characteristics. This means that allocation will be closer to a random distribution and thus entropy levels will increase.

A salient point here is that not only is there a relationship between the levels of the six global variables and the five mutable distributions, but there is also a relationship between the levels of the global variables, the five distributions, and the mutable and immutable characteristics. Thus, a specific mutable property of an individual (e.g., educational level) or immutable property (e.g., skin color) does not have a universal effect on allocation into the five mutable distributions. Rather, the effect of these variables on allocation is *dependent* upon the levels of the six global variables and the five mutable distributions, most notably the relationship between population size and number of organizational positions. Thus, there is a relationship between global properties of societies and mutable and immutable properties of individuals, and this relationship constrains the allocation of individuals into positions in the five dimensional structure.

Change in the Mutable Distribution Structure

Bear in mind that the mutable properties have a dual macro-micro nature. Properties such as wealth (L), technology (T), organization (O), space (S), and information (I) have an existence *independent* oı ᴛhe individual and when aggregated form the macro global properties of the society sui generis. However, each of the five mutable properties (besides, population) can be linked to the population of individual actors. In mathematical terms, the *population* (P) is in turn *mapped into* each of the five mutable distributions. Further, each given individual, at a given point in time, is mapped onto a particular configuration of values on each of the five mutable variables, as he or she has a residence (S), wealth (L), technology (T), organization (O), and information (I).

Each individual carries a value on each of the five mutables, even if it is zero. That is, he or she always carries an organizational value (O), even if it is no value (unemployed). It is tempting to think of allocation as the assignment of individuals with a particular configuration of five mutable values into a relatively *rigid structure* of the five mutable distributions, but in reality the distributions can change (have "mobility") just as can the individuals who occupy positions in them. That is, one can improve one's informational level by "achieving" more education and, as a result, may attain a different job (O) that has increased prestige and a better salary (L). This is the sort of social mobility we are accustomed to analyzing. In reality, the distributional structure can change while the individual stays the same (or changes but at a different rate of speed). For example, the organizational position of college professor (O) over time may see an increased information level (I) necessary for entry (the Ph.D. instead of the M.A.). Thus, over time, a person who does not achieve the extra years of education (from M.A. to Ph.D), lags behind the (O) distribution, while one that achieves the additional education (I) only retains the same relative position in the organization distribution. Further, new organizational positions may be defined rather frequently (e.g., director of research) and quite independently of incumbents. Another way that the distributional structure can vary, of course, is simply for organizational positions (e.g., "jobs") to literally move spatially, as when a manufacturing plant relocates.

The point is that in terms of mutable characteristics, we are not talking *only* about changes in individual mutable characteristics that serve to relocate individuals in a static structure composed of five distributions but are talking about achieving an overall congruence between changeable distributional structures *and* changeable individual characteristics. Thus, the individual not only can change to fit the structure, the structure can change to fit the individual or both can change. Whatever occurs, the goal is to achieve congruence between the individual and the mutable five-dimensional space. That is, to find a position in the structure that the individual is "qualified" for or that does not exhibit "status inconsistency" or some similar evidence of discontinuity.

From a societal point of view, the allocation problem is simply one of creating the proper distributional form of each of the five mutable distributions—this is of course constrained by the levels of the six global variables—and then allocating persons into them. Thus, the first goal for the society is to decide upon optimal levels of the six global variables and the five mutable distributions and to attempt to achieve them. This latter aspect involves mapping the population into the other five global variables.

The first problem, attainment and maintenance of adequate levels of the global variables, was discussed in Chapter 4. If this cannot be achieved, then societal goals may be jeopardized, regardless of how efficient allocation of persons into distributions is. Assuming that adequate levels of the six global variables can be achieved and maintained, the next problem is to adequately allocate persons into the existing positions.

If population size (P) is adequate, and so are the other five global levels, then there should be a position for each person in the population in each of the other five mutables, so as to form five adequate mutable distributions (at a given point in time—we recognize that global, mutable, and immutable levels can change quickly). How, then, does the concrete acting system allocate the population into the five mutable distributions? Certainly, the three-level model is central in this process. There must first be a perception (X) of the existing positions (X') on each of the five mutable distributions. As indicated earlier, it often will not be possible for any one person to have a direct type A isomorphism; that is, to have perceptions based directly on observation. Rather, the perception (X) of the available positions in the empirically existing global and mutable variables (X') will often be based on mapping these available positions (X') onto markers (X''), a type C mapping, and then having perceptions (X) of the positions represented on markers (X''). Of course, the actual global and mutable variables are not mapped onto the markers but only symbols representing them. Thus, a power holder or group of power holders responsible for allocating persons into positions in the mutable structure will generally not have direct perceptions of all positions, particularly in a large and complex society, but must rely on other persons mapping positions onto markers (perhaps by local area), where they can be aggregated into the total number of available positions. Generally, allocation is locally made not nationally.

Difficulty in achieving congruence between the structure and the individual arises because very often neither the structural mutable positions nor the individual mutable characteristics are visible to the observer. Even though a position (e.g., a job opening $[O]$) may exist empirically (at the X') level of the three-level model), and an individual may exhibit empirical characteristics (X') commensurate with that position (i.e., is "qualified" for the position), neither the empirical job nor the empirical mutable characteristics of the individual may be directly amenable to observation by persons who can facilitate allocation of the person into the position. That is, the individual cannot "see" the job and has no knowledge (I) of an "opening," while the prospective employer cannot "see" the "qualifications" in terms of mutable characteristics of the individual. Furthermore, even the employer who "sees" the applicant in person may not be able to "see" his or her "educational level."

There may be rare instances, particularly in a very small, noncomplex society (such as Durkheim's mechanical society), where an individual can directly perceive (X) an actual organizational task (X'), such as observing crops that require harvesting. Further, there may be instances where various mutable or achieved empirical (X') characteristics of the individual (e.,g., his or her residence $[S]$) can be perceived directly (X). The reader will recall from discussion of the three-level model in previous chapters that the establishment of a direct relationship between the conceptual (X) and empirical levels (X') is called *type A isomorphism*. Since this is generally lacking in allocating individuals into positions in the five mutable distributions, societies must instead rely upon indirect establishment of the isomorphism between perceptions (X) and empirical entities (X') through mapping both into the indicator level on markers (X'').

Let us use as an example the dilemma just posed. The society has an organizational position, in the form of a job opening, that must be filled: an empirically existing position as assistant professor in a university department of sociology (X'). Assume that there are individuals who are empirically qualified, meaning that they possess the mutable characteristics (education, etc.), listed as entry requirements for the position. However, assume further that the qualified applicants cannot "see" the open position (because they reside elsewhere or for some other reason), and the prospective employer cannot "see" the mutable qualifications of the applicants and may not even know that they exist. Thus, the employer has no direct perception (X) of the qualified applicant (X'), and the applicant has no direct perception (X) of the empirically available structural position (X'). How can these two be coordinated? This is done through social interaction; specifically, through mapping a description of the available position (X') onto a marker (X''), such as an employment bulletin, listing at a professional meeting, or help wanted newspaper classification. This is, of course, a type C mapping (from X' to X''). Similarly, the applicant maps a description of his or her empirically existing qualifications (X') into a marker, such as a letter of application (X''), also a type C mapping. If the prospective employer deems there to be sufficient congruence (isomorphism) between the job description in the employment bulletin (X'') and the mutable characteristics of the applicant as mapped into the application letter (X''), then the applicant literally may be moved to the university for an interview.

However, even after the applicant arrives on campus, the prospective employer will not be able to achieve direct type A isomorphism between his or her perception of the applicant's mutable characteristics (X) and the actual empirical (X') mutable characteristics of the applicant. *This is because the mutable ("achieved") characteristics of individuals are basically relational. They are relations between the individual and the five mutable properties and are generally not directly observable in the empirical realm (X') and so not subject to direct type A verification.* They are observable only when mapped into markers (X'') such as curriculum vitae and so are amenable only to type B isomorphism or verification, as when the prospective employer generates a perception (X) of the candidate's qualifications by reading his or her vita (X''). This, of course, is type B isomorphism and ensures accurate type A isomorphism $(X–X')$ only indirectly and only if type C isomorphism exists. This occurs if the vita (X'') or marker is isomorphic with empirical reality (X') in terms of the mutable properties of the individual.

Relevant Theories

A number of theories, many of them middle range, deal with various aspects of the allocation process. Among them are Parsons's (1951) systems theory and action theory, Blau's (1977) theory of inequality and heterogeneity, Bates and Harvey's (1975) systems theory, and Blalock and Wilken's (1979) micro and macro formulation. All of these touch upon various aspects of allocation but do not deal with it as specifically and generally as will be done here.

Similarly, a number of narrower theories deal quite specifically with various aspects of allocation but generally not with the whole process, as will be analyzed here. Salient among these, of course, is role theory (see, for example, Rosenberg and Turner 1981; Biddle 1979; and Biddle and Thomas 1966). Specific examples of allocation of persons to roles are discussed by Kingsley Davis (1949) and by Weinstein and Deutschberger (1963) in their discussion of "altercasting." Also directly relevant are the discussions of socialization into roles by such role theorists as Thornton and Nardi (1975), Emmerich (1973), Brim (1960), and Ralph Turner (1974). Other topics encompassed by allocation theory include aspirations (e.g., Ralph Turner 1964), "need to achieve" (e.g., McClelland 1961), cognitive dissonance (Festinger 1957), balance theory (Heider 1958), status inconsistency (Lenski 1954), exchange theory (Homans 1961; Blau 1964; Thibaut and Kelley 1959; Stryker and Macke 1978; Emerson 1981), as well as Weber's (1947) discussion of rationality.

I should stress that allocation theory in no way subsumes these various approaches. In fact, the richness of detail afforded by middle-range theory is lacking here. Rather, allocation theory is consistent with our goal, as stated earlier, of providing a holistic framework. No attempt per se is made to build upon these and other middle-range theories. The chief goal is to provide an allocation theory consistent with the general framework of SET and with the discussion in other chapters. Thus, it will utilize the three-level model, the distinction between pattern and acting systems, R and Q analysis, and the global-mutable-immutable distinctions. I hope that this holistic theory aids in integrating the various middle-range theories while retaining the richness of detail that is necessarily lacking in a framework constructed at a holistic level of generality.

Overview

The aim of a general theory of allocation is to specify the manner in which individuals are allocated into various positions in the structure composed of the five mutable distributions. Some aspects of this theory have been alluded to in the previous chapter and earlier in this chapter. The basic SET model views society as a concrete human system with both acting (diachronic) and pattern (symbolic, generally synchronic) aspects. Thus, human actors interact with each other within the confines of the systems boundaries. Much of the discussion here will focus upon the allocation of individuals into occupations (O), but bear in mind that the individual is also allocated into the other four mutable distributions and remember that all four of these are correlated with occupation (O). Thus, not only does an individual apply for and secure a job (O), but he or she also learns a certain value system, religious dogma, or political ideology (I), uses a particular tool (T), resides in a certain area (S), and earns a certain income (L). All of these link an individual with the mutable structure, and all can be seen as processes of allocation (allocation of the individual into L, S, T, O, and I). Since this is done for every individual in the population (P), the entire population is allocated into the other five variables, thus forming the five dimensional mutable structure.

As SET is generally cumulative, allocation theory thus builds on the basic conceptual distinctions discussed so far. These basic components include:

1. The notion of human society as a concrete system located in physical space.
2. The distinction between acting and pattern (symbol) components within the concrete system.
3. The distinction between Q and R analysis.
4. The distinction between diachronic and synchronic analysis.
5. The three-level model, comprising the empirical (X'), conceptual (X). and indicator (X'') levels and the relationships among them.
6. The six global variables.
7. The five mutable distributions.
8. The set of immutable characteristics that are socially recognized as criteria for interaction within the given society.

Although these eight elements have been separated analytically they are all highly intercorrelated and are all facets of holistic analysis. The human actors linked with the mutable structure act diachronically, over time, within the space formed by the societal boundaries. Relationships among the actors form the Q-system, whereas relationships among variable characteristics (whether global, mutable, or immutable) form the R-system. The diachronic action of the actors (process) utilizes pattern or symbol systems (generally, symbolic representations of R-system variables). Although variable (R) systems certainly change over time, synchronic or generalized symbols from one point in time are often used to guide diachronic action at a later time. This latter point, touched on in Chapter 2, should become clearer in this chapter and will be discussed in detail in Chapter 7.

Organization

Since positions in the mutable structure (e.g., organizational positions) may be chiefly visible only on the marker, some persons may be tempted to say, a la "social construction of reality" theory, that they exist only "on paper" (X'') and lack empirical existence (X'). Although power holders can certainly define positions and eliminate them, positions are certainly not purely defined, perceptual, or "exist only on paper." Rather, each organizational position (O) empirically has a relationship to other persons in the organization, a resource level (L), a technological base (T), an information structure (I), and a given spatial location ($[S]$; e.g., an office).

Take the case of an organizational position that clearly exists empirically—(an accountant in corporation X). This position has existed for many years, but the incumbent died, and so it is now vacant. How is a new incumbent allocated to it? This involves, at the very least, a dyadic interaction between one power holder or decision maker (the employer) and one applicant. Often a group of employers makes a joint decision on a group of applicants, and a group of persons give advice to each applicant. For the sake of simplicity let us first consider the dyadic case. The power holder has a perception (J) of the actual position (J'). This perception (J) is mapped into a marker in the form of a help wanted advertisement (J''). However, a job as represented in a marker such as a classified advertisement (J'') often does not have type C isomorphism $(J''$ does not accurately portray $J')$, or omits important information such as salary (L).

Successful allocation is achieved when there is isomorphism at all points—when the employer's perception (J) of the job accurately represents reality (J') and both are accurately represented on the marker (J''). If this occurs, types A, B, and C isomorphism exist for the *job* as perceived by the employer. The employer also has a corresponding set of perceptions regarding the applicant: perception (A) of the empirical applicant (A') that is congruent with the position (J') and a description of the applicant mapped into a marker such as an application letter and resume (A''). Successful allocation again requires types A, B, C isomorphism on the part of the *employer* for the applicant $(A, A'$, and $A'')$. Bear in mind that the empirically existing applicant (A') as well as the perception (A) and the representation on the marker (A'') all ideally represent *all* five *mutable* variables for the applicant and all *immutable variables that are relevant* in the particular society. Notice that not only does the employer need to achieve isomorphism of all three types for J and for A, but "horizontal" isomorphism should be attained also *between* A and J as well as within each model. That is, J and A should be isomorphic; J' and A' should be isomorphic; and J'' and A'' should be isomorphic. Bear in mind that, in each case, isomorphism is multidimensional, consisting of isomorphism on the five mutable characteristics as well as on relevant immutables.

Unfortunately the complexity does not end here. The applicant also has a set of job perceptions and expectations $(J, J'$, and $J'')$ and a set of personal perceptions (as A, A', and $A'')$. Again, there should be all three types of isomorphism within each set (within J and within A) as well as between them. In addition, there should be interpersonal isomorphism between the overall configuration of A s and J s for the employer, and the overall set of A s and J s for the applicant. The situation is even more complicated if the applicant has a range of possible job goals $(J$ s) and employer has a range of possible applicants in terms of education, income, and so on, $(A$ s).

The perceptions of the position and the applicants that both the employer and the applicant have are basically *expectations* of what will occur in the future. If any of these expectations (X) is not isomorphic with reality (X'), then the expected outcome will not occur. There are a number of reasons that such isomorphism (type A) is lacking. One is that the information on the markers (type C) is erroneous. Another is that expectations may be based upon past knowledge of the mutable structures (including information components such as norms) and immutable variables, and the situation may have changed. That is, if it has been a long time since the employer filled a position, then he or she may have obsolete knowledge concerning the abilities and desires of applicants. Similarly, an applicant that has not sought a position recently may be unaware of technology, information requirements, and so forth. Further, new developments such as legal constraints may force employers to alter their expectations (e.g., affirmative action laws or legislation prohibiting discrimination by age). Often employers and applicants will not have direct knowledge of the situation and must base their expectations and goals upon past performance (which may be obsolete) or other persons' performances, perhaps in other regions (S). Employers who are unwilling to alter their perception of the applicant (A) to match reality (A') in terms of one mutable or immutable characteristic may find themselves with a pool of applicants that violate their expectations on other characteristics. For example, an employer who expected to hire a person at a certain wage (L), with certain levels of the other mutable characteristics, and with certain immutable characteristics may find it possible to maintain that expected low wage level (L) only by changing the expectations of the applicant's other mutable characteristics (e.g., education [I] and technological skills [T]) or immutable characteristics (e.g., gender, race, age).

Seen holistically, then, it is clear that the process of allocating even a single person into a single position in the mutable structure is quite complex, even if the structure itself does not change in the time period studied. Even a minimal interaction involving only two persons (the prospective employer and the applicant) is complex. There exists first the idealized perception of the applicant (A) as held by the employer, and the idealized conception of the job (J) as held by the applicant. Often, type A isomorphism is lacking in one or both of these cases; that is, the idealized perception (A) may not be isomorphic with any existing applicant (A'), and the idealized position (J) may not be isomorphic with any existing available jobs (J'). Further, the idealized job may be isomorphic with reality on some of the mutable dimensions (e.g., technology [T] or spatial location [S]) but not on others such as salary (L).

A further complication involves the frequent lack of isomorphism between the marker, such as the printed advertisement that describes the job (J''), and the actual job duties (J'). This is, of course, type C isomorphism. Lack of type C isomorphism can also exist between the qualifications of the actual applicant (A') and the printed representation of the applicant (A''), for example in a vita. An interesting point is that selection of an applicant for a position is often not made solely on indicator (X'') level characteristics such as a vita, although this is sometimes done. Similarly, such selection is generally not made solely on the basis of empirical observation (X') of the characteristics of the individual applicant, although this is sometimes done. More commonly the employer's perception (A) of the applicant is based on a *combination* or aggregate assessment of both the mapped characteristics on the vita (A'') and the observable characteristics.

The characteristics mapped onto the vita can include both mutables and immutables. Why is the assessment of the applicant by the employer made *both* "on paper" (A''), by perusal of the vita, and "in person" (A') in an interview? Although the interview might serve to corroborate the vita, and thus is a reliability check, the two analyses have more fundamental differences and complementarities as well. As stressed, the mutable characteristics of the individual (residence [S], income [L], technological skills [T], and knowledge or education [I]) are generally not observable to the employer when the person is applying for a position on one of the other mutable distributions (in the present example, this is organization [O]). In most cases the employer would be able to discern little or nothing about the applicant's position on the mutable distributions of interest without the indicator level mapping (A'') as manifested in the vita.

Thus, the first step in selection is often the perusal of the data on the five mutable characteristics that the applicant has mapped into his or her resume (A''). These data generally represent the so-called qualifications for the job, such as education (I) and experience in a prior job (O). In addition to data on mutable characteristics that can only be assessed via mapping on a marker (A''), data on immutable characteristics may also be mapped onto the resume (A''). Assessment of either the mutables or immutables, as mapped on A'', may be used to terminate the evaluation or to proceed to the face-to-face phase. In this latter phase, the employer can assess the applicant's immutable characteristics such as skin color, gender, age, and so on (although not without some degree of error, of course). This is type A isomorphism, while assessment of the resume involves a combination of type C isomorphism (degree to which the actual empirical characteristics of the applicant [A'] are represented on the resume [A'']) and type B isomorphism (the degree to which the characteristics on the resume [A''] are accurately assessed by the employer [A]). If both types C and B isomorphism exist, then the resume will represent the applicant adequately, and the employer's perception will represent the resume adequately. In this case, the perception of the applicant's qualifications (both mutable and immutable) should represent the actual applicant (A') even though this was achieved indirectly through the marker. Thus, the establishment of type C and type B isomorphism results in type A isomorphism.

The latter phase (the face-to-face interview) allows the employer to assess immutable characteristics. Although these often are not the so-called qualifications for allocation to the position, they can certainly be a factor in the decision, even a predominant one. The overall allocation is made on the basis of the five mutables and the salient list of immutables. In actual practice, only one or a few of these might be actually used. Often, different ones are used for different applicants.

A classic (if simplistic) view of self-conception (X) a la Cooley is for the individual to have a "looking-glass self" formed through face-to-face interaction. Our more holistic view shows that this is only a part of the larger picture. The self is clearly affected by feedback from face-to-face interaction. Such face-to-face interaction, especially in secondary interaction among relative strangers, predominantly deals with immutables such as gender, skin color, age, and so forth. Thus, the classic looking-glass self may be largely a self derived from immutables. The total self consists of this immutably derived self (X_i) in combination with the other portion of the self derived from information transmission concerning the mutable variables (X_m). Once a person has been allocated into the mutable distribution structure, this immutably derived self (X_i) may predominate on a day-to-day basis. More likely, however, it will be augmented by the mutably derived self (X_m), and this is particularly true during allocation into the mutable distribution. Here the mutable "qualifications" represented on a marker, such as a resume, form the primary basis on which the applicant is judged by the prospective employer, and thus these mutables provide the primary basis for this portion of the self. However, since communication of these mutable characteristics of the applicant is generally via markers (such as resume or personnel file, and is thus indirect, it is amenable to selective information control. Therefore, the feedback that the applicant receives is often controlled and managed. Often the perception of the applicant (A') relayed back to the applicant is not wholly representative of the actual perception (A) the employer derived. The feedback is distorted, and the applicant's mutably derived self-concept may be inaccurate. This may impinge in various ways on the applicant's immutably derived self. To summarize, the total "self" is derived both from immutable characteristics (this is more likely the face-to-face or "looking-glass self") and mutable characteristics (more likely the "paper self" indirectly derived through information transmission over some marker, e.g., as when an impression that the employer derives from a paper resume is fed back to the applicant through a paper letter).

The role of markers (X'') in the allocation process is a very interesting one. Not only do markers very efficiently convey information on mutables (and to a certain extent on immutables), they also are very amenable to control of information and thus are important tools to power holders. However, information control, of course, proceeds both directions in the allocation process. Not only can employers conceal or alter the feedback given the applicant to conceal their true perception of the applicant (so the applicant's paper self is affected), but the applicant can also control the information that goes to the employer on the resume. This can include alteration or outright falsification of information on both immutables and mutables. The mutables are particularly susceptible to information control since they generally cannot be directly observed. If someone alters information on an immutable (such as skin color), this becomes evident in the second phase of allocation (the interview). If someone alters information on a mutable (such as educational level [I]), this may be much more difficult to detect. Ironically, since mutable information is not subject to type A isomorphism or direct observation, often the manner in which it is checked is by appeal to yet another marker (X''). Thus, in the "credential society" (Collins 1979), a particular educational level listed on a resume is verified not by type A validation but by type B. That is, by the employer observing some other marker (X'') such as a diploma or transcript, which in turn could have been falsified. There is a form of infinite regress here. Further, one is not really checking isomorphism with empirical reality (X') but only checking isomorphism among indicator level markers (different cases of X''). This is perhaps an example of a point made in Chapter 2, during the discussion of the "social construction of reality" and the degree to which society is empirically observed: much of "society" seems to exist as the resulting *symbolic structure* of empirical behavior processes (X'). For example, the empirical act of attending school (X') results in mapping certain symbols onto a diploma (X'') "certifying" that one "graduated." The resulting permanent structure exists empirically only as the mapping of X' into X'', and we interact with the letter $(X''$, or the paper diploma) in the allocation process, rather than with the empirical behavior itself.

To summarize the allocation analysis to this point: allocation is a general process of mapping symbols (both mutable, such as education, and immutable, such as gender) onto markers. Symbolic structure (synchronic) from one point in time is mapped onto markers (such as resumes and personnel files) and used to guide the *process* (diachronic) of allocation into the mutable structure in a later period of time. This process involves some combination of all three levels $(X, X'$, and $X'')$, but X'' is seen as instrumental in translating between X and X' (particularly in the case of the mutables, where direct observation of X' to form X is lacking). In this latter case, a combination of type C $(X'-X'')$ and type B $(X''-X)$ isomorphisms is used to indirectly substitute for a direct type A link $(X'-X)$. Thus, the use of X'' in the allocation process involves not only mere transmission of information between persons (e.g., employer and applicant) but transmission of information among all three levels $(X, X'$, and $X'')$ as well.

Thus far, the discussion has centered on organizational position (O). This specific example of the allocation process, with some modification, can be generalized to allocation into the other mutable distributions (I, S, T, L), too. In general, allocation into these other four distributions will also involve evaluation by employers of both the mutable and immutable characteristics of the applicant. As with organization, markers may be utilized and all three levels $(X, X'$, and $X'')$ may be utilized.

As discussed in some detail in Chapter 4, the five mutable distributions are somewhat correlated, although the degree of correlation will vary from society to society. The correlation is imperfect. Thus, knowing a person's occupation, for example, will probably not allow the absolute prediction of his or her status on the remaining distributions but may permit prediction within a certain range. There will often be sufficient correlation between mutables that a person who exhibits extreme differences on two or more (e.g., very high education [I] but low income [L] and nonprestigious neighborhood of residence [S]) may likely be sanctioned by others. This is essentially a form of "status inconsistency" (Lenski 1954).

Technology

Although allocation into the other mutable distributions follows roughly the same procedure as with organization, it may be useful to comment on each in turn, as some have particular vagaries that may be of interest. In examining allocation into the technological distribution, it becomes clear that the type of technology utilized by an individual is not random (maximum entropy), rather allocation into technological positions is correlated with both mutable and immutable characteristics. For example, gender is the single variable that comes to mind as displaying nearly maximum entropy in most populations. In most populations, the percentage of each sex at birth is close to 50 percent (this, of course, can be altered through differential mortality as the cohort ages). Given a condition of maximum entropy for gender, we might expect joint entropy (gender-technology) to approach maximum entropy (zero correlation). This is often clearly not the case. The distribution by sex of persons who can operate electronic equipment in the United States is not 50-50 but skewed so that more men operate it. Thus, there is some ordering procedure that converts the univariate maximum entropy for gender into a nonmaximum value of bivariate (joint) entropy for gender and technology.

It is clear upon inspection that at least two separate factors operate here, both components of information (I). One is allocation to information necessary to operate the given technology (e.g., mathematics). The second is the existence of sanctions operating to enforce *norms* governing utilization of a particular tool. Thus, a woman can be, at an early age, guided away from technical information such as mathematics that she would later find necessary for utilization of a particular technology (e.g., electronic equipment). Further, even if she had the requisite knowledge from years of early training, she might still be normatively sanctioned away from certain technological utilizations, particularly if they conflicted with norms governing feminity (e.g., guided away from "dirty" tools that conflict with feminine standards of beauty).

The degree to which markers (X'') are used in allocation to technology varies widely with the type of tool. Many tools require little or no certification for utilization, and may be relatively inexpensive. Thus, any American can utilize an electric saw at relatively little expense and with no certification. The only thing to keep one from using it, if desired, is the implementation of normative sanctions (e.g., women may be thought "unfeminine"). In contrast, other types of technology are very expensive (e.g., a jet aircraft), so that an individual can generally operate one only by being extremely wealthy or by receiving permission from the power holder for the group that owns them. Further, for dangerous tools, certification (generally in the form of a license or other paper marker $[X'']$) may be required. Here the person may have to present extensive paper documentation (X'') to certify that he or she is properly credentialled to operate the tool. Often access to such tools is only feasible through allocation to a particular organizational position.

Space

Allocation into a particular area of space (e.g., first into a particular area of the country, and second into a particular residence within that local area) is also clearly governed by both mutables and immutables. The correlation among the five mutables can affect the allocation of the individual into both the regional and local residence. Area of the country (S) may be dictated at least partially by the other mutable distributions. For example, a person with a certain education (I) and technological skill (T) desires a certain income (L) but can achieve this only by accepting a position (O) in a certain city (S). After the city of residence is determined, normative sanctions concerning both mutables and immutables can operate to allocate individuals into particular local residential areas.

One of these is, of course, the immutable characteristic of skin color. Persons of a given income level may be differentially allocated into black areas, Chinese areas, and so on. Mutables obviously affect residential allocation as well. Although a given income level (L) fixes the maximum-priced area that an individual can afford, normative sanctions working to ensure "status consistency" sanction individuals who live in the "wrong" neighborhood when they could afford a "better" one.

Information

Information demonstrates the reciprocal systemic nature of the social process, as it clearly operates as both an independent and a dependent variable in the allocation process. As an independent variable, information possession may be crucial for operation of technology (T), allocation into an organization (O), knowledge of the optimal residence (S), and attainment of wealth (L). Conversely, power holders often operate by withholding information. Thus, for example, allocation of women and blacks into certain technological and organizational positions is affected by information in the form of norms that indicate to individuals the "proper" technologies and organizational positions for them to pursue. Additionally, differential access to information affects positions chosen as goals. Thus, blacks, women, or farm youths may not be allocated into a particular position simply because they never had access to information about it and essentially lack knowledge of its existence.

Obviously, information possessed by the individual is also an important dependent variable in its own right. Clearly, one's position in the mutable I-distribution is a function of the other four mutable distributions. One's income level (L), residence (S), organizational position (O), and technology (T) differentially affect access to the information one has as well as the norms dictating the appropriate information. For example, persons in certain organizations (O) may have to learn information (I) pertinent to their position, while persons at certain upper income levels may be sanctioned by colleagues to learn information (I) concerning fine wines and gourmet foods.

Information is the most "invisible" of the mutables. All of the others have external manifestations, even though they can sometimes be disguised. Information possessed by the individual has no such external manifestation. Direct discernment is very context-specific and can only be ascertained through face-to-face conversation. Much determination of an individual's level of information is thus indirect, relying heavily upon markers. We judge persons' knowledge through their written work (X'') and rely upon diplomas (X'') to certify a certain level of knowledge. Obviously, such a marker has some degree of error, as two persons with the same diploma (X'') can vary quite widely in terms of the actual degree of information possessed (X').

Level of Living

As discussed in Chapter 5, level of living (L), can be operationalized in many ways, depending upon the particular society. In less-developed societies, the life expectancy or the amount of available calories may be the proper operationalization. In other societies, wealth or income may be preferred. It is clear once again that access to income and wealth is highly correlated both with the other mutables (where it serves systemically as both a dependent and an independent variable) and with the immutables that are salient in the particular society. As an independent variable, (L) helps determine the residence one can afford (S), the access to informatioon through "proper" schools (I), the type of technology (T), and the type of position achieved (O). As a dependent variable, information (I), technology (T), organization (O), and residence (S), are all instrumental in determining how a person is allocated into the level of living (L) mutable distribution.

So much has been written about income, wealth, and status attainment, and about "class" in general in sociology, that the issue will not be belabored here. The systemic nature of the allocation process should be stressed, however. Stratification theorists should not look solely at "class" (*L*) but systemically analyze its relationship to the other four mutable distributions as well as to immutables. Further, they should recognize the important role of markers (*X″*) in allocation to wealth. For example, to borrow money (*L*), one generally must complete a detailed paper application form (*X″*) listing a comprehensive variety of mutable information (e.g., residence [*S*], occupation [*O*], income [*L*]), as well as information on immutables (e.g., age, gender). As with alloction to occupation (*O*), such use of a marker (*X″*) maximizes the power holder's control of the allocation process. The application (*X″*) is a permanent record that can be checked against other markers (e.g., in credit bureaus) and used to intimidate the applicant if it is found to be falsified. Further, use of the marker allows the power holder to delay the decision regarding allocation. When the decision is made, it is usually in private and subject to information control. The applicant is generally given some "feedback" concerning the decision and "reasons" for it, but this information can be incomplete, incorrect, or distorted (as when a deficiency on some mutable is given as the reason for loan rejection, whereas the true reason concerned some immutable such as age, gender, or race).

In summary, the same general allocation process operates for all five mutable distributions, and each set of four mutables helps determine the individual's location in the fifth. In studying allocation, this systemic nature should be stressed. It is true, however, that a single instance of the allocation process may not necessarily utilize all other mutables directly or utilize all salient immutables. Rather, different variables can be the key on which the decision hinges in different allocation instances. For example, one employer filling an organization position (*O*) may prefer someone with more education (*I*) but nevertheless will hire a particular applicant who lives in the local area (*S*), rather than expend the time and money for a national search. In this case, a mutable (*S*) is the "swing" variable. In another case, an employer may eschew a local person (*S*), who has sufficient education (*I*) but who is a woman, and search nationally for a man (although this fact may be carefully disguised). In this case an immutable (gender) operates as the swing variable.

There has been much speculation in sociology and the lay public as well regarding the degree to which the "class structure" is "open" or "permeable"; that is, the degree to which long-range social mobility can be accomplished. Horatio Alger and the American Dream notwithstanding, our holistic analysis shows that "mobility" is not a simple matter of making money and thus rising in the "class" (*L*) structure. Rather, one is mobile (either upwardly or downwardly) or not *on all five intercorrelated mutable distributions*. Each set of four, plus the set of salient immutables, determine one's position in the fifth mutable, including (*L*).

This being the case, it is clear that mobility (e.g., allocation into a position in the mutable structure that is different, and perhaps distant from one's initial position) can often be subject to myriad constraints. One might have to occasionally satisfy eight or ten conditions (four mutables plus a number of immutables) in order to progress on a single mutable. Sometimes any one of these is sufficient to retard mobility. The immutables, by definition, can be formidable barriers to mobility, as they cannot be changed by the individual. Rather, mobility must proceed by changing residence (S) and going somewhere where the particular immutable is not negatively evaluated in the allocation process (assuming such a location can be found and one's position in the mutable structure allows it—such as being able to afford the move $[L]$). If this is not feasible, the chief recourse is to change the power holder's attitude with regard to the immutable (e.g., so there is no discrimination by gender or skin color)—often an impossibility in one's lifetime.

Thus, this holistic analysis demonstrates why many people end about where they begin in the mutable structure—the five-dimensional mutable net, along with the immutables, holds them there. Much heralded independent variables such as "intelligence" and "motivation" or "drive" obviously have an effect on mobility. However, if one is blocked from a particular organizational position (O) by a mutable such as area of the country lived in (S) or by an immutable such as race or gender, a high degree of intelligence may prove of little value in mobility, as one does not really get an opportunity to use it.

An interesting thing about the degree of mobility possible is that it is clearly correlated with one's initial position in the mutable-distributional structure. Persons who begin low on (L) have the potential for the greatest gain but also face the most formidable obstacles, necessitating the greatest expenditures of energy and information (which they are least able to afford). Persons in intermediate levels of (L) can experience intermediate mobility (both up and down). Persons in high initial positions in (L) can experience only downward mobility. They have the greatest potential for long-range downward mobility but generally also have the greatest resource base to help them retain their position. If one is at the bottom on all mutables (low income or wealth $[L]$, little education $[I]$, no possession or utilization of technology $[T]$, no job $[O]$, and low prestige residence offering little access to other mutables $[S]$), then barriers to mobility are truly formidable, especially if the individual possesses one or more negatively evaluated immutable characteristics as well.

Now that the general process of allocation has been discussed in some detail, the study turns to a more "micro" level and analyzes cognitive perceptions (X) developed by both applicants and power holders in the allocation process. We will be particularly concerned with *expectations* that participants in the social allocation process develop, and also with how these guide the *goals* that applicants set for themselves.

Expectations and Goals

Generally, mobility (allocation into a new mutable position) occurs when the individual forms some *expectation*, then sets a new position as a *goal*. Initial expectations are constrained by the amount of information available to the person in a given position (one cannot expect something that one is unaware of). Within these initially conceived expectations, a smaller set may be normatively prescribed as appropriate for the given person (e.g., a woman), while others may be proscribed as inappropriate or "unrealistic." This final set of expectations can be utilized to set goals for mobility through reallocation into the mutable distributions. Again out of the initial set of goals, some may be prescribed as appropriate for the individual, while some may be normatively proscribed.

Norms bind goal choice for an individual both in terms of position on the set of five mutable distributional variables and position in the set of N immutable variables. The norms governing the mutable statuses chiefly dictate levels of one distributional variable that are deemed appropriate for a person at a given level of other distributional variables. For example, a person who is the progeny of a family at a certain income level (L) will be expected to obtain a certain set of knowledge and values (I) and a certain occupational level (O). That is, the person is expected to achieve a certain education or knowledge level and its correlated ideological package and to pursue an occupation within a given range commensurate with his or her (L) and (I) levels. Those choosing goals outside this given range may be subject to sanctions by others.

Norms governing the proper goals for immutable variables tend to be more restrictive. Since the status is "ascribed," the norm will apply to the individual generally throughout his or her lifetime, although it may vary with age and, of course, the norm may vary over time. These norms will specify goals prescribed and proscribed for given immutable ("ascribed") status categories. For example, persons under a certain age will be expected to attend school and not work. Females are expected to aspire to and to accept certain jobs and not others. The prescribed and proscribed goals are those consistent with the label of a person in a certain immutable category. That label supports the prevailing ideology (I) of the society for that individual. For example, if the ideology supports the label of a female as beautiful, weak, and dainty, then jobs that require getting grease on one's self (mechanic or printing press operator) or lifting heavy objects will be proscribed.

The person's goals are a function of all immutable statuses. Thus, out of a total set of goals that are technologically feasible (T) in a given society, a subset y may be prescribed as appropriate for blacks, a subset x as appropriate for women, and a subset z as appropriate for persons under a certain weight and height. A given person who is black, female, and under this height and weight thus has acceptable ("nonproscribed") goals only at the intersection of sets x, y, and z, and thus may be severely restricted in goal choice. Such prescription and proscription of goals on the basis of ascribed statuses, if successful, is a very effective social control mechanism in differentially allocating wealth (L) throughout the society and is a major cause of the maintenance of stratification systems. This will be discussed in more detail in Chapter 7.

Given an array of possible goals perceived by an individual as realistic for someone in his or her position in the mutable and immutable status distributions, the person chooses goals that (1) are rewarding and (2) can be reasonably fulfilled. It is very important to the ego to be labeled as successful by other individuals. Thus, goal choice is also a function of past performance by both the individual and others in similar positions that he or she is aware of. Remembrance of past performance provides data for estimating whether, if a given goal is chosen, action to attain this goal will be successful. Inasmuch as the success-failure label is important to the individual's self-concept, and failure is subject to sanction from others, a goal that might have much to offer but that is relatively difficult to obtain may be eschewed in favor of an alternative goal that is safer and has a higher probability of success but offers a lower reward. The choice of difficult goals requires a great deal of confidence if the person is to avoid a high level of anxiety.

Goals attained relatively easily in the past afford secure choices. Thus, much goal selection centers around goals similar to those achieved in the past. Also, many goals are accumulative. A person confident from past successes is not only likely to choose more difficult goals, but may find them easier to attain if perceived by others as successful and capable and labeled that way, because this encourages and facilitates goal attainment. For this reason negative or positive cycles are set up. A person who has a history of failure and few resources will be labeled a failure and a bad risk to help, and thus can easily remain a failure. Likewise, a person who is successful may find it relatively difficult to fail, as she or he will be labeled a success by others because of status symbols manifested and will find that others encourage setting difficult goals and even negatively sanction lack of goals. They give the individual encouragement and the benefit of the doubt. They presume that the mission will be completed successfully.

This assumption of success of the individual by others greatly facilitates accomplishment, just as assumption of failure greatly impedes it. Persons occupying low-level mutable configurations plus immutable positions with little power will be presumed in advance to be unsuccessful by others if they set proscribed goals, and this presumption can be used to deny them the tools that they must obtain through social interaction in order to be successful. These include money, information, energy, encouragement, and so forth.

Thus, persons in low mutable positions (for example, if all five mutable positions are low) and negatively labeled immutable statuses (race, gender, physical size, physical appearance, and so forth) may find a universal assumption of failure on the part of powerful persons they need to interact with for success. These persons wield power through the differential distribution of grades, credit, and so forth. These necessities for success may be universally denied to presumed failures, thus fulfilling the prophecy of failure. Conversely, persons high in all five mutable distributions, and with only positively labeled immutable characteristics, may find great pressure from others to set high goals and automatic approval of credit, acceptance to schools and clubs, and so forth, thus making failure difficult.

Persons in this latter category find a universal assumption of success, thus making motivation on their part (a positive mental attitude) unnecessary. Persons low on all of the mutable and immutable categories find a positive mental attitude crucial, as they are subject to apathy and fatalism as realistic attitudes.

The information and energy available to a person help him or her set goals by defining a range of potentially eligible goals. Normatively prescribed and proscribed information channels define certain goals as appropriate, and position in the mutable structure provides persons with the necessary information and wealth to pursue certain goals and not others. For example, an older, nonminority wealthy male may have powerful goals prescribed for him by existing norms and will have the wealth and knowledge at his disposal for attainment of these goals. Conversely, a young woman minority member will have only a few relatively menial jobs prescribed, will have little knowledge of other positions due to limited information channels, and little wealth to seek other positions even if she were cognizant of them. The goals having the highest probability of successful attainment are those prescribed by the norms for the individual in his or her particular position in the five-dimensional mutable structure and with his or her particular set of immutable characteristics.

In a relatively constant situation of no social mobility and no change in norms, success of goal attainment is maximized, and thus defiance of expectation and the resulting feelings of unjust betrayal are minimized. Such occasions as do occur are often the result of faulty information sources, as when the undergraduate peer grapevine defines a sociology class as a place to earn an easy B in, but the student finds the grading tough and receives a D. In such a case the student often does not place the blame on either the information source or himself or herself but blames the source of the defied expectation (the instructor grading the examination) for not having behaved as expected. Thus, students will leave a class in droves if they can be convinced early in the term to have low expectations of their grades but will be extremely resentful and blame everyone but themselves if they expect a high grade and an easy work load and their expectations are defied. Since healthy ego development is attained by successfully fulfilling goals and ensuring that expectations are not defied, individuals will generally select realistic goals they know they have control over and increase the difficulty of their goals only gradually (a person will not try to alter seasons).

In the usual cases of slow social mobility or no social mobility and relatively constant or gradually changing norms, most actors experience defied expectation of highly valued goals only rarely, usually on the basis of incorrect information or miscalculation. Even if persons are drastically mobile, going from low class to high class or vice versa, they can usually learn to choose proper goals and successfully attain them if their rate of mobility is slow enough, thus minimizing the number of defied gratifications.

As long as an individual remains in the same position in the mutable and immutable structures over time, the normative structure generally remains relatively constant, approving the same goals and same means of attaining these goals, with little change over time. This normative structure is not as visible as a physical structure, although its effects can be just as concrete. One cannot see the norm dictating the role of the housewife and mother for women as one can see a mountain. However, the punitive sanctions that are quickly forthcoming for norm violations are very concrete and easily observed. Norms save actors from many unnecessary decisions about many alternative (and perhaps arbitrary) actions, by defining appropriate goals and appropriate means of achieving them. This relieves the actor of a great deal of ambiguity and accompanying anxiety. Beyond that, norms serve to orient the individual by providing reference points that guide perceptions of the situation and provide a basis for decision making.

There are three distinct cases where an individual may suffer from impaired perception of normative structure:

1. Where there is sudden change in the individual's position in one or more of the mutable distributions (by definition, sudden change in the immutables is extremely rare, as in sex change operations), with little or no change in the norms governing each position or configuration of positions.

2. No change in the individual's position in the mutable and immutable variables but rapid change in the norms governing appropriate goals

and means for action within each position or configuration of positions.

3. Both rapid long-range change of the individual from one position to a drastically different one in the mutable and immutable structure and rapid change of norms governing the new position.

The first case (1) can be recognized as Durkheim's (1951) classical case of anomia, which in severe cases is said to result in anomic suicide due to inadequate regulation of the individual's expectations. As Durkheim (1951) carefully pointed out, anomia can result from upward mobility as well as downward mobility, since the upwardly mobile, too, must adjust to a new position in the mutable structure and must learn a substantially different set of norms governing social conduct. For example, upwardly mobile persons who have always mowed their own lawns and cleaned their own home might be quite severely sanctioned in their new neighborhood for this heretofore appropriate behavior.

The term anomia or normlessness is somewhat of a misnomer here as there is no lack of quite clear and consistent norms. It is only that the new norms are not perceived fully by the mobile person. The rapidly mobile person faces severe identity problems as she or he, in effect, has been reclassified and is now treated entirely differently by the society. The society now has distinctly different expectations. A great deal of adult socialization is required in order for the individual to learn these new expectations as dictated by the norms. The difficulty of this task is a function of how many of the five mutable distributions she or he experiences changes on and how great is the degree of change on each. For example, a person who is greatly mobile in a short period of time in the L distribution (a lottery winner or someone suffering a business failure), but who experiences no changes in residence (S), occupation (O), values and knowledge (I), and type of technology utilized (T) can doubtlessly adjust more easily than someone who experiences changes in all five mutable distributions (notice that we are expanding the discussion considerably beyond Durkheim's [1951] discussion of anomic suicide, as he primarily confined himself to rapid economic change [L]). However, since these five mutable distributions are rather highly intercorrelated, it may be relatively rare to experience great change in one without some accompanying change in the others. That is, a lower-class lottery winner, who overnight wins a great deal of money (L), is very likely to experience subsequent change in values (I), residence (S), occupation (O), and technology (T).

Situation 1, just discussed, primarily concerns change of an individual's position in the portion of the social space composed of distributional or relational variables (mutable distributions), as the immutable individual variables are generally very difficult to alter over a lifetime. Case 2 involves no change in the individual's position in the social space but a change in the norms regulating this particular position. Although rapid norm change could occur for the mutable distributional positions such as wealth (L), occupation (O), technology (T), residence (S), and values (I), as well as for immutable individual statuses such as skin color and gender, it seems more likely for the latter. This is because immutable characteristics are generally permanent and difficult for the individual to change, and they are also highly visible immediately in social interaction. Thus, they serve as optimal mechanisms for social control for majority power holders. The individuals with these characteristics are thus relatively easily discriminated against and subjugated at low positions in terms of the five mutable distributions.

When pressure for norm change comes, we would generally expect it not from persons who are satisfied with their roles as prescribed by prevailing norms but from persons who are dissatisfied. A dissatisfied individual may first turn to traditional avenues of mobility such as education, residence change, occupational change, technological change, or value change. Often this is impossible because prevailing norms regulating individuals with his or her ascribed characteristics mitigate against success, such as precluding women and blacks form entering certain occupational, residential or educational channnels.

The result is that individuals with sufficient economic power, information, and ego strength will press for change in the norms regulating the immutable characteristics. For example, women with relatively favorable positions in the mutable structure will apply pressure to open formerly proscribed occupations to women.

Since the mutable positions are "achieved" positions, individuals in a certain mutable position can opt to leave that position rather than attempt to change the norms. A person who is currently a manager in a business concern (O) may opt to return to school (I). Once there, he or she may chafe at the manner in which superiors act (teachers act as though he or she knows nothing at all, even though he or she has been a boss for years) and may wish to leave this powerless position for the former more powerful position with authority over others. Thus, the person simply leaves school rather than putting pressure to bear upon the norms defining students as powerless. The more temporary the achieved position is, the less pressure there is for norm change on the part of incumbents.

Situation 2 (retention of the individual's position in the property space of mutable variables and immutable individual characteristics, accompanied by rapid change in norms regulating this position) is closer to an actual state of anomia or normlessness than the situation 1 discussed by Durkheim. Here norms cease to exist in their present form and change so as to either prescribe formerly proscribed behavior or to proscribe previously prescribed behavior. Generally, there is initial proscription of certain goals, followed by pressure to prescribe this formerly proscriptive behavior (birth control, abortion, or professional careers for women, for example). A true case of anomia, or complete absence of norms, has probably never occurred on a large scale over a long period of time. It would probably prove debilitating to the individual and would elicit norm constructing behavior. Conversely, most social situations are partially anomic, with flexibility maintained by not having every single action dictated by norms. This is often an optimal situation for authority figures, as it allows the power holder to construct norms on the spot to suit his or her purposes.

Behavior not dictated by norms is often treated normatively by the individual. For example, in many elementary classes students are assigned seats. In later years students not assigned a seat will appropriate one and sit in it daily, thus obviating need for a daily decision about where to sit. Similarly, commuters with several available routes home from work will habitually use one, just as if a norm existed prescribing that route and proscribing others.

The last situation, 3, in which both an individual's position and the norms regulating that position change rapidly, is probably relatively rare, as its occurrence is the multiple of the probability of individual changing from position a to position b, and the probability of norms regulating one or more variables constituting position b changing rapidly. In such a case the effect of rapid norm change would be minimal if it occurred immediately before the individual assumed the new position, as he or she would have to learn all norms anew regardless of the length of time that these norms had been in effect. Such a person might actually be in an advantageous position relative to long-term occupants of the position, who might have difficulty in learning new norms and might consider the necessity of such relearning unjust.

Perhaps the most traumatic case is that of an individual who experiences rapid mobility into a new position, learns the new norms, then shortly after this finds that the norms that he or she has just learned have changed. This should be a rare occurrence since, as noted, the easiest mobility is to new mutable positions where norm change is less probable. Further mobility to new immutable statuses that may be susceptible to great norm change is rare.

Summary

I have endeavored in this chapter to show that individual action takes place within a context provided by the global macroproperties and mutable distributions of the society in which the individual resides and that individual action is in addition constrained and guided by the particular set of immutable characteristics that the society regards as salient. It should be evident from this analysis that although "free will" and individual initiative are certainly important in determining mobility, individual mobility is substantially constrained by the mutable distributions (which are themselves constrained by global levels of the six macro variables) and by the immutable variables. Where one ends in the mutable distribution is generally affected by where one begins. Further, mobility is generally not solely a process of changing position in the income distribution (L). Rather, since the five mutable distributions are highly correlated, it is best to analyze mobility in terms of the individual's position on all five. For example, upward mobility in terms of income (L) is often achieved through change in education (I), which enables one to secure a better paying job (O), but this also entails a change in technological utilization (T) and residence (S).

This chapter discussed the globals, the mutable distributions, the immutables, and the expectations (X) that participants in the allocation process form and that enable them to set goals; hence, the role of the individual within the macro boundaries of the entire society. This, of course, neglects the fact that myriad intermediate groups function between the macro level and the individual's action. These also provide a context for action and are themselves constrained by globals, by the mutable distributions for the whole society, and by larger groups of which they may be a part. In Chapter 6 attention is focussed on these intermediate groups that provide local (and sometimes conflicting) contexts for individual action.

Chapter 6

Organizations

The last two chapters studied the societal and individual levels of analysis. Chapter 4 discussed how societal members monitor and attempt to regulate six macrosociological global variables: population size (P), spatial area (S), level of living (L), technology (T), organization (O), and information (I). Further, the population (P) of individuals was shown to be distributed among the other five mutable variables to form five mutable distributions (analytical rather than global properties of the society).

Chapter 5 was primarily concerned with analyzing the mechanisms whereby individual members of the society are allocated into specific positions in the five-dimensional mutable structure (I, S, T, O, L), a complex process. Initial location in the structure is highly relevant but allocation is based upon both mutable and immutable characteristics of individuals. Other factors instrumental in allocation are the information that the individual has regarding positions, the norms dictating appropriate positions for a given set of mutable and immutable characteristics, and the expectations and goals that are held to be "realistic" or normatively "appropriate" for an individual with a given particular set of mutable and immutable characteristics.

In a very real sense, then, the citizens of each society are distributed within each of the five mutable distributions. Further, these distributions are monitored and regulated (however imperfectly, and this is empirically highly variable across societies) in each society. This is true even though very often an individual may be relatively unaware of his or her position in the societal distribution, but more acutely aware of his or her position in a given organization. One gets hired or fired from an organization not from a societal distribution (O). With this in mind, attention turns to an analysis of organization, a level clearly intermediate to the global level of Chapter 4 and the individual level of Chapter 5.

However, keep in mind that organizations (of whatever size) are not *independent* of the organizational mutable distribution (O) for the whole society but are merely a portion of it. As such, although they may operate autono-

mously to a degree, they are constrained not only by the remainder of organizations in the (O) distribution but also by the other four mutable distributions
(I, S, T, L), as well as by the six globals that constrain all of the mutables.
This intermediate level entered into the discussion of allocation in Chapter 5,
here the analysis continues at a high level of generality. Thus, there will be no
separation between groups and organizations, as in Miller (1978), or between
micro, meso, and macro organizations, as in Hage (1980). Rather, the discussion will focus on the general properties of all organizations or groups that are
intermediate to the individual actor, on the one hand, and the entire society,
on the other hand.

It is convenient here to reassert the belief that only a holistic view can
construct an adequate explanation of society. Allocation into the mutable distributions has been shown to be a holistic process. It does not depend solely
upon a single mutable or single immutable characteristic but rather is determined by a particular holistic configuration of mutables and immutables. The
same is true of organizational growth, and of behavior within organizations.

It is commonplace in everyday life that such mutables as residence (S),
expectations, attitudes, values, and knowledge (I); class position (L); and
technological utilization (T), along with various immutable characteristics
(age, race, gender, etc.) combine to determine allocation into an organization
(O). Yet ironically, in sociological theory, this holistic, intuitive model, which
is isomorphic with empirical reality, is often abandoned in favor of a number
of analytically discrete middle-range models. Thus, gender is analyzed in "sex
role" theory; race studied as a factor in "race and ethnicity" theory, residence
and migration (S) studied in demography or community sociology; income
(L) studied by stratification theorists; or organizational change (O) by organizational specialists. Such piecemeal analysis may have certain advantages but
cannot model the synergistic reality of actual society and precludes a full understanding of how persons are allocated into mutable positions and how interactions and organizations are formed and sustained.

Organizational Formation

In terms of social entropy theory (SET), an organization is essentially a
system intermediate in size between the individual, and the entire society.
Speaking very generally, the focus of analysis in this chapter can range from
a dyad to an organization encompassing virtually the entire population of the
society. However, generally an organization will be intermediate to these two
extremes.

Although the term *organization* is used quite generically, we must distinguish between *interaction* and *organization*. An *interaction* is any exchange of information or matter-energy between two or more persons. Thus, although the individual can alone engage in *action* (which will generally consume matter-energy or information), the dyad can engage in *interaction*. Much interaction within larger groups can be seen as multiples of dyadic interaction, either sequential or simultaneous.

Generically, an organization is simply a system of members interacting within certain boundaries. Thus, it is a concrete system in Miller's (1978) terms. Generally, an organization has a particular goal, or goals, and processes information and matter-energy in order to achieve this goal. Some organizations will be spread across several or many geographic settings (*S*), and thus their physical boundaries may be amorphous (although the central headquarters will often have a clear geographical location). However, virtually all organizations have some symbolic "boundaries" in the form of mutable or immutable characteristics that separate members from nonmembers. This generic systems definition of an organization would seem to encompass the terms *group*, *association*, and perhaps even *institution*.

As mentioned, everyday social activity (e.g., the process of allocation into mutable positions) is holistic and thus a model capable of understanding this activity must be holistic. This emphasis on holistic analysis is borrowed from general systems theory (e.g., Bertalanffy 1968; Buckley 1967),and the emphasis on intuitive analysis of commonsense activity from early ethnomethodology (e.g., Zimmerman and Pollner 1970). Carrying this latter point a bit further, and assuming that there are indeed parallels between methods that scientists and lay members of the society utilize as Zimmerman and Pollner (1970) suggest, it may be instructive to analyze scientific grouping techniques in more detail.

If it is true that scientific method is a *subset* of methods used by the larger society, then study of the *structure* of the former can provide insights into the *structure* of the latter. For example, a large number of statistical grouping methods have been developed in numerical taxonomy (Sokal and Sneath 1963; Sneath and Sokal 1973; Bailey 1974). Traditionally, interest has centered on the *results* of applying these methods, as with other statistical techniques. However, since these methods are used to form groups, perhaps examination should not focus solely on their applications but also on their *structure* for clues as to how groups are formed in the society as a whole. There are actually two interrelated reasons to examine the structure of the statistical techniques themselves:

1. Because, according to early ethnomethodological tenets, these scientific grouping methods have similarities with grouping methods in the larger lay society.

2. Because many of these methods are designed to replicate naturally occurring groups (Sneath and Sokal 1973) and thus should be isomorphic with the "natural" processes by which these groups are formed.

If these two premises hold, then numerical taxonomic grouping methods are isomorphic with societal grouping processes in general, and therefore analysis of the former (whose properties are well known) is instructive in understanding the latter. To this end, let us briefly examine some properties of grouping processes in numerical taxonomy.

A little reflection will show that there are two basic methods for forming groups from a population (P) of a given societal system. One is to view the population P as a single group initially. The task then becomes successively *dividing* the population into subgroups of lesser size. The alternative procedure is to view each of the (P) members of the population as a single system initially. The task then becomes *agglomerating* individuals into larger groups. Although combinations of these two processes can be utilized, divisive and agglomerative methods are the two chief processes for formation in numerical taxonomy (see Sneath and Sokal 1973; Bailey 1974).

The primary goal of any grouping technique is to form a relatively homogeneous group. If the group is truly homogeneous in terms of *all* characteristics, then it is said to be *monothetic* (Sneath and Sokal 1973; Bailey 1974). Thus, for a given organization to be monothetic, its members would have to be identical on *all* characteristics, both mutable and immutable.

Naturally occurring social groups will rarely be monothetic. However, they generally will not be completely dissimilar on all characteristics. Rather, their membership will show *overall* similarity across the set of mutable and immutable characteristics. Whereas the members will not be identical on all characteristics, they will share most of them and a given characteristic will be shared by most but not all members of the group. A group that demonstrates such overall similarity is called a *polythetic* group. If no one characteristic is shared by all members, the group is said to be *fully polythetic* (see Sokal and Sneath 1963; Sneath and Sokal 1973; Bailey 1973, 1974).

In terms of entropy, a monothetic group will exhibit perfect correlations among all variables, and thus will be characterized by minimum (zero) joint entropy on the full set of mutable and immutable characteristics displayed by its members. Needless to say, a monothetic group is rare, and perhaps never occurs in the social system, particularly for a large number of persons on a large number of variables (although monotheticism on one or a few variables is common, particularly in small groups).

However, the opposite extreme (maximum entropy) is also generally lacking in human groups. If maximum entropy occurred, group members would not be similar on any characteristics, but rather group formation would be random. This goes far beyond full polytheticism, and there does not even seem to be a distinctive term in numerical taxonomy or classification theory for it, as groups are assumed to display some minimal level of internal homogeneity. In general, a social group will not be randomly formed but also will fall short of monotheticism. It thus will display entropy levels between maximum and minimum and will be polythetic but often not fully polythetic. Once again this discussion shows the efficacy of holistic analysis, as terms such as *polytheticism* and *monotheticism* have little meaning for univariate analysis but only apply to groups of variables measured on groups of objects.

Divisive Grouping Processes

According to Sneath and Sokal (1973, pp. 18–27), most naturally occurring groups are polythetic and best replicated through agglomerative grouping procedures. In their view, divisive methods (especially in the multivariate case) will form monothetic groups that are largely "artificial" and unrealistic for modeling empirical phenomena. Relying on the three-level model, we see that we can construct a divisive statistical model (X'') that will form monothetic groups. However, these will be "artificial" and not isomorphic with empirically occurring groups (X'), which are generally polythetic. Thus, while such divisive models (X'') are not useful for studying empirically occurring groups (X'), they may be analytically helpful in the cognitive understanding (X) of the generic nature of grouping processes.

Although divisively formed monothetic groups may be largely analytical in the biological applications discussed by Sneath and Sokal (1973), such models (X'') are more likely to be isomorphic with empirically occurring groups (X') in sociology (type C isomorphism). That is, divisive monothetic classes are common in society. These are often univariate, sometimes bivariate, and occasionally trivariate or multivariate. These initial divisions are essentially just divisions into classes rather than functioning groups; that is, division by gender will not necessarily result in men functioning as a group or women functioning as a group. Rather, the process of group formation is often sequential, with two or more distinct stages. First, division into classes is recognized (e.g., by gender, race, residence $[S]$, etc.), and subsequently, persons within each class form a pool of eligibles for agglomerative group formation. The agglomeratively formed group will have goals, criteria for selection of members, and information networks among members and will process energy and information to achieve its goals. For example, persons from among a divisively formed eligible pool of women are selected to agglomeratively form a women's group with particular goals (e.g., the League of Women Voters). One will often see division on two variables simultaneously (e.g., black women's groups), or three variables (black, church, youth groups). Division by more than three or four simultaneous variables is rarer.

Notice that division can occur not only on immutables (age, gender, race), but also on mutables such as religious beliefs (I), class (L), residence (S), interest in computers (T), and so on. Since the mutables are correlated, and position in the mutables is correlated with immutable characteristics, it is not unusual to see some resultant clusters of divisive characteristics (such as an association composed of women [an immutable characteristic] who are pilots [T], and all reside within a certain geographic area [S]).

Agglomerative Grouping Processes

The bulk of group formation within a given social system is clearly agglomerative, although as noted this is often accomplished after a preliminary division (e.g., agglomeration into groups for the purpose of achieving physical fitness may be parallel, with one group for men and one for women, perhaps in the same location). Occasionally, one might find a group that is open to all persons, regardless of any mutable or immutable characteristics. Such a group could potentially be maximally entropic (random) in terms of all mutable and immutable characteristics, but this would be exceedingly rare, as even without formal entrance requirements of any sort, there will likely be selectivity of various sorts (e.g., by residence [S] or income [L]). It is generally the rule that groups will not be open to all persons but will have at least some minimal entrance requirements that serve as the basis for agglomeration.

A number of different criteria for agglomeration have been distinguished within numerical taxonomy. For example, agglomerative methods may be classified as single linkage or complete linkage (Sneath and Sokal 1973; Bailey 1974). In a single linkage method the prospective group member need have a link with only one current group member, whereas in the complete linkage method similarity must exist between the prospective member and *all* current members. Examples are clear in society. In some associations, every member must approve the prospective member, and even one veto is sufficient to deny membership. This is clearly a complete linkage procedure. Other groups grow by single linkage methods where any member has the power to accept one new person into membership regardless of the wishes of other members. Another salient distinction in numerical taxonomy that is found in the larger society as well is the hierarchical-nonhierarchical distinction. Many (but not all) clustering techniques in numerical taxonomy are hierarchical. Only a cursory glance at the organizational literature or at an organizational chart shows the hierarchical nature of the social group as well, and there is a clear resemblance between the organizational hierarchy chart and the dendogram used in numerical taxonomy to illustrate hierarchical clusterings (see Sneath and Sokal 1973). Sneath and Sokal (1973) have observed that the bulk of clustering techniques are sequential, agglomerative, hierarchical, and nonoverlapping, which they term the *SAHN models*.

Like human social groups, these models form groups sequentially or in stages, rather than adding all members simultaneously. These models result in hierarchical polythetic groups—the type that abounds in the society at large. Further, the groups produced by these models are nonoverlapping. Although human society certainly displays overlapping groups (i.e., groups that have one or more members in common), nonoverlapping groups abound as well, and it is not uncommon for employers to attempt to restrict outside employment (dual work-group membership) among their employees. All in all, then, the SAHN grouping procedures and the groups that result have some clear parallels with group formation in the larger society. However, as noted, many social groups are agglomeratively formed only after prior division on one or more variables. They are thus monothetic on one or more divisive variables (e.g., all are women), and this ensures that the subsequent agglomeratively formed group is polythetic rather than fully polythetic.

Agglomerative groups are generally known as organizations or associations. They generally are goal oriented, with one or more clearly defined group goals. They generally possess a communications network or interaction network. These networks are either horizontal, such as an information newsletter sent from headquarters to all members, or a vertical chain of command, with one individual communicating with one or more subordinates. Many agglomerative groups have both horizontal and vertical interaction networks.

Some divisive subgroups usually do not engage in face-to-face interaction among all members of the group simultaneously or have common communications networks linking all members. They generally have a group existence only as a class or category for statistical purposes, where they may be widely utilized (for example, in comparisons of black income with white income). Divisive subgroups are homogeneous or monothetic (Bailey 1974) on the defining characteristic but are generally polythetic on remaining ascribed and achieved characteristics.

Agglomerative groups are generally polythetic in terms of ascribed characteristics. However, if an ascribed individual characteristic is salient enough to define a socially recognized divisive category, then there will often be some correlation between divisive category status and membership in an agglomerative group. By definition, membership in an agglomerative group is an achieved status, which the individual achieves by being agglomerated (admitted) to that group. However, may times the requirements for entering the achieved agglomerative group are based upon achievements, credentials, or skills that are highly correlated with a divisive class. For example, the goals of one agglomerative group may entail skills almost entirely acquired by men. Further, some agglomerative groups have as their goal the betterment of a certain divisive class (for example, NOW or NAACP), so that the membership of an agglomerative group may become highly correlated with, or perhaps even identical with, a divisive group (see Figure 6.1).

	Network	No Network
Divisive	NOW (subgroup of all women)	All women
Agglomerative	A business	Undefined

Figure 6.1 Divisive and Agglomerative Groups.

Virtually all work groups are agglomerative and goal oriented. Persons are hired on the basis of some achievement, such as credentials or experience, and membership in the group thus becomes an achieved status. Most social interaction takes place within the immediate context of an agglomerative group, be it a factory, store, family household, religious service, or social club. The agglomerative group generally has a physical setting (for example, a building) that constrains the relationships of its members, as well as group norms that dictate how interaction is carried out.

Thus, the immediate context for social interaction is (1) the physical setting of the agglomerative group (for example, a factory); (2) the physical resources of the group (for example, raw materials, money, information); (3) the norms of the group (for example, rules and regulations, norms for each role position in the group); and (4) the size of the group. In addition, each subgroup has its own set of the five mutable variables (L, O, T, I, S). These are all defined for the subgroup only and are not to be confused with the larger distribution configuration for the whole population. Each subgroup distribution is a part of the total distribution for the whole society. The group and its individual actors are subject to wider societal norms and the limitations of the societal mutable and global variables. Into this context each individual actor brings his or her own position in the mutable and immutable distributions. Within this total context, interaction between individuals takes place.

Social interaction between two or more individuals involves exchange of matter, information, or energy in order to achieve a certain goal. Interaction is clearly more complex than simple goal attainment action by a single person as discussed earlier. However, such interaction also has the potential to achieve greater goals, as one-person action is obviously quite restricted.

As with individual action, the individual must set a goal that he or she thinks is worthwhile (thus giving purpose to life). The chosen goal should have goal value for the individual. It should be consistent with his or her ego strength, have a reasonably high probability of successful attainment, and not unduly deplete his or her resources. If the goal is proscribed by norms (illegitimate), this has to be counted as a cost, causing anxiety or potential loss of ego strength. In addition, in social interaction with one or more additional persons, the actor must assess the future actions of the other individual. The fact that these actions are guided by norms helps in this prediction.

Boundaries

The social processes of boundary formation, maintenance, and alteration are crucial not only to the ongoing societal system but to the organizational subsystems as well. Boundaries for the larger society have been discussed at some length already, here organizational boundaries are discussed.

Although, in social theory as a whole, the literature on boundaries is terribly fragmented, there has been greater systematic attention to boundaries in the organizational literature, with some declarations of their great importance. For example, in discussing leadership, Gilmore says that "Leadership is centrally concerned with the management of boundaries" (1982, p. 343). However, he notes two distinct views of boundaries in the extant organizational literature (Gilmore 1982, pp. 343–44). Katz and Kahn's (1978) open systems theory takes the boundary as essentially a given, and concentrates on the analysis of flows across the open boundary, rather than how boundaries are formed. In contrast, other theorists stress that boundaries are socially constructed rather than discovered as "givens" (Gilmore 1982, p. 344).

This issue is in part just one way of questioning whether boundaries are independent variables (givens) that constrain human action and serve as both barriers and buffers that must be dealt with; or whether boundaries are in fact dependent variables that social groups construct and utilize. Gilmore views the issue of whether boundaries are taken versus given as a "figure-ground reversal. Rather than examine flows across an assumed boundary, we are looking explicitly at the boundary and the politics of its social construction" (p. 344).

The problem of which was first, the boundary or the organization, is once again largely a false dilemma when viewed from the larger perspective of a holistic, diachronic model rather than from the perspective of two divergent middle-range theories. As mentioned earlier, boundaries serve both as independent and dependent variables. Concrete human groups construct bound-aries and then in turn are constrained and affected by them.

Boundary Formation

There is no question that boundaries are socially constructed; this is not even an issue. The concern here is with the specifics of this construction. Examination of the matter in greater detail shows that there are at least three types of organizational boundaries:
1. The actual physical boundaries of the physical plant occupied by the organization.
2. The bounding characteristics of the members of the organization.
3. The territorial limits or "outreach" of organizational operations (e.g., the limits of a salesperson's territory).

It has been stressed that SET regards the society as a concrete system in Miller's (1978) terms. In a concrete system, the units of analysis are individu-als or aggregates of individuals.. These individuals interact in physical space and time and within societal boundaries. Such boundaries are physical but are socially constructed and socially significant. Organizations are concrete sys-tems as well and have socially significant physical boundaries surrounding their "physical plants" or "headquarters." Of course, there can be myriad sub-boundaries within the outside walls.

The external boundaries are entropy breaks that may divide rather se-verely different entropy levels; that is, entropy levels inside the organizational boundaries may be much lower or higher that in the external environment beyond. Klapp (1975) speaks in terms of controlling boundaries in order to, among other things, restrict the entry of entropy into the system. Generally, the problem is the reverse. Boundaries must be manipulated in order to bring energy and information (negentropy) into the system, to combat the internal increase of entropy. At one time, information was primarily conveyed on markers (X'') such as paper, and thus entered through physical openings in systems boundaries (e.g., mail deliveries through doors), as does matter-energy. Increasingly, information can be conveyed alternatively either through physical conduits such as telephone lines or computer "hardwire" or through sound waves. *Ceteris paribus*, the lower the ratio of internal entropy to exter-nal entropy, the greater is the task of boundary maintenance. Miller (1978) shows in detail the mechanisms groups use to maintain themselves.

Physical boundaries may be established by group members when the or-ganization is begun, even though no boundaries existed previously. Another common pattern is for organizations to succeed prior organizations and to adopt their boundaries, perhaps with some alterations. Regardless of whether the organization has initiated new boundaries or adopted old ones, boundaries are constantly monitored and controlled by organizational members and may be altered (e.g., expanded or contracted) to meet various needs. Keep in mind that a physical boundary is the perimeter of spatial area (S). As stressed repeatedly, (S) is highly correlated with the other five globals. Further, the six globals for any given organization are subsets of the globals for the entire society in which the organization resides.

Thus, each organization has its own set of six globals and its own five mutable distributions, in addition, of course, to the particular set of immutable characteristics possessed by organizational members. Thus, it is important to remember that boundary formation and maintenance of the global property (S) is not an isolated process but is closely constrained by levels of the other five globals (P, I, T, O, L), and four mutable distributions (I, T, O, L), depending upon the specific degree of correlation among these variables that exists empirically in the organization. Also remember that, as a subset of the global and mutable distributions for the host society, the organization's globals and mutable distributions are constrained by those of the larger society. Thus, changes in the six global levels or the five mutable distributions in the society at large can affect the six globals and five mutables for the organization, including boundary placement.

In summary, then, placement of the organization's physical boundaries is determined by its level of living (L), or the resources available for boundary construction and maintenance, by the technology (T) utilized by the organization; by the population size of the organization (P); by the number and type of organizational positions, including the hierarchical arrangement (O); and by the type of information (I) to be utilized and processed by the organization. For example, an organization that processes top secret information (I) or utilizes sophisticated and delicate technology (T) may require different boundaries than an organization with low energy or information levels and unsophisticated technology. Note that an organization with advanced technology and secret information may require not *only* more secure boundaries but also greater inputs of information and matter-energy into the system to meet its technological (T) and informational (I) requirements. This means that the boundary must be capable of control so that persons maintaining it can alternatively close it very tightly (e.g., to maintain secrecy) but alternatively must open it very efficiently (e.g., to admit energy or information). Computerization complicates the task of information control as unauthorized persons are able to gain access to information banks. One way to deal with this is to open the system's boundaries to information transmission but to code the information during transmission. Although neither the sender nor the receiver reads the code, the person attempting to break boundaries must. The scrambled message appears highly entropic to the transgressor, while it has low entropy value (high information value) to the sender and receiver. Thus, computer technology (T) and information coding (I) allow organizations to have open boundaries for information while they appear closed to intruders.

Membership Boundaries

One major problem for information and energy control at organizational physical boundaries is that information and energy processing technologies are often quite cumulative, thus exacerbating control problems. For example, although a new generation of information-carrying markers such as computer terminals (X'') may quickly render an older terminal obsolete, it probably will not hasten the demise of alternative traditional markers, such as paper (X''), and may even exacerbate the paper problem, since the information on the terminal (itself accessible to thieves) can be printed onto paper. Thus, modern organizations may not only have the new problem of preventing information theft from computers, they still need paper shredders (maybe more than ever). Further, this technological accumulation may be exacerbated by increases in population size (P) of the organization. In any case, there is always a continuing problem of monitoring physical boundaries so that only the proper persons (members and "official visitors") gain entry.

Physical entry by nonmembers may be buffered by a number of factors. One may be the existing norms that proscribe entry to a building for nonmembers. Another is physical buffers such as large grounds surrounding the building, lack of nonmember parking, locked parking areas, and so forth. Further, nonmembers may lack information on entrance routes, entry codes, and so on. It is often crucial that organizations find some manner of closing their boundaries to nonmembers, who can harm organizations in many ways: they can deplete resources, steal information, or damage surroundings. Also, as those in the study of social research are acutely aware, outsiders can affect group functioning and cause reactivity (Bailey 1982a).

There may be some empirically occurring groups (X') that are monothetic, meaning that all members have identical characteristics. In such a case it might be relatively easy to distinguish members from nonmembers. However, as already noted, such monothetic groups are rare or nonexistent. Most groups are polythetic and have an array of characteristics displayed by members. Organizations that are not fully polythetic are thus monothetic on one or more variables. Often these are immutable characteristics such as age, sex, or race. Thus, a men's club or women's gymnasium can bar persons who clearly do not possess the correct immutable characteristic, and a young person can be refused admittance to a senior citizen's club. However, because most organizations are polythetic (if not fully so), the gatekeepers often cannot determine membership *solely* by the observation of immutable characteristics. Further, membership is often based on mutable characteristics, and as observed, these are generally not visible in interaction. Thus, boundary guardians have to utilize some form of marker (X'') to indicate membership status. This may be some form of employee identification card or something worn by the members, such as a badge or uniform (e.g., a white laboratory coat).

How does a nonmember become a member? Organizational membership is an achieved (mutable) characteristic of the person. Allocation into a particular organization is merely a "local" instance of the general process of allocation into the (O) distribution discussed in detail in Chapter 5. To recapitulate, the power holder for the organization has particular goals and expectations for the organization (based on the five mutables of the organization and perhaps on his or her own immutable and mutable characteristics) and has particular expectations (X) of the applicant desired (X'). The applicant also has expectations (X) of the particular position (X') desired (based upon the applicant's immutable and mutable characteristics, including residence, past experience, etc.). If the expectations of the employer (X) and the applicant (X) are sufficiently isomorphic, then the applicant is deemed to be "qualified" or "acceptable" for admission. He or she then receives particular markers (X'') such as identification cards or uniforms that allow members to pass through organizational boundaries.

Occasionally there are instances of forced membership, where some entity more powerful than the organizational power holders forces the extension of membership to a certain person or persons. Generally, the only entity powerful enough to accomplish this is some government body, and such forced membership and promotion is on the basis of immutables (age, race, or gender). Other instances of mandated entry in which the entrants do not become full members, but do cross organizational boundaries, are various government inspections (health, safety, etc.) or evaluations required in government programs. Evaluation researchers may find that the organization admits them because it is required to, but that various internal boundaries are faced even after admittance. Whether entrance is forced or not, a person who crosses external boundaries will often be faced with myriad internal boundaries, particularly in hierarchical organizations, with the vital information often far away from external boundaries and securely within layers of internal boundaries.

Members also exit. Exit may be quick if the expectations (X) of either the new member or the power holder are not fulfilled, or if information concerning mutable or immutable characteristics that the applicant had mapped onto some marker such as a resume (X'') cannot be confirmed through checks with other markers, such as diplomas. To exit, the member must relinquish membership status and all markers (X''), such as identification cards or uniforms, and all technology (keys, company car) that allow him or her to cross boundaries.

Outreach

The third type of boundary that organizations maintain is generally overlooked in the literature, probably because it is often not a continuous demarcation. This is the "outreach" or the extent to which the organization has relationships in the environment outside of its physical boundaries. Examples include sales territories, leases for extraction of raw materials, and so on.

Summary

We must remember that *all* organizational boundary operation (including boundary formation, monitoring, maintenance, and control) is concerned with spatial area (S) and thus is correlated with the other four mutables (I, T, O, L) for the given organization. This applies to boundaries of all three types: physical, membership, and "outreach." For example, an increase in the number of organizational positions (O) may necessitate larger boundaries. Also, special kinds of technology (T) may require special boundaries. Even information (I) may require special boundaries if it is extremely sensitive and requires extra protection. However, boundary construction and maintenance requires expenditure of money (L). An organization with special boundary requirements because of special needs regarding its organizational positions (O), its information (I), or its technology (T) may have funds (L) to maintain only minimally adequate boundaries, while an organization with minimal capital outlays (L) for (O), (T), and (I) may be able to afford to enlarge its boundaries (S).

Bear in mind also that many SAH organizations (sequentially and agglomeratively formed, with hierarchical structure) have numerous inner partitions and subpartitions. Although "horizontal" organizational positions may utilize minimal subboundaries such as partitions or curtains, or even the classic "open office," hierarchical positions are generally marked by boundaries. The highest offices may encompass a large inner spatial area (S), where boundaries are secure and strongly protected; for example, by gatekeepers such as receptionists and security guards or by electronic surveillance (T). Generally, the highest office and the most sensitive information will be located at an inner point far from external boundaries, so that intruders can encroach only by penetrating several layers of inner boundaries.

Entropy and Information in Organizations

Organizations are open systems (Bertalanffy 1968; Katz and Kahn 1978; Klapp 1975). As such, they are not bound by the perpetual increase in entropy dictated by the second law of thermodynamics. Rather, power holders in the organizations (such as the president, board of directors) set certain goals and work to achieve them. These goals are generally to maximize profit (L). Other globals possessed by the organization may serve as goals also, particularly if this can be done without too great a sacrifice of capital (L). Thus, acquisition of the latest-generation computer (T) may really not be necessary for information processing (I) but may add prestige to the organization.

The attainment of organizational goals is achieved through processing of information and matter-energy. Some organizations process raw materials; others are service organizations, perhaps dealing only with information (e.g., computer software). In any case, even with "self-help" organizations, information and matter-energy must be processed to some degree in order to maintain organizational structure and functioning (entropy levels safely below the maximum).

Obviously sufficient supplies of matter-energy must be brought into the organization to ensure healthful working conditions. This necessitates opening system boundaries to bring in heating fuel and energy for lighting as well as food for organization members. Such reduction of physical entropy necessitates maintenance of adequate levels of the six globals within the organization; deficiencies in any one could threaten the organization. For example, if capital (L) were unavailable to import fuel or raw materials, or if information (I) on how to do so efficiently were unavailable, or the population were too large (P), or the number of positions (O) were insufficient for this population, or the technology (T) utilized was inadequate for processing energy and information, or the spatial area (S) were too large to be properly maintained, then the organization would have difficulty in maintaining entropy levels sufficiently below the maximum. Any of these global deficiencies, or any combination of them, could be life-threatening for the organization, particularly if they existed for some period of time.

In analyzing an organization it is crucial to remember that the given organization is merely a subsystem, of the larger system (the society); thus, it has a share of the larger system's globals. Societal shifts in the six globals can change the levels of the six globals for the organization. This is because, as an open system, open boundaries allow the organization to lose resources as well as gain them.

When an organization forms, it sets physical boundaries (e.g., acquires a certain amount of floor space [S], perhaps 5000 square feet, with clear boundaries such as walls within the building). It then uses its capital (L) to construct positions (O)—at first these may be merely "paper positions" (X'')—to recruit persons (P) to fill these openings and to acquire information (I) and technology (T). If any of these six entities become scarce over time in the larger society, then the organization may be threatened. A societal shortage of persons (P) with the necessary information (I) to operate computers (T) could mean that these people demand more income (L) than the local organization can afford, and thus they will migrate to other areas (S).

Assuming that the organization's globals are properly secured at adequate resource levels, the organization then processes energy and information to achieve its particular goals, whatever they may be. This processing is done by monitoring and maintaining not only the six globals but also the five mutables at levels below maximum entropy. Such maintenance involves the processes discussed in Chapter 5 and earlier in this chapter—successful allocation of persons into positions and successful boundary maintenance, both of which involve monitoring of information on various sorts of indicators (X''). As noted in Chapter 4, power holders will generally not state their organizational goals as the maintenance of entropy levels below the maximum. Rather, they will state the goal as maximization of profit (L). But, besides closely monitoring profit (L), they will also monitor the other five organizational globals that closely affect profit (P, O, S, T, I). Thus, if profit (L) declines, power holders may change the values of the other related globals in order to restore profit. For example, they may leave positions (O) unfilled, may reduce the number of employees (P), may reduce spatial area (S) occupied by the organization, and so forth.

In addition to monitoring the six globals, organizational power holders monitor the five mutables. Again, perhaps maintenance of (L) will be their chief concern, but the four other distributions (I, S, T, O) also must be monitored, since all five are so highly intercorrelated. Although power holders will not phrase their monitoring in terms of entropy levels, the result of their actions will be maintenance of entropy below the maximum in all of the mutable distributions. That is, allocation of members (P) into (L), (I), (S), (T), and (O) is never random (maximum entropy). Power holders' allocation of personnel within the organization is not random but based on the person's mutable and immutable characteristics. Allocation into mutable distributions may not always be "optimal," just, or even "rational." It may certainly be discriminatory in some sense. However, it will never, in the long run, be random. Whereas the resulting degree of order may fall far short of minimal (zero) entropy in any given distribution or any set of five or fewer mutable distributions (conditional or joint entropy), it will not be random, and this entropy level will be below the maximum. Norms, values (I), and the resulting expectations (X) of both employers and applicants maintain order and thus reduce entropy. Entropy build-up generally occurs when power holders have lost their ability to properly monitor and control the system.

In order for organizational goals to be attained, it is crucial that adequate levels of the six globals be maintained and that organizational members (P) be allocated adequately within the five mutable distributions (S, I, T, O, L). Even if global levels are adequate, organizational functioning depends upon the proper allocation of persons into the mutables. It is not sufficient to simply have the same number of people (P) as positions (O). Rather, these people must be adequately allocated into (O) in terms of their knowledge (I), technological skills (T), and spatial placement (S), if profit (L) is to be maximized. This may entail moving Mr. Smith to the Des Moines office (S) or retraining Ms. Jones (I). Allocation is a continual process and is particularly acute when major changes are made in one of the globals, such as moving the organization itself to another geographical area (S) or changing the technology (T) utilized.

Maintenance of the mutable distributions requires rather constant monitoring. An organization is a controlled system in cybernetic terms (Kuhn 1974), meaning that key variables (in this case the globals and mutables) are monitored and maintained adequately. Control is based upon information processing. The power holder must have adequate information on all of the six global levels and five mutable distributions for the organization, and preferably for the host society as well. Further, it is not sufficient to merely possess accurate information on key variables, decision making and implementation of decisions must be adequate. It is possible to have adequate monitoring of information (e.g., accounting, personnel reports) on the six globals and five mutable distributions but still have insufficient implementation. For example, if power is divided, two power holders could make contrary decisions and effectively cancel each other's actions, with a basically entropic result.

If information and implementation of decisions based on that information is not carefully maintained, over time, maintenance of the six globals and allocation of persons into the five mutable distributions will become less orderly (more random, thus tending toward maximum entropy). Such an entropy increase, if allowed to continue, could jeopardize organizational operations.

This emphasis on monitoring and control within social systems was neglected (or perhaps taken for granted) in functionalism, and this was one of the chief reasons that functional models often appeared deterministic and tautological. Systems do not just "take care of themselves" and do not merely "respond to economic factors (L)" or "respond to population pressures (P)." In fact, intermediate and smaller size organizations are very vulnerable to societywide shifts in the six globals and five mutables. Such shifts can occur quickly and can quickly affect the mutable distributions, largely because systems boundaries open in both directions. The six globals must be constantly resupplied as they are consumed. Further, not only finished products but also personnel can exit systems boundaries. The opening of a new plant in another geographical area (S) by a competitor who is paying higher salaries (L) could quickly decimate the population (P) of persons with certain necessary knowledge (I) and necessary technological capabilities (T), leaving the organizational positions (O) of the first organization in shambles. Such a condition must be quickly responded to, and this requires continual information processing. Thus, the real situation is one of potentially rapid change (even in technology $[T]$) at any given time—quite a contrast from the picture of "equilibrium" painted by functionalists. Readers of some functionalist models might think that power holders could simply "sleep" and that constant monitoring was not really needed, because if the system's equilibrium were disturbed it would quickly return. The fact is that if "equilibrium is disturbed" in a small or vulnerable organization, the organization can be out of business (i.e., experience maximum entropy or the "ultimate equilibration") in a very short time.

Thus, it is important to emphasize that *continual monitoring and processing of information regarding the six globals and five mutable distributions is necessary for the maintenance of adequate levels of these variables within the organization.* Therefore, information is an important commodity. This does not imply that information is always used efficiently to attain group goals. Further, information control has other uses than the attainment of organizational goals. It can be used by power holders within the organization to pursue their personal goals, even if contrary to organizational goals. Also, information control is a powerful implement of social control. It can be used to allocate personnel within the organization so as to maintain morale (X) and regulate expectations (X). Employees who are currently satisfied with their status within the organization might not be if they had access to certain information. Power holders can utilize the hierarchical structure of the system, their control of external and internal boundaries, their control of information processing technology, and their control of information processing personnel to determine how information is utilized.

Multiple Membership

Throughout this book, it has been stressed that the organizational mutable positions (O) of the society exist, sui generis, independent of the society's population (P). Thus, an organizational position can survive a whole series of incumbents, who are allocated to the position and subsequently leave for a variety of reasons (e.g., death, failure of the position to live up to expectations, change of residence). Conversely, organizations sometimes do not survive the life-span of their members. An organization can become defunct because of technological changes (T), loss of money by the power holder (L), or even because the power holder makes a large profit (L) and decides to liquidate the organization and retire.

Not only are organizational positions independent of their incumbents, but a given person can hold multiple membership, both sequentially and simultaneously. Often membership in one organization can lead to membership in others at similar levels. In such a case it is quite possible for an individual to cross organizational boundaries without any radical change of position in the levels of the six globals and five mutables that provide the context for his or her action. For example, Mr. Smith, who is the president of company A, leaves his company's headquarters en route to another city. At the airport he waits in the VIP lounge and upon arrival at his destination city, stays at a private club. The next day he leaves the club for the headquarters of company B, where he serves on the board of directors. Although the individual has changed spatial area (S) and crossed several organizational boundaries, the organizations traversed all had similar levels of the six globals and five mutable distributions and thus occupied similar positions in the societal set of six globals and five mutables that forms their larger context. Further, these global and mutable levels are all similar to the individual's position in the mutable distributions in his home organization and in society at large. Thus, even though he crosses organizational boundaries, he has little need to drastically alter his expectations (X) of his surroundings and of the sort of individuals he will interact with and their expectations (X) of him.

This, of course, is not always the case when one crosses organizational boundaries or has multiple memberships. A person who holds high positions in the mutable distributions within a given organization can experience what amounts to virtual disenfranchisement merely by crossing organizational boundaries. An executive in a corporation can, merely by crossing organizational boundaries (S), leave the prestige of his or her position (O), lose access to company technology (T), lose use of classified information (I), and lose economic benefits such as company food, beverages, and supplies (L). It is possible for a person who commands a great deal of respect within the organization to become a "faceless" individual merely by crossing boundaries. Essentially, what often happens is that a person's position in the five mutables is recognized by others within organizational boundaries, with or without the aid of internal boundaries (which separate executives from others), or markers such as identification cards or door plaques.

Often by merely crossing the physical organization boundary and going "out on the street," one loses reliance on the mutable characteristics in social interaction. Secondary interactions among strangers may not be based on mutables but primarily upon immutables. This does not mean that the mutables will not become important if a sustained interaction is generated with strangers. During the course of interaction, all parties can establish their positions in the mutables through the use of markers (X''), such as business cards, certification by third parties, and so on. It only means that interactions on different sides of the organizational boundary will begin from different social contexts. Within the organization, initial interaction and the expectations of interacting others are influenced by the particular holistic pattern of mutable variables possessed by the person (e.g., vice-president of sales). Outside of the boundaries, the person's position in the mutables is unknown (save for clues from dress, indicating wealth [L], or speech, indicating education [I], etc.), and so the interaction proceeds from initial emphasis on the person's configuration of immutable characteristics. Inside the organizational boundaries the person is initially the vice-president. Outside the boundaries, he is initially a middle-aged white man, five feet, ten inches tall, black hair, blue eyes, weight, 165 pounds.

A sudden switch from interaction relying upon mutables, with one actor high on all mutables, to interaction where mutables are not salient and all expectations and action are based upon immutables can be potentially quite anomic for the displaced person, as he or she is essentailly declassified. What was recently a major source of power is now not useful in interaction. Rather, immutable characteristics are now central, and the individual who sufffers from a sudden loss of power faces the added frustration of inability to change the situation, as the immutables by definition cannot be changed. The individual may have the same self-concept and the same expectations but now may be treated very differently by other persons in the course of social interaction.

The declassification problem may be particularly acute if the individual not only exits the boundary of the organization where he or she had high position on the mutables (and thus had power in interaction) but also crosses another boundary *into* an organization where his or her mutable characteristics are not visible, but where his or her highly visible immutable characteristics do not meet the membership standards of the new organization. Thus, the white male executive who only hours before enjoyed power and deference may merely, by crossing the boundaries of a women's club or a racially segregated bar (of another race), find himself the subject of contempt and maltreatment. Since his immutable characteristics are the source of the problem and since they cannot be altered, he has little recourse except to quickly exit the organizational boundaries.

If the nonmember does not quickly exit the unfamiliar organization and if interaction is sufficiently friendly that it can be sustained, persons will in time determine the mutable characteristics of each other. Strangers will often ask, "What do you do (O)?" followed by "Where do you live (S)?" Further interaction leads to subsequent determination of the other mutables: education (I), technology (T), income (L). Thus, finding oneself declassified, and one's position in the mutable distributions unknown to the other parties in the interaction, one can establish one's position through extended interaction. A less strenuous and less anxiety-producing circumstance ensues from simply avoiding such rapid reclassification, which puts one in hostile social situations with potential danger or at least with potential anxiety. Such reclassification is avoided by avoiding multiple group memberships that have conflicting demands (e.g., such as joining a temperance group and a wine-tasting group at the same time). Minimally, many persons will be in at least two different interaction situations—at work and at home. If these are similar in terms of the mutables and are occupied by persons with similar mutable characteristics, then boundary crossing will necessitate minimal readjustment and minimal change in interaction.

Concluding Remarks

The extended discussion of the globals, mutables, and immutables in Chapters 4 and 5, plus the discussion of organizations in this chapter, provide ample evidence that operations within social systems are not random but show a substantial amount of order. For example, the form of a particular mutable distribution is not randomly determined but is a function of the level of the six globals and the other four mutable distributions, among other things. Similarly, allocation of persons into positions in the mutable distributions is not random but is a function of the person's mutable and immutable characteristics, as well as a function of particular levels of the globals and mutables. Nor is the existence of organizational boundaries random. Boundaries determine the size of (S) and so are a function of the six globals and the other four mutables. In addition, the borders are maintained only through constant monitoring and care.

Thus, evidence for the existence of nonrandom processes is overwhelming. The task in Chapter 7 is to analyze the nature of these nonrandom processes in detail. The central problem of social order will be discussed, with considerable attention given to the attendant concepts of power and conflict.

Chapter 7

The Central Problem of Social Order

Introduction

This chapter is concerned with the central problems—social order—and its attendant concerns—power and conflict. In order to discuss the problem of social order we will need to draw upon most of the concepts discussed in the first six chapters.

Social Order

At least since Hobbes, sociologists and others have been preoccupied with the notion of social order and the question of how societies cohere. However, for the most part, these discussions have yielded few, if any, definitive results. One reason for this is that *order* generally is not clearly defined and certainly not operationalized. Often, the unit of analysis (the society) is not rigorously defined, and this is certainly a prerequisite to any discussion of its properties (such as order). *Order* has been discussed with a large number of adjectives. It is common to see discussions of social order, political order, cultural order, religious order, and so on. Such middle-range verbal discussions generally lack operationalization; and, it is often unclear how these various types of *order* relate to each other. If we were to assume some rather consistent order that persisted over time and returned if disturbed, such as the functionalists' equilibrium, then we might have less need to be precise about the nature of order. However, since we choose to eschew reliance on the concept of equilibrium for reasons discussed in detail in earlier chapters, the concept of order is much more central and problematic and thus cannot be taken for granted or considered a given.

Here the concern is not with relatively narrow conceptions, such as political order, philosophical order, or cultural order. The concept of order here differs from the usual concept of *order* in at least two ways:

1. Order in terms of SET is not a constant value, or absolute, but a matter of degree and empirically variable from system to system and within one system over time.
2. Order is not merely an abstract concept but refers to the position of persons in the mutable distributions. Thus, it is a much more structural and materialistic concept than is generally discussed.

One can easily make the notion of order much more rigorous than it has generally been in verbal analyses in sociology, simply by looking to the statistical meaning of the term. As will be shown in Chapter 8, measures of association or of correlation assess the degree of order. Order in this sense is the degree of departure from randomness (maximum entropy). When order is defined thus, the H measure discussed in Chapter 4 serves as a convenient and adequate (if not sophisticated) operationalization.

Thus, the generic notion of order is simple enough—order is departure from randomness. This is consistent with the work of Parsons (see Parsons and Shils 1951, p. 107), and with verbal formulations generally, and is also consistent with the statistical operationalizations to be discussed in Chapter 8. Applying this definition to various middle-range concerns, political order can be seen as a departure from randomness in political affairs, religious order as a departure from randomness in religious affairs, and social order, generically, as a departure from randomness in all social affairs. However, such definitions are still disquietingly vague and not very useful. Unfortunately, this is the level of many discussions of social order.

It is clear, however, that this definition (lack of randomness) is central to any discussion of order. Regardless of its area of application or its vagueness, virtually any notion of social order will encompass the notion of lack of randomness. Subsequently, departure from randomness affords the possibility of predictability with regard to a system state, also a key notion of order as generically defined.

At this point it is easy for the discussion of order to break down without the introduction of additional analytical distinctions and their attendant complexity. For example, suppose that we all agree that order constitutes departure from randomness. Several questions arise. Specifically, exactly *what* is departing from randomness, and exactly what does it mean to say that this something is departing from randomness? Also, does the existence of order mean lack of conflict, or does the existence of conflict signal lack of order (e.g., randomness)? This is precisely the point where functional equilibrium theorists encountered problems. They spoke of order in a dichotomous fashion (as with equilibrium), as either existing or not existing. Order was thus an absolute rather than a matter of degree. This conception led to theoretical difficulties of large magnitude. Equilibrium theorists will vitrually never conceive of a society where order does not exist. However, if it does exist, can conflict also exist? There is really not much room for conflict in such a model, except at a very low level or as a short-term occurrence before equilibrium is reestablished.

The discussion of order can be clarified considerably through a holistic approach using the several distinctions introduced earlier. The confusion concerning the relationship between order and conflict can be clarified immediately, and this is crucial. If one clings to the absolute model of order, then a dilemma immediately arises. This order model will immediately be criticized by conflict theorists. More fundamentally, it will be obviously contradicted by any of the many cases of conflict (such as war) that can usually be observed around the world at any given point in time. On the other hand, the recognition of conflict as a long-term ocurrence in a society would threaten the dichotomous (exists or does not exist) order model. To some adherents of the dichotomous model, this concept would threaten the whole foundation of social science, for if order does not exist, how can societies exist?

The conflict ends when one recognizes that order is not a dichotomous absolute that a society either possesses or does not but merely a matter of degree. *All* societies identifiable as such possess some degree of order, virtually by definition. On the other hand, many (if not all) societies exhibit some degree of conflict at any given point in time, some a rather high degree. Furthermore, this conflict can be a persisting condition and not merely a brief occurrence before equilibrium is reestablished.

Thus, it is axiomatic in SET that all societies have some degree of order; that is, they display H values below maximum entropy (randomness). However, this degree of order generally will not be maximum (minimum entropy or an H value of (0). Further, the degree of order can remain relatively constant over time, but it need not. It may fluctuate somewhat over time.

At this point, attention can turn to the difficult analysis concerning the relationship of order to conflict. This has been a particularly troublesome area for functionalism, as seen earlier. Order has been defined as the departure from randomness, and that this definition is consistent with both verbal theory and statistics. Further, this definition seems to be minimally adequate and allows us the notion of predictability, also a feature of both verbal and statistical discussions. However, when the anlaysis turns to conflict, the congruence between verbal and statistical discussions ends. Although the relation of conflict to order is a central area of concern in verbal theory, it is not an issue in statistical discussions of order, and in fact, the concept of conflict is not found in statistics. Thus, the question for this model is whether it can accomodate the study of conflict, if indeed the model has a basic compatibility with statistical notions that do not study conflict. The answer is yes, but this issue can only be clarified by introducing further analytical distinctions.

The next question concerns the relationship of conflict to the notion of order. Specifically, can conflict and order exist in the same society? The answer is clearly yes. The next question is whether conflict and order are inversely related; that is, does high conflict indicate low order, and does low conflict indicate high order? This question is more complex and at this point, the usual verbal discussion becomes insufficient. There is clearly some relationship between order (defined as departure from randomness) and conflict, but it is not a perfect relationship. Complete lack of social order (randomness), though rarely if ever found, would not necessarily indicate a high degree of conflict. A high degree of conflict could of course be one way that a condition approaching randomness could occur, and a very high degree of conflict would hardly be conducive to a low-entropy society. On the other hand, one could conceive of other conditions, such as a complete lack of norms (anomia), that could result in randomness. Although such an anomic situation might foster conflict, if would not necessitate it. *Thus, theoretically, conflict is a sufficient but not necessary cause of lack of order.*

Bear in mind, however, that conflict, like order, is not absolute but a matter of degree. A low degree of conflict would not likely result in maximum entropy, unless accompanied by other conditions (such as normlessness). A very high degree of conflict could result in maximum entropy (complete lack of order), but it is not the only way that such lack of order could occur (normlessness, for example, could also cause it). At the other extreme, complete order (minimum entropy or an H value of zero) could probably not occur with a high degree of conflict, but it might exist with a low degree of conflict. However, at extreme levels this discussion is academic, as complete order (minimum entropy or H of zero) and complete disorder (maximum entropy or H of log K) will virtually never occur empirically, although they may be approximated. The average case displays some degree of order intermediate to maximum and minimum entropy. This can occur with or without conflict, although conflict will also often be present to some degree.

Our discussion to this point is somewhat more rigorous than many discussions of order and conflict but is still overly vague. Further, we still have not answered the question of why conflict is an issue in the verbal analysis of order but not in the statistical, although verbal and the statistical conceptions share the same generic notion of order as departure from randomness. Although this question would not arise as an issue in a middle-range theory, from a holistic perspective this is a very important issue indeed, as it arises from an important distinction. Why, indeed, have only verbal order-theorists discussed conflict? The answer is clear enough. It is because generally *only ver-*

bal theorists have discussed social order in terms of relationships between individuals. Recalling the earlier discussion, relationships between concrete individuals are a form a Q-analysis. On the other hand, the statistical notion of order is generally concerned with order in terms of relationships between variables (R-analysis). Conflict is only defined in terms of relationships between actors (Q-analysis), as variables (R-analysis) do not fight one another.

Two Types of Order

The significance of this discussion is that it reveals that order is not a unitary concept as has often been assumed. Rather, it involves two conceptually and empirically distinct though highly related aspects, which can be conceived of as two types of order: *order among persons* (order in social interaction) and *order among variables*. The statistical literature in sociology has been concerned almost exclusively with the latter (R-analysis). The verbal conception of order is sufficiently broad to include both types of order, but these have not been consistently distinguished, which has led to confusion and ambiguity in verbal analyses. These two types of order are highly interrelated. Order in interaction among persons leads to order among social variables, such as the mutables and immutables. But causation is not one way (from actor order to variable order only), it also proceeds in the other direction in the sense that a pattern of order among variables (which was produced by action at an earlier time) serves as a symbolic guide to future human action, thus serving to order it.

Therefore, in order to understand the central problem of social order, it is necessary to understand the *Q-R* distinction and that there are two interrelated types of order:

1. *Diachronic or process order* in the actions of concrete individual actors, acting over time, within the limits of the concrete social system.
2. *Synchronic order* among variables, which is a product of past actor process order, but which also serves to pattern future order by actors.

Q- and R-Relationships

The two types of order (actor order and attribute order) are based upon two types of relationships (respectively, relationships among human actors and relationships among attributes). The *Q-R* distinction, as an analytical distinction, has been widely studied and applied in statistics and research methods (for example, see Bailey 1972). However, the fact that two types of relationships (actor and variable) exist and that two corresponding types of order (actor and variable) exist has not been consistently distinguished and maintained by verbal theorists. This is not a minor point but can be a major point of confusion. Without this distinction, theorists may sometimes be discussing one type of relationship or order and sometimes another, without realizing that the focus has changed. This unwitting shift from one sort of relationship to another is similar to the problem of "displacement of scope" discussed earlier. This displacement problem must be solved if order theory is to be successful. If displacement occurs, the subsequent confusion will preclude adequate order theory.

However, simply because relationships between actors and relationships between their variables must be kept analytically distinct, this does not imply a connection between them. There is a definite and crucial connection, and understanding of this connection is fundamental to the understanding of social order. In one sense, the object (in this case human actors) relationships and variable relationships are two sides of the same coin. The link between Q-relationships and R-relationships is easiest to understand for the synchronic case as shown in Table 7.1. Table 7.1 portrays the familiar S (score) or data matrix, showing a sample of objects (listed in the rows) and a set of variables to be measured for each object (shown in the columns). Correlations of pairs of columns (as is usually done in sociology) yield R-correlations. Merely transposing the matrix and correlating pairs of rows instead of pairs of columns results in a set of Q-correlations, or correlations among objects (persons). The salient point here is that although there are two types of relationships (Q and R) and thus two types of order (Q-order and R-order), there is only *one set of data (numbers in the interior of the table) from which these relationships are computed.*

Table 7.1
The Score (S) Matrix of Objects and Variables

Objects	1	2	3				N
Jim	$Score_{11}$	$Score_{12}$	$Score_{13}$	•	•	•	$Score_{1N}$
Bill	$Score_{21}$	$Score_{22}$	$Score_{23}$	•	•	•	$Score_{2N}$
Jane	$Score_{31}$	$Score_{32}$	$Score_{33}$	•	•	•	$Score_{3N}$
•	•	•	•	•	•	•	•
•	•	•	•	•	•	•	•
•	•	•	•	•	•	•	•
O	$Score_{O1}$	$Score_{O2}$	$Score_{O3}$	•	•	•	$Score_{ON}$

How is it possible that two types of relationships can be computed from one set of data? This is because Q-analysis represents the P-facet in Guttman's (1959) terms and R-analysis represents the I-facet. Both are in a sense alternative views of the same thing because each person (listed in the rows) *possesses* a set of attributes, characteristics, or variables (listed in the columns). Thus, each person is represented by an array of scores on each variable (looking across the row). Conversely, each variable can be represented by its scores across the sample of persons (looking down the column). Note that Table 7.1 represents only one of several alternative means of portraying the connection between persons and their attributes. This is discussed in more detail in Chapter 8. Both the Q- and R-relationships that can be computed from Table 7.1 are synchronic relationships; that is, they are "cross-sectional" or static relationships. A high Q-correlation among two persons shows a "relationship" in terms of their similarity on the variables listed in the columns. It is not an "action" or dynamic relationship, in which the two actors participate. Such dynamic processes are fundamental to understanding social order, and attention is now turned to them.

To sketch a holistic model of social order, virtually all of the previous distinctions utilized in this book must be incorporated. For example, the model must begin with the notion of a concrete system but show how an abstracted system is derived by the concrete actors. It must utilize the three-level model consisting of the conceptual level (X), the empirical level (X'), and the indicator level (X''), as this is used extensively in maintaining social order. The notions of global variables, mutable distributions, and immutable characteristics must also be included, and it must incorporate the discussions of allocation theory and expectation theory, which show how persons are allocated into positions in the mutable distributions. Lastly, in the course of the holistic discussion, it will be necessary to examine in greater detail how and why individuals are categorized and labeled by society, in order to control them so that orderly actions will result. Also, power and conflict will be given a separate section. The holistic model may be seen overly complex by some, who may prefer to confine their attention to a single dimension (e.g., the mutables) rather than combining them all. On the contrary, the combined holistic model (X'') is not overly complex but remains overly simplistic, as it still is not as complex as the society (X') being analyzed and thus not completely isomorphic with it. Further, although these elements have already been discussed separately in various chapters, they have not yet been adequately combined, so the central problem of social order has not been analyzed as well as the model is capable of. Attention now turns to the holistic model.

The Holistic Model of Social Order

All of the elements just reviewed (the three levels, the globals, mutables, and immutables, etc.) are constantly in force in the living society and are intertwined in various complex fashions. Thus, a model can only touch the surface. However, this surface must be touched in order to provide a foundation for more complex analysis.

Analysis of the central problem of social order begins with a description of the elements common (but empirically variable) in every society. Every society is a concrete system composed of a population of P individuals. The society has political borders that are monitored and maintained. They are regulated (alternatively opened and closed to some degree) to control the flow of matter-energy and information, including the flow of individuals. Every society, in addition to the global properties of population size (P) and space (S), has global properties of level of living (L), information (I), technology (T), and organization (O). Its members also possess numerous immutable characteristics, many of which are essentially biological and generic to all societies (e.g., skin color and sex). However, societies may vary in which immutables are socially salient and thus are categorized and monitored.

The mutable distributions form the chief context for the central problem of social order. The central problem is for the society to allocate its persons into the mutables in some orderly fashion—ideally, in the optimal fashion—however, this is difficult. For one thing, the form of the mutable distributions is constrained by the level of the globals and by the levels of other mutables. Thus, it would be nice to allocate everyone into a position of wealth on the level of living (L) mutable distribution. However, this is impossible if the global level of wealth is too small (L) to accomodate all persons (P), for example, or if the technology (T), organization (O), or information (I) levels are insufficient to process wealth (L) available within the borders (S).

Successful allocation of persons into the mutable structure is the material foundation of social order. It is not enough for societal members to merely work or process energy and information, if they are doing so in a random or nonorderly fashion. Random work will lead toward maximum entropy and certainly will tend to lower the level of living (L), as it will expend resources without productive return. Thus, it is crucial to the society to have its members (P) organized (O) in such a way that the society's technology (T), information (I), and space (S) are used as efficiently as possible, if the level of living (L) is to be maximized.

Even if the society cannot optimally allocate persons into the mutables, it must allocate them in some manner. That is, all societies will allocate into the mutables, but some will do so more successfully than others. The society's level of living (L) depends first upon global levels, and then upon successful allocation into the mutables. A given citizen will still be poor, even if allocation is perfect, if global levels are simply insufficient to yield an adequate (L). Thus, societies with low global levels of wealth such as little oil (L), poor information resources (I), inadequate technology (T), and inadequate spatial area (S), will find it *crucial* that persons (P) be allocated efficiently into the organizational structure (O). Societies with higher resource levels may be able to afford a less efficient allocation process but certainly not random allocation.

As mentioned previously, human interactions that allocate people into the mutable distributions will generally show some degree of order. The degree will vary empirically among societies but will fluctuate between maximum entropy and minimum entropy. How is this order achieved? What constitutes "orderly allocation"? Order has been defined as the departure from randomness, but what constitutes departure from randomness? The answer is simplicity itself. By definition in SET, *orderly action is replicated action*. Simply going to work every morning is replicated action. It is orderly behavior rather than random behavior, and it thus affords predictability. In answer to the question, "What is Mary going to do at 8:00 A.M. Wednesday?" we can answer that "She is going to work."

Although this seems overly simplistic, it is really all there is to social order in the univariate case. All that is needed for action (behavior) to depart from randomness is for the same action to be replicated (repeated) over and over, *certeris paribus*. If you go to lunch at exactly 12:00 p.m. every day, your action is a perfectly adequate example of orderly action. From the perspective of SET, *generic social order is defined by the action not by its cause*. Thus, within the concrete social system, your replicated action of going to lunch at the same time is an example of orderly social action, regardless of why you replicate. Action may be replicated for many different reasons. One, of course, is adherence to a norm. If a norm says one *ought* to go to lunch at noon, then you may go because you are afraid of sanctions (even if they are mere remarks from your friends) if you deviate. Or, it may simply be long-term habit from childhood, or this might be when your boss tells you to go to lunch, or you might be afraid that you will be too hungry before dinner time if you eat earlier, and so forth.

From the standpoint of the concrete social system, the crucial element in orderly social action is that it is replicated action within the societal boundaries. The reason for this replication is somewhat secondary at this point. Doubtlessly a prime reason for replicated social action is the internalization of norms, a la Parsons, but this may not be the only reason.

Lest the reader at this point is not quite clear what going to lunch at the same time each day has to do with social order, let us look quickly at Figure 7.1. The figure shows five possible lunch times. If each time were equally likely, then lunch would be random, and the H value would be maximum, or log 5 ($H = 2.320$). This would indicate no replication, and thus no orderly action. However, in the current example, assume that Mary goes to lunch at the same time each day in the week we observe her. Thus, the H value indicates minimum entropy, as $H = 0$. This is an example of perfect orderly action. Most of the time, as we have said, H values will be in between log K and 0, meaning that orderly action exists as shown by departure from randomness (log K), but that it is not perfectly orderly (H is greater than zero).

Figure 7.1
Example of Perfectly Replicated Social Action (H = 0,)
Frequency of Lunch for Five Alternative Times.

10 A.M.	11 A.M.	12 P.M.	1 P.M.	2 P.M.
0	0	7	0	0

Although this simplistic example illustrates what orderly action is, it is not sufficiently instructive, since most orderly actions are much more complex. The action in Figure 7.1 is merely *social action*, as contrasted with *social interaction*. As defined previously, social action is action by a single individual in which he or she expends energy and information. In contrast, social interaction is between two or more persons and involves not only expenditure of energy and information by both, but generally the interchange of energy or information between them. Whereas a simple action like going to lunch basically involves only a single person and a single variable (time of the action), more important instances of orderly social interaction involve two or more persons and are often multivariate, with several variables affecting the outcome of the interaction.

Particularly, we can see that the crucial interaction in which one or more power holders allocate one or more persons into the mutable structure is generally orderly to some degree and is generally multivariate (at least, bivariate). That is, since the five mutables are all interrelated, allocation into one of them usually entails predictable values on the other four, even though the other four may not be utilized specially as criteria for the allocation. For example, orderly allocation into the organizational structure (O) involves a particular location (S), particular educational level (I), particular technology (T), and particular salary (L). Thus, even though the power holder may be allocating the person to the position solely on the basis of educational level, the fact that educational level (I) is correlated (within some range, but not perfectly) with the person's level on the other mutables will mean that they also display H values significantly above maximum entropy.

Although allocation to all five of the correlated mutables is orderly, for analytical purposes we confine ourselves to the familiar case of allocation into the organizational (O) distribution. As a simplistic example of orderly bivariate action, assume that a power holder decides that the organization needs to expand by two positions, one high ranking and one low ranking. These positions first exist solely as perceptions in the president's mind (X), who subsequently transfers them onto paper in the form of two job descriptions (X''). The task now is to find persons with the particular empirical qualities (X') needed to adequately fill these positions. Suppose that the power holder decides to hire solely on the basis of education, with high education required for the high-level position, and low education for the lower-level position. However, suppose also that a power holder in another organization were subsequently to hire a highly educated person for the low-level position and a poorly educated person for the high-level position. In this case, the second hiring phase would not have replicated the first, and there would thus be no orderly action.

A more likely scenario is that recurrent hiring in most organizations allocates highly educated persons into higher-level jobs and lower-educated persons into lower-level positions. In this case there is replication, and thus social order exists (at least in terms of process, or orderly social interaction). Such replication, or orderly interaction, over time, will result in distributions such as those shown in Figure 7.2. Panel (a) of the figure shows the criterion case of no replication or randomness. Panel (b) shows the criterion case of perfect replication, whereas panel (c) shows the more realistic case of high replication, but with some nonreplication due to some uncontrolled variation. Examples of such uncontrolled variation could include nepotism or political influence, which allowed a person with low education to gain allocation to a high-level position, or racial discrimination, which resulted in a minority person's allocation into a lower-level position despite higher education. Focusing on the pure case of Figure 7.2 (b), orderly interaction between actors can be seen to result in an orderly pattern of statistical relationship or correlation among variables. That is, if power holders hire on the basis of education, with more educated persons being allocated to higher-level positions, this will result in a relationship between the variables of education and occupation.

Again, the significance of this nexus may not be clear but understanding of the connection between actions between persons and relationships between variables is necessary to the understanding of the central problem of social order and the understanding of the operation of social system in general. This point is emphasized by SET's basic axiom of social order: *Orderly process relationships between human actors (diachronic Q-relationships), when based on specific variables, will result in orderly relationships (correlations) between these variables (synchronic R-relationships).*

Figure 7.2
Effect of Replicated Social Interaction on the Correlation between Educational Level and Job Level
(hypothetical frequencies)

	Position					Position		
	High	Low				High	Low	
Education					*Education*			
High	25	25	50		High	50	0	50
Low	25	25	50		Low	0	50	50
	50	50	100			50	50	100

(a)
No Replication
(Randomness)
(No Order)
(Maximum $H[XY]$)

(b)
Perfect Replication
(Maximum Departure
from Randomness)
(Perfect Order)
(Minimum $H[XY]$)

	Position		
	High	Low	
Education			
High	40	10	50
Low	2	48	50
	42	58	100

(c)
High Replication
(Substantial Departure
from Randomness)
(High Degree of Order)
($H[XY]$ between Maximum
and Minimum)

The nexus between human action and statistical correlation is so basic and familiar that we tend to overlook it or take it for granted. This is a mistake, as without a focus on such central connections we can never attain a truly holistic understanding of the social system. One reason that this nexus is de-emphasized is that most sociologists, particularly statistcians, think principally in terms of R-relationships. Thus, they think that high levels of one *variable* lead to high levels of another *variable*. In fact, the variables are merely characteristics that do not "touch" each other and cannot causally affect each other without a human agent. In short, as a *variable*, more education does not *cause* or even "lead to" a higher-level occupation. There will only be a relationship between two variables when they are chosen by human actors as a basis for replicated social interaction.

This may still not be sufficiently clear to those persons used to thinking in terms of higher education "leading to" a better occupation (O) or more income (L). To take a different example, assume that, over time, many organizations wish to allocate persons into two positions: automobile mechanic and secretary. If gender or variables highly correlated with it (such as type of technology utilized [T], type of education achieved [I], etc.) are not used as a basis for replication, then the conditional entropy H ($Y|X$) will be random (maximum). That is, given a person's gender, there will be no pattern of allocation. We would be very surprised to see such a condition empirically. The distribution shown in Figure 7.3 is more realistic. The figure illustrates a hypothetical example showing that gender is the basis for replication into the organization. This hypothetical case shows minimum bivariate entropy $H(XY)$ $=0$, indicating that every interaction was replicated, with no exceptions, thus yielding a perfect correlation (phi $=1.0$) between the variables of gender and occupation. Notice that at a given time the content of the replication could conceivably be reversed, so that henceforth only women were hired as mechanics and only men as secretaries. The correlation between the two variables would still be 1.0 (but with opposite signs), and bivariate joint entropy as measured by $H(XY)$ would still be minimum (0). Thus, *it is not the content of the variables that decides their degree of correlation but only the degree to which they were used in replicated interaction.* If half the companies hired women as mechanics while the other half did not, or if they alternated their hiring by gender, then replication would not exist, and order would not be present.

Category Theory

Which characteristics, variables, or attributes (various terms are used), serve as bases for orderly social interaction? The manner in which the five mutable variables, and a number of immutable personal characteristics, are used as a basis for orderly interaction has already been discussed at length. The immutable characteristics may vary from social system to social system; but, is most social systems, they are likely to include gender, skin color, and birthdate (age). Others that may be used include characteristics such as eye and hair color, physical height and weight, and physical beauty.

Figure 7.3
Example of Perfect Replication Using Gender as a Basis for
Allocation into the Occupational Distribution
(hypothetical frequencies)

Occupation
High Low

Gender

	High	Low	
Female	0	50	50
Male	50	0	50
	50	50	100

(Maximum Correlation—
Minimum Bivariate Entropy)
(Phi $= 1.0$—H[XY] $= (0.0)$

In addition to the five mutables and the basic immutables are numerous categories or labels that may be applied to people and used as a basis for orderly allocation. These are basically "achieved" or mutable characteristics. For example, a power holder, when deciding which persons to allocate from among a pool of eligibles, may apply labels to some of them such as *lazy, self-starter, aggressive, resourceful,* or *arrogant* and use these as a basis for orderly allocation. Thus, there may be a correlation between perceived "aggressiveness" and allocation to administrative position, with aggressive men being allocated to administrative positions, and passive men to lower positions. However, statistical interaction can exist, so that when gender is controlled for the relationship disappears, because women are allocated differently (passive women are allocated into higher positions than aggressive ones).

Regardless of whether the particular characteristic used for allocation is a mutable, an immutable, or merely a label (e.g., "honest") applied by the power holder, the characteristic serves as a category. As each individual has only one given value or score on a given variable, this score can always be categorized in some way, and this category is then used for allocation. Very often, even continuous or interval variables are categorized into ordinal or nominal variables. For example, for allocation purposes within the legal system, the individual's age is recorded as a score of an interval variable but is then categorized into the ordinal dichotomy of juvenile or adult for disposition of the case. Similarly, a person's educational level may be recorded only as "less than high school" or "high school or above".

Category theory is a general application of labeling theory (e.g., see Becker 1963) in which individuals are labeled in some way. This label is then used by others as a basis for their treatment of that person. Further, the person also often reacts to the label as well. Category theory is specifically concerned with the use of categories for the allocation of persons in the orderly process of social replication. As noted before, immutable characteristics provide a convenient basis for allocation because they are so visible and, since they are immutable and cannot be changed, offer nearly perfect predictability. Mutable characteristics also serve as categories and are crucial to the society. However, since they are often "invisible" in interaction, they generally must be conveyed upon markers. That is, the individual can be categorized as a college graduate only if he or she provides documentation on a marker (e.g., a college transcript or diploma).

In addition to using mutable and immutable characteristics as categories for allocation, numerous other labels can be applied. These can be used in residual cases, where for some reason the mutables and immutables are not adequate for allocation, or they can be used to supplement the mutables and immutables. For example, if a person has the immutable characteristics that the power holder desires (e.g., is a white man) but does not have the proper mutables (e.g., his education level is low), then other labels may be utilized to compensate for this lack of education (e.g., labeling him as *intelligent, ambitious,* or *capable*). Conversely, if the person has immutable characteristics that the power holder does not desire (e.g., is a black woman) but has the required mutable characteristics (e.g., a high level of education), then other category labels can be used to disqualify that applicant (e.g., *temperamental, imperious,* or *unmotivated*).

Effect of Symbolic Structure on Action

As emphasized earlier, action by individuals and interaction among two or more individuals is a direct *cause* of symbolic, or variable, order. For example, two key concepts in sociology are race (an immutable) and organization

(O) (a mutable). If we conduct a statistical analysis and find that race and occupation are correlated, we would know from the discussion that this order is the result of replicated action—race was a salient factor in interaction, so that persons of certain races were allocated to certain occupations. Further, this was not a chance or short-term occurrence but *replicated* over a long period of time in order for the relationship to be evident.

The salient point here is that the interaction that gave rise to the correlations between variables was interaction between *concrete human actors*. A key decision earlier in this book was whether to use concrete human actors as the basic components of the system (a concrete system in Miller's 1978 terms) or variables such as the social role as the basic units (an abstracted system in Miller's terms). This was a key point of contention and debate between Miller (1979) and Parsons (1979). We opted to use the concrete system, saying that its analysis was the only way to make a model that was truly holistic and sufficiently isomorphic with the functioning society. Further, we contended that the use of a concrete system would not preclude analysis of the symbolic interrelationships that are the focus of the abstracted system but would facilitate such analysis. Here, it is evident that *the relationships between variables (R-relationships) that are the focus of the abstracted system are generated by interaction among concrete actors (the focus of the concrete system). Thus, the holistic model deals with both concrete and abstracted systems and shows their nexus.*

However, the relationship between symbols and action is reciprocal and circular (and cyclical). That is, symbolized concepts are used to guide human interaction. This leads to a transformation of the synchronic symbol structure (both in terms of the concepts and their interrelationships), which leads to a transformation of concrete action in the next period, and so on. This point was illustrated earlier in the distinction between diachronic or process order (1) and synchronic order (2): human action and interaction at one point in time (1), through replication, *caused* order (correlation) between two variables (2), sex and occupation. Here process Q-order (1) causes R-order (2). However, note that the reason the replications caused order between sex and occupation was because the replicated interaction *was based upon* and guided by these concepts. Thus, the prior existence of these concepts (2) caused them to be used in the replication (1). Here the causal ordering is reversed, with R-order causing Q-order, but in different time periods. Careful reflection shows that such a cyclical process is *not* tautological but merely a long-term sequence embodying both process and product.

Human interaction during a given time period generates *both* basic concepts and their interrelationships. The basic concepts include the mutables and immutables, but also abstractions (loyalty, patriotism, etc.). These concepts

(X), whether or not they are listed in indicators (X'') or have empirical counterparts (X'), form the cultural content of information (I). This is a basic global property of the concrete society, of course. This information content (I), as stressed, is correlated with the other five globals and also is crucial to human interaction. Interaction is impossible without information transfer. A chief reason that the synchronic symbol structure affects the interaction process is because interaction is based on the actors' expectations, and these in turn are based on perception of the past synchronic symbol structure. The role of expectations is discussed in greater detail later in this chapter in the analysis of order and the three-level model and also in the analysis of power.

The basic cycle is neverending, as shown in Figure 7.4. In this process, human interaction (Q) between concrete actors is conducted in time period 1.

Figure 7.4
Relationship between the Diachronic Process of Human Interaction (Q-relationships) and the Synchronic Symbol System (R-relationships)

Human Interaction Based upon Earlier Symbolic Structure	Results in Shaping Synchronic Symbol Structure	New Phase of Human Interaction Based upon Synchronic Symbol Structure of Time 2
Time 1	Time 2	Time 3

This action is guided by information processed through earlier interaction and itself shapes the store of concepts and their interrelationships (time 2). These symbols are generally synchronic in the basic sense that they are not living, do not process energy, and cannot themselves act. However, simply because they are essentially time-invariant by nature (synchronic) does not mean that they cannot be changed. They can be changed but only by the Q-action of human actors. Thus, diachronic process leads to synchronic structure, which guides the next wave of diachronic process, which in turn shapes the synchronic symbol structure by adding some new symbols and deleting or altering some old ones. The cycle of diachronic process—synchronic structure—diachronic process, continues forever. The reciprocal process-product relationships form a social situation that has orderly properties but that can be altered over time, yielding both structure and change. That is, the synchronic symbol structure can be altered simply by altering human actions. If human action in a given time period is replicated *exactly* as it was in the prior time periods, then the same symbolic structure will result. No new concepts will be constructed, no old concepts will be deleted, and the statistical (R) relationships between existing concepts will remain the same (e.g., the correlation coefficient between sex and occupation will remain the same over time). If the actions are not replicated, then the symbol structure will be changed by these changed actions.

Conversely, if the symbol structure is not changed from time period 1 to time period 2, then action in these time periods will be guided by the same concepts (X) and will be unlikely to manifest sweeping change. If actions are changed radically without change in the symbol structure, it means that actors are using the same information differently than before. However, if the symbol structure is changed, then actions will be changed, as they are guided by processing this new information.

The result is that the symbolic R-structure does change and actions do change, but this change is generally rather slow. Replication is generally not perfect, so that perfect order (minimum H) does not result between variables. Thus, some variation in the degree of replication from one time period to another also can be expected. For example, imagine that in time period 1 persons with more education received higher positions 96 percent of the time and in period 2 only 90 percent of the time. However, in each period the majority of cases are replicated, and there is a rather high degree of order. Similarly, changes in action will result in the formation of new symbols, leaving the old ones altered in meaning or deleted; however, the entire symbol system will not be changed. If it were, random (maximum) entropy of information would result. This would be essentially an anomic situation, and there would be no basis for actions. Generally, actions will not change completely in a given time period because they are based on symbol systems that did not change very much. To see in more detail why the process changes rather slowly, we need to examine *why* actions are replicated.

Why Actions Are Replicated

Each society decides which concepts and variables to use in social interaction, and what value these will have (e.g., will a particular racial designation be utilized positively or negatively in the allocation process). Decisions to use certain attributes rather than others are made in various ways. They may be enforced by a power holder (e.g., one who does not like women or blacks and so assigns them to inferior status) or because they are consistent with a prior body of information (I), such as religious dogma. In rare cases, concepts may be consciously selected through a "rational" decision process. More likely, they will simply be "inherited" from past practice but may be altered, over time, if they do not prove efficacious or if they cause internal conflict within the society. The choice of immutable characteristics as salient concepts in social interaction may be relatively arbitrary and may be enforced by power holders. However, as part of this enforcement, power holders may enforce ideology (I) that claims a functional basis for allocating persons according to particular positions (e.g., minority group members are not sufficiently intelligent for the position, women do not have sufficient strength or "mechanical ability," etc.). As for mutables, the six globals and five mutables have already been shown to form the material base for the operation of all societies and thus *must* be utilized in day-to-day operation in order for the society to operate efficaciously and maintain (or improve) its level of living (L).

It is easy to compile a list of reasons (although probably not an exhaustive one) why actions are replicated using certain variables as a basis for replication. The basic question is why *any* actions are replicated. That is, why is there any social order? Is it really needed for societal operation? The answer is clearly yes.

To see why this is true, one needs only to holistically analyze any simple series of mundane social actions, as is easily illustrated with the five mutable distributions. As demonstrated repeatedly, the five mutables are correlated, and such correlations can arise only from replicated (orderly) action. Let us simply examine the null hypothesis of no correlation. The relationship between any two mutables (on the societal level) can be used for purposes of illustration; for example, the relationship between organizational structure (O) and technology (T). An example of no correlation would occur when, for a given occupation, the technology used was random. For example, a farmer (at a given spatial location [S] and level of living [L], with a given knowledge [I] of farming) has a rather vast array of tools (T) at his or her disposal but uses them randomly. Thus, one day a motorcycle might be used in plowing, the next day a refrigerator, the next day a laser beam, and so on. The example seems even too ludicrous to comprehend, however, the point is clear—an actor at a given position in the mutable structure cannot perform random actions. To do so means a random use of technology, random knowledge (really no useful knowledge at all), random organizational allocation, random movement within space, random boundaries, and ultimately a random (low) level of living. To put it bluntly, random action does not meet societal needs and cannot work. Random action will deplete resources with no accumlative results in terms of the mutables. The result is maximum entropy (chaos). Thus, from the standpoint of SET, orderly action has to occur. This action need not approach minimum entropy and can vary from society to society, but it must exist to some degree. The absence of orderly action precludes organization. In information theory terms this would represent zero information, and the society would effectively be attempting to operate with a zero level of knowledge or a zero level of the information global variable (I). This would effectively preclude societal operation as we know it.

Summary

To summarize the discussion of replicated action:

1. Replicated (orderly) human action leads to orderly statistical relationships between the attributes (of individuals) on which the replication was based.

2. The proportion of actions that are replicated varies from system to system and from time period to time period. In the usual case, not all actions will be relicated (this would be an H value of zero, or minimum entropy) but some will. In no case will all replication cease (maximum entropy as measured by H).

3. Some replicated action is necessary with regard to the five mutables in order to provide the correlations between them that are necessary to maintain the material existence of the society.

4. Other "nonmaterial" replication based upon considerations other than the mutables will generally exist.

5. Replicated action is generally based on more than one variable at a time, thus leading to correlations among them.

6. The bulk of replicated action in a given society is probably sustained by norms, but some replication may be the result of custom or ritual.

7. Not all replicated action is "rational" or even goal-oriented.

8. Replicated action that bases allocation into the mutables on certain immutable characteristics will produce correlations between a person's immutable characteristic and his or her position in the mutable structure (e.g., between sex and occupation).

9. The choice of immutable characteristics on which allocation into the mutable structure is based varies empirically from society to society, but these immutables generally include race, sex, and age.

10. Mutable (e.g., education) and immutable characteristics (e.g., sex) of persons are often chosen as bases for allocation into the mutables because they are deemed to be "required" for successful adaptation to the task. Often, however, it is clear that persons with a range of characteristics (e.g., both men and women) could successfully perform the required tasks and that the use of an immutable such as sex is reinforced by custom, norm, and the use of power, as it behooves power holders to maintain the status quo. Thus, in many cases it is not clear that certain immutable characteristics (e.g.,

race, sex, or age) are really necessary to occupy a certain place in the mutable distributions. However, the synchronic symbolic structure hinders rapid change in replicated action, particularly in regard to the immutables. This is one reason why not only power holders (who would obviously benefit) will favor the status quo but also people who would seem to benefit from change (such as women against the ERA). This is a complex matter and sometimes involves combinations of mutables and immutables (e.g., persons with a certain immutable characteristic such as women will be hired only if they already have higher positions in the mutable structure than do men: have more education, come from an upper-class family, etc.). Before turning to the discussion of power, conflict, and inequality, we examine the important issue of how the three levels are used to construct both types of order: orderly interaction among humans and orderly correlations among variables.

Order and the Three-Level Model

Adequate understanding of the central problem of social order requires examination of the role played by the three-level model—conceptualization (X), the empirical world (X'), and information markers (X'')—in the process of replicated action and in the storage and transmission of orderly symbolic structure that results from this orderly replicated action. As already seen, the process of replicated action, the resulting symbolic structure, and its effect on the next wave of replicated action form a continuous and permanent cycle. This cycle utilizes all three levels of the three-level model. Analysis of this process is complex and can become confusing, as each given entity has a counterpart on all three levels. For example, sex is a theoretical concept (X); it is also an actual attribute of a concrete individual (X') and can also be symbolized on a marker, such as the pages of this book (X'').

Further, decisions concerning such issues as which immutables to utilize in allocating individuals into the mutable structure can be based upon all three levels. For example, a power holder could sit alone and make decisions concerning which characteristics to use. This would be a purely cognitive process occurring solely at the conceptual level (X), although it could certainly be argued that it would be impossible without prior information concerning the other two levels. Alternatively, the power holder could initiate the decision-making process by referring to markers (X'') such as company manuals or rule books. As a third alternative, the power holder could make a "grounded" decision; that is, forego thinking about the immutables to be used (X) or reading about them (X'') until after empirical observation (X') of the population. By observing the population the power holder could make some decision in terms of the immutable characteristics (X') observed. Thus, the same decision-making process (hiring) could be initiated in any of the three levels $(X, X'', \text{ or } X')$.

Direct empirical (X') decision making is probably relatively rare, except perhaps in very small societies such as Durkheim's mechanical society or in small subgroups within a larger society. It is safe to say that most face-to-face interactions among persons (X'), such as an employer and job applicant, are preceded by information processing on either the conceptual (X) or indicator (X'') levels, or both. That is, the employer may decide the characteristics of the person to hire (X) without consulting company records (X''), or alternatively, may not have any perception (X) whatsoever of the characteristics of the person to hire until checking company regulations (X''). Once the employer has formed the expectations of the applicant's mutables (e.g., education required), and immutables (e.g., age, sex, race), either purely cognitively (X) or from the written job description (X''), these expectations are then used to seek a candidate who embodies them empirically (X') for allocation into the position.

The cyclical and permanent relationship between the process of interaction among human actors,—the resulting symbolic structure, and then the action again,—clearly is facilitated by use of the three levels, although the relationship between the process-product model and the three-level model is complex. At the very minimum, human interaction and the formation of the resulting symbolic order require use of the conceptual level for symbol formation (X) and actual action among concrete individuals at the empirical level (X'). Thus, virtually all human action, particularly orderly action, utilizes both the empirical (X') and conceptual (X) levels. It is theoretically possible to have action by one human, and perhaps even interaction between two or more humans, purely at the empirical level (X') and not directed nor informed by cognition (X). In fact, we all have seen such "mindless" acts, where the person "acts before thinking." In truth, though, most interaction at the empirical level (X') is guided by cognition (X) using various symbols, although this does not ensure that the cognition is not faulty or that the action is "rational."

Further, in complex society, a large measure of interactions, particularly in certain settings (such as within organizational boundaries) will rely at least to some degree (and often heavily) upon guidance from markers (X''). Much interaction is guided by information stored on markers (X''). Examples are numerous, with the most familiar being instructions for income tax, procedural manuals for organizations, or even books of etiquette, which list proper interaction procedures in social situations.

Since the process-product cycle of human interaction can utilize the three levels in various ways, numerous interactions are possible between the process-product cycle and the three-level model. Thus, there is no single sequence of three-level model usage but rather many sequences. For example, as noted in passing, a particular interaction sequence (say, in a given organization) could begin at the cognitive level (X), at the empirical level (X'), or at the indicator level (X''). Further, from each alternative starting point the sequence can proceed in different ways (e.g., from X to X', or from X to X' to X'', or from X to X'' to X'). Similarly, another sequence may proceed from X' to X'' to X, and still another proceeds from X'' to X to X'.

Thus, it will not be feasible to discuss all possible sequences. One familiar sequence is illustrated in Figure 7.5. This is the concept (X)—indicator

Figure 7.5
Illustration of Order and the Three-Level Model:
The Basic X–X″–X′ Sequence

New Position Conceptualized by Power-holder (X) $\rightarrow$	Position Mapped onto Markers Such as Personnel Manual and Newpaper Advertisement (X'') $\rightarrow$	Position Made an Empirical Reality with Actual Funding, Facilities, Duties, and an Incumbent (X')
(a)	(b)	(c)

(X'')—empirical level (X') sequence used very often in human interaction. This sequence was used extensively in the discussion of the allocation process in Chapter 5. In this familiar example, the sequence begins with one actor (for example, a power holder) conceptualizing (X) some goal, which is to be accomplished through the interaction process. For example, the concept (only a gleam in the actor's eye) may be a new organizational position. Perhaps, this is important to the power holder, as it realizes a long-term goal of company expansion that economic conditions previously precluded. The position is defined in terms of conceptual symbols and includes a vision of the type of person (in terms of mutable and immutable characteristics) who could fill it. The symbolic structure used to formulate this concept (X) was derived from past orderly action. That is, past action provided the symbolic structure that the actor now uses to conceptualize the position and to form expectations of mutable and immutable characteristics. These expectations (X), based as they are on the existing order, will entail certain mutable levels (e.g., a certain level of education) and probably certain correlated immutables, which are correlated with mutables in the current order and usually are expected for such a position (e.g., race, sex, age).

The next stage in the sequence is to map this new position (X) into the company's markers, in the form of a job description in the personnel manual (X''). This description probably will not be fully isomorphic with the power holder's initial expectations. Specifically, it will probably list most of the duties but not necessarily all. More important it will probably describe the minimum mutable characteristics required for the position (education, technological skills, etc.) but may not list immutable characteristics. These may remain latent but are still contained in power holder's expectations (X), as his or her past experience has shown them to be correlated with the required mutable levels. Thus, the written description (X'') and the actual conception (X) may differ somewhat. The next step is to construct another marker, a letter or advertisement (X'') that carries information concerning the nature of the position and its availability to prospective applicants. Again, some isomorphism may be lost even within the indicator level, as the advertised job description (X'') is rarely as fully detailed as the job description in the personnel manual (X''). At this point, the sequence that began at the conceptual level (X) and proceeded to the indicator level (X'') now moves to the empirical level (X') as actual candidates possessing actual configurations of mutable and immutable characteristics apply for the position. When a suitable candidate is found, the position becomes an empirical reality, with an incumbent, full funding, and facilities (X').

Since this example of orderly interaction is minimally a dyad comprising a power holder and an applicant (and may, of course, include many others), there is another half of the sequence. The power holder's sequence was X—X''—X', as it progressed from initial conceptualization, to formation on paper to the search for an empirical incumbent. The applicant's sequence is often a mirror image in the other direction: the applicant conceptualizes the sort of position needed (X), sees it described in an advertisement (X''), and then visits the organization as an applicant to observe the actual position (X').

The sequence of Figure 7.5 is just one of many common sequences. Another is where the personnel director, new to the company, has no prior image of what the position entails and what the characteristics of the applicant should be. In this sequence, the power holder begins with the written job description (X''), which provides him or her the mental image of the candidate (X), and then the search for an actual candidate (X') is begun. In the parallel sequence, the applicant had no intention to apply for a position and thus no prior expectation (X). This sequence also begins with X'', when the applicant reads the advertisement (X''), forms an image of the position (X), and then decides to investigate the actual position (X'); these are parallel X''—X—X'

sequences. Notice that sequences of one actor (e.g., the power holder) are easily matched with other sequences of the other actor (e.g., the applicant).

In the "ideal-type" interaction, all six occurrences (X, X'', and X' for each of the two actors) would all be isomorphic with one another. In this case, the power holder's perception of the position (X) would be identical with the written description (X'') and with the actual job (X'). Also, the applicant's three levels would be identical and match those of the employer. In the actual case, there is generally some lack of isomorphism, for example, some discrepancy between the expectations (X) of the employer and those of the applicant. However, these expectations can be similar if both actors have formed their expectations for the interaction from the synchronic symbolic order that resulted from past actions. For example, if both the power holder and the applicant perceive (X) on the basis of past social order, that a woman will be hired for a secretarial position and a man for the position of mechanic, then the interaction may proceed orderly, with little conflict and with a relatively high degree of isomorphism at all points. Such orderly interaction between actors, based upon synchronic symbolic order, will perpetuate this order (the status quo).

Occasionally instances of deliberate lack of interlevel isomorphism will occur, as when a power holder deliberately places a misleading advertisement (X'') containing a job description that does not match the available empirical position (X'). However, most instances of severe lack of isomorphism will occur from some sort of rather abrupt change in either the mutable or immutable distributions at the empirical level (X'). If actors still have perceptions and expectations (X) based on the prechange empirical solution, then there will sometimes be a large degree of discrepancy between the conceptual level perceptions (X) and the empirical reality (X'). One common example of this is when one actor experiences a rapid change in a mutable such as spatial location. A person moving from one region of the country to another (S) may find that his or her expectations (X) for a position are not met in the new location (e.g., the salary [L] may be much lower than he or she is accustomed to). Similarly, an employer relocating a plant to another region may find his or her expectations of worker's salary levels confirmed but have a severe discrepancy between expectations of worker's education and the actual levels. Also, rapid technological changes (e.g., computerization) may render past expectations inadequate, so that neither actor in the interaction has a clear expectation, but rather the entire situation is rather anomic.

Lack of isomorphism among the three levels may also arise due to the correlations among variables, particularly between the mutables and immutables. One example of this is when an organization experiences economic difficulties (L) and must pay less for a given position than previously. If the correlations that previously held between the mutables and immutables are maintained, we would expect the lower (L) value now paid by the position to be accompanied by different values of the applicant's mutable characteristics (such as education $[I]$, technology $[T]$, and residence $[S]$, and immutable characteristics (age, race, sex, etc.). This can cause lack of isomorphism between the power holder's expectations of (X) of applicants and the actual applicants (X') *if* the power holder expects to see applicants with the same immutable characteristics as before. The power holder, who has traditionally hired a young, white man for the position, may now find that, due to correlations with lowered income, the applicants are women, black, or old.

Another cause of lack of isomorphy among the three levels is *change* in the correlations among the mutables and immutables. For example, suppose that more women suddenly study engineering (I) and that blacks suddenly dramatically increase their educational levels (I). This rapid change in orderly action during a given time period will result in changes in the correlations between education and sex and education and race.

An interesting thing about expectations in interaction is that often they are overtly univariate essentially, although the mutables and immutables involved are actually correlated, so that the (covert) interaction context is multivariate rather than univariate. As an example, a personnel manager in an aerospace firm may have hired engineering graduates for years. This hiring has been essentially univariate (and monothetic, to recall the discussion of Chapter 6, as it is based primarily on education). All persons hired are identical in the sense of being engineering graduates. If there are too many applicants, distinctions may be based on grades or on other mutables, such as region of resistence (S). Due to the strong correlation between education and gender and education and race, this manager may never have had a woman applicant or a black applicant. Thus, although the manager's decision was based on only one variable (education), the hiring was actually a "package deal" in which the manager was receiving a number of immutable properties (age, race, sex) that were effectively held constant by the correlation with education. If this correlation changes quickly, the manager who expects a young, white man (X) will now face a severe lack of isomorphism with these expectations, as applicants (X') are women or black.

The Synchronic Nature of Markers

Before turning to the discussion of power and conflict, it is necessary to discuss the role of markers in the orderly process in a little more detail. As discussed, over time, orderly interaction between actors results in a synchronic symbol structure, which affects the next cycle of interaction among actors. The nature of the orderly process and of the resulting symbolic order can be changed, over time, but that change is often slow. There may still be some confusion as to the synchronic nature of symbols. Some work in ethnomethodology has stressed the nongeneral nature of concepts (Garfinkel and Sacks 1970). According to this view, some (or even all) concepts are indexicals whose meaning is not fixed. Thus, the meaning of an indexical such as *you* is not context-free but rather context-specific; that is, the referent of *you* cannot be identified outside of a given context and changes with each context.

It might seem at first glance that the notion of an indexical is inconsistent with the notion of a synchronic symbol structure. That is, can an indexical concept (whose meaning *varies* with the context of social interaction) be synchronic (time-invariant)? Closer reflection shows that there is no contradiction here. A given symbol can be vague in meaning, can have dual meanings (only a cursory glance at the dictionary shows that many words have several meanings), or can be an idexical and still be synchronic. The only requirement is that the symbolic representation and the way it is reacted to (even if it is context specific) must not be changed over the given time period. For example, the concept *you*, although clearly an indexical, is also clearly synchronic, as its meaning does not change over time nor does its status as an indexical.

Actors in nonliterate societies must work largely without the indicator level. Rather than storing their symbols on markers such as paper (X''), they simply must remember them, thus only using two levels of the three-level model $(X$ and $X')$. The number and complexity of symbols that can be stored is thus limited by memory, and symbols are subject to distortion and change of meaning over time, thus losing their synchronic nature.

Complex societies probably could not exist in their present form without markers and certainly could not maintain their present levels of social interaction. One important function is the transmission of information between actors at different spatial positions in the system (S). If actors are at different spatial locations, face-to-face interaction is impossible, but they can still interact and transmit information via markers such as letters or the telephone (X''). Another important function in orderly interaction that markers such as paper and computers serve is the storage of information. Without the aid of markers, the replication necessary for social order would be much more difficult. That is, as earlier, the ordered relationship between two variables (e.g., sex and occupation) is caused by replicating human interactions based on these variables over an extended period of time. Without markers to store information, persons involved in complex interactions and those interacting over a long period of time would forget the exact content of information. The synchronic nature of the symbol system would be slowly eroded and this would result in changes in the human interaction that the symbol system guides. The result would likely be some loss of ability to replicate, especially over a long period of time, and thus also some subsequent loss in the order displayed in the symbolic structure. This slow erosion would be in the direction of randomness and maximum entropy.

Thus, it may be only a slight exaggeration to say that the use of markers, such as paper, make replicated action possible and thus make social order possible. Put another way, without markers, social order would be much more difficult to construct and maintain. It is indisputable that, if markers were suddenly removed from modern society, a state of anomia would reign (at least temporarily) and the degree and efficiency of social interaction would drop drastically. Social order would not disappear, but there would be a trend toward maximum entropy and a tremendous reduction in the information content (I) of the society and thus corresponding changes in the other globals and mutables that are correlated with I.

There are numerous examples of the ways that markers (X'') are used to construct and maintain social order. The ability to replicate depends upon access to the synchronic symbol structure constructed by past replication. This ability to replicate often depends upon reference to some particular marker. For example, even the ability to replicate the spelling of symbols depends upon the existence of a dictionary (X''). The dictionary is the prime example of the role that markers play in maintaining social order. The dictionary is essentially synchronic (the same words are in there with the same meanings in 1980 as in 1900). However, some change is noted, as some meanings are listed as archaic. It is an interesting testimony to the synchronic nature of the symbol structure, though, that even archaic or obsolete meanings are still retained in the marker and are still a part of the symbol-structure. The dictionary also illustrates that the symbol structure, while orderly, is not perfectly orderly. The dictionary exhibits basic consistency and clarity but with a number of multiple meanings for words, thus attesting to their indexical nature and their basic lack of complete clarity and generality. It is clear from perusing a dictionary that the symbol structure it contains allows one to replicate actions with a high degree of order but not without some ambiguity.

Another interesting example of the power of the marker in complex society is the signed legal document. The results of many human interactions, even if made face-to-face and with complete agreement among all parties involved, are not legally binding if made only orally. The agreement made on a marker such as paper and signed by all parties has a much higher status in the society—almost a sacred status. Also, an interesting testimony to the synchronic nature of the document is that a person's signature is synchronic. It is reconstructed over and over through replicated action, and alterations in it (e.g., forgeries) can be determined (by experts) with a high degree of success. Perhaps, the epitome of the marker as an important tool in social interaction is the will. The will, properly written and signed, has tremendous power in the orderly transfer of property.

To summarize, social structure resides in markers to such a great degree that control of markers and their information content is a great source of power. That is, although power results from control of all of the globals and mutables, control of information (I) is particularly crucial. The ultimate power is the power to change the information content of markers or to rule upon their exact meaning in case of disputes. Thus, lawmakers, such as the United States Congress, who actually have the power to determine the information content of markers affecting all citizens, have a high degree of power. Also very powerful are the Supreme Court justices who can decide disputes concerning the exact meaning of the synchronic symbolic structure.

Markers and Mutables

Although markers play a crucial role in all replicated action, their role is particularly salient with regard to the mutables in a complex society. As mentioned earlier, mutable characteristics, unlike immutable characteristics, are not generally visible during interaction. Thus, for example, a power holder interviewing persons for a position in an organization cannot see mutables such as educational level the way race or sex can be observed (although epiphenomena of education such as grooming or diction might be visible). Thus, markers become the *only* way that replication can be achieved, for only markers (e.g., diplomas and school transcripts) can be used to determine which people have the minimal educational levels required for the job. Without markers such as school records, there would be much more variance in the mutable characteristics (e.g., educational attainment) of persons allocated into a particular position. Thus, over time, the correlations between education and occupation would diminish in the synchronic symbol structure.

Replication of interaction is so common that we tend to take it for granted. However, it is a central matter of social concern, for it is the source of order in the symbolic structure. Because it is so familiar, there may be a tendency to think that social replication is "natural" or "easy to attain." The truth is that there are many barriers to replicated interaction. For example, inadequate reserves of any of the globals are a great barrier to replicated interaction. Thus, if the actors have insufficient money and energy reserves (L), inadequate or false information (I), inadequate technology (T), or are too widely separated in space (S), replicated action may be difficult. Unless these obstacles are overcome there is a tendency to lessen of the percentage of acts that are replicated, which of course weakens the degree of social order and tends in the direction of maximum entropy. Markers play a crucial role in overcoming these barriers by providing information needed to document the applicant's mutable characteristics, so that actors are allocated into the mutable structure in the intended manner, rather than randomly.

Power and Conflict

The generic sociological definition of power is clear enough, although there certainly is not complete consensus regarding it. Basically, power is the ability to control the actions of another, with or without his or her consent. However, such a bland and context-free definition is only minimally useful in a holistic theory such as SET. The purposes of SET require a much expanded, much more materialistic notion of power.

Power has many facets. From the viewpoint of holistic systems theory it is easy to see that one crucial feature in the attainment and retention of power often neglected by theorists is boundary control. Remember that a concrete social system was defined as a population of concrete human actors operating in a particular spatial area within systems boundaries. Perhaps, the first requirement for the retention of power is proper maintenance and control of these boundaries. If the person or persons in charge are not able to control the flow of matter-energy, persons, and information across systems boundaries (in both directions), their degree of power will be questionable.

Control of boundaries, including their proper opening and closing, is an aspect of intersystem power. Assuming that this power is solidified, the power holders can concentrate upon intrasystem power. Again, a prerequisite for adequate power is control of intrasystem boundaries, such as local spatial boundaries. The central societal power holders, who control the entire system, can allocate power over local jurisdictions to local leaders. However, they must reserve the right to intervene, specifically the right to cross local boundaries. Thus, federal officials must be able to cross local boundaries (such as state boundaries) at will and must have the power to monitor or even close such subsystem boundaries if they deem it necessary.

As should be evident from the discussion throughout this book, the basic source of system power is the set of globals. The power holders must control the globals. Put another way, any persons who control the globals for the society are its power holders. Further, the power holders are the ones who shape the mutable distributions, for they are the ones with the power to allocate persons into positions in all five of the mutable distributions. However, allocation is generally not based upon all of these simultaneously but is likely to be univariate (e.g., allocation into an occupation), with the other allocations on the other distributions subsequently following overtly due to their correlations with occupation.

It should also be evident that there is generally not a sole power holder in a complex social system, although there can certainly be a person who has more power than any other person. Rather, there are many power holders, as many positions in the mutable distributions afford at least some degree of power. Put another way, many positions *demand* that the incumbent exercise some power. Thus, although we are accustomed to thinking of power as a desired quality and one that many persons would like to attain, the truth of the matter is that there are also many reluctant power holders. These are persons who because of their particular configuration of mutable and immutable characteristics were allocated into a particular position in the mutables that requires them to exercise power whether they want to or not.

The persons with the greatest power are, of course, the systems leaders, as they control the globals. The central power holders have the responsibility of monitoring and maintaining the global levels. They have great power, as the global levels have a crucial effect upon the mutable distributions. The central societal leaders also have control over allocation of persons into the mutables.

A person who has been allocated into the mutables has a specific amount of power. At this stage the exercise of power becomes a rather routine exercise of replicating actions according to the norms and written rules and regulations that proscribe and prescribe actions for the incumbent of the position.

Expectations and Power

It has been stressed that the societal system does not operate deterministically. Rather, its operation is conducted by concrete human actors who set system goals, monitor the system, and alter its operations if necessary in order to meet the goals. For example, system leaders often monitor the existing state of the globals and mutables, decide which areas need improvement, and then formulate a plan to meet these goals. This, of course, entails use of information (I) and generally utilizes markers. Only in a very small society could leaders gain a perception (X) of the mutables and globals from direct observation of the empirical situation (X') and thus attain type A isomorphism. In complex societies, type A isomorphism between the power holders' perceptions of the real situation (X) and the actual empirical situation (X') can only be achieved indirectly by accumulating empirical observations (X') from local areas onto markers (X''), such as reports by agricultural officials. These reports can then be aggregated to produce a final report (X'') listing empirical conditions (X') for the entire system (type C isomorphism). The power holders then gain an overall perception (X) from reading the reports ([X''] a type B mapping or isomorphism). Thus, type A isomorphism is achieved indirectly through sequential type C and type B isomorphisms.

System power holders are the only persons who have access to this central information concerning the globals and mutables for the entire system, unless they decide to release it to others, of course. This control of central information is necessary for proper system operation and thus is a major source of power, even though the information rarely is completely accurate, particularly for a very large and complex society. This information is cognitively processed by the leaders (X) who use it to make decisions regarding the system.

Another facet of information control that plays an important role in the maintenance of power is the control of expectations. Let us speak in terms of the ancient free will versus determinism distinction, although this dichotomy is not sufficiently complex for the analysis of complex society. Individuals, acting within the concrete social system, certainly do have free will. Young persons are often dramatically aware of this and even find free will to be painful, as they attempt to choose among a wide variety of occupations that the complex society offers them, in an attempt to find the perfect career. However, it is also clear from the discussion in Chapters 4, 5, and 6 that this free choice is constrained by the particular levels of the globals and mutables at the particular point in time that the decision is being made and is permanently constrained by the immutables (which can never be changed, although the manner in which they are reacted to by others can change). Thus, we definitely have free will, for example, in terms of choosing the positions in the mutable structure that we would like to occupy, but this free will is constrained—sometimes highly constrained—by the globals, mutables, and immutables, which are often highly intercorrelated.

Thus, the role of an individual's cognitive expectations (X) and the cognitive goals based upon them (X) is crucial in determining the position that he or she will occupy (be allocated into) in the mutable distribution. Expectations and goals were discussed extensively in Chapter 5, so here they will only be analyzed in relation to power. The truth is that any person, in any social system, has freedom of perception (X), and during that moment of cognition, other persons (including power holders) have no awareness of it. Thus, each person is free to set any expectations that he or she desires regarding any position in the mutable structure. However, persons do not generally choose from among the full array of positions, because, even though one has "free will," there are constraints upon it.

To begin with, as in Chapter 5, the array of expectations to choose from is correlated with the person's initial position in the mutable structure. For example, persons in certain positions (especially low in the mutables) may never have even heard of some occupations, as they have no access to information concerning them. Persons will often preclude some expectations because of their position on a particular mutable (e.g., residence [S] precludes many expectations if the person does not wish to move, or [T] may preclude an expectation if the person considers the particular technology too dangerous). Thus, power holders find that some of their power is maintained for them, in the sense that individuals over whom they exercise power have their expectations shaped by their given position in the mutable structure, so that the power holder need take no overt action. A person's goals are chosen from among a given array. These expectations are shaped by his or her mutables and immutables and perception of the synchronic symbol structure, and certain goals are formulated. At this point the person still has "free will." He or she can aspire to be the leader of the country, for example. However, it is clear that given his or her array of mutables and immutables and the manner in which such characteristics were allocated in the past (as reflected in the correlations in the symbolic synchronic structure), that various goals will have highly varying probabilities of success. There will be a set of goals that the person probably can attain; a set that he or she might be able to attain under the present social order; and a set that he or she will definitely *not* be able to attain.

Mutables and Conflict

The goals that can be easily attained within the mutable structure, at any given point of time, will almost by definition probably not threaten power holders at all levels of superior positions in the mutables. This is because the power holders (presumably) accept their own positions in the mutable distributions and perform adequately (or else they would be replaced). Since the power holders accept the order displayed by the mutable structure, they condone expectations by others that are consistent with the present form of the mutable structure. When persons aspire to positions in the mutables that are difficult or impossible to attain, there is a potential for conflict; and power holders can be expected to first utilize all recourse within the present structure then resort to overt use of power (even force), if they deem it necessary. At the very least we would expect the persons with the improbable goals to be closely monitored.

Because the distributions of mutables are correlated, and a particular individual's mutable characteristics are also intercorrelated, most individuals formulate relatively realistic expectations of positions to be attained in the mutable structure. These are often relatively close to their initial (or their family's initial) position in the mutable structure. A complex society offers such a wide range of choices that, even if an individual is constrained to positions relatively close to his or her starting point in the mutables, this still affords a rather substantial freedom of choice.

What sort of individuals are most likely to formulate goals that are improbable for persons with their characteristics in the present mutable structure, and thus have the most potential for conflict with power holders? Persons lowest in the mutable structure obviously have the most to gain by formulating lofty goals (by definition, persons at the top of the structure cannot be very upwardly mobile but strive to maintain their positions and prevent downward mobility). Thus, all things equal, it would seem that persons lowest in the mutable structure (particularly in L) would have the greatest potential for conflict with power holders. However, the situation is more complicated than this. Many people lower in the structure have only sketchy information (I) concerning positions (O) that pay more (L). *Moreover, these positions are often very technical (T),* demand high education (I), and often are concentrated in distant areas (e.g., Wall Street or Silicon Valley) and require expensive relocation (S). Thus, many persons are simply unlikely to have expectations that differ so drastically from their present situation, as they are too unrealistic and too unfamiliar to consider.

A major point here is the multivariate nature of these goals: specifically, that they involve *five* factors (residence [S], education and information systems including ideology, religious beliefs [I], technology [T], and an unfamiliar organizational position with unknown obligations [O]—all for the sake of increased income [L]). In such a situation, the more realistic and more psychologically rewarding choice is to strive for modest gains in salary (L) or for a change in occupation (O) that is relatively similar to the one now occupied (or is at least familiar) but that affords an advantage such as self-employment. Such goals are often realistic. Thus, laborers aspire to owning small businesses and rarely apply for positions as neurosurgeons or atomic physicists. However, they certainly hold such aspirations for their children, who may acquire the education (I) that makes them aware of the particular positions (O), the economic rewards that they offer (L), and the technical (T) and locational (S) requirements of these positions. Their parents are more likely to focus on financial independence or salary gains through unionization.

Thus, most of the conflict between persons lower in the mutables and power holders will come in terms of one mutable at a time (principally, income [L] rather than as a broad assault on all five mutables. Conflict will generally center around expectations that, from the standpoint of the total societal globals, are rather modest (such as union efforts to increase wages by a rather small percentage.) Conflict can also center around any of the other mutables, such as required training (I), plant relocation (S), or technological change (T). The major point here, though, is that such conflict between individuals and power holders is based on *mutables*. Most individuals will not have unrealistic expectations that involve great change on all five mutables, although they may have such intergenerational aspirations for their children. Rather, conflict will focus on issues, such as pay raises, where the individual feels his or her expectations are not only realistic but "just." These demands are often strongly resisted by power holders and can lead to genuine conflict, but generally do not represent long-distance moves within the mutable structure and generally do not threaten the social order, as represented either by replicated action or by the resulting synchronic symbolic order.

Immutables and Conflict

One situation where there is considerable potential for direct conflict between aspirants and power holders concerns the immutable characteristics of aspirants. Although the mutable characteristics of aspirants are largely "invisible" in direct interaction and must be documented by markers (X''), immutable characteristics are very visible in face-to-face interaction and within the physical setting of the organization. Real potential for conflict between aspirants and power holders exists whenever aspirants possess the mutable characteristics that ostensibly "qualify" them for the position but possess immutable characteristics historically not possessed by incumbents of the position to which they aspire. As we have stressed, the existing correlations between the mutables and immutables often preclude such a situation. Thus, a personnel manager in an aerospace firm who is hiring mathematicians may find that virtually all applicants are men, and thus will not be confronted with the potential conflict of "sexism," as women have not studied mathematics in large numbers.

Since there are multiple, correlated obstacles to rapidly making very large changes from a low position to a high position in the mutables, most persons in lower mutable positions do not have such expectations, and conflicts are averted. Similarly, racial minorities who have low positions in the mutables are kept from rapid mobility not only by direct discrimination based on race, but also by their five low positions in the correlated mutables. That is, any person, regardless of race, who has little money (L), little education (I), few technological skills and little access to advanced technology (T), and a disadvantageous and unprestigious spatial or residential location (S) will not be in a position to rapidly and drastically improve his or her occupational position (O). Thus, the power holder can often reject such an applicant on the basis of one of the mutables, often education (I) or occupational experience (O), without having to face the potential conflict of the racial discrimination issue.

The issue of gender and power is particularly interesting from the standpoint of entropy theory, as births display a gender value near maximum entropy, *regardless of other factors*. Thus, births are near 50 percent male and 50 percent female (actually generally slightly more males), regardless of the parents' position in any of the five mutable distributions. Thus, gender entropy at birth is maximum regardless of parents' income (L), education (I), residence (S), technology (T), or occupation (O). In other words, both men and women represent "expected values" at birth. In terms of social entropy theory, then, women are a "false minority": they are not a numerical minority at birth; they are not economically disadvantaged relative to men (approximately as many women as men are born to upper income families); and they are the only "minority" who are born to "nonminority" (at least as far as the father is concerned) parents. Thus, women do not begin at a disadvantage relative to men at birth and do not need to "make up" any deficiencies but only to maintain their initial entropy values across other variable categories, particularly the mutable distributions.

Only a cursory look at empirical data such as occupation classified by sex shows that the maximum entropy values that gender exhibited at birth have changed, sometimes drastically. The univariate entropy, which was maximum at birth for gender, has changed, so that conditional and joint entropy values display nonmaximum entropy values. The point is that discrimination against women in terms of allocation into the mutables is more evident than discrimination based upon other immutable characteristics such as age or race, as women begin from a position of statistical equality (maximum entropy) in terms of their distribution, and *any departure from maximum entropy* is evidence of change in their original allocation. This departure, over time, from maximum entropy can only be due to replicated social action based upon the immutable characteristic of gender, which causes correlations between gender and each of the five mutable variables. These correlations are not limited to simple zero order linear correlations or multivariate linear correlations but are also curvilinear correlations resulting from interaction among the five mutables (e.g., the correlation between the immutable variable of sex and the mutable variable of education may differ depending upon the value of the spatial variable $[S]$, meaning the women in different regions receive different levels of education).

Entropy and Inequality

Entropy theory has some interesting implications for the study of inequality. Maximum entropy is randomization; it is also, statistically speaking, the "most probable" distribution. Another way to say this is that, in the absence of replicated human action and interaction that create order, we would expect any given distribution to approximate randomization. Thus, without replicated social action, any given immutable characteristic should be distributed along any given mutable distribution in a random fashion (maximum entropy). Consider the mutable distribution for income (L). For a given global level of total income possessed by the concrete society (L) and for a given population size (P), the mutable distribution is formed by allocating each person in the population a certain amount of income out of the total global amount that is available.

In the absence of replicated action and the resulting social order, the best guess is that each person in the population will be allocated with equal probability into a given income category. In other words, each person in the population, under random allocation, would have the same probability of allocation into a given high-income category (but also into a low-income category). This holds regardless of the individual's immutable characteristics. Thus, each woman would have a probability of selection equal to each man and each black person would have a probability of allocation equal to each white person. *Equality is thus maximum entropy and is the most probably statistical state, certeris paribus.* If, statistically speaking, equality is the *most probable* state, why do many social systems demonstrate a rather rigid and persistent departure from equality? Would not this mean that persons would not have to work to attain equality but could in fact just wait for a trend in that direction? This would be consistent with entropy theory in the sense that equality or randomization is maximum entropy, and according to the second law of thermodynamics, over time, systems tend toward maximum entropy—and thus towards equality.

However, open systems *do not necessarily* tend toward maximum entropy if there are forces that combat this trend. Thus, as seen in this chapter, replicated social action, based on immutables such as race and sex, effectively prevents these distributions from approaching randomness. The immutable characteristics are very visible and predictable (since they cannot be changed) and thus are susceptible to utilization as a means for allocating persons into the mutable distributions. In other words, replicated action is not random action. As long as the social system allocates persons into mutables in a replicated (orderly) fashion and as long as this replication is based upon immutable characteristics, so that persons with different immutable characteristics (e.g., male or female) are differentially allocated, then maximum entropy will not be approached and inequality will continue.

Concluding Remarks

We have seen that social order does not occure either by chance or merely as the result of deterministic forces of some sort. Rather, it is the result of replicated human action. This replicated action and interaction is conducted by utilization of all three levels of the three-level model. The role of markers on the indicator level (X'') is particularly important. This replicated interaction among human actors constitutes Q-relationships. These in turn result in R-correlations among the symbols representing characteristics on which this replicated action is based. These characteristics include all of the mutable characteristics of the individual (education $[I]$, income $[L]$, technology $[T]$, organization $[O]$, and residence $[S]$), as well as many immutables (e.g., race, sex, and age) and other selected labels that are applied to individuals (e.g., mentally ill, incompetent, ambitious). These symbols and their correlations form a synchronic symbol structure that is carried both in the actor's perceptions (X) and on markers of various sorts (X''), such as code books and manuals.

The synchronic symbol structure, for example as recorded in a rule book, provides the information on which interactions are based, and thus it is a major source of the social ability to replicate and to form social order. Conversely, the interaction among actors, which is a process occurring over time, forms, maintains, and alters the synchronic symbolic structure. For example, although the rule book guides the interaction process, the interaction process can result in a new rule book in a new time period, which may be the same or altered (revised). Thus, we see a continual and neverending process-product-process-product sequence (a form of dialectic, if you will). This continuing sequence allows the society to have order, in terms of both process and product (i.e., both action order and symbolic order), but to alter this order dialectically over time. This sequence is thus a historical event. To understand a particular person's actions, then, we need to know the point in time (the point in the continuing and cumulative process-product sequence) in which the action occurred, as symbolic meaning could be different in different time periods. For example, whereas both the terms Negro and black remain in the synchronic symbol structure of the United States in the 1980s and both can be found in the dictionary, a particular actor in a particular context in 1950 would be more likely to use the term Negro than black, while the converse is true in the 1980s. However, in either case some term is used to categorize persons of a particular skin color and to allocate them in the mutable structure in a replicated manner.

Thus, a salient point in understanding the central problem of social order is the understanding of the nexus between process or interaction order (Q-order) and product or symbolic (variable) order (R-order). Although the former may not seem important to statisticians nor the latter to verbal theorists, they both are crucial from a holistic perspective. The next task is to analyze the manner in which persons are mapped into symbolic categories at the indicator level (X''). The central focus is on tabular representation and statistical analysis. To begin with, we will analyze how tables are constructed and the impact of this construction on measurement, including the measurement of entropy. We then examine the relationship of the statistical concept of entropy to the variety of extant statistical formulations currently in use in sociology.

Chapter 8

Statistical Entropy

Social entropy theory, as a holistic model, emphasizes the symbiotic complementarity between verbal and numerical analysis in everyday social life. Although sociologists and other social scientists often separate verbal and quantitative analyses, actors in everyday social interactions generally do not make such a separation. Rather, everyday interactions depend upon the use of closely intertwined formulations of both words and numbers. Thus, a holistic analysis that seeks isomorphism with the actual society *must not* analytically separate statistics from verbal analysis but must study both quantities and qualities and their nexus.

The synchronic symbol structure (R-structure) that forms the basis for the diachronic process structure of human interaction (Q-structure) necessarily includes both words and numbers as basic symbols. In addition, after symbols are coded into markers (X'') from either the econceptual level (X) or the empirical level (X') or both, these symbols are often sequentially manipulated by humans in order to further interpret the basic data inherent in the symbols. Such further analysis and interpretation involves recasting the symbols into numerical formulations of various sorts, such as percentages, measures of central tendency, measures of correlation, and so on.

Some social scientists see themselves as "theorists" and eschew numerical analysis, while others see themselves primarily as "statisticians" and pay little attention to strictly verbal analysis. Yet scientists of either persuasion will routinely utilize an interplay of numerical and verbal symbols in their everyday life, as this combination is central to the successful operation of concrete society. For example, when the verbal theorist, who displays disdain for numerical analysis, goes on a simple trip to the supermarker, this shopping venture will often include all three levels of the three-level model, as well as segments of the synchronic symbolic *product*–diachronic *process* chain. Further, the shopping will generally entail use of *both* numbers and verbal symbols. A typical process is as follows. The shopper first conceptualizes (X) the products to be bought and often the number of items and prices as well.

This conceptualization may begin at the conceptual (X) level with decisions about which items to buy, or it may begin at the empirical level (X') with a search through the cupboard to ascertain which items are needed. Thus, while still at the conceptual level, numerical symbols have already entered the process. Next the shopper maps the concepts (X) decided upon onto the indicator level (X'') in the form of a shopping list. This is a type B mapping $(X$ onto $X'')$ and serves primarily as a memory aid. The shopper then goes to the store and selects the items empirically (X'). The items selected are mapped onto the shopping list, and this is a type C mapping $(X'$ onto $X'')$. This mapping results in change in the symbols that were originally on the list (X''). For example, items that are purchased are checked off the list, items that are missing or too expensive are marked out, new items are added to the list, and revisions are made in the number of a specific items that is purchased. This revision of the shopping list (X'') involves both verbal symbols and numerical symbols (e.g., three oranges were purchased instead of two). The shopping process also entails the use of markers (X'') to identify the products to be purchased. For example, vegetables such as green beans may be sealed in a can that represents a relatively closed physical system, as the tin boundary is relatively impervious to information and matter-energy flows across it. This means that the shopper cannot identify the contents without a marker (X''), such as a paper label that indicates the contents. The price will also be shown somewhere, either on the label, the can, or the shelf (all thus serving as markers), as well as in some other marker (X'') such as a newspaper advertisement. Thus, here again is a verbal-numerical combination (e.g., whole green beans, 2/98¢).

When the shopper takes the purchases to the check stand, the checker produces still another marker in the form of a cash register tape (X'') that again lists both verbal and numerical symbols in the form of the item name, quantity, and price. The shopper will often use this marker (the receipt) by "checking its accuracy" (e.g., by verifying that type C isomorphism exists between the items purchased $[X']$ including their quantity and price, and the mapping of this data on the marker or receipt $[X'']$). Further, a little reflection will show that markers such as the revised shopping list and the cash register receipt contain so much numerical information that they facilitate a variety of statistical manipulation. For example, upon returning home the shopper can use these markers (receipts) to compute the total amount of money spent and the average cost per item. In addition, other measures can be classified based on the items purchased, such as percent of the budget spent on produce, and so forth. Not only will the cash register receipt show the price and type of item (e.g., oranges) but may also classify the department of the store from which it was purchased (e.g., produce). The point here is that once verbal and numerical symbols are recorded on markers in the course of everyday societal interaction, these symbols can be used, through successive and sequential reanalysis and symbol manipulation, to produce a whole array of statistical measures. Often this entails not only the reanalysis of data on a single marker, such as figuring the mean and median cost of items and the percentage of the budget spent on dairy products, but also entails comparison of different markers. For example, by comparison of the store receipt (marker one) with the newspaper advertisement (marker two), one can compute the percentage of items sold at higher than the advertised price, while comparison of the original shopping list (marker three) with the cash register receipt (marker one) reveals the correlation between the items one intended to buy and items actually purchased.

Thus, even mundane interaction involves statistical analysis, albeit rudimentary in many cases. Further, the *markers commonly used in mundane social interaction form the basis for sophisticated data analysis*. A little reflection will show that even the familiar cash register receipt will yield, through proper recoding, listing of the frequency of items of each classification. This facilitates the construction of a contingency table, for example, that shows the proportions of dairy items and produce, and facilitates the computation of gamma, chi square, and many other statistics. Most sociologists would not compute such statistics, as they lack a sound theoretical base, and thus are difficult to interpret. Nevertheless, the illustration proves the point that statistical and verbal analysis need not be empirically distinct academic enterprises but are inextricably interwoven in day-to-day interaction (see Bailey 1984$_d$). We are all statisticians as well as verbal analysts (at least to some degree) in our everyday life, and we cannot easily separate the two enterprises. Thus, if we are to successfully model everyday interaction holistically, we can separate the statistical and verbal realms only at the risk of greatly damaging the holistic nature of our analysis.

In sum, then, statistical analysis is not solely an academic enterprise but part and parcel of everyday life, although it is practiced in a rarified and refined fashion in academia. Other examples abound. By comparing two documents such as all members' membership applications for a voluntary association (Club A) with the minutes for the October meeting of Club A (which lists members present and absent), we can construct a contingency table listing presence or absence by race, gender, age, residence, and so on and conduct a variety of statistics from chi-square to gamma. Statistical analysis is thus not limited to the analysis of data gathered through adademic surveys, although such data may certainly be superior in terms of theoretical interpretation, suitability for statistical inference, validity of statistical assumptions, and so forth.

This analysis illustrates a principle of early ethnomethodology (Zimmerman and Pollner 1970), as discussed earlier: that the methods of sociology are

similar or identical to methods in general use in the lay society. In this particular case, this principle shows that statistical analysis is not unique to academic
endeavors but is in general use in lay society. Thus, as in Chapter 6, this principle can be turned on its head by analyzing academic methods (statistical
analysis) in order to see how such methods are used in the lay society. However, this principle *never* says that academic sociology uses *all* of the methods
extant in the general society. Further analysis shows that statistical analysis in
sociology is generally limited to only one form of mapping, the mapping of
individuals into dimensions formed by properties of individuals, and this is
the type conducive to R-analysis, the form predominant in American sociology.

Before examining mappings for R-analysis in more detail, let us examine
some alternative mappings, some of them only rarely used in sociology.
Perhaps an example will help in this analysis. Let us begin by imagining that
persons are being allocated into two positions (security guard and secretary)
within an organization. One variable that may be salient in this allocation in
gender.

Consider the following table:

	Male	Female
Security Guard		
Secretary		

There are a number of ways to map content into the interior of this table, and
thus a number of ways to analyze this table. One form of analysis for this
skeletal table is with alphabetic (as opposed to numeric) terms representing
not only the content of the column and row headings but also the content of
the interior cells. Here the symbols are represented by alphabetical labels. For
example, the following symbols can be mapped into the interior cells of the
table:

	Male	Female
Security Guard	Traditional	Feminist
Secretary	Feminist	Traditional

Such a table entails no quantification. This sort of mapping is known
within sociology as a typology (Stinchcombe 1968). Until relatively recently,
the utilization of such typologies has been almost solely the province of verbal
theorists. Interestingly enough, the number of sociologists conducting ethnography, observational analysis, or other forms of "qualitative methodology" has
been increasing, and many of these researchers utilize typologies in their data
analysis (see Spradley and McCurdy 1972, for examples). As used by verbal

theorists, such a typology is likely to be "heuristic" in Winch's (1947) terms. Such a heuristic typology is likely the product of an X to X'' (type B) mapping. However, if the labels (feminist and traditional) were in use in the actual society being studied, then types A and C isomorphism might exist as well. This is more likely the case with the typologies utilized by ethnographers, some of which are the result of "grounded theory" (Glaser and Strauss 1967).

In addition to such an alphabetic-alphabetic mapping with labels in the cells, another form of mapping is widely used in statistics outside of sociology (in psychology, for example) but used relatively rarely in sociology. This form uses alphabetic symbols to represent row and column headings of the table as in the typology. These headings usually represent categories of nominal or ordinal variables. The cell entries are not alphabetic symbols, as in the typology, but are numbers representing the values of some third variable (the row and column headings respectively each represent a single variable). In contrast to the alphabetic-alphabetic representation of the typology, this new form is an alphabetic-numerical representation, with alphabetical symbols forming the exterior of the table and numbers occupying the interior cells. The following is an example:

	Male	Female
Security Guard	83	86
Secretary	94	93

Here the cell entries are *not* frequencies but scores on some continuous variable, for example mean scores on an aptitude test administered by the personnel department. This sort of mapping is widely used in analysis of variance in psychology and other fields. It is taught within sociology (e.g., Blalock 1979, pp. 335–79) but is used relatively infrequently compared to symbol-object mappings. Notice that three variables are represented in this mapping, two of which are nominal (gender and occupation) and one of which is continuous (test score). Thus, this is a variable-variable (symbol-symbol) mapping, because the numbers in the interior cells represent variable scores rather than frequencies of objects (persons).

Note that both tabular forms discussed so far (the typology and the analysis of variance table) represent *only* variables in both the headings and interior cells and nowhere show frequencies of *objects*, such as human beings. This is in direct contrast to the variable-object table, which shows variables as headings and frequencies of objects in the interior cells. The latter is the most familiar representation in sociology. In fact this basic variable-object mapping is virtually the *only* mapping ever used by most sociological statisticians and the mapping referred to in the discussion of the link between diachronic social interaction and synchronic symbolic structure. This mapping uses symbol categories for the row and column headings, and persons (concrete individuals) constitute the cell frequencies. The table thus shows the basic congruence between acting and pattern systems in its synchronic form, as follows:

	Male	Female
Security Guard	8	2
Secretary	2	8

Virtually the only variation on this that many sociologists seem to know is the use of percentages (with the base being either the row total, column total, or grand total) as the cell entry.

However, sociologists should be aware that not everyone has adopted their convention of mapping individuals into the symbol space. For example, consider the analysis of inequality. Following the sociological convention of using symbols (variables) as table headings and objects (frequencies) as interior cell entries, we could construct a table such as the following one in which hypothetical percentages of the population are shown in various income categories:

Lowest Fifth	Second Fifth	Middle Fifth	Fourth Fifth	Highest Fifth
40	30	15	10	5

In such a table, the column headings are symbol categories (categories of the income variable) and the cell entries are persons, expressed either as frequencies (or, as in this case) as percentages. This is the standard symbol-object mapping seen so often in sociology.

However, if we examine mappings into the indicator level (X'') compiled by persons who are *not* sociologists, we quite often encounter the opposite— the object-symbol mapping. Here the column headings are divisions of the population, and the cell entries refer to categories of some symbol (variable) as in Table 8.1 The columns are fifths of the population and the cell entries are percentages of the total annual income. The same table (United States Department of Commerce 1980, p. 62) also reports income as number of dollars (as the cell entries) when the headings are again divisions of the total population.

This discussion of alternative mappings is not merely academic or analytical. These *different mappings result in different values of various statistical measures, including different values of the entropy measure.* Since the symbol-object and object-symbol mappings are two sides of the same coin, there is fortunately a rather simple mathematical transformation from one to the other.

Still, the distinction between them must be clearly understood if we are to avoid confusion when computing entropy. In this book, we bow to sociological custom and generally adopt the symbol (variable)-object mapping. However, this will sometimes entail remapping if the data sources utilized (X'') constitute the object-symbol mapping (or some other mapping).

Table 8.1

Percent Distribution of Aggregate Income, by Fifths of the Population, for Families and Unrelated Individuals, United States, 1978.

	Percent Distribution of Aggregate Income				
	Lowest Fifth	Second Fifth	Middle Fifth	Fourth Fifth	Highest Fifth
1978	45.2	3.7	9.7	16.4	24.8

Source: United States Department of Commerce, *Money Income of Families and Persons in the United States: 1978*. Washington, D.C.: U.S. Government Printing Office, 1980.

The relationship between object systems and variable systems in synchronic analysis can be clearly seen if we examine the S, or score matrix. This matrix was presented in Chapter 7 (see Table 7.1). Table 7.1 utilized objects as row headings and variables as column headings with scores mapped into the interior cells. Notice that each score represents both a corresponding object or person (in the row) and a variable or symbol (in the column). Thus, this basic table can be used either in a symbol-object mapping, or an object-symbol mapping. Figure 8.1 shows the former, the particular mapping identified as that generally used by sociologists. In this figure the variables form the dimensions of the property-space, and the dots represent objects (persons). The dots can represent the position of the concrete individual in the multivariate property-space. The particular configuration of dots illustrates the strength of relationship between the variables. This is, of course, the familiar scatter diagram found in the discussion of correlation in any sociological statistics text (e.g., Blalock 1979). This R-analysis, or correlation of variables, is accomplished by correlating the columns of Table 7.1.

Q-analysis, or correlation of objects, is accomplished by correlating the rows of Table 7.1 instead of the columns. This simply amounts to matrix transposition, the graphical representation of which is shown in Figure 8.2. In this figure the dimensions of the property-space represent objects, and the dots in the space represent variables.

Figure 8.1

R-Mapping, with Variables as Dimensions, and Persons as Points in Space

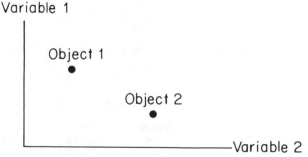

Figure 8.2

Q-Mapping, with Objects (Persons) as Dimensions, and Variables as Points in Space

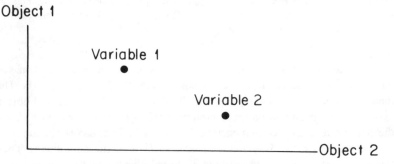

Notice that there is only one set of data in Table 7.1 (the numbers in the interior cells of the table). This data can be read either in terms of the concrete individuals (rows or Q-analysis) or in terms of their characteristics or variables (columns or R-analysis). Since the former represents the concrete system of human individuals and the latter represents the pattern (symbol) system, Table 7.1 shows clearly that these two systems are interrelated, two sides of the same coin. Remember that we are now discussing synchronic analysis. The diachronic acting system of human actors creates symbolic structure, over time, and actually maps itself (the population of concrete individuals) into the symbolic categories as cell frequencies. Thus, in synchronic analysis, a cross-sectional view shows that the concrete system and the pattern system are inter-related, as there is only one set of interior numbers. In a sense, the concrete and pattern systems represent two alternative views of the same phenomena.

This discussion specifies the relationships, both diachronic and synchronic, between the concrete system (concrete, acting, Q-system, P-facet) and the symbol system (conceptual, pattern, R-system, I-facet). However, the exact relationship of Miller's (1978) abstracted system to the concrete and pattern systems still needs to be clarified.

As defined by Miller (1978, p. 19) the basic unit of the abstracted system is a relationship. Strictly speaking, a relationship is neither a variable nor an object, and thus does not seem to fit directly into the Q- versus R-distinction. A glance at the manner in which abstracted systems are operationalized, however, sheds more light on the problem. The classic example of an abstracted system is Parsons's (1951) social system, in which the social role rather than the individual person is the stipulated unit of analysis. In almost every case where examples of the social role are given, they can easily be coded as variables. For example, Parsons (Grinker 1967, p. 328) discusses two roles that "John Jones" has: he is Mary Jones' husband and also the mail carrier. The first instance specifies his marital status; the second, his occupation. Both are commonly considered to be variables. Both are routinely recorded on questionnaires as characteristics of a person, and so the analysis is clearly R-analysis, with a variable as the basic unit. That is, although the social role is the vehicle for diachronic social interaction by actors, it can be synchronically coded as a variable and thus as part of the symbol or pattern system.

Notice that a common everyday marker (X''), such as the grocery receipt (or certainly an application for a job or a major loan), will often contain sufficient information for *all* of the types of mappings just discussed. The typology with labels in the cells, the analysis of variance table with the mean of a continuous variable in its cells, and the R- and Q-mappings of Figures 8.1 and 8.2 could all be constructed from such common markers. Although it is clear that not all such mappings will be explicitly constructed in the course of everyday social interaction, the fact remains that *the data needed for such mappings are ubiquitous in everyday interaction, and an adequate understanding of social life requires recognition of this fact.* This ubiquity also implies that sociological methodologists should utilize forms of analysis in addition to the standard R-analysis in order to achieve a broader picture of social reality. Further suggestions of such analyses are found in work published elsewhere (Bailey 1983a).

Probabilistic Entropy

The basic notion of statistical entropy was discussed in some detail in Chapter 3. This chapter delves more deeply into the statistical properties of entropy measurement and the relationship between entropy and various statistical measures commonly found in sociology. We will first consider entropy analysis for categorical data (e.g., gender or race), either at the nominal or ordinal level (or interval or ratio data such as income, which have been categorized for some reason). This is probably the form of statistical entropy analysis familiar to most people, and the form discussed heretofore. This form of analysis utilizes categorical data and analyzes the probability of occurrence of each category. Later in the chapter, attention will turn to the entropy analysis of continuous variables such as interval or ratio data that have not been categorized.

We have already discussed some of the advantages of the entropy concept, including that it has verbal or theoretical as well as statistical interpretations. In the last chapter, social order and its relationship to entropy were discussed in detail. This chapter examines the statistical features of entropy.

One very interesting and appealing statistical feature of entropy is that it is a generic univariate measure that is easily extended to multiple dimensions with little loss of interpretability (but with increasing computational difficulty). A little reflection will show that this cannot be said of the bulk of statistical measures currently in use in sociology. Most are rather rarified measures based on a number (sometimes a large number) of assumptions. Further, many of these assumptions are routinely *not* met in sociology. Often, the measures are so familiar and established (such as Pearson's r or multiple regression analysis) that they are routinely used, but there is little routine examination of the underlying assumptions (such as normality). Often such assumptions are thought tenable provided certain procedures are followed (such as random sampling). However, attempts at randomization are not always successful. Further, even if adequate sampling is achieved, the underlying assumptions of the technique may be threatened by factors such as attenuation of the range of values on a given variable. A common example of such attenuation is the use of closed-ended categorical variables from questionnaires. Such questionnaire variables are often attenuated to a relatively few categories, such as the commonly used Likert-style answer categories. Another way that the assumptions of parametric statistics are threatened is by the frequent use of categorical data instead of continuous data, or by the "ad hoc" categorization of data by coders or others who handle the data during the course of the collection and analysis process. Violations of assumptions of familiar methods, if not blatant, are often overlooked. If challenged, researchers often respond that the analysis is adequate because the method is "robust." Some methods are indeed robust, but the term *robust* is very vague and unquantified. That is, we do not know exactly *how* robust a given statistic is, because we do not quantify the degree to which the assumption can be violated before the method must be abandoned. Thus, researchers who plead "robustness" without quantifying the degree of robustness are in a rather ironic position when they continue to be very precise in other parts of the analysis, such as rigorously adhering to a particular level of significance such as .05.

In addition to having a larger set of assumptions than entropy (to be discussed later), most methods in use in sociology today *have no clear univariate interpretation*. The bias in sociology is almost entirely toward correlational techniques and inferential statistics, with the chief exception being work on measures of segregation or population diversity (see Lieberson 1969; Teachman 1980). Whereas measures of central tendency and dispersion such as the mean and variance, respectively, are used for univariate analysis, there are virtually no sociological measures that are used first for univariate data and then extended to the multivariate case (again, measures of population diversity are one exception). A correlation coefficient such as Pearson's r is in a sense a measure of bivariate variance, but with some adaptations that limit its interpretation strictly as covariance. For data of all levels in sociology, there is a clear bias toward correlational techniques (measure of association for the nonparametric case and measures of correlation for parametric data). The one exception that comes readily to mind is chi-square. Although it does have a univariate interpretation, this is rarely seen in sociology. Further, rather than being a direct measure of the distribution of scores through categories, as in entropy, chi-square compares the departure from *maximum entropy* (in the form of squared differences between observed score and maximum entropy) with maximum entropy ("expected values"). These ratios are then summed and interpreted in terms of the degrees of freedom. Chi-square will thus always be a positive value unless the observed values are purely random; that is, chi-square can be exactly zero only in the rare case when the observed or actual values display completely maximum entropy.

In contrast, entropy has a clear and unambiguous univariate interpretation. Whereas chi-square measures a particular entropy value (maximum entropy), it uses it only as a criterion point. Thus, the chi-square value always shows the degree of departure from a particular value of entropy—*maximum* entropy. An entropy measure such as H will measure *not* just a single value of entropy such as maximum entropy but *all* possible values of entropy from maximum to minimum. In general, correlational measures such as those that predominate in sociology do not measure entropy directly, although most have a clear relationship to it, but rather measure departure from maximum entropy. As in the last chapter, order is departure from randomness or maximum entropy, and thus virtually all correlational measures and predictive measures such as regression measure departure from randomness, though different ones measure different aspects of this departure and have different algorithms for doing so.

In a real sense, in fact, correlation and regression measures *depend* upon departure from randomness and tend to lose their usefulness in the case of randomness. Maximum and minimum entropy are important criterion points for entropy measures such as H. H measures these points quite well, however, correlational measures such as Pearson's r have some difficulty with them. If one variable (or both) is randomly distributed and so would have a univariate maximum value for the H measure, the bivariate or zero-order correlation as measured by Pearson's r between the two variables will be zero, since a variable whose values are randomly distributed displays no relationship with another variable. It cannot be accurately predicted or used in prediction. Similarly, the case of minimum entropy (maximum order) is a vexing case for correlational measures and is essentially an anomaly. If all cases display the same value on one variable, the result is a straight line (either horizontal or vertical) on a scatter diagram for R-analysis such as Figure 8.1. In the sense that all points are on the regression line and there is no scatter around the line, correlation is perfect and displays an r of 1.0. Further, prediction of the variable displaying minimum entropy is perfect. However, the problem is that the minimally entropic variable is, at least for the given sample, a constant. Thus, its values are all the same and any case gives perfect prediction (a sample of 1 suffices), as there is no variance. Thus, the second variable is worthless in prediction, and a correlation coefficient in useless. Granted, most cases in sociology are neither maximum nor minimum entropy, and thus correlation does function for them. Nevertheless, most correlational techniques lack the clear univariate analogue provided by entropy and provide comparatively inadequate specification of the theoretically crucial values of maximum and minimum univariate entropy.

The unidimensional interpretability of entropy is also useful theoretically. By comparing the original entropy value for univariate entropy of a variable (either dependent or independent) with the measure of joint entropy for that variable and an additional variable, we can get a rather clear intuitive picture of the effect of the second variable on the first. This is most dramatically illustrated in the case of the entropy of gender at birth. The last chapter discussed at length the role of immutable variables such as race and gender on allocation into the mutable structure. Gender at birth displays an entropy variable very near maximum. There are generally slightly more males born than females but to generalize it can be said that roughly 50 percent of each gender are born. This means that a given baby had approximately equal probability of being male or female, and so univariate entropy computed for gender at birth is maximum.

It is a simple matter to recompute univariate gender entropy at various times in the life cycle and at different positions in the mutable structure in order to see whether entropy has changed from its original maximum value. Doubtlessly other characteristics also occasionally display maximum entropy, particularly for a small area or a short time. However, gender is the only one that comes to mind that almost universally displays maximum entropy at birth. This is thus a "natural" occurrence of the expected values (in chi-square terminology) for gender and offers a very fortuitous reference point. For example, since gender occupies only two categories, we know that the maximum entropy value is always log K, and so will be log 2 for this example. Thus, entropy at birth will always fluctuate closely around log 2. The particular value will depend upon the base for the logarithms. However, as McFarland (1969) shows, this decision is rather arbitrary, as it is a relatively simple matter to translate from one to the other. For theoretical and computational ease base 2 is preferred, but tables are not always readily available, so base e (natural logarithms, or ln) are also an obvious choice. For purposes of illustration we will use base 2, using the table provided in Theil (1967). This is convenient as the table (Theil 1967, p. 429) shows $\log_2 2$ to be exactly 1.00.

This means that gender entropy at birth is 1.0. We only need compare this criterion with entropy values in various positions at later stages in life to see the effects that social interaction have wrought on the gender ratio. For purposes of illustration let us make such a comparison from published markers (X'') that are readily available. Turning to the *Guide to Graduate Departments of Sociology 1980* (American Sociological Association 1980), we see that the faculty listing for a certain major department shows 22 men's names and 2 women's names among the tenured faculty (listed as associate or full professors). Computation of entropy for this data yields an entropy value of .40. We know that maximum entropy in 1.00 in this case and minimum entropy is 0.00.

Of course, we cannot attribute all of the reduction in entropy from birth to the present time (a drop from 1.00 to .40) to hiring and promotion practices of the sociology department for which the computations were made. There is no doubt that the pool of students and faculty from which departments select candidates departed from maximum entropy. In fact, there was probably a steady progression of changes (decreases) in entropy throughout the life of the cohort from birth to attainment of the faculty position. Further, the computation of gender entropy can be affected by demographic changes in the sex ratio caused by differential mortality or migration (although such demographic effects are relatively unlikely to result in the computed decrease in entropy).

The interest here is not with any one particular value of entropy but rather with the nature of the analyses that can be made with univariate entropy. In addition to computing gender entropy within an organization (O) such as the university, it could also be computed for the other four mutables. For example, gender entropy could be computed in a particular spatial or geographical area (S), for a particular technology such as operating an airplane (T), for a particular class position (L), or for a particular belief such as a religious belief (I). This has a correlational flavor in the sense that two variables are being analyzed each time. However, although all the values of gender enter into the analysis, only a single value of the mutable (e.g., O) is utilized; that is, gender entropy is analyzed for a given value of a particular mutable. In terms of control of other variables and imputation of causation, this analysis lends itself to an interpretation similar to that for a correlational measure such as Pearson's r. The particular level of the mutable cannot be said to have *caused* the particular value of gender entropy just as one variable in a zero-order correlation cannot be said to have *caused* the particular distribution of values of the other variable. Further, just as with Pearson's r nothing is known about the role of other variables (including those whose influence may have been in the past) in affecting the values of a particular dependent variable.

Thus, although this utilization of univariate entropy is not superior to correlational techniques in terms of control or imputation of causation, it nevertheless allows an interpretation not available with standard correlational techniques—*the analysis of changes in univariate entropy in various salient social settings*. This is in one sense analogous to "dummy variable correlation," where all values of one variable are used (e.g., gender, or the variable for which univariate entropy is computed), but the other variable (e.g., a mutable such as organization) is only coded as existing or not, and the analysis is limited to the confines of its existence.

The utility of such univariate analysis should be obvious, especially since we get it for "free"; that is, this univariate analysis does not preclude multivariate analysis. To the contrary, since multivariate entropy has a statistically clear relationship to univariate entropy, the latter forms the basis for the generic interpretation of the former. A little reflection will show that although the standard bivariate analysis commonly found in sociology is certainly useful, it has a distinct disadvantage in not providing the measurement of the degree of order found separately in each variable. Entropy allows not only bivariate measurement but comparison of bivariate and univariate measurement. Further, the sequential univariate analysis of entropy is very useful in such things as time series analysis or life course analysis (for example, to see how gender entropy values change over the life course of a cohort). Bear in mind that most univariate entropy measures are not maximum as is gender entropy at birth, and so will not yield the convenient criterion value of 1.00 for maximum entropy (base 2) that gender entropy at birth does. Nevertheless, comparisons of entropy values for different times or for different mutables (e.g., *O, S, T, I,* or *L*) can still be very illuminating, especially when complemented by multivariate entropy analysis.

When the univariate analysis of statistical order was said to be not only very valuable and unique to the entropy measure but also free, the latter meant that multivariate entropy is a rather straightforward entension of univariate entropy. This obviously has clear interpretative advantages, because it allows us to proceed from a univariate to a bivariate to a multivariate interpretation. It not only provides us with an interpretation of each of these levels but also with a comparison of levels. Further, there is not one form of multivariate entropy measurement but two: joint entropy and conditional entropy. Formulas for the joint and conditional measures of *H* were presented in Chapter 3. Perusal of equation (3.3) for joint entropy shows that it is basically a simple extention of the univariate measure, except that whereas univariate entropy measures the probability of occurrence of a category of a single variable, bivariate conditional entropy measures the probability of occurrence of the combined categories of variable 1 and variable 2. For example, whereas univariate entropy for gender would measure the probability of occurrence of each gender category (e.g., male) and univariate entropy for race would measure the probability of occurrence of each category for race (e.g., black), bivariate joint entropy for gender and race would measure the probability of the joint occurrence of all possible combinations of categories of race and gender (e.g., black male).

Bivariate joint entropy is merely computed from the categories of the basic bivariate contingency table so common in sociology. Further, joint entropy for more than two variables is a simple extension of the formula for however many variables are to be analyzed. Even with a million variables, the multivariate measurement of entropy would simply be based on the probability of occurrence of all possible combinations of categories of the million variables. Although computation becomes increasingly difficult as the number of variables increases, it is nevertheless still a distinct advantage to be able to understand and interpret the notion of multivariate joint entropy for any number of variables (even though it may not be technically feasible to actually compute that value, as such computation would exceed the storage space of computers currently available). The maximum value for joint entropy is also a straightforward extension of the maximum *H* for the univariate case. Maximum *H* for a single variable is log *K*, where *K* is the number of categories (see equation 3.2). Maximum joint entropy (*H*) for *n* variables is $\log K_1 \ldots K_n$, where K_1 is the number of categories for variable i.

Note that joint entropy is analogous to correlational analysis, in the sense that it shows the degree to which all of the variables covary. In addition to joint entropy, it is possible to compute conditional multivariate entropy, which is analogous to regression. Conditional entropy (equation 3.4) shows the entropy value of variable Y when the value of variable X is known. Whereas joint entropy measures the symmetrical relationship between variables as does correlation, without providing any statistical bases for imputation of causal direction (although intuitive bases may exist), conditional entropy provides a directional or asymmetrical measure. It is analogous to regression in this sense. As with regression, there are *two* conditional entropy measures that can be computed for each bivariate analysis, but only one joint (correlational) measure. The two conditional entropy measures are $H\,(Y|X)$, or the entropy of Y when X is known, and $H\,(X|Y)$, or the entropy of X when Y is known. As with regression, the statistical computation will not specify one variable as causally independent and the other variable as dependent. Rather the researcher must specify one variable as independent (the one whose values are known), and the conditional entropy will be computed for the variable designated as dependent. For example, in computing the entropy for the mutable variable of occupation (O) when gender (an immutable) is specified, the immutable property of gender serves intuitively as the "causal" variable that determines the particular occupational category one is allocated into. However, the conditional entropy of gender (the immutable) can also be computed when the mutable (occupation) is known. This is similar to the strategy outlined earlier to compute univariate entropy rather than conditional entropy but for a particular occupation. This interpretation, as with regression, may seem counterintuitive in the sense that occupation is now being treated as the "cause" and gender the "effect," even though we know full well that occupation cannot change gender. However, as with regression, this is a perfectly valid statistical operation, because the measure of conditional entropy does not specify an independent variable. Further, even though occupation cannot change gender, it may be useful at times to look at the gender distribution for a particular occupation and see how occupation affects gender distribution. That is, although occupation cannot change gender, the processes of allocation into occupations discussed in great detail in earlier chapters will result in particular gender entropy values for particular occupations. By computing conditional gender entropy when occupation is known, we can see graphically what these gender entropy values are (i.e., what the results of the allocation processes are). Thus, a full entropy analysis includes all measures: univariate entropy, univariate entropy for different times and different values of the five mutables, joint entropy, and two conditional entropy values, one for each variable when the other is known. All of these are clearly interpretable and comparable and provide a more comprehensive analysis portrait than correlation and regression, which afford only a zero order correlation coefficient and two regression coefficients for the bivariate case. Of course, for the multivariate case, correlation and regression afford multiple and partial r as well as the several regression coefficients, but as we have seen, entropy provides further analogous interpretations as well. Further, for H, the most direct comparison is not with correlation and regression but with the various nonparametric statistics available in sociology. Only cursory examination of the most popular ones (e.g., gamma, phi) will show that they have many assumptions and limitations and do not yield the myriad interpretations and comparative possibilities of entropy. These interpretations are discussed in more detail later.

Number of Categories

It is well known that the number of categories affects the value of virtually all of the commonly used nonparametric statistics in sociology, such as Yule's Q, gamma, phi, Cramer's V, and so on. Entropy measurement is not exempt from this restriction, as indeed no measure based on categorical data can be. Nonparametric measures are affected not only by the number of categories but by change in this number such as the collapse of categories (Blalock 1964). The effect of the number of categories on entropy measurement has been discussed in some detail by McFarland (1969).

Obviously, any measure of the distribution of values into a set of categories is going to be affected by the number and size of categories, as change in category boundaries can alter the cell frequency of each category and thus alter the probability of occurrence of that category. This affects the H measure in two ways: (1) the value of maximum entropy is altered, and (2) the value of a given empirically computed entropy value is altered. Since maximum univariate entropy as computed by H is log K where K is the number of categories, an increase in the number of categories increases the maximum value and thus increases the range of potential H values (because minimum entropy remains fixed at zero). Change in the number of categories can also affect the probability of occurrence of a given category and thus can affect the computed value of·entropy in a particular empirical measurement. Although the potential minimum entropy value will remain zero (when the probability of occurrence of one particular category is 1.0, meaning that all cases lie in that category), the actual *computed* value of entropy could change from the minimum to some value above zero if categories were changed in such a manner that the original category were split, so that some cases now fall in each of two or more categories. That is, although previously the whole sample of cases (N) occurred in one category, it now occupies two or more categories.

However, even though the number of categories will affect entropy, as well as other standard nonparametric statistics used by sociologists, this effect for entropy will often be small. There are a number of reasons why the number of categories does not greatly affect the interpretation of entropy. One is that if the value of entropy is zero (minimum), gerrymandering of boundaries, unless extreme, will not enable one to change the value very far from zero. At the other pole, if values truly are distributed randomly, then entropy will be maximum *regardless* of the number of categories. One can change the computed numerical value in this case (by changing the number of categories, K) but cannot change the fact that this value is the maximum. That is, if values are randomly distributed through K categories, the maximum H value will be log K. If the number of categories is increased to $K + 1$, the maximum value will change to log $K + 1$. In either case, the important point is that the computed value is still the maximum, and changing the number of categories did not change this fact. A random distribution remains random, no matter how many categories it is divided into. In fact, if the distribution of cases is truly random, category boundaries can be assigned randomly, without changing the fact that the computed entropy value is the maximum for that set of categories. Further, the change in computed values will be slight. The major point is that unless the change in the number of categories is *extreme* and the distribution of values is highly unusual (e.g., highly skewed), changing the number of categories will have relatively little effect on entropy values.

Thus, usually changes in the number of categories will have only a minor effect on the computed value of entropy. For example, Treas (1983) reports only minor change in her entropy measure of family income inequality when the number of categories was changed. More important, usually the number of categories are *not* arbitrarily changed at the whim of the researcher but are essentially fixed. If they are fixed, then the number of categories does not affect the interpretation, and the whole matter is moot. Since this point is important, it behooves us to delve a little more closely into the question of how categories are constructed. Here it is helpful to analyze the situation in terms of the three-level model.

Type B Mapping. One common way in which data categories are constructed is through the mapping of concepts (X) onto the marker level (X''), type B mapping. A familiar example of this occurs in survey research, where the researcher chooses the answer categories for a closed-ended question (see Bailey 1982a). One common format is the Likert-style format of five categories (strongly agree, agree, neutral, disagree, strongly disagree). Here the number of categories is chosen by the investigator. The value of computed entropy will be affected by the number of categories, but it is only one of several aspects of research (and indeed the *last* aspect) that will be affected. Any scale score constructed by combining such categories will be immediately affected. Also, the reaction of the respondent may be affected, and thus the number of categories may affect the response rate and the adequacy of the response. So, seen in context, it is clear that the number of categories affects virtually the whole of the research process, from data gathering to index construction to statistical computation of entropy or some other nonparametric statistic. The other side of the coin is that *computation of the entropy measure does not depend upon some given number of categories.* The measure is quite flexible with regard to the number of categories, and almost any number will suffice as long as they are chosen with regard to standard rules of classification (are all of the same size, mutually exclusive, exhaustive, etc.). A problem arises only when an investigator changes the number of categories to unethically manipulate the value of the measure. For example, any of the standard formats currently used in measurement and scaling (such as five categories or seven categories, see Bailey 1982a) will suffice. Further, there is a great deal of standardization in measurement (the five Likert categories are common), and this facilitates comparison of two different entropy measures as it standardizes the value of maximum entropy.

Type C Mapping. It is thus true that in some cases, for example in survey research, the researcher will have some control over the number of categories, and this will have an impact on all stages of the research project, including the potential maximum value of H and the computed value of H. However, in other cases the researcher will have less control over the number of categories in a particular variable. One example of the latter is where the variables are simply symbolic representations of empirical entities. Thus, they are formed by mapping empirically occurring categories (X') onto markers (X''), type C mapping. A familiar example is that of gender. Since only females and males exist empirically, the researcher cannot usually change the number of categories when mapping onto markers. Here, the number of categories is not a problem for entropy measurement because it is fixed. However, it is a rather severe problem for commonly used sociological statistics such as regression, because there are so many of these variables in sociology (sex, race, religion, etc.). These nominal variables are perfectly adequate for entropy measurement but pose a real problem for regression, both because they violate the basic assumptions and because use of attenuated "dummy" variables subverts the whole interpretation of correlation and regression, which is in terms of explained variance. The whole notion of explained variance is difficult to apply to nominal dummy variables, and the results are generally unsatisfactory. Entropy has no such interpretative barriers.

The Marker (X″) Level. Most research utilizes a combination of type B and type C mappings, and thus has both conceptual (X) and empirical (X') categories as part of the information mapped onto its marker level $(X″)$. Further, it is common for researchers to "recode" data on markers, including collapsing categories. Recoding may also include construction of new categories and division of existing ones, but collapsing categories is probably the most common procedure. Again, such collapse is a general issue (as is the treatment of missing values) that affects any statistic used, including entropy (see Blalock 1964 for a valuable discussion of the effects of collapsing categories).

All in all, then, when viewed holistically it is clear that the number of categories affects virtually the whole of the research process and *not* just the statistical computations. Further, it affects almost all statistical computations and *not* just entropy. Still further, the effects of such category changes in most cases are rather slight (see Treas 1983, p. 550). However, some readers may still be troubled by the fact that the maximum value of H varies with the number of categories, thus clouding the comparative interpretation of H for different numbers of categories. Again, the issue requires clarification. For one thing, many categories are standardized, whether analytical categories conceived by the researcher and thus a type B mapping or empirically derived and a type C mapping. For example, cross-cultural comparisons of gender entropy do not encounter a problem because gender has the same number of categories in all societies. As another example, most American income inequality studies rely upon *Current Population Survey* (CPS) data that all utilize five categories, and so again number of categories is not an issue. For cases where the number of categories is different, one can easily solve the problem by transforming H so that it varies between zero and 1.00 in all cases. This is easy to do and is often dictated by other considerations, as shall be seen in the discussion of inequality. When so standardized, the measure will have a maximum of 1.0 regardless of the number of categories (as in equation 3.12). However, bear in mind that a number of other statistics in use in sociology also lack a standard maximum value. Further, the attainment of a standard maximum such as 1.0 does not preclude data problems (such as attenutation).

In summary, even though entropy is like other nonparametric statistics in its sensitivity to the number of categories, this is generally a minor problem for a number of reasons. One is that the number of categories is often fixed and not an issue. Another is that, in those cases where the number of categories is not fixed, entropy has no required number of categories and so is flexible in this regard. Finally, if one wishes to standardize the value of maximum entropy for comparative purposes, this is accomplished easily enough through various transformations.

Sample Size

The determination of sample size, like the number of categories, can obviously affect any statistic, and entropy is no exception. Again, as with the specification of number of categories, a number of factors often enter into the determination of sample size besides requirements of the particular statistic being computed. Often samples are constrained simple because respondents are unavailable or the costs of gathering sufficient data are prohibitive. Although one can find a formula for setting sample size in many statistics and sampling books (e.g., see Mendenhall, Ott, and Scheaffer 1971), this generally requires the investigator to specify a level of sampling error and estimate the population variance. The latter is a dilemma, for if this were known, sampling would often be unnecessary. Further, this procedure generally specifies sample size for only a given variable, and sociological samples routinely gather data on *many* variables simultaneously, with each likely to have a different population variance.

Thus, to say the least, the specification of sample size for any statistic is less precise in sociology than may sometimes appear. In general, however, the sample sizes routinely utilized for other statistical analyses will suffice for measurement of entropy as well. As a rule of thumb, we minimally need several times as many persons as categories (in the R-analysis such as Figure 8.1) to escape degree-of-freedom problems. Obviously the more categories, the larger the sample that will be required. Sudman (1976) reports modal national sample sizes of "1000 + " and these should generally be sufficient if they are a representative random sample.

Sampling Distribution

Only a relatively small amount of work has been done in the area of developing the sampling distributions of various entropy measures. As Theil puts it: "Informational measures based on a random sample are obviously also random, and the question then arises of how they are distributed around the corresponding population values. Some work, but not much has been done by various authors in this area" (1971, p. 662) Theil then presents the variance for univariate H. Remember that H is a function of the probabilities of occurrence of the various categories. Assume that H is estimated by $\hat{H}$, where $\hat{H}$ is the same function of the observed frequencies $f_1 \ldots , f_N$ as H is of the probabilities $p_1, \ldots, P_N$. Then $\hat{H}$ is asymptotically normally distributed (n—>∞) with mean H and variance of

$$\hat{H} = 1/n \sum_{i=1}^{N} p_i(\log p_i + H)^2 \qquad (8.1)$$

Theil (1967, pp. 18–19) elsewhere derives the sampling variance for information (h). The measure of information (h) is a component of entropy (H). Specifically, from Theil (1967, p. 24):

$$H(x) = \sum_{i=1}^{n} x_i h(x_i) \qquad (8.2)$$

Thus, the variances have been derived for both h and H, with the latter being of most concern here. These variances hold only for large samples, but small sample corrections are presented by Theil (1971, p. 662). In addition, some recent discussions in the sociological literature focus on sampling distributions for measures of inequality, including entropic measures (see Jasso 1982; Treas 1982).

For joint entropy chi-square can be used as a test of significance, just as in other nonparametric statistics in sociology. For example, a common practice in bivariate contingency table analysis in sociology is to compute chi-square as a significance test to determine whether the relationship between the two variables departs significantly from independence. If so, a measure of strength of relationship can be computed and interpreted. The same procedure can be followed exactly with bivariate joint entropy (equation 3.4). For a given two-dimensional table we first compute chi-square. If the relationship is found to be statistically significant (e.g., at the .05 level for the appropriate number of degrees of freedom), then it is clear that there is a nonzero relationship between the two variables. In that case the analysis of joint entropy (and conditional entropy for that matter) can proceed. See Sneath and Sokal (1973, p. 142) for discussion of the relationship of H to chi-square.

Relationship of Categorical Entropy
to Continuous Variables

So far the discussion has centered on the computation of entropy (H) for categorical variables, such as nominal variables (e.g., gender), ordinal variables (e.g., years of education completed), or continuous variables that have been categorized (e.g., age). Stevens's (1951) classification of levels of measurement as nominal, ordinal, interval, and ratio is commonly used in sociology, with the widespread assumption that continuous measurement such as interval and ratio is superior for research purposes.

The problem arises, of course, when we attempt a type C mapping by including actual data in the model to yield numerical results. In the most fortuitous situation we will find that all of the variables we wish to analyze meet the assumptions of the linear least-squares model. The assumptions of the OLS (ordinary least squares) model are well known and need not be listed here. Briefly, the model requires independent continuously measured (interval or ratio) variables that are not highly intercorrelated with each other, so that multicollinearity is not a problem. The data should be gathered through a random sample of sufficient size to ensure a multivariate normal distribution. Further, we assume homoscedasticity, or equal variances in independent and dependent variables.

Of course, what we immediately find when we attempt a type C mapping is that a large number of variables (we stop short of saying a majority) of interest in sociological anaylses *do not* meet these assumptions. Many of them are categorical, for example, including race, gender, occupation, religion, area of residence, marital status. The problem now is that, in terms of the three-level model, we do not have type A isomorphism, as the empirically occurring variables (X') are *not* isomorphic with the conceptualized variables (interval or ratio) assumed by the model (X). In more standard language, the data do not meet the assumptions of the model. What are we to do now? There are only three basic strategies: (1) choose only those data for analysis that fit the assumptions of the model; (2) tailor the model in some manner to attain isomorphism with the empirically occurring data; or (3) reject the OLS model in favor of a model better suited to the data. All three strategies are common in sociology. As regards the first, Coser (1975) fears that the "methodological tail can wag the theoretical dog," if sociologists choose problems not by their theoretical importance but because the data meet the assumptions of their favorite statistical model. Utilization of the third strategy is evidenced by the frequent use of nonparametric statistics for contingency tables in sociology (for discussion of the popular gamma statistic see James Davis 1971).

However, nonparametric statistics are generally not as multivariate as multiple regression and correlation and do not have the interpretations of these techniques. For example, it is difficult to analyze more than three variables simultaneously in a contingency table. Thus, when sociologists wish to analyze variables that are not continuous and do not meet the assumptions of regression, about the only alternative is the second—to attempt to alter the OLS model in such a manner that the desired data may be utilized. There has been a marked tendency in this direction in sociology in the last decade. This is understandable, since so many sociological variables are categorical and so many questionnaire items have response categories that are ordinal at best. One strain of evidence of this is the use of the popular "dummy variable" regression and the utilization of ordinal data in models designed for continuous data (see O'Brien 1979; Bollen and Barb 1981; Johnson and Creech 1983). Another approach is "log-linear" analysis (Goodman 1971, 1972; Swafford 1980). Perusal of a recent issue of a major sociological journal reveals one article using "logistic regression" (Robinson 1984) and another using "logit regression" (Shavit 1984). Both techniques are adaptations (critics might say "weakenings") of the standard OLS model. Only casual reflection will show that it is difficult to meet the assumptions of regression, particularly the assumption of homoscedasticity, with probabilistic data. Since there is clearly a recent demand for probabilistic models and since entropy is a probabilistic model, the time seems to be ripe for entropy analysis. There is clearly a demand for it and a niche in sociological statistics for it—not to the exclusion of existing methods but to supplement the existing statistical armory. For example, why would one who desires a probabilistic analysis utilize the categorical data in a modified regression model? Doing so almost ensures attenuated variance, thus resulting in a low amount of explained variance as measured by R^2. Rather than attempting to fit categorical data into a model not designed for them, it might be a better procedure to simply utilize an entropy analysis. If a symmetrical analysis (such as correlation) is desired, then joint entropy can be computed. If an asymmetrical analysis (such as regression) is desired, then conditional entropy can be computed. As suggested earlier, the recommended procedure is to compute univariate entropy for each variable and then both joint and conditional entropies for the combined set.

Categorical and Continuous Entropy

Entropy is a measure of disorganization or uncertainty. Thus, it would be reasonable to guess that entropy is basically a measure of dispersion or an analogue to variance. This is confirmed by Theil:

> The use of informational measures is particularly appropriate when the variables are qualitative rather than quantitative. The modal value (the outcome with the largest probability) may then be used as a measure of central tendency, the entropy as a measure of dispersion, and the expected mutual information as a measure of dependence. These three should be compared respectively with the mean, the variance, and the convariance (or the correlation coefficient) of the more conventional type of statistics. . . .
>
> Pursuing this line of thought a little further, we should note that the difference between the average conditional entropies $H_Y(X)$ and $H_{YZ}(X)$ is concep-

tually related to the partial correlation coefficient of X and Z given Y. (1971, pp. 662–663)

That is, for a dependent variable X and independent variables Y and Z, the term for unexplained variance in the regression equation is $1 - R^2_{X \cdot YZ}$. This is a measure of "uncertaintly," or variance in X that cannot be explained by knowledge of Y and Z. Thus, this term is analogous to the conditional entropy $H_{YZ}(X)$.

Continuous Entropy

Although entropy has been discussed for categorical variables, it is relatively easy to compute it for continuous variables as well. Remember from equation (3.2) that

$$H = -\sum_{i=1}^{K} p_i \ln p_i.$$

Alternatively, another way to write the same formula that is mathematically equivalent and may be easier as a computing formula is

$$H = \sum_{i=1}^{K} p_i \ln 1/p_i \tag{8.3}$$

Assume that instead of a categorical variable we have a continuous variable, such as income, measured for a sample of N persons. As Theil (1967, pp. 91–92) shows, H can easily be computed for income simply by computing the income fraction for each person. That is, assume that each of the N persons has an income that is some proportion of the total. Let x_i be the proportion of total income earned by the ith person. Then the sum of the incomes (x) of all N is 1.0, or

$$\sum_{i=1}^{N} x_i = 1$$

Then, following equation (8.3) and using logarithms to the base 2,

$$H = \sum_{i=1}^{N} x_i \log_2 1/x_i \tag{8.4}$$

Note that this is the same equation for H that was computed for categorical data. The only difference is that now each of the N values of the continuous variable is, in a sense, utilized as a category, so that x_i can be interpreted as the probability of occurrence of that particular income category. Also note that the maximum value of H, which was the log of the number of categories for categorical data, is now

$$H_{max} = \log N \tag{8.5}$$

Minimum H is, of course, still zero.

When computed for continuous variables, entropy is still a measure of dispersion and directly analogous to the variance. Thus, H can be seen as measuring degree of departure from the mean income in this case.

As in Chapter 3, entropy was originally defined by Clausius as a continuous variable and conceptualized in terms of change (dS), or diachronically rather than synchronically. The synchronic variable (S) could be defined only through integration. Thus, entropy has always been conceptualized in terms of differential and integral calculus (see Rothstein 1958, p. 4). If one wishes to write Shannon's H in terms of differential and integral calculus, this is a rather straightforward procedure involving the specification of the probability density function. For an example of this see Batty and Sikdar (1982), also see equation 8.12.

In summary, then, it is relatively easy to compute entropy for either continuous or categorical variables, which helps remove some of the previous resistance to entropy because it was thought to be only applicable to categorical data. For example, Sneath and Sokal (1973, p. 145), in discussing entropy measures as used in numerical taxonomy, say that "It has proved difficult to adapt them to continuous, quantitative characters." One implication of this situation would be that entropy analysis is a special case of information analysis that holds only for categorical data, and in the more general instance, some other concept is preferable. The application of entropy to continuous data effectively erases this implication.

Measuring Inequality

Thus, entropy analysis is *not* limited to categorical data, and either continuous or categorical entropy measures can be used. One way to examine this more closely is through the application of entropy to the study of inequality (e.g., in income or wealth), where entropy measures have proven very efficacious. Theil (1967) analyzed the entropic measurement of inequality in some detail, and his measures have received considerable attention from sociological students of inequality such as Allison (1978) and Treas (1982; 1983).

Continuous

Let us first analyze income inequality as a continuous distribution. This is easily done by applying equation (8.4.). In this case, H is applied to income shares (x_i is the share or fraction of the total income held by person i). Maximum inequality exists when one person has all of the income ($x_i = 1.0$) and all other persons have none at all ($x_i = 0.0$). In this case, inequality is a maximum but entropy (H) is minimal or zero, as it will be any time that a single category or value contains 100 percent of the cases. Conversely, inequality is minimized when all persons have the same income. In this case, for a sample of N persons, each person's income is exactly $1/N$ of the total income for the group. This is defined as zero inequality or complete equality. Notice that this is represented by the maximum value of H, or $\log N$. Also notice that the lowest possible value of inequality (zero inequality) is represented by *maximum* entropy, whereas maximum inequality is represented by *minimum* (zero) entropy. Therefore, entropy as measured by H is *not* a direct measure of inequality but a measure of *equality*. Income or wealth certainly can be studied in terms of the equality of the distribution, but most theory is directed toward the concept of inequality, so it seems preferable to measure inequality directly.

This is easily done. The simplest way to reverse the entropy measure is to simply subtract it from its maximum, which is $\log N$. This is the approach adopted by Theil (1967, p. 91).

$$\log N - H(y) = \sum_{i=1}^{N} y_i \log N y_i \tag{8.6}$$

The right-hand side of equation (8.6) varies from 0 (when entropy is maximum) to $\log N$ (when entropy is minimum or zero). Since the former represents minimum (zero) inequality and the latter represents maximum inequality, this measure now is an inequality measure rather than an equality measure. Note, however, that its upper bound still varies with sample size.

This measure serves quite adequately as a measure of inequality. It facilitates both aggregation and decomposition (as, for example, when we wish to compare groups, such as income of blacks and whites). It also has a number of advantages over other popular inequality measures, such as the Gini concentration measure. The entropy measure is easier to compute and interpret (see Allison 1978), and as Treas (1983, p. 550) notes, the Gini is relatively insensitive to inequality changes. For this reason, among others, Treas chose the entropy measure over the Gini for the study of family income inequality. Allison (1978) evaluated this particular entropy measure of inequality (equation 8.9) along with the Gini and other inequality measures. He found that the entropy measure fared very well on a number of criteria, including scale invariance, sensitivity to transfers, and adequate upper bounds.

This measure not only fares well in Allison's (1978) evaluation but also has proven efficacious in empirical research, such as the study of family income inequality (see Treas 1982, 1983; Treas and Walther 1978). However, as is often the case in entropy research, these various investigations are in danger of losing their visibility as cumulative research, simply because this visibility is masked by variations in presentation of these measures. It has been noted earlier that the cumulative body of entropy research is masked by the fact that *H* is called, variously, *uncertainty, information, entropy,* and even *surprisal* (Sneath and Sokal 1973, p. 141). The same sort of thing is developing in inequality measurement.

Both Allison (1978) and Treas (1983) utilize Theil's (1967, p. 92) measure, presented in this chapter as equation (8.6). Theil does not label this index but presents it just as it is presented in equation 8.6. Yet, Allison (1978) labels it *T*, and Treas (1983) calls it *I* (one can only speculate that Allison named the measure after Theil, and Treas named it after inequality or even income inequality). The cumulative impact of these studies is further masked by the fact that Treas presented the formula in the same form and using the same symbols as Theil (the right-hand side of equation 8.6), yet Allison presented a *different* formula that, although mathematically identical, is written in terms of deviation from the mean and shows *T* as a measure of dispersion divided by the mean. Treas's formula is presented in equation 8.7. Allison's formula is presented in equation 8.8. From Treas (1983):

$$I = \sum_{i=1}^{N} y_i \log Ny_i \tag{8.7}$$

From Allison (1978, p. 867):

$$T = 1/n \sum_{i=1}^{n} \frac{\varkappa x_i \log_2 x_i - u \log_2 u}{u} \tag{8.8}$$

Combining these, we see that

$$I = T = \sum_{i=1}^{N} y_i \log Ny_i = 1/n \sum_{i=1}^{n} \frac{\varkappa x_i \log_2 x_i - u \log_2 u)}{u} \tag{8.9}$$

Thus, Allison's careful evaluation and Treas' careful empirical analysis concern the same measure and so complement each other quite well. These studies, along with the present analysis and with other work on entropy measures of inequality (Bailey 1985), form the nucleus for a cumulative body of entropy analysis of inequality.

Decomposition

Theil's measure (equation 8.6) facilitates the decomposition of inequality measurement into subpopulation components and conversely facilitates the aggregation of subpopulation inequality analysis. The process of decomposition can become confusing, but it is clarified by the distinction between globals and mutables. Remember that population size (*P*) and level of living (*L*) are two basic global properties of *all* social systems. In general statistical analysis in sociology, if we are analyzing only income, we would label this a *univariate* analysis. However, in Theil's measurement of income inequality, it is very clear that we are *not* just studying a single global variable (*L*) but the *distribution* of people (*P*) into the (*L*) distribution.

For undeveloped countries the optimal operationalization of level of living (*L*) might be the total number of food calories possessed by the society, the total number of energy sources (e.g., fossil fuels), or even the total life expectancy. It will generally be either a direct or indirect measure of the amount of energy the society possesses. For industrialized societies the number of such energy variables is too large and diverse to always be directly accountable, so the best operationalization of (*L*) is probably either the total wealth or income possessed by the society. In the United States, it is common to analyze inequality for both wealth and income, and the difference in inequality between the two is often of interest. The same inequality measure should generally be applicable to either.

What we wish to stress here is that the analysis of inequality (let us focus on income for the present) begins with the two distinct global variables of *total income possessed by the society* (*L*) and *total population size* (*P*). Note that these are *globals* and not yet *mutables* in our terminology. To conduct the inequality analysis, we must first envision the *mutable* distribution formed by distributing all individuals in the population (*P*) into *total societal income* (*L*) in order to construct the mutable income distribution (*L*). Thus, we see that each of the *N* individuals has a share (fraction) of total (global) income, so that each of the *N* individuals in the concrete living societal system has a nonnegative amount of income. There are then a total of *N* nonnegative amounts of individual income (Theil 1967, p. 91).

Thus, the basic analysis of income inequality utilizes *two* global variables (population and level of living, or [*P*] and [*L*], respectively), but this is not always recognized, because they are combined into one mutable distribution of income. Unless it is clear that *two separate elements* (P and L) are involved, analysis of income inequality can become tremendously confusing. It is even more complicated when another variable is added. In this case, total income (L) remains the same for the societal level (that is, the global value of income [L] possessed by the society does not change); however, the global population value (P) is now being divided on some other basis. The basis for division of population (P) can be either one of the other four globals ($O, I, S,$ or T) or any of the socially salient immutable variables (such as race, sex, or age). Also bear in mind that *all* global variables are interrelated, as are all five mutables. Further, many immutables are related to the mutable distributions. Thus, this same analysis, with H or its various transformations, can be applied to *other* mutables besides income (L); for example, occupations (O) or sub-system spatial areas (S).

For the analysis of income inequality in economics or sociology, some standard variables are used to divide or "decompose" the population to discern income inequality differences between groups. In a sense, then, these selected variables will serve as controls, or at least additional independent variables. Among the variables that Theil (1967) uses for decomposition and aggregation are an immutable variable (white-nonwhite) and the mutable of spatial area (S), the latter being used both at the societal level (where the internal subdivisions are states) and at the supranational level (where the subdivisions are countries).

The basic formula for decomposition into component subgroups is presented by Theil (1967, p. 95, equation 1.9), and can be written in various symbolizations. The decomposition formula is derived by decomposing the right-hand side of equation 8.6 into between-set and within-set inequalities, where the sets are the subcomponents of the total population N (e.g., a white set and a nonwhite set or a male set and a female set). Remember that the left side of equation 8.6 is simply the computed entropy value (H) subtracted from the maximum possible value of entropy (log N). The right side is

$$\sum_{i\,=\,1}^{N} y_i \log N y_i.$$

This right term suffices as long as we do not wish to examine income inequality for different groups, such as different occupations, sexes, or races. *Any* sets could suffice as bases for division, even hypothetical ones. However, notice that the most common bases for decomposition (gender, race, occupation) are categorical variables rather than continuous variables. Thus, even if one analyzes income as a continuous variable, this suffices only for a rather nondiscriminating analysis. One who wishes to add independent variables through decomposition is likely once again to be working with categorical variables. The chief point is that the population global variable is divided into groups or sets on some basis. When this is done, the inequality measure (equation 8.6) has a very attractive interpretation. As Theil says:

> We now find that this measure has a simple interpretation in terms of income shares and population shares; moreover, that it can be aggregated in a straightforward manner. In that respect it is more attractive than most well-known inequality measures such as Gini's concentration ratio. (1967, pp. 95–96)

Theil's decomposition formula (his equation 1.9) is shown in equation 8.10:

$$\log N - H(y) = \underbrace{\sum_{i=1}^{N} y_i \log \frac{y_i}{1/N} = \sum_{g=1}^{G} Y_g \log \frac{Y_g}{N_g/N}}_{(a)} + \underbrace{\sum_{g=1}^{G} Y_g \left[\sum_{i \in Sg} \frac{Y_i}{Y_g} \log \frac{y_i/Y_g}{1/N_g} \right]}_{(b)} \quad (8.10)$$

where G is the number of population sets; Sg is one of the G population sets; Y_g is the income share of a particular set (the ratio of the income of set g to total income); N_g is the population of set g; N is the total population; and N_g/N is the population share of the particular set. Therefore, for each given set, we need to compute the share that set possesses of the global variable of income (L) and the share that set possesses of the global population variable (P), called the income shares and population shares, respectively.

Term (a) of equation 8.10 measures *between-set inequality.* Note that this is computed from the income share for the set (Y_g) and the population share of the set (N_g/N). *Term (b)* of equation 8.10 measures the within-set inequality. This is derived from the income share of the set (Y_g) from the ratio y_i/Y_g, which is a conditional income share (y_i is an unconditional income share), and from $1/N_g$, which is the population share within the particular set.

In summary, this book has discussed the merits of entropy measurement. This particular entropy measure of inequality (equation 8.6) has a distinct advantage over the popular Gini measure. As Theil says: "The concentration ratio is rather popular, but it has the serious drawback that it does not lend itself to between-set and within-set decompositions. This is due to the use of absolute differences, which are awkward for such purposes" (1967, p. 123). Such decomposition into between-group and within-group inequality analysis is important both statistically and theoretically for a number of reasons. Theoretically speaking, the between-group distributions are fundamentally important. Consider the two global variables of population (P) and income (L).

If we decompose (P) into occupational groups (O), we have now formed the *occupational* mutable distribution. If there is no within-group occupational inequality, this means that *all* occupations have the same income. Further, decomposing on the immutable of race, if there is no between-group income inequality, this would show that race is not a factor in inequality. The fact of the matter is that there *will* be some degree of between-group inequality. If this were not true, we would have no real reason to study inequality, and poverty would not be a "social problem." Thus, between-group inequality is of basic theoretical importance. The notions of between- and within-group inequality are also of fundamental statistical importance and thus have tremendous integrative potential (integration of knowledge is one of the goals of holistic analysis). Beginning with inequality measures, we see that the notions of between-group and within-group inequality also directly link Theil's entropy measure (equation 8.6) to at least two other useful inequality measures: the variance of the income logarithms, and the squared coefficient of variation. Both of these have rather straightforward decompositions into between-group and within-group inequalities and are discussed by Theil (1967, pp. 124–127).

In addition, the between-group and within-group decomposition facilitates the integration of entropy-based measures with a large class of group-based statistics. A primary link is to analysis of variance (ANOVA), which uses a categorical independent variable (e.g., race) and a dependent continuous variable (e.g., income) and so has a direct parallel to the entropy-based inequality analysis. The F test of ANOVA is based on the ratio of between-group to within-group variance. Thus, through ANOVA, the entropy analysis has a direct link to experimental causal analysis; unless F is greater than 1, between-group variance does not exceed within-group variance. This indicates that the independent variable is *not* an effective cause of the change in the dependent variable. The between-group sum of squares (SS) to within-group SS analysis is fundamental to many categorical statistics, including multiple discriminant analysis and a host of numerical-taxonomic techniques. For further discussion see Sokal and Sneath (1963) and Sneath and Sokal (1973).

Categorical Income Data

A somewhat ironic fact is that even though income is a continuous variable, the reported macrosociological data are often categorized before users see them. There are a number of reasons for such grouping. One is to protect the identity of persons who do not wish their income revealed. Another is that global data from the whole society are simply unmanageable unless grouped, as millions of individual cases cannot be effectively transmitted and analyzed. Thus, the data received are generally going to be presented in relatively few groups. If one desires the basic measurement of inequality, without decomposition on additional variables besides population and income, then it is necessary to *remove* the groupings in order to compute Theil's continuous measures (equation 8.6), which can be cumbersome (see Treas 1983). It is somewhat ironic that, for United States data, the *Current Population Survey* (see Treas 1983) categorizes the income data, and these efforts must be undone to use the data in a continuous inequality measure. If these data could be *decat*egorized exactly back to where they started, with *no loss* of information or accuracy, then only time and energy would have been expended. However, it is difficult to accomplish this; there is no clear way to decategorize the data, and this process must be based on assumptions.

In essence, what is done is to assume some underlying distribution for the categories (often *not* multivariate normal). For example, Theil (1967, p. 96) uses the log normal and Pareto distributions. He shows that the continuous inequality measure of equation 8.6 is equal to a derivative written in terms of individual income and average income. When speaking of a number of individuals, $Nf(z)dz$, who earn an income in a particular income range:

$$\sum_{i \in S} y_i \log Ny_i = \left(\frac{z}{Nm} \log \frac{z}{m} \right) Nf(z)dz \qquad (8.11)$$

where z is the income of any individual; m is the average income of all N individuals; the total income is Nm, and an individual's income share, y, is equal to z/Nm. What has been done here is to begin with categories that do not tell an individual's income but only the number of individuals in a given income category. This relates the inequality measure (the right side of 8.6 is the left side of 8.11) to the individual income z. The final step is to simply integrate the derivative over all individuals to remove the category boundaries. Specifically, the right side of 8.11 is integrated:

$$\int_0^\infty \left(\frac{z}{m} \log \frac{z}{m} \right) f(z)dz \qquad (8.12)$$

The process of decategorization necessarily involves making basic assumptions about the distributions of incomes within a category; that is, categorizing requires giving up the within-group information. Therefore, as Theil says, referring to the inequality measure, the right side of which is shown in equation 8.12:

The table shows also a difficulty in the application of the inequality measure. When the income distribution is only specified in terms of percentages of income recipients for rather wide intervals, we have to use approximate methods to compute the measure . . . . One acts as if the income recipients within each interval have the same income, viz., the amount which corresponds to the midpoint of the interval. (1967, p. 99)

In other words, this particular assumption assumes that there is *no* within-group variance in income. There obviously *is* some within-group variation, but this information *was lost* during categorization and cannot really be regained without returning to the original individual continuous data. Thus, the optimal procedure is not to use categorical data but only the individual continuous data. However, this is probably impossible, as we cannot obtain the data for an entire population and would probably not be able to manage the analysis of so many cases if we could obtain it. However, there is another alternative to decategorization. This is simply to compute inequality for the categories and not attempt to use a continuous measure, such as equation 8.6. This is relatively straightforward and probably the best procedure under the circumstances as long as what we are doing is clearly understood.

Categorized data of the type discussed earlier in this chapter was presented in Table 8.1, which shows the income distribution for the United States. Note that this table yields no direct information on individual income, and so we cannot directly compute the individual income shares used in our prior analysis. Rather than having a distribution of income shares, we now have what Theil (1967, p. 96) calls an "ordinary" income distribution, or the distribution showing only the *number* of individuals in a given income category. Note further that this table does not actually show income categories but only rank orders of categories. Thus, a considerable amount of information has been lost compared with the distribution of individual incomes. To understand such tables it is helpful to again turn to the global variable distinction. These tables both provide information on the population global (P) and the income global (L). However, the population global has been decomposed into five categories, *not* on the basis of some additional variable such as race or occupation, but solely on income rankings. The effect of this is that there are now five population groups, each with 20 per cent of the population. In other words, *the population shares have been arbitrarily set at maximum entropy.* In order for a value below maximum entropy of population to be obtained, the cell percentages would have to be unequal. Since the population shares of each group have been effectively standardized, the only entities left to vary (unless we decompose on some third variable) are the income shares of each category. Further, we do have some ordinal information on income, as the population categories have been ranked in terms of percentages of income (or wealth).

The chief difference between the present categorical analysis and our earlier continuous analysis is that we can only ultimately analyze income inequality in terms of population categories and not in terms of individuals. That is, in the individual, continuous analysis, maximum entropy or maximum H occurs when each of the N individuals has an equal share of the income, or $1/N$ of the total income (this represents minimum inequality). In the present K categorical table in effect the *category* not the individual is used as the unit of analysis. Thus, maximum categorical entropy does not necessarily indicate maximum individual entropy, or minimum individual inequality. That is, maximum entropy or minimum inequality in Table 8.1 is *not* log N, as in the individual analysis, but log K, where K is the number of categories (in this case, log 5). The result is that neither entropy (nor the Gini nor any other measure) can measure absolute individual equality or inequality but can measure it only categorically. Thus, the minimum amount of inequality is constrained by the difference between log K and log N. The maximum amount of inequality will give a measured value of entropy of 0 in either care, but for the individual analysis this will indicate that a single individual possesses all the income, while for the categorical analysis it will indicate only that a single group has all of the income.

In other words, the primary difference between the individual analysis and the categorical analysis is that in the latter all information concerning income variation within each of the five population groups has been lost. Thus, finding a value of maximum entropy for the categorical case means that each group has 20 percent of the income (in which case the groups could not be ranked as they are now). This is the minimum amount of inequality that can be measured for this data, but *it is not necessarily minimum individual inequality*. This would occur if all individuals within each group also had equal incomes, in which case entropy would be the maximum (log N). To make the assumption that there is no within-group difference in income (an assumption that is sometimes made in decategorizing data), effectively decategorizes Table 8.2, and we are back to basically an individual or continuous analysis.

If we choose to simply analyze the data as presented, which is the most straightforward approach (as long as we recognize that this means interpreting entropy in terms of categories rather than individuals), we can proceed as for the continuous analysis. We can simply measure inequality by H, but this is inversely related to inequality (H is a measure of *equality*), so we can reverse it as Theil did for the continuous case in equation 8.6. This is shown in equation 8.13:

$$B^* = \log K - H \tag{8.13}$$

This is the same as equation 8.6, except maximum entropy is now log K instead of log N. $B*$ is now a direct measure of inequality. For a categorical table, minimum inequality exists when all categories have the same income probabilities. This is maximum entropy, or a $B*$ of zero (log K − log K). Conversely, when inequality is a maximum, H = zero and so $B*$ − log K. Thus, $B*$ is the categorical equivalent of Theil's continuous measure (equation 8.6) and will be identical with Theil's measure if all N persons each has his or her own category, so that $K = N$. Generally, however, K will be smaller than N, often greatly so, and so this constrains the range of variation of entropy and inequality measurement for categorical data.

One other adjustment that may be desired is to standardize the maximum value of the inequality measure (see Theil 1967; Allison 1978; Treas 1982). This can be done easily enough by simply dividing the measure by the maximum possible value of entropy or log K. This is shown in equation 8.14:

$$B = \frac{\log K - H}{\log K} = 1 - \frac{H}{\log K}$$

$$\text{(8.14)}$$

B varies between zero and unity. It is zero when inequality is a minimum, and unity when inequality is a maximum. Thus, it is zero when $B*$ is zero, but is 1.0 when $B* = \log K$. There are basically two schools of thought on whether $B*$ or B should be used. The problem with $B*$ is that it does not have a fixed maximum value, but rather the maximum will vary with the number of categories. Theil (1967) argues that this is a positive feature (his measure of equation 8.6 also varies with population size, having a maximum value of log N). Theil argues that if one person has all of the income in a large population, this represents more inequality than if one person has all of the income in a dyad. If one wishes to stress this feature, $B*$ should be used. However, for comparative purposes, and to make the measure conform to standard sociological statistical interpretations, it may be preferable to utilize B. When using B, though, keep in mind that by using categorical data, one has already attenuated the degree of entropy variation from $0 - \log N$ down to $0 - K$. By categorizing a population of size N into K categories, one loses the ability in essence to measure entropy in the range log K) to log N (this applies both to $B*$ and B). Further dividing by log K further reduces the maximum measured entropy value from log K to 1.0. Thus, from equation 8.6 (Theil's continuous measure) to equation 8.13, the maximum entropy value is attenuated from log N to log K, and from equation 8.6 to equation 8.14, the maximum is attenuated from log N to 1.0. This could have a number of effects on the analysis and interpretation. For example, such attentuation may inversely affect the ability to effectively utilize the technique of decomposition (see Theil 1967, pp. 92–94), because such attenuation can certainly narrow the between-group inequality variations, among other things.

Measures of Population Diversity

This chapter, which has concentrated on the statistical properties of entropy and its relation to other statistical measures, concludes with an analysis of a class of sociological measures directly related to inequality measures and thus related to entropy. These are called *measures of population diversity* (see Lieberson 1969; Teachman 1980). Since authors such as Lieberson (1969) already have related some of these measures (see also Duncan and Duncan 1955), we may relate entropy to their discussions, thus relating it to a whole class of measures whose similarities are known.

There are a number of bases for determining the "diversity" of a given population, just as there are a number of bases for decomposing the population in inequality analysis. Not surprisingly, some of the chief variables used for decomposition are also used as the basis for studying population diversity. Among the bases for diversity mentioned by Lieberson (1969) are religion, ethnic origin, and political party. Since diversity has a direct parallel to decomposition, it is not surprising that it, too, involves the study of within-group and between-group diversity. Further, since *diversity* is almost a synonym for *uncertainty* (a term often applied to the entropy measure *H*), it is clear that analysis of diversity is in a real sense entropy analysis (both deal with variation in qualitative variables). Since the integration of such parallel efforts utilizing different terms is one goal of general systems theory, we can briefly compare diversity analysis and entropy analysis (and at the same time inequality analysis) in the interest of parsimony, scholarly efficiency, and the accumulation of knowlege.

The literature on diversity also is similar to that on entropy and inequality in maintaining (although not emphasizing) the distinction between the population global and the other global variables—an approach that is *very* rare in sociological statistical analysis, where the population variable is virtually invisible (although certainly used in computation of the mean and variance). The literature on diversity differs from many other statistical analyses, however, in taking a pairwise approach to the problem. That is, in studying the diversity of the population within four religious groups (Lieberson 1969), a distinction is made between the proportion of pairs with a common religion (*S*) and the proportion of pairs without a common religion (*D*). This refers to pairs of persons, out of the total sample size of *N* persons. Then, $D + S = 1.00$. If there are four religious groups, the proportion in each group is p_i and

$$\sum_{i=1}^{K} p_i = 1.0$$

Notice that again this refers to two variables: shares of population, and shares of religion. In Table 8.1 population shares were standardized at maximum entropy in the sense that an equal share of the population ($1/K$ or .20) was in each group and only income shares were left to vary. Here, *religion* is standardized in the sense that each category contains an equal share of the total number of religions ($1/K$ or .25) and only population shares are left to vary. The difference is due to the distinction made at the beginning of this chapter between different modes of presenting tabular data. In Table 8.1, the population (objects) are the categories, and a characteristic (income) is mapped in. In this case the converse is true—the characteristic of religion is used to form the categories, and the objects (persons) are mapped in. Therefore, Table 8.1 is in the basic format for a Q-analysis that relates objects, whereas this analysis is in the format for the standard R-analysis among variables usually seen in sociology.

The diversity measure (D) is basically an entropy measure, although this is difficult to discern due to the pairwise computation and the differences in terminology. The number of pairs (two-person dyads) that can be randomly sampled from a population of N persons without replacement is

$$\frac{N(N-1)}{2}.$$

Lieberson (1969) assumes sampling with replacement to simplify the approach and X_i rather than p_i as the proportion of the population in each of the four religious categories. Then, the proportions of pairs with all possible combinations is the total of 1.0, and this is represented by the square of the multinominal

$$(X_1 + X_2 + X_3 + X_4)^2 + \tag{8.15}$$
$$(X_1)^2 + (X_2)^2 + (X_3)^2 + (X_4)^2 = \tag{8.15a}$$
$$+ 2[(X_1X_2) + (X_1X_3) + (X_1X_4) + (X_2X_3) + (X_2X_4) + (X_3X_4)] \tag{8.15b}$$

In this pairwise formuation, S is the sum of squares for all groups and the proportion of pairs with a common religion. It is the sum of the four terms in 8.15a. The remainder of terms (8.15b) when summed yield D, which is diversity, or the proportion of pairs *without* a common religion. Since $D + S = 1$, the simplest way to compute D is through $1 - S$. Lieberson (1969) uses the symbol A_w (following Greenberg 1956) for D, which symbolizes *within* population diversity. Lieberson (1969, p. 851) says: "If everyone has the same religion, A_w would be 0. If every resident has a different religion, then the index would be 1.00" (1969, p. 851).

Let us compare A_w directly with entropy (H). If everyone is in the same religious category of the four, then $H = 0$, the minimum possible value of entropy. If there are only four persons in the sample $(N = 4)$ and everyone has a different religion, then $H = \log K$. Looking in Theil's (1967, p. 429) Table A, for base 2, $\log 4 = 2.0$. Thus, whereas A_w varies between 0 and 1 for this particular illustration, H varies between 0 and 2 (remember that the maximum value for H varies and is $\log K$). Thus, all that is necessary is to divide H by $\log K$ in order to standardize the maximum value at 1.0. Such a standardization procedure has been utilized for other statistical measures in sociology, such as Pearson's r, and chi-square (see Stavig and Acock, 1980). In other words, Lieberson's (1969) measure of diversity within a population, A_w, is clearly related to entropy, as

$$A_w = H/\log K \qquad (8.16)$$
$$\text{or } H = \log K/A_w \qquad (8.17)$$

Note that this is only an approximate relationship. It holds for maximum and minimum H but not for all values of H. For a more accurate statement and further discussion of this relationship, see Teachman (1980).

Now that H has been related to A_w, Lieberson's integrative analysis can be used to link H to numerous other measures, as Lieberson has already linked A_w (or $H/\log K$) to these measures:

> Except for the fact that some authors prefer to measure diversity in terms of the probability of agreement $(1 - A_w)$, this index is essentially identical to (1) Gini's index of mutability proposed in 1912 and Bachi's index of linguistic homogeneity [both cited in Bachi 1956, p. 197]; (2) the measure of diversity described by Simpson (1949); (3) the P^* index employed by Bell (1954) in his modification of the Shevky-Williams index of isolation; and (4) the measure of industry diversification proposed by Gibbs and Martin (1962) and also used by Gibbs and Browning (1966). Except for modifications due to sampling without replacement or an effort to take into account the true range of possible value for a given number of categories, A_w is basically the same as the index of qualitative variation described by Mueller and Schuessler (1961, pp. 177–179); the index of economic differentiation proposed by Amemiya (1963); and the adjusted D measure employed by Labovitz and Gibbs (1964). (Lieberson 1969, pp. 851–52)

This quote is very revealing, as it shows that, *far from being some heinous measure of heat whose application to sociology is misplaced or at best scientistic, the statistical formulation of entropy bears a clear relationship to*

*many common measures used by social scientists, and in fact forms the basis
for the integration of these measures.* Leiberson (1969) also analyses the be-
tween-population measure (A_b). This is a direct extension of A_w, and the interested reader is referred to Lieberson (1969). In addition, a number of other
indices, not mentioned by Lieberson, are almost direct measures of entropy
(or of H divided by log K). These include the index of dispersion (D), which
is 0 when entropy is minimum and 1.0 when entropy is maximum, and Ken-
dall's measure of variation. For further discussion of these measures see
Loether and McTavish (1980, pp. 154–60).

Proportional Reduction in Error

Costner's (1965) evaluation of statistical measures in terms of their proportional reduction in error (PRE) has proven very useful in understanding and
integrating statistical measures in sociology. As discussed in Chapter 3, Horan
(1975) and Teachman (1980) have shown that entropy (H) also has a clear and
direct PRE interpretation. However, both authors follow the practice of labeling H as a measure of "uncertainty," and so designate their measures as PRU
rather than PRE (see equations 3.8 and 3.9). Although Teachman and Horan
use very different symbols and reverse the positions of the X and Y variables,
their formulations are identical. Let us rewrite this formula, utilizing basically
Horan's (1975) symbols, except that H is used for entropy rather than U for
uncertainty. Then:

$$PRE_{yx} = \frac{H(Y) - H(Y|X)}{H(Y)} \tag{8.18}$$

Here Y is the dependent variable and X is the independent variable. $H(Y)$ is
just the univariate entropy of the dependent variable Y. Note that this term appears in both the numerator and denominator. The only other term in the equation is the conditional entropy $H(Y vX)$, which shows the entropy of the dependent variable Y when the entropy value of the independent variable X is
known. Equation 8.18 can also be written:

$$PRE_{yx} = 1 - \frac{H(Y|X)}{H(Y)} \tag{8.19}$$

Equation 8.19 shows that PRE is simply 1.0 minus the ratio of conditional bivariate entropy to univariate entropy of the dependent variable. Thus,
the entropy value computed when the values of the independent X variable
(and thus the computed univariate entropy for X) are known is $H(Y|X)$. If this
is equal to the entropy value computed *without* knowing X (which is $H[Y]$),

then the PRE value is $1 - 1 = 0$. This shows that *knowledge of X has yielded no increase in information*, as the bivariate case $H(Y|X)$ yields the same value as the univariate case $H(Y)$, which means that analysis of the independent variable X is unproductive. Thus, if $H(Y) = H(Y|X)$, the PRE $= 0$. At the other pole, if $H(Y|X) = 0$, then PRE $= 1.0$. An entropy value of zero, or $H(Y) = 0$, can be attained only one way—when entropy is a minimum, with all cases in a single category of the table. This is *perfect predictability* in that the category in every case can be predicted with *no error*, as they are all in the same category, as long as the value of the independent variable X is known. Note that technically speaking, $H(Y) = 0$ is not allowed, as division by zero yields infinity. All this says is that if univariate entropy is minimum (0), then the PRE measure cannot be used effectively because the dependent variable is a constant in this case (all cases are in a single category). Thus, knowing the value of a second variable (X) cannot improve the prediction and so a bivariate analysis is unnecessary, the PRE measure will not be used if $H(Y) = 0$. Note that *this is true not only for entropy, but for all categorical statistics*, as there is no reason to correlate a constant with a variable.

The terminology has been changed from PRU in equations 3.8 and 3.9 to PRE in equations 8.18 and 8.19. Does this change merely reflect the use of the term entropy rather than uncertainty, so that we now have proportional reduction in entropy, or is this measure in actuality a true proportional reduction in error, or PRE measure? This measure (equations 3.8, 3.9, 8.18, and 8.19) *is a true proportional reduction in error (PRE) measure*, and it fits all of the requirements of such a measure as discussed by Costner (1965). Any PRE measure applied to categorical data measures dispersion from the modal category, with a value of 1.0 when knowledge of the independent variable allows predicting the modal category of the dependent variable with complete accuracy, meaning that all cases are in the mode. This is of course minimum conditional entropy or $H(Y|X) = 0$. For further discussion see Costner (1965), Horan (1975), and Teachman (1980).

Summary

This chapter began by discussing the relationship between verbal and numerical theorizing. The categorical table, with verbal symbols describing its categories (e.g., in Theil's [1967] decomposition into racial groups, or Liebperson's [1969] within-population analysis of diversity among religious groups) provides a perfect example of this. Such a table deals with salient social categories that verbal theorists rely heavily upon (e.g., race, occupation, religion, political affiliation, gender) but combines them with numerical cell entries, usually frequencies or probabilities. The manner in which the verbal-numerical data are mapped into the X'' level in the form of tables (e.g., characteristics as cell headings, as in Table 8.1) has ramifications for the results from any statistical analysis, whether the analysis uses H or some other statistic. Later in the chapter, this problem was resolved by dividing the analysis of such tables into two component parts, the population global (P) and the income global (L). By analyzing a table in terms of population shares and income shares, for example, we can effectively avoid confusion regardless of the type of table format that is used and translate between tables with different formats.

The focus next turned to a rather intensive analysis of the statistical H measure in terms of sample size, sampling distribution, number of categories, and so forth, including the use of type B and type C mappings for the construction of data categories on the indicator (X'') level. The analysis also explored the relationship between entropy measurement for continuous and categorical variables, where categorical entropy is the analogue of variance for continuous variables, providing a clear link to correlation and regression and entropy can be computed for continuous variables by conceptualizing the distribution in terms of population shares and variable shares (e.g., income shares). If categorical data are used, the equivalent units are category shares of the total population global (e.g., P) and category shares of the total income (L). Thus, entropy is not limited to categorical analysis. However, categorical analysis is so prevalent and important in sociology that it should not be deemphasized merely to pursue some continuous method, such as multiple regression.

The chapter also studied various entropy formulations useful for the study of inequality, relying heavily upon Theil (1967) for this analysis. Inequality analysis is very important in sociology, and entropy has proven to be an effective means for inequality study. One major advantage that entropy has over commonly used measures, such as the Gini, is that it facilitates decomposition (e.g., into racial or sexual groups), and this is crucial to the effective study of inequality in sociology. That is, although analysis of the overall inequality distribution is very important, this measure allows delving more deeply into the basic dimensions of inequality by decomposing so that inequality differences both within and between groups can be analyzed for theoretically important variables such as race, age, religion, sex, and region. Indeed, a comprehensive study of inequality would decompose for all of the mutables and for a large number of the most salient immutables. Entropy is the supreme tool for accomplishing this, both from a statistical and theoretical standpoint.

In the course of this chapter, the entropy measure was shown to have numerous transformations and applications, only a few of which were studied. For further discussion, see Theil (1967; 1970; 1971), Shannon and Weaver (1949), McFarland (1969), or any of the numerous other discussions of information theory. Entropy was also shown to be a basic generic measure of variation in *any* variable, and as such, it is easily related to virtually *all* of the statistics used in sociology. A number of these relationships have been discussed. Other analyses are available in Teachman (1980) and Magidson (1981).

The inescapable overall conclusion is that *H* is entropy and not information, and that *H* and various other entropy formulations have great utility in sociology and will be increasingly used. As shown, *H* can be used for continuous variables, and in the joint and conditional forms, it has analogues to regression and correlation. Further, it is also useful for categorical variables, and there is a link between the categorical and continuous analyses (itself a valuable integration of knowledge). But beyond this, so many categorical variables (e.g., race, sex, religion) are so basic to sociological analysis, that the establishment of sociological knowledge is not well served by relegating them to inferior status and either neglecting them in favor of continuous regression analyses or forcing them into models (e.g., dummy regression) that do not yield optimal explanatory power.

Sociology is better served by utilizing methods that effectively analyze categorical data, and entropy, in the form of *H* and other statistical formulations, is optimal for this. Indeed, probabilistic analysis of categorical data is clearly the statistical frontier in social science, and entropy is a major generic component of this class of measures. Log-linear methods (Goodman 1971; 1972), probit analysis, logit analysis, entropy, and other probabilistic techniques will supplement traditional analyses such as regression and, as such, will help to fill the voids in sociological knowledge left by emphasis on these traditional methods (principally with regard to the analysis of categorical data). Theil calls such methods (including entropy) the *frontier of econometrics* (Theil 1971), and this is equally true for sociology, as entropy analysis is the frontier of sociological analysis as well, both theoretically and statistically (for example, see Krippendorff 1986).

It should be clear from this chapter, particularly from the discussion of the conjunction between population shares and variable shares in the inequality analysis (see Theil 1967) that such statistical analysis (e.g., entropy statistical analysis) is basically the measurement of the results of *allocation processes*. These allocation processes utilize mutables and immutables to allocate persons into various positions in the mutable structure. Inasmuch as these actions are replicated over time, the allocation processes will be orderly, and the measured entropy values will be below the maximum (but probably above the minimum). These processes had been analyzed in detail in previous chapters, this chapter analyzed statistically the results of such processes, and it is possible to summarize our endeavors, offer hypotheses, and discuss the tasks that remain.

Chapter 9

Reflections and Hypotheses

It is time, in this final chapter, to reflect upon social entropy theory, to suggest testable hypotheses, and to identify remaining areas of investigation. A holistic, macrosociological approach has proven capable of identifying and confronting some important sociological problems. One advantage of a broad approach over a more specialized one is its ability to illuminate sociological vistas precluded or cut by a narrower viewpoint, and I trust that SET has accomplished this to some degree. As one example, the whole problem of the relationship among the globals, mutable distributions, mutable characteristics of individuals, and immutable characteristics of individuals is clearly an important issue from a macrosociological systems perspective, but would not emerge as an issue at all in many narrower approaches (e.g., criminology, small group research, gerontology, race and ethnicity). As a related example, the allocation of the society's population into subsystems, such as organizations, emerges as a major theoretical issue from the macrosociological systems perspective but again might not come to view at all in a narrower perspective that did not focus upon relationships simultaneously among the society, the individuals within it, and the myriad subsystems, such as business organizations, voluntary associations, and families.

It is impossible to repeat all that has been said in the previous eight chapters or to summarize it easily. Thus, the goal of this chapter is to merely comment upon salient features of each chapter in the hopes that such recapitulation can yield an integrated overview of the SET approach to sociology; also, some hypotheses will be listed for chapters where this task seems appropriate. However, no attempt will be made to test these hypotheses or even to generate an exhaustive list of them. However, it is important that an approach such as SET be at least potentially operationalizable and testable, even though this operationalization and verification may not be begun immediately for myriad reasons, such as the need to complete further theoretical tasks.

Reflections

Chapter 1

The beginning chapter broached the issue of how best to construct a theory of complex society. There is some controversy over this, primarily generated by Merton (1968). It is even of issue whether sociology should construct such models at this time or continue to concentrate on middle-range theory. The chapter argued that the time is ripe for a macrosociological model, as sociology seems somewhat fragmented, with a large number of substantive and methodological specialties but few, if any, integrative superstructures. Further, macrosociology is perhaps the only unique purview that sociology does not share with other social sciences, which are specialty sciences. If sociologists do not study complex society holistically, who will?

The next question was how best to proceed? Although Merton (1949) had implied that, when the time was right, such theory could be constructed by aggregating middle-range theories, others (e.g., Opp, 1970) questioned the efficacy of this approach and identified certain problems with an aggregative approach. How could disparate specialties be added together to arrive at a coherent holistic theory? Doing so implies that sufficient specialties exist and that they can all be mastered by persons attempting the integration (in itself, highly problematic). This task further requires the aggregation of a great many concepts, some of which are vague, ambiguous, or contradict other concepts (e.g., equilibrium theory and conflict theory). It was concluded that strict aggregation was *not* feasible for the present study, although perhaps other theorists can successfully utilize such a strategy. A better approach was not to aggregate but rather to sketch a model sufficiently broad to accommodate all the various specialties and middle-range theories, including methodological as well as substantive specialties. The task at this stage was not to exhaustively *include* middle-range approaches but only to ensure that no middle-range approach were *precluded*. A perusal of the respective chapters shows that the study was apparently true to this aim. The chapters vary in the number of specialty areas cited, with some chapters (e.g., Chapter 5) showing special effort to relate the analysis to particular specialty literatures. Other chapters have fewer references but still were written so as not to preclude existing approaches when they are deemed to be valid.

In deciding against the aggregative strategy, the question arose of how to constuct a holistic model of the complex society. There are at least two other strategies: the divisive and the direct. The divisive in the opposite of the aggregative: it begins with larger theories (e.g., of world or supranational systems) and divides or reduces them to theories of society. A host of problems confront this strategy, among them fundamental problems of emergence and reduction and the unfinished nature of most current world and supranational theories. Thus, it seemed that the best strategy was neither the aggregative nor divisive but direct, which entails viewing the complex society as well as possible and constructing a model isomorphic with it. Chapter 1 is based on the assumption that societies have sufficient unitary character to make them suitable subjects of scientific investigation and that the object is to understand the general nature of the structures and processes that allow societies to go about their everyday operations. In other words, the task of understanding the operations of complex society is appropriate, timely, and compatible with the purview of sociology.

At this point the basic question that arises concerns the proper model for achieving such aims. General systems theory (GST) offers a model that is clearly compatible with the belief that society is a set of interrelated components: the systems model. GST is sufficiently general to comprise the complex isomorphic model desired. Further, it offers many useful principles that can be applied to sociology, while adding a minimum of theoretical baggage that might conflict with some middle-range paradigms, thus hindering the desire not to preclude specialty areas.

Chapter 2

However, there are some hindrances to the goal of developing a systems model of complex society. One hindrance is that systems theory is closely identified by many sociologists with functionalism, which has suffered major and sustained criticism. Thus, the basic question at this juncture is whether the problems of functionalism are in fact inherent in all systems approaches (in which case the mission seems doomed) or are largely specific to the particular approach of structural-functionalism. This book, of course, takes the position that the flaws that engendered criticism for functionalism were largely those of functionalism and *not* of contemporary systems theory. Thus, a systems theory can be written without these major debilitating flaws, and the preceding chapters attempt to demonstrate this contention.

A basic point that may be overlooked in evaluating systems theory in sociology is that functionalism is *old* systems theory. Even though some of it may have been written within the last twenty years, its systems principles often stem back to the nineteenth century, with equilibrium (nineteenth century equilibrium) as a foundation. Further, the concept of equilibrium is used indiscriminately and often incorrectly from the standpoint of its thermodynamic roots. One can search the functional literature in vain for any mention of modern systems tools, such as the Prigogine (1955) entropy analysis for open systems, the open systems concept in general (it is mentioned in Parsons 1951 but not systematically pursued), the *H* measure of entropy, the concept of marker, and the distinction between abstracted and concrete systems, and acting and pattern systems (Kuhn 1974). Such concepts in concert are crucial to an adequate systems analysis of the complex society.

Chapter 2 lists thirteen challenges to a successful macrosociological systems theory. The reader is the best judge of whether SET has met these aims. Again, keep in mind that the immediate objective is to ensure that we do not *preclude* important theoretical elements, as we obviously cannot *include* everything about the complex society simultaneously in one book. However, sketching a viable skeletal system that can be filled-in in a cumulative fashion is a reasonable goal, and I trust that this has been accomplished. These issues are dealt with briefly in Chapter 2.

Perusal of Chapter 2 shows that a large number of these thirteen challenges are dealt with in Chapter 2, which sketches the basic systems model. These are all general issues dealing with the nature of the system, such as the basic definition of system, specification of boundaries, isomorphism between model and society, relationships among systems parts and micro and macro levels, and a defense against the criticism that the systems model is an inappropriate organic, or mechanical analogy. The basic definition of a concrete system, discussed in Chapter 2, deals succinctly with many of these issues. Although an abstracted system alone does not allow one to adequately deal with these issues, the problem can be solved by beginning with a concrete system, then deriving the abstracted aspects (e.g., role analysis) from it.

Other issues presented in Chapter 2 are dealt with in other chapters. For example, the vital issue of the measure of system state is dealt with in Chapter 3, in the extended discussion of equilibrium and entropy. Macro variable selection is the topic of Chapter 4. Relationships between component parts and the micro and macro levels are discussed in detail in Chapters 4 and 5 and to some degree in Chapters 6 and 7. Individual and group needs and goal setting are discussed in Chapters 5 and 6. Matter-energy and information processing are discussed in detail throughout Chapters 2-7. Information is treated more systematically than energy, and the latter might be the focus of future work. However, examination of the marker as an information carrier, though treated in detail here, deserves much more analysis, specifically in the context of the three-level model. Diachronic analysis is also discussed in some detail through Chapters 2-7, often in contrast to synchronic analysis. This work is central to the understanding of complex society and to a certain extent deals with the classic problem of structure-process. Explanation, prediction, and verification have been treated less systematically. It is discussed in Chapter 2, and discussions in various chapters (such as relationships among variables in

Chapter 4) are also germane to this issue. However, hypotheses have not yet been specified, due to preoccupation with the generation of the holistic model. Thus, later in this chapter operationalization and testing will be disscussed in more detail and a nonexhaustive list of hypotheses from various chapters generated. All in all, then, all thirteen problems have been addressed in what is believed to be a viable and promising manner.

Chapter 2 is the crucial theoretical chapter from a systems standpoint. The chapter argues in detail why the analysis must begin with a concrete rather than an abstracted system and how this *does not preclude* analysis of abstracted systems (e.g., role analysis), which would be inconsistent with the goal of not precluding important analysis. If it precluded role and action analysis in the Parsonian sense, such concrete analysis would cut the heart out of the model. Rather, Chapter 2 shows that the reverse is true—that concrete analysis does not preclude abstracted *but rather facilitates such analysis by providing the only suitable foundation for it.*

The controversy over abstracted versus concrete analysis demonstrates the likelihood that the actual complex society contains both and both are relevant for it. Thus, the *only* strategy consistent with an integrative, holistic approach is one broad enough *to include both the concrete and abstracted and show how they are related.* Unless these two elements are studied together, the analysis is *very limited.* For example, only study of the abstracted-concrete complementarity can allow sufficient study the conjunctions of R- and Q-analysis, synchronic symbol structure and diachronic process, allocation processes, micro-macro conjunctions, and the three-level model. That is, only an isomorphic model broad enough to show both concrete and abstracted features can achieve sufficient breadth to analyze all the myriad phenomena that must be simultaneously understood to allow understanding of the workings of complex society. In particular, the *conjunctions* between various diverse elements (such as R-relationships and Q-relationships, or abstracted and concrete systems) constitute the frontiers of the understanding of society and are the crux of holistic analysis. These things have been studied separately; their interrelationships must now be understood. Another way to say this is that every *versus* in sociological analysis is an intellectual problem that sociology must deal with in the future, such "versus" analysis is basically the analysis of theoretical boundaries. Sociology is replete with such *versuses*: micro versus macro, abstracted versus concrete, theoretical versus empirical, structure versus process, equilibrium versus conflict, free will versus determinism, are but a few.

The model sketched in Chapter 2 is specifically designed to deal with these versuses. A considerable number of them (all those just mentioned) have been discussed in detail, and the model seems sufficiently broad to deal with others that we may not have specifically addressed. A convenient rule of thumb is that *each time a versus cannot be dealt with adequately, this is a sign that the model is insufficiently holistic and must be broadened*. No such versuses come easily to mind for the societal level, because the components and boundaries of the model (X'') were specifically designed to be isomorphic with an actual complex society (X'). The interior is not yet filled in completely, but sufficient breadth has been allowed for the various versuses through the aim of establishing such type C (model-society) isomorphism.

Later chapters show that the three-level model presented in Chapter 2 has a crucial role in social entropy theory. It is used in virtually all facets of the analysis, including the study of information processing, the allocation of persons into groups, epistemology, and construction of statistical tables. It is particularly crucial to the understanding of the relationship between diachronic process, by acting human individuals, and the synchronic symbol structure, which both shapes human process and is in turn shaped by it. It should be noted in passing that the analysis of the three-level model as used in everyday society has just touched the proverbial tip of the iceberg. The matter is much more complex than can be pursued here. For example, one reason many persons have difficulty identifying the marker or indicator level (X'') is that it blends so easily into the empirical level X', as virtually every marker or information carrier also has some other physical identity. Thus, an observer who was not cognizant of the information content of the given marker (e.g., did not know the language or code) might not even recognize the object as a marker. For example, a piece of paper could be recognized as *a piece of paper* (X') and thus identified as part of the empirical (X') realm, *without* being identified as an information carrier and thus as a part of the marker level (X''). Only the mapping of cognitive information (X) onto an empirical object (X') allows one to form the indicator or marker level (X''). Thus, (X'') is formed by mapping concepts (X) and the empirical level (X') into it, and this overlap between (X'') and the other two levels often makes it difficult for the observer to distinguish it, either analytically or empirically.

Another problem in identifying markers (X'') within the social system, and with analysis of the indicator level (X'') in general, is that a marker is simply a name for an object or some form of matter that has *as its function the storage and transmission of information*. As emphasized in classical functionalism, an object can have many *other* functions besides information storage and transmission. Some objects have a dual function and carry information (thus, serving as a marker) in addition to their other function or functions. Many times the information carried is simply in conjunction with the other function, and the information simply facilitates accomplishment of the other function. For example, a metal container (tin can) functions adequately for food storage but some attached marker (a paper label on the can) identifies its contents. The information on the can is a true marker (X'') but the function of the can is to store food not information, and information transmission is a secondary function that facilitates the primary function of food storage. Other physical objects have no information function at all, however, they have a surface that could be used to store and convey information, if desired. Thus if the object is not to be utilized as an information carrier, it must carry random information; that is, every physical object is a marker in the sense that it carries some socially salient level of information, from maximum entropy (no information) to minimum entropy or maximum negentropy (maximum information).

Therefore, every object will carry some information, even if it is a zero amoung (maximum entropy). To ensure that it conveys no message, it must be completely blank (e.g., a solid color) or convey a message that is maximally entropic (no information). The latter is often accomplished by a pattern that is uniform, or random, thus conveying no patterned information. A common example is the repetitious square tile pattern of a bathroom floor, or the green and white squares on the wall paper in my closet. This pattern can be read by the observer (type B isomorphism) and I can glean a cognitive perception (X) from the marker (X''). However, the information content of the message is zero because entropy is maximum.

An example of the complexity of the three-level model is the fact that each level may be mapped into itself and into each of the other two. This was discussed briefly in Chapter 2. Here, it will only be mentioned as a topic for future epistemological analysis, as it is crucial to the understanding of complex society. Concepts (X) and empirical entities (X') can be represented on the marker level (X''). For example, a given marker such as a book can represent ideas (X), empirical entities (X'), and also other markers (X''). Similarly, on the cognitive level (X), it is possible to conceptualize about not only markers such as books (X'') and empirical objects such as babies (X') but also other concepts (X). Further, markers are themselves empirical entities (X') to begin with (even before they carry information), and the cognitive level (X) of the human is housed in the concrete individual (X', see Laszlo 1972). Thus, each of the *three levels (X, X', and X'')* *is represented in each of the three levels (X, X', and X'')*. The complexity does not end here. The number of cross-level or intralevel mappings that can be made is virtually endless and basically an infinite regress. For example, consider the marker level, and a particular marker (X''_1), such as a book on literature. This marker (the book) can represent another book (X''_2), representing another book (X''_3), representing another book (X''_4), representing another book (X''_5), and so on to the final book (X''_N). Ultimately, this becomes a mapping of an infinite number of books into one. The most convenient analogy is that of two of mirrors, with one mirror (X''_1) reflecting all the images in the other (X''_2) that contain all the images in the first (X''_3), and so on. This can be done on the conceptual and empirical levels and across two levels $(X$ and X'; X and X''; X' and $X'')$, or across all three levels (which really becomes complex).

Although this analysis will not be pursued now, it is clear that such processes occur constantly in the complex society, even though all of them may not be seen (similar to the unawareness of what is happening in the next room or in the house across the street). It should also be clear that only a holistic model can effectively deal with such complexity. But holistic models must be evaluated holistically. If one is accustomed to use of the simple conceptual-empirical distinction, with its one isomorphism, and its one form of validity, then the three-level model can seem an annoying complication, as it broadens the analysis from one type of validity to three. However, in order to study the real world of complex society, *three levels is the minimum*, as they are used constantly in our everyday life, and it may turn out to be the case in the future that the three-level model is inadequate and even more levels really exist. However, for the present, in order to progress in the study of sociology, it is *crucial* to utilize all three levels. Another interesting area of study that will be pursued in the future is the notion of human markers. It is clear upon reflection that humans serve as markers. Their genders, ages, heights, races, and so on are examples of *information* visible to participants in human inter-action. In addition they carry cognitive information and give out information through nonverbal cues and various biological signals (see James Miller 1978). Further, human individuals carry other markers upon their persons. For example, their clothes provide information on their gender and social class and perhaps on age and residence. Also, the number of additional markers that individuals carry, such as identification cards, driver's licenses, and credit cards seems to be increasing (see Rule, McAdam, Stearns, and Uglow, 1983).

Many of the issues addressed in Chapter 2 are pursued throughout the book. They cannot all be mentioned here, and many will be addressed in the discussions of other chapters. However, it is necessary here to comment further on the conjunction between statistical analysis (e.g., as discussed in Chapter 8) and the boundaries of concrete systems. It is axiomatic that entropy levels will always be somewhat different, often radically different, on different sides of a given system boundary. Such a sharp difference in entropy is termed here an *entropy break*. The existence of an entropy break is one means of boundary determination. If no entropy break exists (if entropy levels are identical on each side of the boundary), then the boundary is either *completely* open in terms of matter-energy and information, in which case it hardly functions as a boundary in the real sense, or the boundary is artificial and simply marks differentiations between system parts rather than demarcates one system from another. Such instances are so rare empirically that any true system boundary is fairly sure to be an entropy break, and entropy levels will differ on different sides of it.

This has clear ramifications for sampling theory. Any sample of N persons that samples across an entropy break will yield a heterogeneous sample that, when entropy is measured, will show a mixture of the two entropy levels of the two systems included in the sample. As an extreme example (which would never occur empirically), assume that B is the boundary between system 1 and system 2; that the entropy for system 1 is maximum log N_1, the sample size in system 1; and the entropy for system 2 is 0. Such extreme values of entropy probably could never coexist, because no boundary could be sufficiently closed to keep all of the energy in system 2. Nevertheless, it is clear for heuristic purposes that if samples were taken across the boundary B, the measured entropy value would be a mixture of maximum and minimum entropy and would thus be some intermediate value representative of neither system.

The conclusion is that *regardless* of the type of statistical analysis to be conducted, *sampling should be within system boundaries and not cross boundaries*. Theoretically, all areas within system boundaries should be represented. Any samples across entropy breaks will result in a misleading mixture of entropy values and a misrepresentation in the amount of variance explained. Without realizing it, most researchers sample within systems and do not cross entropy breaks to a great extent simply because, without realizing it, they do not sample across geographical boundaries. This constitutes recognition (probably implicit rather than explicit) that the components within such geographical boundaries are concrete systems and to sample across boundaries is to mix systems and thus weaken the interpretability of the data gathered. However, it is inevitable that some sampling across systems boundaries does occur for various reasons, including failure to recognize existence of boundaries. Most of this probably occurs across subsystem boundaries but still undoubtedly weakens the analysis.

Chapter 3

In fairness to classic functionalism, a school of thought that began in the nineteenth century certainly cannot be faulted for using nineteenth century principles. The problem was not in the initial stages of the functional paradigm so much as in the end. In the beginning *everybody* was using the concept of equilibrium in many fields (for example, see Samuelson, 1983). The problem occurred in mature functionalism, when the school dabbled with modern concepts such as the open system and homeostasis. However (and homeostasis is a good example), these newer concepts were not used in a way that *improved* the analysis through analytical distinctions, but rather they were simply overlaid on the original equilibrium superstructure (and in fact homeostasis was devalued as a "special case of equilibrium"; see Parsons 1961b), so that the value of these new concepts was largely lost.

It is really equilibrium itself that is a "special case" in terms of systems analysis. As Pikler (1954; 1955) shows, equilibrium in economics is useful for specific and rather localized analysis but, in generalizing to a large scale analysis, equilibrium becomes inadequate, and one must resort to the parent entropy analysis.

To illustrate this point, let us return to the passage by Pareto cited in Chapter 3:

> Somewhat similar to the artificial changes mentioned are those *occasional* changes which result from some element that *suddenly* appears, has its influence for a *brief period* upon a system, occasioning some *slight disturbance* in the state of equilibrium, and then passes away. Short wars waged by rich countries, epidemics, floods, earthquakes and similar calamities would be examples. (1935, p. 1436, emphasis added)

The artifical changes that Pareto refers to are the hypothetical changes in an isolated thermodynamic system. Although they never actually occur, they were assumed in classical thermodynamics for heuristic purposes. Pareto is saying that in the actual empirical society, changes occur that are similar to such hypothetical or artificial changes. Note, though, how *minor and even irrelevant* these changes from outside the system are. First of all, these threats to equilibrium are *occasional*. This implies that the system will not be barraged by a whole sequence of threats, but they will occur only occasionally. They appear *suddenly*, rather than build up strength over a long period of time. These threats only occur *briefly* and are not sustained. They occasion only a *slight disturbance* in equilibrium. Overall, it would seem that such occasional, sudden, brief, and slight changes are not theoretically salient. They are not very serious or important and are easily fixed. In summary, such occurrences are simply not very relevant to a comprehensive and complex systems analysis of society. And if long-term, frequent, severe threats to the system occur, it is quite clear that the system *will not* regain equilibrium. If the outside threat is from a more powerful system, that system will most likely absorb the less powerful one.

But, if equilibrium is of specialized and local rather than generalized empirical importance, how did it become defined as *central* to analysis of the social system? This was done by linking *equilibrium to order*, a link shown to be erroneous. To repeat a passage from Parsons and Shils: "In other words, interdependence is *order* in the relationship among components which enter into a system. This order must have a tendency to self-maintenance, which is very generally expressed in the concept of equilibrium" (1951, p.107, italics in the original). Thus, Parsons defines *equilibrium as the self-maintenance of order*. As stated in Chapter 3, *this is simply not correct*. Equilibrium (as opposed to homeostasis or a steady-state) is defined only for an isolated system and only for maximum entropy (or its mathematical equivalence in terms of the states of the salient extensive and intensive system properties). This means that *true equilibrium is not the maintenance of order but the maintenance of randomization (maximum entropy), which is the most stable and statistically probable state of the system.*

Again, all that is needed is to broaden the analysis. Instead of depending upon a dichotomous measure (equilibrium-disequilibrium) that measures constancy but not order, it is obviously necessary to switch to a broader, continuous, direct measure of the degree of order (defined as departure from randomness). This measure is entropy, which for the present analysis is represented by H. This measure will represent randomness (maximum entropy); maximum departure from randomness or maximum order (minimum entropy, or $H = 0$); or any degree of order in between. Also, it has the theoretical advantage that entropy (through negentropy) can be interpreted in terms of information and organized complexity (see Buckley 1967; James Miller 1978). By studying change in H over time (dH/dt), it can also be seen if the measured degree of order is static or not. If so, this condition can certainly be labeled *equilibrium*. This allows use of equilibrium without depending upon it in the many cases where this static condition *cannot* be documented.

Chapter 4

The first three chapters were largely programmatic and definitional. Although of central theoretical and epistemological importance, these chapters were prefatory to applications or substantive analysis. Such substantive analysis begins in earnest in Chapter 4, where the level of living (L) of a society is used as a basic systems variable (which, like the others derived, can be measured in terms of entropy). The chapter then searched analytically for all correlates of L (direct or inverse), keeping the analysis sufficiently broad that no empirically existing societies were precluded. The model was designed to apply to societies at all stages of development. This means, of course, that the model must be very general, and specific operationalizations, which apply only to particular societies, must be avoided.

The search yielded six global variables: population size (P), total information content (I), spatial area (S), total technology possessed (T), total number of organizational positions (O), and total level of living (L). The term *global* means that in each of these variables the concrete social system is the unit of analysis, and each represents *the total amount of the component possessed by the total society*. Thus, these six components are the total amount of space within the boundaries of the system, the total population of human actors within the system, the total amount of information these actors possess, the total amount of technology they possess, and the total amount of organizational positions (whether listed on markers [X''] or not) that they possess. All of these have long been studied separately, and most are the subject of a specialty or discipline (e.g., demography studies population). However, from the standpoint of social entropy theory, it is the *conjunction* or interrelationship of these six globals that is most important, and that constitutes the key to our understanding of complex society. In other words, although these six variables have long been studied independently, SET studies them in concert, to see how they work together in the everyday operations of complex society. These variables can be represented by a system of simultaneous differential equations—this mathematical work remains to be done. It is likely that there are a number of interactions among these six variables, which indicates that the differential equations will be nonlinear. Also, depending upon the specific operationalizations utilized (which may depend to some extent on the particular society studied and the data available), difference equations may have to be used instead of differential equations.

In addition to each global representing the *total amount of that variable that the society possesses*, it is also important to understand that each of these six components is *actually multivariate*, and each may have a number of distinct operationalizations, especially when applied to a complex society. The same could be said of population, organization, environment, and technology (POET) as presented by Duncan and Schnore (1959). The information component is crucial to the understanding of complex society (as indeed, all six components are) but as presented here it is quite broad. In subsequent analyses the information component itself could be broken down into a whole set of interrelated information subcomponents. For example, for nonindustrialized societies (such as Durkheim's mechanical society), there may be a relatively few information subcomponents, principally those dealing with agriculture, societal mores, and religion. In modern industrialized society, there are myriad information components, including scientific and technical information, political ideology, religious information, and so on. Each of these can be highly complex in itself. Again, following the aim not to preclude important elements of complex society, it may not be feasible to separately analyze these myriad information components, but the model must have room for them.

The other globals can similarly be broken down into subcomponents, and operationalized in many different ways. For example, for many societies, the L component might be better symbolized by energy (E), as the main and primary source of wealth is the energy resources that the system either extracts from its spatial area through utilization of its information, organization, and technology, or imported across systems boundaries from other systems. Since a social system (or any system) cannot exist at the level of maximum entropy and since energy utilization is the only way to avoid approaching this level according to the second law of thermodynamics, it is clear that any society must have sufficient energy, either through production within its own boundaries or through importation. Thus, especially for nonindustrialized social systems, L could generally be replaced by E, the amount of energy, as this is the main source of wealth. However, in industrialized systems, things are more complex and indirect. Here money (in terms of income or wealth, see Chapter 8) is often the most convenient operationalization of (L). This is a standard and convenient operationalization of (L) but it should not disguise the fact that energy is often primary to such wealth (as Middle Eastern countries like Saudi Arabia dramatically illustrate). Energy utilization is a central foundation on which the social system rests and is crucial to the everyday operation of this system. Yet, except in a few limited specialties (e.g., ecology and environmental sociology), energy has been taken for granted by sociologists, who have not effectively analyzed its role in society (see Bailey 1968). Even though SET explicitly takes energy into account, it is also to some extent guilty of its neglect. Faced with so many tasks in outlining the general model, I also often took energy as a given and discussed information processing fairly comprehensively in terms of the three-level model. This will be rectified in later work which will focus on both living and nonliving systems and thus will emphasize energy to a greater degree.

Note that although five of the six globals discussed in Chapter 4 seem to deal with the materialistic basis of society (population, level of living, space, organization, and technology), the information component is also included, thus including a host of ideational factors, from religion to cultural symbols. The addition of information separates the analysis of Chapter 4 from most ecological analyses (e.g., the POET model of Duncan and Schnore 1959) and thus makes it significantly more holistic. Rather than being the "old POET model with just level of living and information added on," the model now seems to be sufficiently holistic to analyze complex society. Leaving out one variable, from a holistic viewpoint, is like leaving out the baking powder while baking a cake—a total disaster.

From the standpoint of a specialty or from a piecemeal perspective, whether the model includes four or six global variables may seem immaterial. From a holistic perspective it is crucial. If there are five basic correlates of (*L*), as hypothesized here then a model that listed only four (or fewer) *could not be isomorphic with the ongoing empirical society.* That is, a four-global model, such as POET, when presented on the indicator or marker level (X''), *cannot* be isomorphic with the empirical society (X') that utilizes six globals simultaneously in its everyday operations. Even in analytical terms, the difference between POET and PISTOL is dramatic, as the former can be represented with four simultaneous differential equations each containing only four variables, whereas the latter consists of six equations, each containing six variables. Thus, although the POET R-systems model only has sixteen terms, the PISTOL R-systems model has thirty-six terms. A systems perspective is interested in the interrelationships among all variables. Thus, what appears to be a difference of only two terms (*L* and *I*) turns out to translate into a difference of twenty relationships between the two models. In terms of the mathematical analysis and the study of interactions, this could be an extremely important difference.

Chapter 5

The global variables represent the total possessions of the social system on six dimensions. They seem to be exhaustive, although each can be easily divided into many subcomponents (for example, information can be divided into scientific information, humanistic information, religious information, political ideology). The next step is to recognize that five of these six globals (level of living [*L*], space [*S*], information [*I*], technology [*T*], and the totality of organizational positions [*O*]) are apportioned among the persons in the population (*P*); that is, the population (*P*) is *allocated* into the other five globals.

As in both Chapters 4 and 5, the population is distributed into the other five globals to form an interrelated system of mutable distributions. Note that although every society possesses six global variables, *none* of these (exclusive of *P*) is an *ascribed* characteristic of persons in the sense of race or gender; that is, neither *I, S, T, O,* or *L* is permanently connected to individuals. Rather, each society must find some bases for *allocating* or *distributing* its population among these other five resources. When the distributions or mutables (e.g., occupational division of labor) are not distinguished from the globals (e.g., total number of organizational positions that the society possesses), there is a considerable loss of analytical clarity. Both the globals and mutables are properties of societies, but the globals are global properties in Lazarsfeld's (1937) terms, whereas the mutables are analytical properties in his terms. Since each individual in the population has a position in the five mutables, each individual possesses five mutable characteristics. Therefore, although the mutables are properties of societies (analytical properties), they are also properties of individuals (relational properties in Lazarsfeld's terms) and thus form the link between macro (global) and micro (immutable characteristics of individuals) properties. Since they are so theoretically important, it is *crucial* that the theoretical distinction between the mutables and globals be maintained.

One good way to achieve this is to analyze the mutable distributions in the same manner that Theil (1967) analyzed the income mutable, as discussed in Chapter 8. This is to distinguish between *population shares* and *variable shares*, where the total population size is N and the total number of categories in the mutable variable is K. Therefore, to analyze the organizational mutable, the organizational shares of each category, and the population shares of each category must be separated. For example, if K/N of the population is in each occupational category, then there is maximum entropy. However, generally the proportion of the population (population share) will depart from the maximum and so one "variable" is the population share in each occupational category. Another "variable" is the number of occupational categories. The number of categories (K) determines the value of maximum entropy ($\log K$), and each "occupational share" is just $1/K$.

Therefore, the *mutables are the link between the macro (societal) properties (the globals) and the micro (individual) properties (such as the immutables)*, and *one of the most crucial theoretical and empirical problems in sociology is the process of allocating individuals into the mutable distributions*. Ironically, while sociology has studied stratification, ethnicity, organizations, networks, conflict theory, and so on, it has *virtually neglected* the general study of allocation processes. This has probably been because sociology has not taken a sufficiently broad approach for this to emerge as a theoretical issue. If one thinks in terms of sociological specializations such as gender roles or ethnic relations, then allocation does not emerge clearly as an issue. Again, this is the advantage of a holistic perspective with the society as the unit of analysis. From the societal standpoint, with the society as the unit of analysis and humans as the components of the concrete system, the relationship among the globals, mutables, and immutables is the crux of understanding the society. Allocation is *so central that virtually every sociological specialization depends upon it in some manner*, often centrally. For example, the centrality of allocation of persons into mutables is clear in the case of various diverse middle-range specializations such, as conflict theory, stratification, gender roles, racial discrimination, and occupational division of labor.

The construction of a macrosociological systems theory such as SET can be very tiring and can seem interminable. Yet, it seems worth the effort when it enables discerning salient issues such as allocation. The centrality of this process to society could probably never be seen through middle-range theories, which tend to slice up the allocation process like a stick of salami. To discern allocation in middle-range theories would probably require knowing what to look for in advance and searching through a large number of specializations. Even then the task would probably be impossible. Since the specialties are not sufficiently broad to discern allocation, they certainly would not emphasize it. Not only would its analysis be neglected and haphazard, but it would be couched in different language in different middle-range theories.

Persons are allocated into the mutable positions (not only O, but also S, I, T, and L) on the basis of both immutables and their existing mutables. The allocation process is so complex that it will not be recapitulated here; instead the reader is referred to Chapter 5 (and also Chapter 7), where it is discussed in considerable detail. However, it is important to emphasize that the process involves the conjunction of a great many social structures and processes: not only the mutables and immutables, but also the three-level model (which is central), the synchronic-symbol structure-diachronic process interaction, the conjunction of R- and Q-analysis, needs, expectations, and goals. For full understanding of allocation it is crucial that it be studied holistically as the conjunction of *all* of these, because a piecemeal analysis will not be isomorphic with the empirical degree of complexity in the ongoing actual society.

Allocation is a general systems process that is central to other disciplines besides sociology. For example, Rozonoer (1973) discusses analogies in thermodynamics and economics and applies the concept of allocation in several areas. There is need for a general multidisciplinary discussion of allocation, including the analysis of allocation across levels (e.g., for groups, organizations, societies; see Miller 1978 for discussion of cross-level studies).

Chapter 6

The topic of allocation is also relevant to Chapter 6, which studied organizations and groups intermediate between the individual person and the larger host society. (This follows the sequence begun in Chapter 4 and continued in Chapter 5.) There are an extremely large number of these groups in a large social system, and each individual can have multiple memberships (see Miller, 1978).

This chapter showed that organizations can be formed agglomeratively, beginning with a nucleus of one or a few members and sequentially adding members; or divisively, by splitting off from established groups. While many groups form agglomeratively, including businesses that grow as their business increases, other groups form by splitting, whether because of friction or factions within these larger groups (e.g., splinter sects in Protestant religious denominations), or even because a more powerful entity decrees a split because the organization is too large (as in antitrust decisions). Of course, aggregation and division can occur cumulatively, as when a number of local groups grow agglomeratively and then merge or when groups split from a larger group and then split again as they themselves become larger.

No matter how the group is formed, it has the salient properties described for the concrete system: boundaries and relationships between concrete human members. As an entity within the context of the larger host society, each group is a *subsystem* that also has its own set of global and mutable properties; that is, each group has the six globals (P, I, S, T, O, L), and its membership (P) is allocated among the five mutables. There is first a process of allocation into the membership (i.e., across the group boundary). All members are so allocated, which entails opening the boundary to admit them (they may be identified with a badge, identification card, parking permit, etc.). After this initial allocation, members are also allocated differentially within the five mutable distributions possessed by the group. The two allocations may be simultaneous (as when a person from outside the system is simultaneously hired as a member and as vice-president), or the allocations may be sequential (as when a person is first admitted without knowing what his or her job title will be, or first admitted to a low position in the mutables and later reallocated to a different position).

Chapter 6 discusses all groups, of whatever size, that are intermediate in size to the total society above them and the individual below them (i.e., they are subsystems of the society and host systems for individuals and smaller groups). Thus, if the population size (P) for the society totals N persons, the groups analyzed in Chapter 6 are of size N_g, where a $1 < N_g < N$.

Like societies and supranational systems above them as well as individuals below them, groups must utilize energy and information to keep their entropy levels low enough for survival. They must ensure that the individual members stay healthy, and then they must ensure that the organization has sufficient energy and information. Thus, boundaries must be opened to allow flow of members, information, and energy into the organization but closed to prohibit the entry of nonmembers, who might deplete resources, and to otherwise minimize the loss of energy and information. To this end, the chapter discussed three sorts of boundaries that organizations must monitor: physical boundaries, membership boundaries, and outreach boundaries, such as sales territories or maximum distribution areas.

Chapter 7

In both Chapter 7 and Chapter 8, the topic is *order*. Chapter 7, in essence, continued the discussion of allocation into mutables, begun in Chapters 5 and 6, into the areas of order, power, and conflict. Although sociologists have often equated order with stability or moving equilibrium in which stability is reestablished (Parsons and Shils 1951, p. 107), order *is not* adequately defined as stability or maintenance of a static condition. Whereas some examples of order are seen to be static or constant over time, this is a secondary rather than a defining characteristic of *order*. The thing that *all definitions of order have in common is that they all require a nonrandom pattern of some sort*. This must be true whether the definition uses a purely verbal and nonquantitative conception of order, such as political order, cultural order, religious order, or social order, or whether it speaks mathematically or statistically, as in the case of order defined as interdependence between variables or rank order (ordinality). This applies as well to either the univariate or multivariate cases.

As reiterated throughout this book, SET studies the interrelationships between various social phenomena, rather than analytically dividing the analysis of these phenomena into specialty areas of analysis. Many people study these specialties, but the link between them is also a crucial subject for study. To this end, *I cannot overemphasize the importance of understanding the nexus between social order as the process of human action and interaction* (the subject of Chapter 7) *and statistical order, such as that displayed in a correlation coefficient, or conditional, or joint entropy below the maximum* (the subject of Chapter 8). Statistical order or interdependence as displayed in a contingency table does not just happen or occur naturally. This order is *produced* and *maintained* by human interaction within the concrete social system. Human interaction takes place through the expenditure of energy and information. *To the extent that this action and interaction is replicated, order exists. In other words, orderly human interaction is replicated interaction.*

It is very important to understand that there are two distinct forms of social order and to maintain this distinction at all times. If the distinction were not maintained, the analysis would not be sufficiently complex to adequately model complex society. These two forms are diachronic *process order* (Q-order), or the orderly actions of individual actors over time, and *synchronic order* (R-order) among variables. They are two sides of the same coin, with the latter produced by the former but also influencing process in the future. This occurs in an ongoing, cyclical manner. The importance of the relationship between Q-process and R-symbolic structure led to the *axiom of social order*, which states the relationship between them. By emphasizing R-relationships between variables in their statistical analyses and by utilizing abstracted systems in their verbal analyses, sociologists have deemphasized the study of Q-relationships and thus effectively precluded the study of the crucial relationship between R and Q stated in the axiom of social order. This Q-R nexus is crucial to an adequate understanding of social order and should not be forgotten.

The relationship between the symbolic R-*structure* and the diachronic Q-*process* is reciprocal over time, with a symbol system and its particular meanings providing the information on which to base future process but with the human actors having the power, through this process, to alter the meaning of the symbol structure in the next time period, and thus to alter the R-relationships among variables (e.g., sex and occupation). If the *information* in the R-structure is random (maximum entropy), then it will provide minimal guidance for process, and *actions* will tend toward randomness (maximum entropy). Thus, the degree of *structure entropy* in one time period affects the degree of *process entropy* in the next time period, which in turn affects the structure entropy in the next time period, and so forth, in perpetuity. This neverending cycle could be characterized in terms of various middle-range concepts, including cybernetic feedback loops or possibly even dialectic relationships.

If every symbol or word in the R-synchronic structure had perfect meaning and there were perfect intercorrelations among them, then R-structure entropy would be minimal (zero). In this case, human actors would have perfect information to guide their actions or Q-process and thus would never face an ambiguous case where they were uncertain what action to take. If they could perfectly interpret and utilize the R-information, then their actions (Q) would be perfectly replicated (minimum or zero Q-process entropy). Obviously, as reiterated, the usual case is somewhere in between, with the statistical relationships between variables (R-structure) showing neither maximum nor minimum entropy and with the Q-process being neither perfectly orderly (minimum entropy) or perfectly disorderly (maximum entropy). Although much more data is available on the R-statistical relationships than on the Q-processes, it is clear that human interaction is moderately replicated and thus orderly, but certainly this replication is often rather far from perfect.

There are many reasons why some replicated Q-action does occur, and many reasons why actions are *not* replicated. Some replication results from persons internalizing norms that stipulate that they behave the same way each time in a certain context and also through learning the proper behavior for their roles. This is the sort of orderly process emphasized by Parsons (1951). However, it is clear that norm and role learning is often very imperfect, especially, for example, if one changes one's position in the mutable structure and thus faces an unfamiliar situation. A great many ambiguous situations arise in process interaction in everyday ongoing societal operation, where the actors do not know which actions to take. If these actors are to replicate past actions and actions of others, there must be information available to guide them in a replicated manner. This is generally provided in the symbol structure represented in myriad markers of every conceivable variety that are used in societal interaction.

An untold number of such markers (X'') exists, in infinite variety, from personnel manuals to federal laws to street maps to street signs to etiquette books and so forth. Assuming no change in the information provided in these markers, human action can be replicated, and thus can generate order, to the extent that *all* actors have access to the markers, interpret them the same way, and follow the directives. Obviously, there is differential adherence in all of these areas. Undergraduates (and also faculty members) in universities do not perfectly replicate those actions required by the university simply because they may not have the university catalogue, often do not read it when they have it, differentially interpret the information, and willfully disobey it in some instances.

Since action often follows norms and signposts in the form of markers of various sorts, the resulting product (symbolic) order will generally not be random, and thus will display an entropy value below the maximum. However, since actors do not always attempt to replicate past actions and sometimes are unable to do so for various reasons (including faulty memory, and inadequate markers, for example), the resulting order will be less than perfect, so that entropy values will be greater than zero. Markers have a very important role in the allocation of persons into positions in the mutable structure. Power holders utilize markers to portray the nature of positions in the mutable structure (e.g., descriptions in personnel manuals) and often use them to disseminate information on the position so that it may be filled (e.g., an advertisement in the classified section of a newspaper). Allocation is based upon both mutable characteristics and immutable characteristics of individuals. If both the person to be allocated and the power holder in charge of allocation agree on the nature of the position and the characteristics of the individual, then allocation may be routine, relatively orderly, and relatively noncontroversial. In such case, there is relatively little conflict in everyday interaction. However, some cases hold a potential for conflict, as when the expectations of either the power holder or the individual being allocated are not fulfilled. The power holder who is unable to allocate persons with the characteristics desired can attempt to alter these characteristics (e.g., increase education [I] through on-the-job training). If the frustrated expectations deal with mutable characteristics, the power holder is unable to change these, but can change his or her own position in the mutable structure (e.g., by moving the manufacturing company to another geographical location [*S*]) where persons with different mutable or immutable characteristics can be hired (allocated into the mutable structure).

Similarly, the individual whose expectations are not fulfilled, denying allocation into the mutable structure in the desired manner, can attempt to alter his or her mutable characteristics so that the desired result is gained. For example, he or she could secure more education (*I*) or move to another area (*S*) where the desired job is available. However, if the person is not being allocated in the desired manner due to immutable characteristics, there is clearly potential for conflict, particularly if the person is in a relatively advantageous position on some of the mutables, providing sufficient resources for conflict. Since immutables cannot be changed, such conflict can be long-term unless something occurs to alleviate the situation, such as change in the allocation process so that immutable characteristics are allocated in a different manner than before. One example is legislation designed to remove the correlation between gender and allocation by decreeing that gender not be used as a basis for allocation. The attainment of such complete statistical independence between gender and allocation into the mutables is unlikely simply because of the other mutables and immutables correlated with each of these.

Chapter 8

To the extent that the replicated processes described in Chapter 7 occur, the resulting order will appear in statistical formulations such as contingency tables. If this happens, the degree of order should be measurable through the use of various statistics. The chapter evaluated the *H* measure and its various transformations as a measure of order, and there is no need to repeat that analysis here. The evaluation showed that the entropy statistic (*H*) is a valuable measure of the degree of disorder in the distribution. By transforming *H*, order can be directly measured as departure from randomization. If desired, the measure can be further standardized by division by log *K* (or log *N* in the case of continuous data), so that the measure varies between 0 and 1, as is customary in sociology. A perfectly disorderly or random distribution of scores on a given variable is indicated by a maximum entropy (*H*) value (log *K*). An orderly distribution of values shows maximum departure from randomization, indicated by a minimum entropy value ($H = 0$). As such, *H* or its various transformations represent a clear and unambiguous operationalization of order for *any variable* to be measured.

Although *H* is still sometimes referred to as *information* (Odum, 1983), there seems to be no logical or intuitive basis for defining *H* as such, since maximum *H* is randomization and there is really *no way* to justify defining *maximum information* as randomization. Thus, the sooner *H* ceases to be identified as information, the better. The only intellectually viable approach is to recognize that *H* is an entropy measure and consistently refer to it as *entropy*.

Hypotheses

Since one theme of this integrative and somewhat holistic effort is to include various formulations rather than to preclude them, there should be room in SET to accommodate the variety of hypotheses currently found in sociology. Thus, although SET may not inform a particular specialized hypothesis in great detail, nothing said in this book should contradict or preclude that hypothesis. In that sense, the operationalizations and hypotheses of social entropy theory include the various operationalizations and hypotheses of middle-range approaches that the larger systemic approach accommodates. In some cases such already existing hypotheses may validate various aspects of SET, and in other cases the skeletal framework of SET may bridge the gulf between two or more such existing hypotheses, thus expanding their power and theoretical viability. In the sense that SET traverses existing operationalizations and hypotheses, it may be said to be already operationalized and formalized and in some cases even tested. However, since SET goes beyond middle-range formulations and covers areas they do not, its breadth should allow generating some additional hypotheses, which are not evident in the prior middle-range formulations. To this end, I will briefly examine various chapters, in a nonexhaustive fashion, to see the sort of hypotheses that can be derived from social entropy theory.

Chapter 1

Chapter 1 is largely programmatic. It argues for a direct approach to macrosociological theorizing and relates the SET approach to other formulations. This definitional chapter was meant to lay the foundation for analysis that generates hypotheses but not to generate such hypotheses itself. It could certainly generate hypotheses of a certain kind (e.g., that the direct approach to macrotheorizing is optimal) but this is not the thrust of the chapter.

Chapter 2

Chapter 2 is also largely epistemological and somewhat definitional. As such it is akin to writings of a theoretical or philosophical sort, which are extremely common in many disciplines and generally not stated in the form of hypotheses or subjected to test. Nevertheless, it may be valuable to state some epistemological hypotheses, even though they may have an unorthodox nature and not be immediately amenable to testing or validation in the usual sense.

Hypothesis 2.1:   There are three distinct levels of social reality: the conceptual (X), the empirical level (X'), and the indicator or marker level (X'').

Corollary 2.1:   Thus, the classic two-level model (conceptual-empirical) is only a partial model of social reality.

Hypothesis 2.2:   There are three paths of isomorphism or validity: path A from X to X'; path B X to X''; and path C from X' to X''.

Hypothesis 2.3:   An adequate model of social explanation must attain all three points of isomorphism.

Hypothesis 2.4:   Any theoretical formulation (e.g., deduction) can be identified on the marker (X'') level and, to be adequate, must be isomorphic with empirical reality (X') (type C isomorphism).

Hypothesis 2.5:   Type A isomorphism (between X and X') often cannot be established directly in sociology and must be established indirectly through type B and type C isomorphism.

Hypothesis 2.6:   Much social phenomena exists on the marker level, X'', even though there may not be type A isomorphism between X and X'.

Hypothesis 2.7:   The congruence between the concrete and pattern systems can be seen in the cyclical relationship between the two systems over time, as societal members sequentially utilize all three levels of the three-level model.

Hypothesis 2.8:   Concrete and abstracted phenomena exist together in actual empirical social systems (X').

Corollary 2.8:   Therefore, use of the concrete systems model with emphasis on physical space-time does not preclude study of abstracted cultural and social phenomena but, on the contrary, provides a necessary foundation for such study.

Hypothesis 2.9:   Boundary specification is difficult or impossible for sbstracted social systems.

Chapter 3

Hypothesis 3.1:   Equilibrium in an isolated thermodynamic system is the most probable state of the system (maximum entropy) or its mathematical equivalent in terms of relationships among the extensive and intensive system properties.

Hypothesis 3.2: The term *equilibrium* applies only to isolated or closed systems.

Hypothesis 3.3: Equilibrium indicates the maximum degree of system disintegration or disorder.

Hypothesis 3.4: Social systems are subject to some degree of control by the persons and groups who construct and maintain them.

Hypothesis 3.5: Persons and groups who control systems attempt to maintain key systems variables and systems boundaries in certain ways.

Hypothesis 3.6: Social system boundaries may be controlled so that the system is alternatively open or closed, but generally it cannot be maintained as permanently closed, as it requires inflow of matter-energy and information.

Hypothesis 3.7: Entropy, patricularly in the Prigogine open systems formulation, can be applied to any social system.

Hypothesis 3.8: The statistic *H* is truly an entropy measure.

Hypothesis 3.9: The statistic *H* has been variously termed *entropy, information, uncertainty,* and *surprisal.*

Chapter 4

Hypothesis 4.1: All social systems possess six global variables: level of living (*L*), space (*S*), organization (*O*), technology (*T*), information (*I*), and population size (*P*).

Hypothesis 4.2: All societies allocate or distribute their population (*P*) into the other five amounts of the global resources that they possess.

Hypothesis 4.3: All social systems possess five mutable distributions: information (*I*), space (*S*), technology (*T*), organization (*O*), and level of living (*L*).

Hypothesis 4.4: The six global variables are all related mathematically.

Hypothesis 4.5: The six global variables can be written in the form of a set of simultaneous differential equations.

Hypothesis 4.6: The five mutable distributions are all related mathematically.

Hypothesis 4.7: The five mutable distributions can be written in the form of a set of simultaneous differential equations.

Hypothesis 4.8: The five mutables are related mathematically to the six global variables.

Hypothesis 4.9: The five mutable distributions are analytical properties of the society (the society is the basic unit of analysis).

Chapter 5

Hypothesis 5.1: After allocation into the mutables, each individual person also possesses mutable characteristics (e.g., occupation, education).

Hypothesis 5.2: Each individual member of society possesses five mutable chatacteristics.

Hypothesis 5.3: Since mutable *distributions* are macro properties of societies but individuals, due to their positions in these societal distributions, possess mutable *micro* characteristics, *the mutables* (I, S, T, O, L) *are the basic micro-macro link in society.*

Hypothesis 5.4: Each individual in the social system possesses immutable characteristics that cannot be changed (e.g., race, sex, birth date).

Hypothesis 5.5: Both mutable and immutable characteristics of individuals are used as the basis for allocation of the individual into the mutable structure of society.

Hypothesis 5.6: The five mutable properties of individuals are generally not directly observable empirically (type A isomorphism) but are generally coded onto markers, and information about them is derived from these markers (type B isomorphism).

Hypothesis 5.7: Expectations (X) of both power holders and the individuals being allocated are crucial in the process of allocation into the mutable distributions.

Hypothesis 5.8: Goals concerning allocation are generally based upon reasonable expectations, often derived from past experience.

Hypothesis 5.9: Markers (X'') play a crucial role in the allocation process.

Hypothesis 5.10: Allocation is most orderly when there is isomorphism between expectations (X) and representation on the marker (X'') (type B isomorphism). This is true for both representation of the postion in the mutable structure and representation of the individual being allocated (e.g., his or her mutable and immutable chatacteristics).

Hypothesis 5.11: Allocation is most orderly when there is isomorphism between the power holder's expectations and the allocated individual's expectations.

Hypothesis 5.12: Immutable characteristics are widely used in the allocation process because of their visibility.

Hypothesis 5.13: There is a correlation between an individual's position on the information mutable (*I*) and his or her position on the occupation (*O*) mutable.

Hypotheses 5.14– There is a correlation between the individual's position on *5.23:* each of the five mutables and his or her position on each of the four remaining mutables.

Hypothesis 5.24: Each social system has a set of immutable characteristics of individuals that are utilized as bases for allocation into the mutables.

Hypotheses 5.25– Each socially salient immutable characteristic is correlated *5.29:* with the individual's position in each of the five mutable distributions (for example, a correlation between race and occupation).

Chapter 6

Hypothesis 6.1:   Some social groups are formed agglomeratively.

Hypothesis 6.2:   Some agglomeratively formed groups are formed through single links between new members and the nucleus.

Hypothesis 6.3:   Some agglomeratively formed groups are formed through multiple (even complete) links with existing members.

Hypothesis 6.4:   Some groups are formed divisively.

Hypothesis 6.5:   Some groups are formed sequentially, being first divided on some immutable or mutable characteristic, then agglomeratively formed within that homogeneous group on some immutable or mutable characteristic.

Hypothesis 6.6:   Some groups are formed sequentially, being first agglomeratively formed, then divided.

Hypothesis 6.7:   Divisively formed groups are more likely to be monothetic on at least one variable than are agglomeratively formed groups.

Hypothesis 6.8:   Agglomeratively formed groups are more likely than divisively formed groups to be polythetic on all variables.

Hypothesis 6.9:   Social groups monitor and maintain physical boundaries around the physical spatial area (*S*) occupied by the group.

Hypothesis 6.10: Social groups monitor and maintain the boundary characteristics of group members.

Hypothesis 6.11: Social groups monitor and maintain "outreach" boundaries, which represent the physical limits of the group's operations.

Hypothesis 6.12: Each social group monitors and maintains its own set of six global variables, that are a subset of the six global levels of the larger host social system.

Hypothesis 6.13: Each social group monitors and maintains its own set of five mutable distributions that are a subset of the five mutable distributions maintained by the larger host social system.

Hypothesis 6.14: Entropy levels within the social group may vary but must be maintained below maximum entropy on certain relevant variables (e.g., on the six globals and five mutables).

Hypothesis 6.15: The group's physical boundary serves as an entropy break. For example, key variables such as the globals and mutables have different entropy levels on different sides of the boundary.

Hypothesis 6.16: If entropy levels do not change when group boundaries are crossed, then the boundary designation is arbitrary and does not distinguish the given system from some larger system of which it is a part.

Hypothesis 6.17: Boundary placement can greatly affect the entropy levels of the six globals and five mutables within the social group.

Hypothesis 6.18: Continual monitoring and processing of information regarding the six globals and five mutable distributions is necessary for the maintenance of adequate levels of these variables within the group or organization.

Hypothesis 6.19: Crossing group boundaries can declassify a member in terms of the mutable distributions he or she possessed within the context of the former group.

Chapter 7

Hypothesis 7.1: Degree of order is degree of departure from randomness.

Corollary 7.1a: All definitions of order have in common that they entail departure from randomness.

Corollary 7.1b: Order is not a constant value but a matter of degree. Order can vary from a low of zero (randomness or maximum entropy) to a high of perfect predictability (maximum departure from randomness or minimum entropy).

Hypothesis 7.2: Order is measured by the positions of persons (P) in a given mutable distribution.

Hypothesis 7.3: Order will generally be intermediate in degree in most empirically observable social systems (i.e., will have a value below maximum entropy but above minimun entropy).

Hypothesis 7.4: Conflict is a sufficient, but not necessary, way for order to be below the maximum (entropy above the minimum).

Hypothesis 7.5: Two basic types of social order exist in the social system: order in terms of the relationships among individual actors (Q-order or concrete order), and order in terms of the relationships among variables (R-order or abstracted order).

Hypothesis 7.6: *Axiom of social order*: Orderly process relationships between human actors (diachronic Q-relationships), when based on specific variables, will result in orderly relationships (correlations) between these variables (synchronic R-relationships).

Hypothesis 7.7: Relationships between variables (R-relationships) that are the focus of the abstracted system are generated by interaction among concrete actors (which is Q-interaction and the focus of the concrete system).

Corollary 7.7: Therefore, the holistic SET model deals with both concrete and abstracted systems, and shows their nexus.

Hypothesis 7.8: The diachronic, Q-process-synchronic R-structure sequence occurs sequentially and permanently over the three levels (X-X'-X'') of the three-level model.

Hypothesis 7.9: Orderly action (Q-process) occurs through replication of actions.

Hypothesis 7.10: Adherence to norms is one chief cause of replicated action, and thus a cause of diachronic process order.

Corollary 7.10: To the degree that social actions are replicated, Q-process entropy, and thus also R-structure entropy, is below maximum entropy.

Hypothesis 7.11: The central system power holders have the responsibility of monitoring and maintaining the six globals.

Corollary 7.11: Therefore, the central system power holders have the responsibility for maintaining entropy levels below the maximum in the system.

Hypothesis 7.12: Goals that are easily attained within the mutable structure at a given point in time will have minimal potential for conflict.

Hypothesis 7.13: Goals held by individuals at relatively high levels in the mutable structure, who are precluded from goal attainment by their immutable characteristics (e.g., gender), will have maximum potential for conflict.

Hypothesis 7.14: Equality of immutable distributions (e.g., maximum entropy of race or gender) is the statistically most probable state of the distribution.

Hypothesis 7.15: Orderly (nonrandom) states of immutable distributions are thus statistically "less probable" and must be maintained by replicated social action, such as adherence to discriminatory norms.

Chapter 8

Hypothesis 8.1: The statistical *H* measure is an entropy measure not an information measure.

Hypothesis 8.2: Entropy as a generic measure of disorder in a given distribution is a property of *all* distributions, even hypothetical ones, and is *not* a unique property of heat systems.

Corollary 8.2: Thus entropy analysis is *not* limited to heat systems.

Hypothesis 8.3: The calculation of entropy and other statistical measures depends upon the manner in which concepts (X) and empirical data (X') are mapped into the contingency table on the marker level (X'').

Hypothesis 8.4: There is a straightforward relationship between categorical entropy and continuous entropy.

Hypothesis 8.5: Categorical measures of univariate, conditional, and joint entropy are clear analogues to correlation and regression analysis.

Hypothesis 8.6: The degree of entropy that is empirically measured by a statistic such as *H* will generally be intermediate (neither maximum nor minimum) and will be the result of the degree of replicated Q-process interaction in that society.

Concluding Remarks

The reflections on social entropy theory and the list of hypotheses has now been concluded. These hypotheses are not meant to be an exhaustive nor a random sampling; rather, they are intended to be somewhat representative of the respective chapters and demonstrate that SET is not purely "verbal theory," but can also be stated in the form of testable hypotheses.

Perusal of the various hypotheses will show that many of them are somewhat unorthodox and original, both in format and conceptual content. Thus, they may provide a valuable supplement to the sometimes stultified and stagnant arsenal of hypotheses presently available in sociology. Note that many of these hypotheses cannot be generated outside of SET, because the language is not available elsewhere (e.g., the concepts of the three-level model). Further, only SET or some equally broad model is able to generate many of these hypotheses, as a narrower middle-range perspective simple lacks the breadth to generate such hypotheses (e.g., statements of relationships among globals, mutables, and immutables). Other hypotheses are of the sort common to contemporary sociology (e.g., Hypotheses 5.13–5.24).

Like all such endeavors, SET leaves some questions unanswered. One such topic is the distinction between model and theory. I have discussed these terms elsewhere (Bailey 1982a). In this book, I adopted the term model in the sense of "model-data isomorphism," as it is used in systems theory (see Bailey 1983c) but meant it "writ large" to include the basic meaning of *theory*.

I would like to close by repeating my statement that the goal of the broad SET formulation is to provide a theoretical framework that will include narrower formulations but not preclude them. As mentioned, any time a middle-range paradigm exhibits either an anomaly or a "versus" dilemma, one alternative to consider is broadening the formulation in order to seek a framework that is better able to deal with the problem. One such anomaly is the confusion concerning the notion of validity in the two-level model. I have noted numerous "versus" situations, where different concepts seem to be in deadlock as theoretical adversaries and the paradigm is unable to resolve the issue. These include theory versus method, conceptual versus empirical, structure versus process, and even free will versus determinism, among many others. I do not claim that SET has resolved these issues and others but claim that it provides a sounder basis for their analysis than narrower formulations and a stepping stone for the future formulation of still broader models.

References

Aberle, David. F. 1987. "Distinguished Lecture: What Kind of Science is Anthropology?" *American Anthropologist* 89:551–66.

Aberle, David F., A. K. Cohen, A. D. Davis, M. J. Levy, Jr., and F. X. Sutton. 1950. "The Functional Preprequisites of a Society." *Ethics* 60:100–11.

Adams, Richard Newbold. 1975. *Energy and Structure: A Theory of Social Power*. Austin: University of Texas Press.

Aiken, Michael. 1981. "Crossing the Boundaries and Building the Bridges: Linking Sociology to the Social Sciences." *Sociological Quarterly* 22:447–70.

Alexander, Jeffrey C. 1978. "Formal and Substantive Voluntarism in the Work of Talcott Parsons: A Theoretical and Ideological Reinterpretation." *American Sociological Review* 43: 177–98.

Alexander, Jeffrey C., Bernhard Giesen, Richard Münch, and Neil J. Smelser, eds. 1987. *The Micro-Macro Link*. Berkeley: University of California Press.

Allison, Paul D. 1978. "Measures of Inequality." *American Sociological Review* 43: 865–80

Amemiya, Eiji C. 1963. "Measures of Economic Differentiation." *Journal of Regional Science* (Summer): 85–87.

American Sociological Association. 1980. *Guide to Graduate Departments of Sociology 1980*. Washington, D.C.: Author.

Arnheim, R. 1971. *Entropy in Art: An Essay on Disorder and Order*. Berkeley: University of California Press.

Bachi, Roberto. 1956. "A Statistical Analysis of the Revival of Hebrew in Israel." In *Scripta Hierosolymitana*, ed. Roberto Bachi, Vol. III, pp. 179–247. Jerusalem: Magnus Press.

Bailey, Kenneth D. 1968. "Human Ecology: A General Systems Approach." Unpublished Ph.D. dissertation. Austin: University of Texas.

_____ . 1972. "Polythetic Reduction of Monothetic Property Space." *Sociological Methodology* 1972, ed. Herbert L. Costner, San Francisco: Jossey-Bass.

_____ . 1973. "Monothetic and Polythetic Typologies and Their Relation to Conceptualization, Measurement and Scaling." *American Sociological Review* 38: 18–33.

_____ . 1974. "Cluster Analysis." In *Sociological Methodology* 1975, ed. David R. Heise, pp. 59–128. San Francisco: Jossey-Bass.

_____ . 1978. *Methods of Social Research*. New York: The Free Press.

_____ . 1980. "Types of Systems." *Systems Science and Science*, ed. Bela H. Banathy, pp. 26–34. Louisville, Ky.: Society for General Systems Research.

_____ . 1981. "Abstracted versus Concrete Sociological Theory." *Behavioral Science* 26:313–23.

_____ . 1982a. *Methods of Social Research*, 2d ed. New York: The Free Press.

_____ . 1982b. "Post-Functional Social Systems Analysis." *Sociological Quarterly* 23: 509–26.

_____ . 1983a. "Sociological Classification and Cluster Analysis." *Quality and Quantity* 17: 251–68.

_____ . 1983b. "Sociological Entropy Theory: Toward a Statistical and Verbal Congruence." *Quality and Quantity* 18: 113–33.

_____ . 1983c. "Relationships among Conceptual, Abstracted, and Concrete Systems." *Behavioral Science* 28: 219–32.

_____ . 1984a. "Beyond Functionalism: Toward a Nonequilibrium Analysis of Complex Social Systems." *British Journal of Sociology* 35: 1–18.

_____ . 1984b. "Equilibrium, Entropy and Homeostasis: A Multidisciplinary Legacy." *Systems Research* 1: 25–43.

_____ . 1984c. "A Three Level Measurement Model." *Quality and Quantity* 18: 225–45.

_____ . 1984d. "On Integrating Theory and Method." *Current Perspectives in Social Theory* 5: 21–44.

_____ . 1985. "Entropy Measures of Inequality." *Sociological Inquiry* 55: 200–11.

_____ . 1986. "Philosophical Foundations of Sociological Measurement: A Note on the Three Level Model." *Quality and Quantity* 20: 327–37.

_____ . 1988a. "Social Entropy Theory: An Overview." *Systems Practice* 1.

_____ . 1988b. "The Conceptualization of Validity: Current Perspectives." *Social Science Research.*

Barber, Bernard. 1970. *L. J. Henderson on the Social System*, ed. Bernard Barber. Chicago: University of Chicago Press.

Bates, Frederick L., and Clyde C. Harvey. 1975. *The Structure of Social Systems*. New York: Gardner Press.

Batty, M., and P. K. Sikdar. 1982. "Spatial Aggregation in Gravity Models. 1. An Information-Theoretic Framework." *Environment and Planning A* 14: 377–405.

Becker, Howard S. 1963. *Outsiders: Studies in the Sociology of Deviance*. New York: The Free Press.

Bell, Wendell. 1954. "A Probability Model for the Measurement of Ecological Segregation." *Social Forces* 32: 357–64.

Berger, Peter L., and Thomas Luckman. 1967. *The Social Construction of Reality*. New York: Doubleday-Anchor Books.

Bergman, G. 1962. "Purpose, Function, and Scientific Explanation." *Acta Sociologica* 5: 225–28.

Berrien, F. Kenneth. 1968. *General and Social Systems*. New Brunswick, N. J.: Rutgers University Press.

Bertalanffy, Ludwig von. 1956. "General System Theory." *General Systems* 1:1–10.

_____ . 1968. *General System Theory*. New York: George Braziller.

Biddle, Bruce J. 1979. *Role Theory: Expectations, Identities, and Behaviors*. New York: Academic Press.

Biddle, Bruce J., and Edwin J. Thomas. 1966. *Role Theory*. New York: John Wiley and Sons.

Bierstedt, Robert. 1959. "Nominal and Real Definitions in Sociological Theory." *Symposium on Sociological Theory*, ed. Llewellyn Gross, pp. 121–44. New York: Haper and Row.

Blalock, Hubert M., Jr. 1964. *Causal Inferences in Nonexperimental Research*. Chapel Hill: University of North Carolina Press.

_____ . 1968. "The Measurement Problem: A Gap Between the Languages of Theory and Research." *Methodology in Social Research*, ed. Hubert M. Blalock, Jr., and Ann B. Blalock, pp. 5–27. New York: McGraw-Hill Book Co.

_____ . 1979. *Social Statistics*, 2d ed. New York: McGraw-Hill Book Co.

Blalock, Hubert M., Jr., and Paul H. Wilken. 1979. *Intergroup Processes: A Micro-Macro Perspective*. New York: The Free Press.

Blau, Peter M. 1964. *Exchange and Power in Social Life*. New York: John Wiley and Sons.

_____ . 1977. *Inequality and Heterogeneity: A Primitive Theory of Social Structure*. New York: The Free Press.

Blumer, Herbert. 1969. *Symbolic Interactionism: Perspective and Method*. Englewood Cliffs, N. J.: Prentice-Hall.

Bohrnstedt, George W., and David Knoke. 1982. *Statistics for Social Data Analysis*. Itasca, Ill.: F.E. Peacock Press.

Bollen, Kenneth, and Kenney Barb. 1981. "Pearson's *R* and Coarsely Categorized Measures." *American Sociological Review* 46: 232–39.

Boulding, Kenneth. 1978. *Ecodynamics: A New Theory of Social Evolution*. Beverly Hills, Calif: Sage.

_____ . 1979. "Universal Physiology." *Contemporary Sociology* 8: 687–91.

Bridgman, Percy W. 1927. *The Logic of Modern Physics*. New York: Macmillan.

Brillouin, Leon. 1956. *Science and Information Theory*. New York: Academic Press.

_____ . 1964. *Scientific Uncertainty, and Information*. New York: Academic Press.

Brim, Orville G., Jr. 1960. "Personality Development as Role-Learning." In *Personality Development in Children*, ed. Ira Isco and Harold Stevenson, pp. 127–59. Austin: University of Texas Press.

Brinton, C. Crane. 1933. *English Political Thought in the Nineteenth Century.* London: Ernest Benn, Ltd.

Brown, Robert. 1963. *Explanation in Social Science.* Chicago: Aldine.

Buckley, Walter. 1967. *Sociology and Modern Systems Theory.* Englewood Cliffs, N.J.: Prentice-Hall.

————. 1968. *Modern Systems Research for the Behavioral Scientist.* Chicago: Aldine.

Butler, E. W., and S. N. Adams. 1966. "Typologies of Delinquent Girls: Some Alternative Approaches." *Social Forces* 44: 401–407.

Campbell, Jeremy. 1982. *Grammatical Man: Information, Entropy, Language, and Life.* New York: Simon and Schuster.

Canfield, J. 1964. "Teleological Explanation in Biology." *British Journal for the Philosophy of Science* 14: 285–95.

Cannon, Walter B. 1929. "Organization for Physiological Homeostasis." *Physiological Reviews* 9: 399–431.

————. 1932. *The Wisdom of the Body.* New York: W. W. Norton.

Capecchi, Vittorio. 1964. "Une Methode de Classification Fondee sur L'entropie." *Revue Francaise de Sociologie* 5: 290–306.

————. 1966. "Typologies in Relation to Mathematical Models." *Ikon*, supplementary no. 58 (September): 1–62.

Capecchi, Vittorio, and Frank Möller. 1968. "Some Applications of Entropy to the Problems of Classification." *Quality and Quantity* 2: 63–84.

Carnot, Sadi Nicholas Léonard. 1824. Réflexions sur la Puissance Motrice du feu et sur les Machines Propres à Développer Cette Puissance. Paris. (Landmarks of Science. Readex Microprint).

Charvat, F. 1972. "On Philosophical Aspects of the System Conception in Contemporary Sociological Knowledge." *Quality and Quantity* 6: 3–16.

Charvat, F., and J. Kucera. 1970. "On the Theory of Social Dependence." *Quality and Quantity* 4: 325–53.

Charvat, R., J. Kucera, and M. Soukup. 1973. "Toward the System Theory of Dependence: Further General Theoretical Remarks." *Quality and Quantity* 7: 69–90.

Churchman, C. West. 1968. *The Systems Approach.* New York: Dell.

Clausius, R. 1850. "On the Mechanical Theory of Heat." Berlin: Poggendorff's Annalen.

_____ . 1879. *The Mechanical Theory of Heat*, trans. Walter R. Browne. London: Macmillan.

Coleman, James S. 1964. *Introduction to Mathematical Sociology*. New York: The Free Press.

Collins, Randall. 1975. *Conflict Sociology: Toward an Explanatory Science*. New York: Academic Press.

_____ . 1979. *The Credential Society*. New York: Academic Press.

Comeau, Larry R., and Leo Driedger. 1978. "Ethnic Opening and Closing in an Open System: A Canadian Example." *Social Forces* 57 : 600–20.

Comte, Auguste. 1986 [1853]. *The Positive Philosophy*, trans. and condensed Harriet Martineau. London: George Bell and Sons.
_____ . 1875. *System of Positive Polity or Treatise on Sociology*. London: Burt Franklin.

Cooley, Charles H. 1922. *Human Nature and the Social Order*, Rev. ed. New York: Charles Scribner's Sons.

Coombs, Clyde H. 1953. "Theory and Methods of Social Measurement." *Research Methods in the Behavioral Sciences*, ed. Leon Festinger and Daniel Katz, New York: Henry Holt and Co.

Coser, Lewis A. 1975. "Two Methods in Search of a Substance." *American Sociological Review* 40: 691–700.

Costner, Herbert L. 1965. "Criteria for Measures of Association." *American Sociological Review* 30: 341–53.

_____ . 1969. "Theory, Deduction, and Rules of Correspondence." *American Journal of Sociology* 75 (September): 245–63.

Davis, James A. 1971. *Elementary Survey Analysis*. Englewood Cliffs, N.J.: Prentice-Hall.

Davis, Kingsley. 1949. *Human Society*. New York: Macmillan.

_____ . 1959. "The Myth of Functional Analysis as a Special Method of Sociology and Anthropology." *American Sociological Review* 10: 757–72.

Davis, Kingsley, and Wilbert E. Moore. 1945. "Some Principles of Stratification." *American Sociological Review* 10: 242–49.

Deutsch, K. 1951. "Mechanism, Teleology and Mind." *Philosophy and Phenomenological Research* 12: 185–223.

Devereux, Edward C., Jr. 1961. "Parsons' Sociological Theory." *The Social Theories of Talcott Parsons*, ed. Max Black, pp. 1–63. Englewood Cliffs, N.J.: Prentice-Hall.

Dore, Ronald Phillip. 1961. "Function and Cause." *American Sociological Review* 26: 843–53.

Duncan, David. 1908. *Life and Letters of Herbert Spencer.* Two volumes. New York: Appleton.

Duncan, Otis Dudley. 1961. "From Social System to Ecosystem." *Sociological Inquiry* 31 (Spring): 140–49.

Duncan, Otis Dudley, and Beverly Duncan. 1955. "A Methodological Analysis of Segregation Indexes." *American Sociological Review* 20: 210–17.

Duncan, Otis Dudley, and Leo F. Schnore. 1959. "Cultural, Behavioral, and Ecological Perspectives in the Study of Social Organization." *American Journal of Sociology* 65: 132–46.
Durkheim, Emile. 1933 [1893]. *The Division of Labor in Society.* New York: Macmillan.

_____ . 1950. *The Rules of the Sociological Method.* Glencoe, Ill.: The Free Press.

_____ . 1951. *Suicide.* Glencoe, Ill.: The Free Press.

_____ . 1954. *The Elementary Forms of the Religious Life.* Glencoe, Ill.: The Free Press.

Eisenstadt, S. N., and H. J. Helle, eds. 1985. *Macro-Sociological Theory: Perspectives on Social Theory.* Beverly Hills, Calif.: Sage Publications.

Emerson, Richard M. 1981. "Social Exchange Theory." In *Social Psychology: Sociological Perspectives.* ed. Morris Rosenberg and Ralph M. Turner, pp. 30–65. New York: Basic Books.

Emmerich, W. 1973. "Socialization and Sex-Role Development." *Life-Span Development Psychology: Personality and Socialization*, ed. P. B. Baltes and K. W. Schaie,pp. 124–45. New York: Academic Press.

Entwisle, Doris R., and Dennis Knepp. 1977. "Uncertainty Analysis Applied to Sociological Data." *Sociological Methodology 1970*, ed. Edgar F.

Borgatta and George W. Bohrnstedt, pp. 200–16. San Francisco: Jossey-Bass.

Erasmus, Charles J. 1967. "Obviating the Functions of Functionalism." *Social Forces* 45: 319–28.

Feldman, J., and M. El Houri. 1975. "Social Classification from Homogamy: A Method Based on Information." *Quality and Quantity* 9: 283–316.

Festinger, Leon. 1957. *A Theory of Cognitive Dissonance*. Evanston, Ill.: Row, Peterson.

Fielding, Nigel G., ed. 1988. *Actions and Structure*. Newbury Park, Calif.: Sage Publications.

Forrester, J. W. 1973. *World Dynamics*, 2d ed. Cambridge: Wright-Allen.

Foster, C., A. Rapoport, and E. Trucco. 1957. "Some Unsolved Problems in the Theory of Non-isolated Systems." *General Systems* 2: 9–29.

Galtung, Johan. 1975. "Entropy and the General Theory of Peace." *Essays in Peace Research*. Volume I, ed. Johan Galtung, pp. 47–75. Atlantic Highlands, Humanities Press.

——— . 1980. *The True Worlds: A Transnational Perspective*. New York: The Free Press.

Garfinkel, Harold. 1967. *Studies in Ethnomethodology*. Englewood Cliffs, N.J.: Prentice-Hall.

Garfinkel, Harold, and Harvey Sacks. 1970. "On Formal Structures of Practical Actions". In *Theoretical Sociology: Perspectives and Developments*, ed. John C. McKinney and Edward A. Tiryakian, pp. 337–66. New York: Appleton-Century-Crofts.

Greogescu-Roegen, Nicholas. 1971. *The Entropy Law and the Economic Process*. Cambridge: Harvard University Press.

——— . 1976. *Energy and Economic Myths*. New York: Peragmon Press.

Gibbs, Jack P., and Harley L. Browning. 1966. "The Division of Labor, Technology, and the Organization of Production in Twelve Countries." *American Sociological Review* 31: 81–92.

Gibbs, Jack P., and Walter T. Martin. 1959. "Toward a Theoretical System of Human Ecology." *Pacific Sociological Review* 2 (Spring): 29–36.

——— . 1962. "Urbanization, Technology, and the Division of Labor: International Patterns." *American Sociological Review* 27: 667–77.

Gibbs, J. Willard. 1874–1877. "On the Equilibrium of Heterogeneous Substances." *Transactions of the Connecticut Academy of Arts and Sciences* III.

Giddens, Anthony. 1979. *Central Problems in Social Theory: Action, Structure and Contradiction in Social Analysis.* Berkeley: University of California Press.

_____. 1981. *A Contemporary Critique of Historical Materialism. Volume I. Power, Property and the State.* London: Macmillan.

Gilmore, Thomas N. 1982. "Leadership and Boundary Management." *Journal of Applied Behavioral Science* 18: 343–56.

Glaser, Barney G., and Anselm L. Strauss. 1967. *The Discovery of Grounded Theory: Strategies for Qualitative Research.* Chicago: Aldine.

Goldschmidt, Walter R. 1966. *Comparative Functionalism: An Essay in Anthropological Theory.* Berkeley: University of California Press.

Goodman, Leo. 1971. "The Analysis of Multidimensional Contingency Tables: Stepwise Procedures and Direct Estimation Methods for Building Models for Multiple Classification." *Technometrics* 13: 33–61.

_____. 1972. "A Modified Multiple Regression Approach to the Analysis of Dichotomous Variables." *American Sociological Review* 37: 28–45.

Gouldner, Alvin. W. 1959. "Reciprocity and Autonomy in Functional Theory." *Symposium on Sociological Theory,* ed. Llewellyn Gross, pp. 241–70. New York: Harper and Row.

_____. 1970. *The Coming Crisis of Western Sociology.* New York: Basic Books.

Greenberg, Joseph H. 1956. "The Measurement of Linguistic Diversity." *Language* 32: 109–15.

Grinker, Roy R., ed. 1967. *Toward a Unified Theory of Human Behavior: An Introduction to General Systems Theory,* 2d ed. New York: Basic Books.

Guggenheim, Edward Armand. 1933. *Modern Thermodynamics by the Methods of Willard Gibbs.* London: Methuen.

Guttman, L. 1959. "Introduction to Facet Design and Analysis." *Proceedings of the Fifteenth International Congress of Psychology,* Brussels, 1957, pp. 130–32. Amsterdam: North-Holland Press.

Laszlo, E. 1972. *Introduction to Systems Philosophy.* New York: Gordon and Breach.

Lazarsfeld, Paul F. 1937. "Some Remarks on the Typological Procedures in Social Research." *Zeitschrift für Socialforschung* 6: 119–39.

———. 1958. "Evidence and Inference in Social Research." *Daedalus* 8: 99–130.

Le Chatelier, H. 1888. "Recherches Experimentales et Theoriques sur les Equilibres Chimiques." *Annales des Mines, Huitième Série, Mémioriès,* XIII, Paris: Dunod.

Leik, Robert K., and Barbara F. Meeker. 1975. *Mathematical Sociology.* Englewood Cliffs, N.J.: Prentice-Hall.

Lenski, Gerhard E. 1954. "Status Crystallization: A Nonvertical Dimension of Social Status." *American Sociological Review* 19 (August): 405–13.

Lieberson, Stanley. 1969. "Measuring Population Diversity." *American Sociological Review* 34: 850–62.

Lingoes, James C. 1968. "An IBM 360/67 Program for Guttman-Lingoes Multidimensional Scalogram Analysis—III." *Behavioral Science* 13: 512–13.

Lockwood, David. 1956. "Some Remarks on 'The Social System'," *British Journal of Sociology* 7: 134–46.

Loether, Herman J., and Donald G. McTavish. 1980. *Descriptive and Inferential Statistics: An Introduction,* 2d ed. Boston: Allyn and Bacon.

Lopreato, Joseph. 1971. "The Concept of Equilibrium: Sociological Tantalizer." *Institutions and Social Exchange: The Sociologies of Talcott Parsons and George C. Homans.* ed. Herman Turk and Richard L. Simpson, pp. 309–43. New York: Bobbs-Merrill.

Lotka, Alfred J. 1956. *Elements of Mathematical Biology.* New York: Dover.

Lundberg, George A. 1939. *Foundations of Sociology.* New York: Macmillan.

Magidson, J. 1981. "Qualitative Variance, Entropy and Correlation Ratios for Nominal Dependent Variables." *Social Science Research* 10: 177–94.

Malinowski, Bronislaw. 1944. *A Scientific Theory of Culture.* Chapel Hill: Univeristy of North Carolina Press.

———. 1948. *Magic, Science, and Religion and Other Essays.* Glencoe, Ill.: Free Press.

Maruyama, Magoroh. 1963. "The Second Cybernetics: Deviation Amplifying Mutual Causal Processes." *American Scientist* 51: 164–79.

Maxwell, J. C. 1871. *Theory of Heat*. London: Longmans, Green.

McClelland, David C. 1961. *The Achieving Society*. Princeton, N.J.: Van Nostrand.

McFarland, David D. 1969. "Measuring the Permeability of Occupational Structures: An Information-Theoretic Approach." *American Journal of Sociology* 75: 41–61.

McKinney, John C. 1966. *Constructive Typology and Social Theory*. New York: Appleton-Century-Crofts.

Meadows, D. H., D. L. Meadows, J. Randers, and W. W. Behrens. 1972. *The Limits to Growth*. New York: Universe Books.

Mendenhall, William, Lyman Ott, and Richard L. Schaeffer. 1971. *Elementary Survey Sampling*. Belmont, Calif.: Wadsworth.

Merton, Robert K. 1949. *Social Theory and Social Structure*. Glencoe, Ill.: The Free Press.

———. 1968. *Social Theory and Social Structure*. Enlarged ed. New York: The Free Press.

Miller, George A. 1953. "What is Information Measurement?" *American Psychologist* 8: 3–12.

Miller, James Grier. 1978. *Living Systems*. New York: McGraw-Hill Book Co.

———. 1979. "Response to the Reviewers of Living Systems." *Contemporary Sociology* 8: 705–15.

———. 1980. "Rapoport's Review." *Behavioral Science* 25: 76–87.

Möller, Frank, and Vittorio Capecchi. 1975. "The Role of Entropy in Nominal Classification." *Quantitative Sociology: International Perspectives in Mathematical and Statistical Modeling*, ed. Hubert M. Blalock, Jr., A. Agambegian, F. M. Borodkin, Raymond Boudon and Vittorio Capecchi, pp. 381–428. New York: Academic Press.

Mueller, John H., and Karl F. Schuessler. 1961. *Statistical Reasoning in Sociology*. Boston: Houghton Mifflin.

Northrop, F. S. C. 1947. *The Logic of the Sciences and the Humanities*. New York: MacMillan.

O'Brien, Robert. 1979. "The Use of Pearson's *R* with Ordinal Data." *American Sociological Review* 44: 851–57.

Odum, Howard T. 1983. *Systems Ecology*. New York: John Wiley and Sons.

Osburn, William F. 1951. "Population, Private Ownership, Technology and the Standard of Living." American Journal of Sociology 56: 314–19.

Opp, Karl-Dieter. 1970. "Theories of the Middle Range as a Strategy for the Construction of a General Sociological Theory: A Critique of a Sociological Dogma." *Quality and Quantity* 4: 243–53.

Pareto, Vilfredo. 1935. *The Mind and Society, Volume IV.* New York: Harcourt, Brace.

Parsons, Talcott. 1937. *The Structure of Social Action*. Glencoe, Ill.: The Free Press.

———. 1951. *The Social System*. Glencoe, Ill.: The Free Press.

———. 1961a. "An Outline of the Social System." *Theories of Society. Volume I.* ed. Talcott Parsons, Edward Shils, Kaspar D. Naegle, and Jesse R. Pitts, pp. 30–79. Glencoe, Ill.: The Free Press.

———. 1961b. "The Point of View of the Author." *The Social Theories of Talcott Parsons,* ed. Max Black, pp. 311–63. Englewood Cliffs, N.J.: Prentice-Hall.

———. 1961c. "Some Considerations on the Theory of Social Change." *Rural Sociology* 26: 219–39.

———. 1967. "Boundary Relations Between Socoiocultural and Personality Systems." In *Toward a Unified Theory of Human Behavior*, 2d ed., ed. R. R. Grinker. New York: Basic Books.

———. 1979. "Concrete Systems and 'Abstracted' Systems." *Contemporary Sociology* 8: 696–705.

Parsons, Talcott, and Shils, E. A., eds. 1951. *Toward a General Theory of Action*. New York: Harper and Row.

Pergler, P. 1968. "Comment on the Problem of Information and Typology." *Quality and Quantity* 2: 85–88.

Pickler, A.G. 1954. "Utility Theories in Field Physics and Mathematical Economics (I)." *British Journal of the Philosophy of Science* 5: 47–58.

———. 1955. "Utility Theories in Field Physics and Mathematical Economics (II)." *British Journal of the Philosophy of Science* 5: 313–16.

Prigogine, I. 1955. *Introduction To Thermodynamics of Irreversible Processes*. Springfield, Ill.: Charles C. Thomas.

_____. 1962. *Non-equilibrium Statistical Mechanics*. New York: Interscience Publishers.

Radcliffe-Brown, A. R. 1935. "Structure and Function in Primitive Society." *American Anthropologist* 37: 58–72.

_____. 1948. *The Andaman Islanders*. Glencoe, Ill.: The Free Press.

_____. 1952. *Structure and Function in Primitive Society*. Glencoe, Ill.: The Free Press.

Rapoport, Anatol. 1980. "Philosophical Perspectives on *Living Systems*." *Behavioral Science* 25: 56–64.

Resnick, Robert, and David Halliday. 1960. *Physics for Students of Science and Engineering. Part I*. New York: John Wiley and Sons.

Rifkin, Jeremy, and Ted Howard. 1980. *Entropy: A New World View*. New York: Viking Press.

Robinson, Robert V. 1984. "Reproducing Class Relations in Industrial Capitalism." *American Sociological Review* 49: 182–96.

Rosenberg, Morris, and Ralph H. Turner, eds. 1981. *Social Psychology: Sociological Perspectives*. New York: Basic Books.

Rothstein, Jerome. 1958. *Communication, Organization, and Science*. Indian Hills, Colo.: Falcon's Wing Press.

Rozonoer, L. I. 1973. "A Generalized Thermodynamic Approach to Resource Exchange and Allocation. I." *Automated Remote Control* 34: 781–95.

Rule, James B., Douglas McAdam, Linda Stearns, and David Uglow. 1983. "Documentary Identification and Mass Surveillance in the United States." *Social Problems* 31:222–234.

Russett, Cynthia Eagle. 1966. *The Concept of Equilibrium in American Social Thought*. New Haven: Yale University Press.

Samuelson, Paul A. 1980. *Economics*, 11th ed. New York: McGraw-Hill Book Co.

_____. 1983. *Foundations of Economic Analysis* [1947], enlarged ed. Cambridge: Harvard University Press.

Sandri, G. 1969. "On the Logic of Classification." *Quality and Quantity* 3: 80–124.

Schnore, Leo F. 1961. "Social Problems in the Underdeveloped Areas: An Ecological View." *Social Problems* 8 (Winter): 182–201.

Shannon, Claude E., and Warren Weaver. 1949. *The Mathematical Theory of Communication*. Urbana: University of Illinois Press.

Shavit, Yossi. 1984. "Tracking and Ethnicity in Israeli Secondary Education." *American Sociological Review* 49: 210–20.

Simpson, E. H. 1949. "Measurement of Diversity." *Nature* 163: 688.

Small, Albion, and George E. Vincent. 1894. *An Introduction to the Study of Society*. New York: American Book Company.

Sneath, Peter H. A., and Robert R. Sokal. 1973. Numerical Taxonomy: The Principles and Practice of Numerical Classification. San Francisco: W. H. Freeman.

Sokal, Robert R., and Peter H. A. Sneath. 1963. *Principles of Numerical Taxonomy*. San Francisco: W. H. Freeman.

Sorokin, Pitirim A. 1943. *Sociocultural Causality, Space, Time*. Durham, No. Car.: Duke University Press.

Spencer, Herbert. 1864–1867. *The Principles of Biology*. Two volumes. London: Williams and Norgate.

———. 1892 [1864]. *First Principles*. New York: Appleton.

———. 1896. *The Principles of Psychology*. New York: Appleton.

———. 1966 [1885]. *The Works of Herbert Spencer, Volume I; Essays Scientific, Political and Speculative*. Osnabrück: Otto Zeller.

Spilerman, S. 1972. "Extensions of the Mover-Stayer Model." *American Journal of Sociology* 78: 599–626.

Spradley, James P., and David W. McCurdy, eds. 1972. *The Cultural Experience: Ethnography in a Complex Society*. Chicago: Science Research Associates.

Stavig, Gordon R., and Alan C. Acock. 1980. "Coefficients of Association Analogous to Pearson's *r* for Nonparametric Statistics." *Educational and Psychological Measurement* 40: 679–85.

Stevens, S. S. ed. 1951. *Handbook of Experimental Psychology*. New York: John Wiley and Sons.

Stinchcombe, Arthur L. 1968. *Constructing Social Theories*. New York: Harcourt, Brace, Jovanovich.

Stryker, Sheldon, and Anne Statham Macke. 1978. "Status Inconsistency and Role Conflict." *Annual Review of Sociology* 4: 57–90.

Sudman, Seymour. 1976. *Applied Sampling*. New York: Academic Press.

Swafford, Michael. 1980. "Three Parametric Techniques for Contingency Table Analysis: A Nontechnical Commentary." *American Sociological Review* 45: 664–90.

Szilard, Leo. 1929. "Über die Entropieverminderung in Einem Thermodynamischen System bei Eingriffen Intelligehter Wesen." *Zeitschrift für Physik* 53: 840–56. Translated by A. Rapoport and M. Knoller as "On the Decrease of Entropy in a Thermodynamic System by the Intervention of Intelligent Beings." *Behavioral Science 9 (1964)*: 301–10.

Sztompka, P. 1969. "Teleological Language in Sociology." *Polish Sociological Bulletin* 2: 56–69.

_____. 1974. *System and Function: Toward a Theory of Society*. New York: Academic Press.

Teachman, J.D. 1980. "Analysis of Population Diversity: Measures of Qualitative Variation." *Sociological Methods and Research* 8: 341–62.

Theil, Henri. 1967. *Economics and Information Theory*. Chicago: Rand McNally and Co.

_____. 1970. "On the Estimation of Relationships Involving Qualitative Variables." *American Journal of Sociology* 76: 103–54.

_____. 1971. *Principles of Econometrics*. New York: John Wiley and Sons.

Thibaut, J. W., and H. H., Kelley. 1959. *The Social Psychology of Groups*. New York: John Wiley and Sons.

Thornton, Russell, and Peter M. Nardi. 1975. "The Dynamics of Role Acquisition." *American Journal of Sociology* 80: 870–85.

Treas, Judith. 1982. "U.S. Income Stratification: Bringing Families Back In." *Sociology and Social Research* 66: 231–51.

_____. 1983. "Postwar Determinants of Family Income Inequality." *American Sociological Review* 48: 546–59.

Treas, Judith, and Robin Jane Walther. 1978. "Family Structure and the Distribution of Family Income." *Social Forces* 56: 866–80.

Tumin, Melvin M. 1953. "Some Principles of Stratification: A Critical Analysis." *American Sociological Review* 18: 387–94.

Turner, Jonathan H. 1978. *The Structure of Sociological Theory*. Rev. ed. Homewood, Ill.: Dorsey Press.

———. ed. 1989. *Theory-Building in Sociology: Assessing Theoretical Cumulation*. Beverly Hills, Calif.: Sage Publications.

Turner, Jonathan H., and Alexandra Maryanski. 1979. *Functionalism*. Menlo Park, Calif.: Benjamin/Cummings.

Turner, Ralph H. 1964. *The Social Context of Ambition*. San Francisco: Chandler.

———. 1974. "Rule Learning as Role Learning." *International Journal of Critical Sociology* 1: 52–73.

United States Department of Commerce. 1980. *Money Income of Families and Persons in the United States: 1978*. Washington, D.C.: U.S. Government Printing Office.

Vodáková, A., and F. Vodàk. 1969. "Contribution to the Validation Problem." *Quality and Quantity* 3: 62–79.

Wallerstein, Immanuel. 1974. *The Modern World System: Capitalist Agriculture and the Origins Of the European World Economy in the Sixteenth Century*. New York: Academic Press.

Ward, Lester F. 1883. *Dynamic Sociology*. Volume I. New York: Appleton.

Weber, Max. 1947. *The Theory of Social and Economic Organization*, trans. A. M. Henderson and Talcott Parsons, ed. Talcott Parsons. New York: Oxford University Press.

Weinstein, Eugene A., and Paul Deutschberger. 1963. "Some Dimensions of Altercasting." *Sociometry* 26: 454–66.

Wheeler, Lynde Phelps. 1951. *Josiah Willard Gibbs: The History of a Great Mind*. New Haven: Yale University Press.

White, H. C., S. A. Boorman, and R. L. Breiger. 1976. "Social Structure from Multiple Networks. I. Blockmodels of Roles and Positions." *American Journal of Sociology* 81: 730–80.

Weiner, Norbert. 1948. *Cybernetics*. New York: John Wiley and Sons.

Wilson, A. G. 1970. *Entropy in Urban and Regional Modelling*. London: Pion.

Winch, Robert F. 1947. "Heuristic and Empirical Typologies: A Job for Factor Analysis." *American Sociological Review* 12: 68–75.

Zimmerman, Don H., and Melvin Pollner. 1970. "The Everyday World as a Phenomenon." *Understanding Everyday Life*, ed. Jack Douglas, pp. 80–103. Chicago: Aldine.

Vodáková, A., and F. Vodàk. 1969. "Contribution to the Validation Problem." *Quality and Quantity* 3: 62–79.

Wallerstein, Immanuel. 1974. *The Modern World System: Capitalist Agriculture and the Origins of the European World Economy in the Sixteenth Century.* New York: Academic Press.

Ward, Lester F. 1883. *Dynamic Sociology.* Volume I. New York: Appleton.

Weber, Max. 1947. *The Theory of Social and Economic Organization*, trans. A. M. Henderson and Talcott Parsons, ed. Talcott Parsons. New York: Oxford University Press.

Weinstein, Eugene A., and Paul Deutschberger. 1963. "Some Dimensions of Altercasting." *Sociometry* 26: 454–66.

Wheeler, Lynde Phelps. 1951. *Josiah Willard Gibbs: The History of a Great Mind.* New Haven: Yale University Press.

White, H. C., S. A. Boorman, and R. L. Breiger. 1976. "Social Structure from Multiple Networks. I. Blockmodels of Roles and Positions." *American Journal of Sociology* 81: 730–80.

Wiener, Norbert. 1948. *Cybernetics.* New York: John Wiley and Sons.

Wilson, A. G. 1970. *Entropy in Urban and Regional Modelling.* London: Pion.

Winch, Robert F. 1947. "Heuristic and Empirical Typologies: A Job for Factor Analysis." *American Sociological Review* 12: 68–75.

Zimmerman, Don H., and Melvin Pollner. 1970. "The Everyday World as a Phenomenon." *Understanding Everyday Life*, ed. Jack Douglas, pp. 80–103. Chicago: Aldine.

Author Index

303

Subject Index